# Psychology
# Is
# Social

READINGS AND CONVERSATIONS IN SOCIAL PSYCHOLOGY

# Psychology is Social

*Third Edition*

Edward Krupat
*Massachusetts College of Pharmacy
and Allied Health Sciences*

HarperCollins*College*Publishers

Sponsoring Editor: Catherine Woods
Cover Design: Jill Yutkowitz
Production Manager: Bob Cooper
Compositor: Publishing Synthesis, Ltd.
Printer and Binder: Malloy Lithographing
Cover Printer: Malloy Lithographing

For permission to use copyrighted material, grateful acknowlegment is made to the copyright holders on pp. 391–392, which are hereby made part of this copyright page.

(Title/Edition) PSYCHOLOGY IS SOCIAL, Third Edition by Edward Krupat
Copyright © 1994 by HarperCollins College Publishers

Library of Congress Cataloging-in-Publication Data
Psychology is social : readings and conversations in social psychology / [edited by] Edward Krupat. — 3rd ed.
      p.    cm.
   Includes bibliographical references and index.
   ISBN 0-673-46918-2
   1. Social psychology.    I. Krupat, Edward.
   HM251.P84 1994
   302—dc20                         93-49661
                                    CIP

94  95  96  97  9  8  7  6  5  4  3  2  1

# Contents

# Preface to the Third Edition

It has been a long time between editions of *Psychology is Social*. In the field of social psychology much has changed, yet many of its most attractive aspects have remained the same. I hope the same can be said of this book. My goal, for instance, has not changed at all. I still want to introduce students to social psychology in a way that captures their interest, to show that social psychology goes well beyond academics and can enlighten and expand their understanding of the everyday world. Reflective of the changes in the field, only two articles from the second edition have been retained, and each of the ten conversations in the book is new to this edition.

To make the book come alive and capture the interest and imagination of readers, I have done the following:

1. The *conversations* that precede each section are meant to give students insight into the thinking of well-known social psychologists. In these we discover, for example, the unorthodox path that led Daniel Batson to study empathy and helping and the equally unusual way that Robert Cialdini has developed his knowledge in the area of social influence. I have tried to allow students to identify with the material by identifying as well with those who have generated it.

2. The *readings* come from a variety of sources, both academic and popular. I have included readings of many types: single studies, reviews, and commentary; recent and classic studies; basic and applied research; and field and laboratory approaches. The idea is to demonstrate the range of social psychology and to give students a view of the breadth of issues that social psychologists have approached, attempted to enlighten, and continue to grapple with. Whether the topic is media violence, discrimination, or the spread of AIDS, students are invited to read about the contributions that social psychology has made.

3. The primary criterion in making selections for the book was *readibility*. I have attempted to choose articles in which the writing is clear and straightforward. In the case of articles from the professional journals, in all cases I have done a good deal of editing, especially in the complex statistical sections, in order to make the findings less technical. Readers can assume that statistical tests meet standard significance levels and should refer to the original article if they should want to pursue the results in greater detail.

I would like to thank a number of people who helped me in this project. The ten social psychologists who agreed to take part in the conversations all proved to be wonderfully interesting and articulate, and I thank each of them. At HarperCollins, I want to express my appreciation to Catherine Woods for having enough confidence in the book to have it revised after many years. Special thanks go to Steve Harkins of Northeastern University and Richard Smith of the University of Kentucky, who offered numerous suggestions and put up with me when I sought their opinions or wavered endlessly about topics and selections. Julie Whelan, Richard Kaplan, Nancy Occhialini, and David Amdur of the library staff at the Massachusetts College of Pharmacy and Allied Health Sciences have been wonderfully helpful in tracking down even the most unusual questions. Thanks for secretarial and typing help go to Mickey McCarthy and Janet Post as well as Jennifer Poole, Rayanne Gonzalez, and William Brazier. And, almost 20 years too late, I would like to thank Zick Rubin, whose graduate school song and skit provided the title for this book.

My personal thanks, of course, go to my family. My wife Barbara has provided constant support and love for the past 25 years and deserves public thanks. As for my children, Jason and Michael were not born when I began the first edition, and it scares me to think that they will both be in college (and possibly using this book?) once this edition is published. I know that I have learned a great deal about social interaction from them, and I would hope they might even agree that they have learned a bit from me too.

Edward Krupat
Boston, MA

# Social Psychology: An Introduction

In order to get a sense of just what social psychology *is*, first it is necessary to deal with some common misconceptions and see just what social psychology *is not*. When I meet someone and I am asked what I do for a living, the simple statement "I'm a social psychologist" usually causes nothing but trouble and confusion. Either I get a blank stare or I receive a response that embodies the misunderstandings people have about social psychology.

The most common reaction is, "Oh, so where is your practice?," revealing a common misconception that all of psychology is *clinical* or *abnormal* psychology. When I answer that I don't have a practice, that I teach and do research, people are often confused because they associate psychology with the study of abnormal behavior and the practice of psychotherapy. The niche that social psychologists have carved out for themselves is unique in that social psychologists study *normal* rather than abnormal processes, they consider the *whole* individual rather than merely reaction times or learning curves, and they believe that behavior is determined by the manner in which the individual sees and makes sense of the world. In short, social psychologists do research that attempts to understand and explain everyday social behavior, the ways in which people interact and influence one another. So while I don't "have a practice," the practice of social psychology can still be useful and helpful to people in many ways.

The second reaction to the statement "I'm a social psychologist" is "Oh, how nice. You're a sociologist. I have a cousin who's a sociologist too." No matter how many times I try to say, "No, not a sociologist. A social psychologist," the answer comes back, "Sociologist, social psychologist. Big deal, no difference."

The point, of course, is that there are considerable differences. One key issue that distinguishes many sociologists from their psychologically oriented colleagues is that sociologists tend to study people at what is known as the aggregate level. Sociological explanations often tend to lose the individual, to submerge the individual in a consideration of group classifications, social structures, and patterns of social organization. Social psychologists in no way deny the powerful effects of culture, religion, and social class on behavior. Yet their interest is not in looking at the class structure itself. Instead, social psychologists focus on the individual and how he or she contributes to, perceives, and is affected by these larger entities.

## B = f(P,E)

Although the focus may be different, social psychology does share one key element with sociology. This is a recognition that the individual's behavior is critically determined by what is happening outside the individual in his or her environment. Referred to as *situationism*, this focus on the role of *external* variables actually sets social psychology apart from many other areas of psychology that deal with *internal* determinants of behavior, such as personality, motivation, drives, and needs.

We can ask: Which are more important, psychological (internal) or sociological (external) variables? Historically, many psychologists and sociologists have spent a great deal of time and energy debating the relative importance of internal versus external influences as if the answer had to be one or the other. Kurt Lewin, who many recognize as the single most important voice in social psychology, made this debate seem trivial in generating a simple but highly sensible formula. It reads:

$$B = f(P,E)$$

Translated, Lewin has said that "Behavior is a function of the person and the environment." He has told us that we will find useful but incomplete answers if we only look inside the individual for answers, just as we will find good but equally incomplete answers if we only look to the person's environment. We must therefore look within *and* without, recognizing that it is the combination or interaction of these factors that determines how and why people behave. In essence, we could say that social psychology's true contribution is not simply giving a situationist look to psychology, but in going beyond that by embracing the perspective of "interactionism."

**An Example: Suicide.** Let us make this point more concrete by taking a social phenomenon, suicide, and seeing how it has been explained by some classic sociological and psychological thinkers. Emile Durkheim, the French sociologist, looked at the sociocultural factors that he believed determined suicide rates. He investigated records of suicide in different historical periods and in different countries and found that people in various social classes and religious categories living under certain political conditions were more likely to commit suicide than others (Durkheim 1897). However, while he made it clear that social conditions do affect suicide rates, Durkheim did not fully provide the "why" of suicide. Although social conditions can make certain groups feel more involved than others, Durkheim cannot tell us why, under identical social conditions, some people did commit suicide while others did not or even why some committed suicide while others committed homicide. His approach leaves out the individual and the subjective impact of the situation on the person. He can explain why suicide rates differ in various groups, not how the individuals within those groups perceived their conditions and reacted to them.

In direct contrast to a purely sociological explanation of suicide, we have the purely psychological. It is different, but also lacking in certain respects. The classical Freudian explanation of suicide is that it represents a case of aggression turned against the self. Some of the personal characteristics associated with suicide are extreme depression, a lack of good interpersonal relationships, and the feeling of being a burden to others. This approach has just what the other does not—a personal description of the feelings and perceptions of the suicidal person—but it lacks what the sociological one has.

In emphasizing the role of internal factors such as personality and emotion, it tends to ignore the complex social forces acting on the person. While some people may feel depressed and contemplate suicide, social forces and complex social norms may influence whether the suicide will actually be carried out and even how. For instance, in World War II those Japanese pilots who flew kamikaze missions felt that they died with honor for their cause, yet the thought of flying a kamikaze mission seemed bizarre to American pilots. The difference was in the norms and values of the two societies. Therefore, to truly understand a phenomenon such as suicide, we need to understand the manner in which both internal and external factors interact.

**Some Practical and Research Examples.** applying the interactionist approach to a more mundane example, imagine that you were working for an advertising agency attempting to develop a campaign to sell auto insurance. Should you expose people to ads that reassure and calm them, like the Allstate commercials that tell consumers they are "in good hands" if they buy that brand of insurance? Or would it be better to shake them up by showing them scenes from gruesome auto accidents, reminding them that your insurance company will take care of their families if they should die?

The question of "high fear" versus "low fear" only asks half of the interactionist question: what kind of situation or environment should we expose people to? The other half of the $B = f(P, E)$ equation suggests that the outcome should also depend on the nature of the people involved. After many studies with conflicting results on the effects of low versus high fear campaigns, researchers began to look into the interaction of fear and personality.

In a classic study in which Irving Janis and Seymour Feshbach (1954) tried to get people to change their toothbrushing habits, for instance, the researchers discovered that subjects who were high in anxiety responded well to low fear, but were overwhelmed when presented with a powerful fear-inducing campaign. However, people who were low in anxiety were able to cope with the high fear message and responded slightly better to that than the low fear message.

More recently, social psychological health researchers have proposed that hospital patients should benefit from being given more information before they undergo threatening procedures such as surgery. Although attempts to provide a more information-filled environment have been generally successful, for some patients information seems to do more harm than good. Reminding us of the interaction of person and environment, Suzanne Miller and Charles Mangan (1983) found that people who typically cope with stress by focusing on their problems benefitted greatly from being provided with information; however, those whose coping style was characterized by denial were actually better off when they received less information.

$B = f(P,E)$ helps us understand why some students choose to go to huge mega-universities while others select small colleges, and why some people thrive in urban settings while others want to be as far away from a city as they can be. Many years ago when I was a graduate student, I got a summer job as a research assistant in New York City. During the course of the summer, I overheard a famous social psychologist complaining about the lack of resources he was being provided with. Aware of his fame, I suggested that he could probably have any position he wanted, and I even had the audacity to recruit him personally to the school I was attending, the University of Michigan. He thanked me and declined to even consider it, saying, "If I ever had the choice between a so-so position in a great city and a great position in a smaller town, I would always opt for the city." Having related this story over the years, I find that some students would agree, but many others would give just the opposite answer. Although I have no idea what Lewin would have answered for himself, I do know that, in order to predict how satisfied people in general would be with their homes and jobs, he would tell you that you had to know about *both* the people and their environment.


## BASIC AND APPLIED RESEARCH

As we have noted, social psychology's response to the person/environment debate, which many people phrased as an "either/or" question, was to say *both*. Another parallel debate has been the so-called "basic/applied" question. Should researchers direct their attention toward basic (or pure) research, whose goal is the development and testing of knowledge and theories? Or should they be focused on the applied side, becoming involved in problem solving and the search for solutions to important social issues?

The answer given by social psychology once again is that this is not an either/or issue; these two interests are not mutually exclusive. Good theories should be testable in and applicable to the real world, and they should help us find solutions to important matters. The real world is the perfect context to test and refine our theories to see if they hold up when exposed to the complexities of life. In a similar vein, good applications and effective interventions need to be based on solid theory. Without important theoretical bases for developing solutions, we wander from one problem to the next without an effective framework. To cite Kurt Lewin once again. "There is nothing so practical as a good theory" (Lewin 1951, p. 169).

After going from one extreme to the other on the basic/applied question, modern social psychology finally seems to be maturing and thereby reflecting and honoring Lewin's words. Once, basic and applied researchers looked down upon one another and had little contact. Then the two camps made an uneasy peace and began to interact and show grudging respect for one another's contributions. But today the basic/applied split shows signs of slowly disappearing. Some of the field's most respected basic researchers are among its most active problem solvers. And those who are looking to prevent the spread of AIDS, who are involved in reforming the legal system, and who are combating discrimination are actively working from and testing new theories as they develop interventions and offer advice and solutions.

## A NOTE ABOUT THE BOOK

This book is divided into ten sections, each reflecting a major area of interest in social psychology. Each section begins with a "conversation" with a social psychologist who is highly respected in that area. Social psychology is all about people, why they act, how they think, what they do—and the conversations demonstrate that, behind all of this research, real people exist. In these conversations I have asked them to explain what their ideas or theories are, how they came up with them, and even how they came to be interested in their topic in the first place. The conversations are unrehearsed and free-flowing, and they are meant to make academic subjects come alive by offering readers a glimpse into the thinking of those people whose names we see in the textbooks.

The articles in the book, usually about three to a section, have been chosen to represent a number of types and viewpoints. They come from popular sources and texts as well as academic journals, but my primary concern in selecting each of them has been readability. In research papers in particular, I have edited the "Results" sections in those instances where the statistical discussions were too complex and technical. In short, I have made every attempt to make this book, to use a phrase that has become a cliche in just a few short years, "user-friendly."

So I invite students to read, to learn, even to *enjoy* as you discover what social psychologists have discovered about you and me, about the nature and causes of everyday social interaction.

## References

Durkheim, E. (1897). *Le suicide: Etude de Sociologie.* (Trans. *Suicide: A Study in Sociology.*) Paris: Alcan.

Janis, I. and Feshbach, S. (1954). Personality differences associated with responsiveness to fear-arousing communications. *Journal of Personality, 23,* 154–166.

Lewin, K. (1951). Problems of research in social psychology. In D. Cartwright (ed.) *Field Theory in Social Science: Selected Theoretical Papers.* Westport, CT: Greenwood.

Miller, S.M. and Mangan, C.E. (1983). Interacting effects of information and coping style in adapting to gynecologic stress: Should the doctor tell all? *Journal of Personality and Social Psychology, 45,* 223–236.

# Psychology
# Is
# Social

**1**

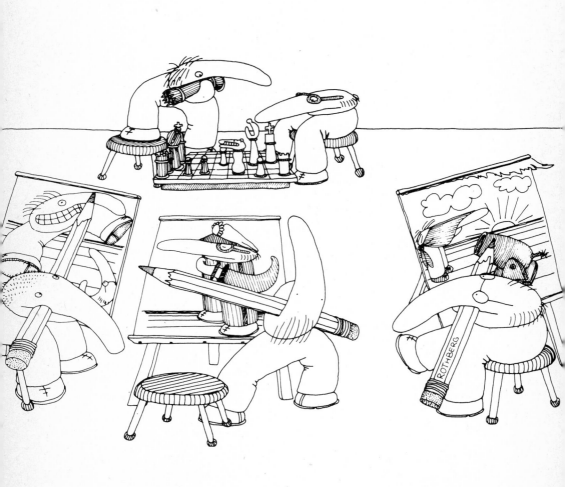

# Social Cognition: Making Sense of the World

An emphasis on social cognition dominates modern day social psychology. This focus on how we think about people and situations is not just an important subfield in itself, but it serves as the framework for so much current research and intervention throughout the field of social psychology.

Susan Fiske, Professor of Psychology at the University of Massachusetts at Amherst, is one the most respected people in this field. Her book, *Social Cognition,* coauthored with Shelley Taylor, is regarded as a uniquely clear and complete presentation of this broad area. Moreover, her recent involvement as an expert witness has helped to further illuminate the ways in which research evidence can be used in judicial proceedings. In our conversation, Prof. Fiske explains the different ways in which we have conceived of people as thinkers and how the manner in which we think about others can affect our everyday lives. Moving us beyond the laboratory, she tells how social cognition has branched out into law, medicine, and politics.

## A CONVERSATION WITH
## SUSAN FISKE

**Krupat:** *If we are going to talk about the field known as social cognition, perhaps you could start out by telling me what it is all about?*

**Fiske:** The simplest answer is that it deals with how people think about other people and themselves and how they come to some kind of coherent understanding of each other. Sometimes what I tell people on airplanes is it's about how people form first impressions of strangers. That's not quite right, but on airplanes it's an effective conversation-stopper when necessary.

**Krupat:** *In psychology we have a broad area known as cognition. What is social about social cognition?*

**Fiske:** There have been endless debates about that. I think at its core social cognition is social on the target end—it is concerned with people thinking about people, as opposed to people thinking about nonperson objects. On the other end it's about the impact of the social situation and social factors on people's thinking. A lot of the most recent work has looked at people's interaction goals, at people actually dealing with each other and forming strategies or tactics for interaction. So we could say it is about "thinking for doing" in a social setting.

**Krupat:** *To pick up on your earlier point, how much of a difference does it make if the object of your perception is a person rather than a thing?*

**Fiske:** When you're thinking about another person or perceiving another person, that's a mutual process. The person is relevant to you. So if you're looking at your new roommate or the person next to you in a lecture, you're not just looking at a chair or a sculpture. How the person is dressed, the expression on the person's face, and how that person responds to you are all important in a way that's simply not true for objects.

**Krupat:** *Another way that I have heard this area described involves the person as an information processor. How is that similar to or different from what we have been talking about?*

**Fiske:** That was a perspective used early on, but the computer metaphor is fading from favor as people are finding it too narrow and too oriented towards sequential, A-leads-to-B-leads-to-C kinds of processes. There are too many things that happen simultaneously, too many things related to emotions, feelings, and behavior.

**Krupat:** *Regardless of the metaphor we choose, how good would you say that we are at this business of social thinking and reasoning?*

**Fiske:** We have a lot of very adaptive ways of thinking socially because we do it so much and because it is so vital to us. We do go astray under certain circumstances, but I think it is fair to say that most of the time people are good enough at perceiving each other and at making sense of each other. Still, it is also true that we are prone to a lot of very specific kinds of errors which get us into trouble in various situations. One of the most common kinds of errors is a bias toward explaining other people's behavior in terms of their unique personality instead of explaining it in terms of the situation or circumstances surrounding them. This is known as the fundamental attribution error. Another kind of cognitive bias has to do with stereotyping people, seeing them as members of some group-based category rather than as unique individuals.

**Krupat:** *You said that these can get us into trouble. How so?*

**Fiske:** Take the fundamental attribution error. That gets you into trouble if you assume that other people are highly predictable based on a particular personality or disposition that you have identified in them. If they are actually responding to situational pressures instead, then you are going to be wrong about what the person is going to do, feel, and think. The same thing is true of stereotypes. To the extent you rely on the person's category to make sense of the person when he or she is a unique individual with a lot of characteristics besides that category membership, you are not going to know how to deal with this person effectively. In both cases you are coming up with simplistic models of what other people are about, and it interferes with your ability to predict and control events.

**Krupat:** *Do these kinds of biases actually get us into trouble?*

**Fiske:** In the majority of your interactions, you can't deal with people as totally unique individuals. So having good enough perceptions of group membership or personality probably gets you through a lot of daily interactions. Even if they're wrong, most of these decisions may not have too many consequences for you. But if that person is somebody's boss, then it's not a good enough decision. I would argue that people are very pragmatic about this. When it matters to them, when they're motivated, then they're more careful or at least try to be more careful, and as a result they think more about the other person. If it is important to be accurate in this situation, then people will engage in more complex thought processes, which gives them at least the possibility of being more accurate. It all depends on motivation. It's as simple as that.

**Krupat:** *So we can be careful if we want to exert the effort. It's just that we are not always motivated to do so. Is that what you are saying?*

**Fiske:** There are two broad-brush strategies to describe our thinking about other people, although I should say that this is really a continuum and not a dichotomy. One extreme is to go with fairly automatic first impressions, with the first thing that you find out about people. I have talked about this in terms of "category-based processes," and other people have talked about "automatic processes." At the other end, an alternative way of making sense of people which is much more thoughtful and takes a lot more information in usually builds a sort of coherent story or a portrait about the person, taking all the pieces of information together. In the attitude literature that is called "systematic processing" or "central processing," and in the person perception literature "individuating" or "piecemeal processing."

**Krupat:** *This sounds a lot like the debate I have heard between seeing the person as a "naive scientist" versus a "cognitive miser."*

**Fiske:** In the late sixties and early seventies, the approach that dominated this area was to look at people as if they were scientists carefully gathering information and combining it in some kind of rational manner in order to come out with considered, thoughtful conclusions. The problem was that people weren't doing that much of the time. And that's where the cognitive miser idea came in. According to this, people have meager cognitive resources compared to the complicated environment that's out there. So in order to deal with the booming, buzzing confusion, people have to be economical about the use of their cognitive resources; so they take a lot of shortcuts. And that was kind of a second wave of social cognition research. The current wave of social cognition research takes that a step further and says that we can be more careful when we are motivated to be. So the term that we've come up with for that is "motivated tactician." This reflects the pragmatic orientation that people have towards having to interact and think about each other in order to decide how to deal effectively with them. It says that people have a number of different cognitive strategies or tactics available to them and that they choose among these, depending on what their goals are in a situation.

**Krupat:** *Are we learning things from the field of social cognition that go beyond some of the things that we already knew from the broader field of cognition?*

**Fiske:** Yes. For example, in research on attention, basic research in cognition has found that people pay attention to things that are novel. When you take that over to people, you have to define novelty more broadly, in ways that include people who are novel in a particular circumstance. In a regular college classroom, somebody who is seven feet tall is definitely novel, but not on a basketball team. Or how about the only woman in a group of men or the only black in a group of whites? Research on novelty in social situations has led to the idea that a novel stimulus person looms large in people's thinking and seems to have had a lot of impact. You wouldn't necessarily find that if you're just thinking about objects, because the objects are not interacting.

**Krupat:** *Are there any equivalent kinds of things in the study of memory, for instance?*

**Fiske:** Within person memory research, researchers have been interested in the differences in how people form impressions and remember things about others. You might think that if I gave you a list of personality traits that you would remember them best if you are told simply to memorize them. But in fact that's not true. People remember them best when they are trying to form an impression of a person who has all those traits. What is interesting about that—and you couldn't have found that within nonsocial cognition research—is that it's because people are constructing a theory of the person.

**Krupat:** *But is it always good to construct a theory of a person? Wouldn't it be possible to have such a strong theory about someone that you virtually assure that your expectancies will end up being confirmed—what has been known as a self-fulfilling prophecy?*

**Fiske:** As you say, when you get into actual interactions, these theories or expectancies can create behavior in the other person. You might ask questions and seek information that confirm your prior ideas. In terms of the courtroom, you can certainly see these effects where people's expectancies or leading questions asked by attorneys lead to biases in what people report, for instance, in eyewitness testimony. An interesting finding, by the way, is that people's confidence and certainty in what they are reporting is totally uncorrelated with their accuracy.

**Krupat:** *I know that you have been personally involved in a couple of important trials as an expert witness, and we seem to see many social cognition researchers involved in a range of social causes and issues. Are more and more laboratory scientists poking their noses into practical arenas these days?*

**Fiske:** There are a number of us who are interested in stereotypes and stereotyping. There are other people who are interested in how people's health beliefs get formed and how they cope with major negative life events. Other people study advertising and how social cognition influences consumers. Still others study what social cognition can tell us about how people deal with political information and how candidates get packaged. The variety of applications is staggering.

**Krupat:** *So you believe that we can really have an impact and make a difference with the knowledge we generate?*

**Fiske:** Social psychology seems to hold an attraction for people who are interested in making the world a better place, but who want to do it as scientists. One thing that interested me in the two legal cases you mentioned was that when you examine a real world problem, like a perfectly qualified person not getting promoted in a firm or the effects of pornography on sexual harassment and try to analyze it in terms of what social cognition researchers know, it's possible to come up with some pretty concrete insights about the situation. Moreover, it's convincing to people outside the field. Our explanations are much less speculative than other kinds of psychological explanations and they are very credible to people in the media, people in the courtroom, and people in politics. You can actually make the world a better place by studying and understanding this and then exporting it to people who have a use for it. To me that's the encouraging part, and that's what's fun about it.

Susan Fiske and Shelley Taylor

# Cognition in Social Psychology

In this selection, Fiske and Taylor explain what it means to take a cognitive approach in social psychology and how the perception of *things* is different from the perception of *people*. As briefly explored in the preceding conversation, Fiske and Taylor consider the different ways in which social psychologists have characterized people as thinkers: naive scientist (careful and systematic); cognitive miser (taker of shortcuts that can mislead); and motivated tactician (careful or sloppy, depending on one's goals and situation).

In contrast to experimental psychology, social psychology has consistently learned on cognitive concepts, even when most psychology was behaviorist. Social psychology has always been cognitive in at least three ways. First, since Lewin, social psychologists have decided that social behavior is more usefully understood as a function of people's perceptions of their world, rather than as a function of objective descriptions of their stimulus environment (Manis, 1977; Zajonc, 1980a). For example, an objective reward like money or praise that people perceive as a bribe or as flattery will influence them differently than a reward they perceive as without manipulative intent. What predicts their reaction, then, is their perception, not simply the giver's actions.

Other people can influence a person's actions without even being present, which is the ultimate reliance on perceptions to the exclusion of objective stimuli. Thus, someone may react to a proffered bribe or to flattery by imagining the reactions of others ("What would my mother say?" "What will my friends think?"). Of course, such thoughts are the person's own fantasies, having perhaps tenuous connection to objective reality. Thus, the *causes* of social behavior are doubly cognitive; our perceptions of others actually present and our imagination of their presence both predict behavior (cf. G. W. Allport, 1954).

Social psychologists view not only causes but also the end *result* of social perception and interaction in heavily cognitive terms, and this is a second way in which social psychology has always been cognitive. Thought often comes before feeling and behaving as the main reaction that social researchers measure. A person may worry about a bribe (thought), hate the idea (feeling), and reject it (behavior), but social psychologists often mainly ask: "What do you think about it?" Even when they focus on behavior and feelings, their questions are often, "What do you intend to do?" and "How would you label your feeling?" These arguably are not behavior and feelings but cognitions about them. Thus, social psychological causes are largely cognitive, and the results are largely cognitive.

A third way in which social psychology has always been cognitive is that the person in-between the presumed cause and the result is viewed as a *thinking organism;* this view contrasts with viewing the person as an emotional organism or a mindless automaton (Manis, 1977). Many social psychological theories paint a portrait of the typical person as reasoning (perhaps badly) before acting. In attempting to deal with complex human problems, as social psychology always has, complex mental processes seem essential. How else can one account for stereotyping and prejudice, propaganda and persuasion, altruism and aggression, and more? It is hard to imagine where a narrowly behaviorist theory would even begin. A strict stimulus-response (S-R) theory does not include the thinking organism that seems essential to account for such problems. In several senses, then, social psychology contrasts with strict S-R theories in its reliance on S-O-R theories that include stimulus, organism, and response. Consequently, the thinker, who comes in-between stimulus and response, has always been paramount in social psychology.

The social thinker has taken many guises in recent decades of research. These guises describe the various roles of cognition in social psychology. Besides the varied roles of cognition, motivation has played different roles in the view of the social thinker. Keeping in mind these two components, cognition and motivation, we can identify four general views of the thinker in social psychology: consistency seeker, naive scientist, cognitive miser, and motivated tactician.

The first view emerged from the massive quantities of work on attitude change after World War II. In the later 1950s, several theories were proposed, all sharing some crucial basic assumptions. The consistency theories, as they were called, viewed people as *consistency seekers* motivated by perceived discrepancies among their cognitions (e.g., Festinger, 1957; Heider, 1958; see Abelson et al., 1968, for an overview). For example, if David knows he is on a diet and knows that he has just eaten a hot fudge sundae, he must do some thinking to bring those two cognitions into line.

Two points are crucial. First, these theories relied on perceived inconsistency, which places cognitive activity in a central role. For example, if would-be dieters can convince themselves that one splurge will not matter, eating a sundae is not inconsistent for them. Objective inconsistency, then, is not important. Subjective inconsistency—among various cognitions or among feelings and cognitions—is central to these theories. Actual inconsistency that is not perceived as such does not yield psychological inconsistency.

Second, once inconsistency *is* perceived, the person is presumed to feel uncomfortable (a negative drive state) and to be motivated to reduce the inconsistency. Reducing the aversive drive state is a pleasant relief, rewarding in itself. This sort of motivational model is called a drive reduction model. Less formally, the sundae-consuming dieter will not be free from anxiety until he manufactures some excuse. Hence, consistency theories posit that people change their attitudes and beliefs for motivational reasons, because of unmet needs for consistency. In sum, motivation and cognition both were central to the consistency theories.

Ironically, as they proliferated, consistency theories ceased to dominate the field, partly because the variants on a theme became indistinguishable. Moreover, it was difficult to predict what a person would perceive as inconsistent and to what degree, and which route to resolving inconsistency a person would take. Finally, people do in fact tolerate a fair amount of inconsistency, so the motivation to avoid it—as an overriding principle—was called into doubt (cf. Kiesler, Collins, & Miller, 1969).

Research in social cognition began in the early 1970s, and with it two new models of the thinker emerged. Cognition and motivation played rather different roles in these two models, compared to the roles they played in the consistency seeker model. In both new models, motivation is secondary in importance to cognition. At present, however, a brief look is useful.

The first new model within the framework of social cognition research is the *naive scientist,* a model of how people uncover the causes of behavior. Attribution theories concern how people explain their own and the other people's behavior; they came to the forefront of research in early 1970s. Attribution theories describe people's causal analyses of or attributions about the social world. For example, an attribution can address whether someone's behavior seems to be caused by the external situation or by the person's internal disposition. If you want to know why your acquaintance Bruce snapped at you one morning, it would be important to decide if there were mitigating circumstances (his girlfriend left him; you just backed into his car) or if he has an irritable disposition (he always behaves this way and to everyone).

Attribution theorists at first assumed that people are fairly rational in distinguishing among various potential causes. In part, this was a purposeful theoretical strategy designed to push a rational view of people as far as possible, in order to discover its shortcomings. The theories started with the working hypothesis that, given enough time, people resemble naive scientists, who will gather all the relevant data and arrive at the most logical conclusion. In this view, you would think about your friend's behavior in a variety of settings and carefully weight the evidence for a situational cause or a dispositional cause of his behavior. Thus, the role of cognition in the naive scientist model is as an outcome of fairly rational analysis.

If you are wrong about why Bruce was irritable, the early theories would have viewed your error as emotion-based departure from the normal process or as a simple error in available information. For example, if you attribute

Bruce's unpleasant behavior to his irritable disposition, it may be because you are motivated to avoid the idea that he is angry at your. Hence, errors arise, mainly as interference from nonrational motivations. In the early attribution theories, motivation enters mainly as a potential qualification on the usual process.

Unfortunately, people are not always so careful. On an everyday basis, people often make attributions in a relatively thoughtless fashion. The cognitive system is limited in capacity, so people take shortcuts. The limitations of the cognitive system can be illustrated by such trivial problems as trying to keep a credit card number, an area code, and a telephone number in your head as you dial, or by more serious problems such as working poorly when you are distracted. The impact of cognitive limitations shows up in social inferences, too. To illustrate, in deciding why Bruce was irritable, you may seize on the easiest explanation rather than the most accurate one. Rather than asking Bruce whether there is something disturbing him, you may simply label him as unpleasant, without giving it much thought. Quite often, people simply are not very thorough.

Hence, the third general view of the thinker (and the second major type of model in social cognition research), comes under the rubric of a *descriptive* model: what people actually do, rather than what they should do. One name for this is the *cognitive miser* model (S. E. Taylor, 1981). The idea is that people are limited in their capacity to process information, so they take shortcuts whenever they can. People adopt strategies that simplify complex problems; the strategies may not be normatively correct or produce normatively correct answers, but they emphasize efficiency. The capacity-limited thinker searches for rapid adequate solutions, rather than slow accurate solutions. Consequently, errors and biases stem from inherent features of the cognitive system, not necessarily from motivations. Indeed, the cognitive miser model is silent on the issue of motivations or feelings of any sort. The role of cognition is central to the cognitive miser view, and the role of motivation has vanished almost entirely, with isolated exceptions.

As the cognitive miser viewpoint has matured, the importance of motivations and emotions has again become evident. Having developed considerable sophistication about people's cognitive processes, researchers are beginning to appreciate anew the interesting and important influences of motivation on cognition. With growing emphasis on motivated social cognition (Showers & Cantor, 1985), researchers are returning to old problems with new perspectives gained from studying social cognition. The emerging view of the social perceiver, then, might best be termed the *motivated tactician,* a fully engaged thinker who has multiple cognitive strategies available and chooses among them based on goals, motives, and needs. Sometimes the motivated tactician chooses wisely, in the interests of adaptability and accuracy, and sometimes the motivated tactician chooses defensively, in the interests of speed or self-esteem. Thus, views of the social thinker are coming full cycle, back to appreciating the importance of motivation, but with increased sophistication about cognitive structure and process.

In summary, social psychology has always been cognitive, in the broad sense of positing important steps that intervene between observable stimulus and observable response. One early major set of theories viewed people as consistency seekers, and motivation played a central role in driving the whole system. With the rise of social cognition research, new views have emerged. In one major wave of research, psychologists view people as naive scientists. These psychologists see motivation mainly as a source of error. In another recent view, psychologists see people as cognitive misers and locate errors in the inherent limitations of the cognitive system, saying almost nothing about motivation. Finally, motivational influences on cognition reemerge in a revitalized view of the thinker as a motivated tactician.


## PEOPLE ARE NOT THINGS

As one reviews research on social cognition, the analogy between the perception of things and the perception of people becomes increasingly clear. The argument is made repeatedly: the principles that describe how people think in general also describe how people think about people. Many theories of social cognition have developed in ways that undeniably build on fundamental cognitive principles, as we will see. Nevertheless, borrowing such principles, we must consider fundamental differences when applying them to cognition about people. After all, cognitive psychology is relatively more concerned with the processing of information about inanimate objects and abstract concepts, whereas social psychology is more concerned with the processing of information about people and social experience.

At this point, the reader who is new to social cognition research already may be saying, "Wait, you can't tell me that the way I think about mental arithmetic or about my coffee cup has anything to do with the way I think about my friends." The wisdom or folly of applying the principles of object perception to the perception of people has been debated for some time (Heider, 1958; Higgins, Kuiper, & Olson, 1981; Krauss, 1981; Schneider et al., 1979; Tagiuri & Petrullo, 1958). Some of the important differences between people and things include the following:

- People intentionally influence the environment; they attempt to control it for their own purposes. Objects, of course, are not intentional causal agents.
- People perceive back; as you are busy forming impressions of them, they are doing the same to you. Social cognition is mutual cognition.
- Social cognition implicates the self, because the target is judging you, because the target may provide you with information about yourself,

and because the target is more similar to you than any object could be.

- A social stimulus may change upon being the target of cognition. People worry about how they come across and may adjust their appearance or behavior accordingly; coffee cups obviously do not.
- People's traits are nonobservable attributes that are vital to thinking about them. An object's nonobservable attributes are somewhat less crucial. Both a person and a cup can be fragile, but that inferred characteristic is both less important and more directly seen in the cup.
- People change over time and circumstance more than objects typically do. This can make cognitions rapidly obsolete or unreliable.
- The accuracy of one's cognitions about people is harder to check than the accuracy of one's cognitions about objects. Even psychologists have a hard time agreeing on whether a given person is extraverted, sensitive, or honest, but most ordinary people easily could test whether a given cup is heat-resistant, fragile, or leaky.
- People are unavoidably complex. One cannot study cognitions about people without making numerous choices to simplify. The researcher has to simplify in object cognition, too, but it is less of a distortion. One cannot simplify a social stimulus without eliminating much of the inherent richness of the target.
- Because people are so complex, and because they have traits and intents hidden from view, and because they affect us in ways objects do not, social cognition automatically involves social explanation. It is more important for an ordinary person to explain why a person is fragile than to explain why a cup is.

For these reasons, social cognitive psychology will never be a literal translation of cognitive psychology. It profits from theories and methods adapted to new uses, but the social world provides perspectives and challenges that are dramatic, if not unique, features of thinking about other people and oneself.

## References

Abelson, R. P., Aronson, E., McGuire, W. J., Newcomb, T. M., Rosenberg, M. J., & Tannenbaum, P. H. (Eds.) (1968). *Theories of cognitive consistency: A sourcebook.* Chicago: Rand McNally.

Allport, G. W. (1958). *The nature of prejudice.* Reading, MA: Addison-Wesley.

Festinger, L. (1957). *A theory of cognitive dissonance.* Palo Alto, CA: Stanford University Press.

Heider, F. (1958). *The psychology of interpersonal relations.* New York: Wiley.

Higgins, E. T., Kuiper, N. A., & Olson, J. M. (1981). Social Cognition: A need to get personal. In E. T. Higgins, C. P. Herman, & M. P. Zanna (Eds.). *Social cognition: The Ontario Symposium* (Vol. 1, pp. 395–429). Hillsdale, NJ: Erlbaum.

Kiesler, C. A., Collins, D. E., & Miller, N. (1969). *Attitude change: A critical analysis of theoretical approaches.* New York: Wiley.

Krauss, R. M. (1981). Impression formation, impression management, and nonverbal behaviors. In E. T. Higgins, C. P. Herman, & M. P. Zanna (Eds.).*Social cognition: The Ontario Symposium* (Vol. 1, pp. 323–341). Hillsdale, NJ: Erlbaum.

Manis, M. (1977). Cognitive social psychology. *Personality and Social Psychology Bulletin, 3,* 550–566.

Schneider, D. J., Hastorf, A. H., & Ellsworth, P. C. (1979). *Person perception.* Reading, MA: Addison-Wesley.

Tagiuri, R., & Petrullo, L. (Eds.) (1958). *Person perception and interpersonal behavior.* Palo Alto, CA: Stanford University Press.

Showers, C., and Cantor, N. (1985). Social cognition: A look at motivated strategies. In M. R. Rosenzweig and L. W. Porter (eds.), *Annual Review of Psychology* (Vol. 36, pp. 275–305). Palo Alto, CA: Annual Reviews.

Taylor, S. E. (1981). A categorization approach to stereotyping. In D. L. Hamilton (Ed.). *Cognitive processes in stereotyping and integroup behavior* (pp. 88–114). Hillsdale, NJ: Erlbaum.

Zajonc, R. B. (1980). Cognition and social cognition: A historical perspective. In L. Festinger (ed.). *Retrospections on social psychology* (pp. 180–204). New York: Oxford University Press.

Richard Nisbett
Lee Ross

# Judgmental Heuristics and Knowledge Structures

Nisbett and Ross deal with the ways in which people go beyond the information before them and make inferences that are not always accurate. They discuss two *heuristics,* or cognitive shortcuts, that people frequently use: the availability and representativeness heuristics. By using the availability heuristic we may overestimate the likelihood of an event to the extent that instances of it come easily to mind, whereas the representativeness heuristic can mislead when we mistakenly assume that a person or event is typical of the general class that it is a part of.

The most characteristic thing about mental life, over and beyond the fact that one apprehends the events of the world around one, is that one constantly goes beyond the information given.

Jerome Bruner

The perceiver, as Bruner (1957) recognized, is not simply a dutiful clerk who passively registers items of information. Rather, the perceiver is an active interpreter, one who resolves ambiguities, makes educated guesses about events that cannot be observed directly, and forms inferences about associations and causal relations. In this chapter we explore the strategies that permit and encourage the perceiver to "go beyond the information given," that is, to venture beyond the most immediate implications of the data.

We will introduce the reader to the "availability heuristic" and the "representativeness heuristic"—two simple judgmental strategies on which people seem to rely, and by which they sometimes are misled, in a variety of inferential tasks. In so doing, the chapter introduces the reader to a set of extraordinarily important contributions by Daniel Kahneman and Amos Tversky (1972, 1973, in press; Tversky & Kahneman, 1971, 1973, 1974).

The heuristics to be explored are relatively primitive and simple judgmental strategies. They are not irrational or even nonrational. They probably produce vastly more correct or partially correct inferences than erroneous ones, and they do so with great speed and little effort. Indeed, we suspect that the use of such simple tools may be an inevitable feature of the cognitive apparatus of any organism that must make as many judgments, inferences, and decisions as humans have to do. Each heuristic or, more properly, the misapplication of each heuristic, does lead people astray in some important inferential tasks. Since this book is particularly concerned with inferential failings, it is the misuse of the heuristics—their application in preference to more normatively appropriate strategies—that we will emphasize.

Although we characterize the heuristics as "judgmental strategies," the term is misleading in that it implies a conscious and deliberate application of well-defined decision rules. The heuristics to be explored should be distinguished from straightforward computational or judgmental "algorithms" (such as the method for finding square roots or deciding whether one's bridge hand merits an opening bid), which generally are explicit and invariant both in the criteria for their use and the manner of their application. The intuitive psychologist probably would not assent to, much less spontaneously express, any general formulation of either heuristic. Instead, the utilitization of the heuristics is generally automatic and nonreflective and notably free of any conscious consideration of appropriateness. As we shall see, the heuristics are not applied in a totally indiscriminate fashion. In many contexts in which a given heuristic would promote error, people refrain from using it and probably could articulate why its use would be foolish. On other logically equivalent and equally unpropitious occasions, people readily apply the same heuristic and may even attempt to justify its use.


## THE AVAILABILITY HEURISTIC

When people are required to judge the relative frequency of particular objects or the likelihood of particular events, they often may be influenced by the relative *availability* of the objects or events, that is, their accessibility in the processes of perception, memory, or construction from imagination (cf. Tversky & Kahneman 1973). Such availability criteria often will prove accurate and useful. To the extent that availability is actually associated with objective frequency, the availability heuristic can be a useful tool of judgment. There are many factors uncorrelated with frequency, however, which can influence an event's immediate perceptual salience, the vividness or completeness with which it is recalled, or the ease with which it is imagined. As a result, the availability heuristic can be misleading.

### Availability Biases in Frequency Estimation

Let us proceed first by introducing and then exploring in some detail three judgmental tasks for which application of the availability heuristic might lead one to biased estimates of the relative frequency of various objects or events. The first two examples are hypothetical.

(1) A pollster who asks a sample of American adults to estimate the "percentage of the work force who are currently unemployed" finds an "egocentric bias." That is, currently unemployed workers tend to overestimate the rate of unemployment, but currently employed workers tend to underestimate it.

(2) An Indiana businessman confides to a friend, "Did you ever notice how many Hoosiers become famous or important? Look any-where—politics, sports, Hollywood, big business, even notorious bank robbers—I couldn't guess the exact figures, but I bet we Hoosiers have far more than our fair share on just about any list in *Who's Who.*"

(3) A group of subjects consistently errs in judging the relative fre-quency of two kinds of English words. Specifically, they estimate the number of words beginning with particular letters (for example, *R* or *K*) to be greater than the number of words with those letters appearing third, although words of the latter type actually are far more numerous.

Examples 1 and 2 seem to present common and familiar errors, although one might not immediately recognize the role of availability factors in produc-ing them. In fact, some readers might hasten to cite motivational or even "psychodynamic" factors that could induce unemployed workers to overes-timate the commonness of their plight or that could prompt proud Indiana residents to exaggerate their share of the limelight. Example 3 seems less intuitively obvious and at first seems quite unconnected to the other two examples. Nevertheless, the chief source of error in all three cases seems to us to be the availability heuristic.

Consider Example 1, about estimates of unemployment. Here the bias in subjective availability can be traced to a bias in initial sampling. Unem-ployed people are more likely to know and meet other unemployed people than are job-holders, and vice versa. The reasons for such a sampling bias are hardly mysterious: The unemployed individual is likely to share the neigh-borhood, socioeconomic background, and occupation of other jobless individ-uals. He also is likely to encounter other unemployed people in such everyday endeavors as job-hunting, visiting employment agencies, collecting unem-ployment benefits, and shopping at stores offering cut-rate prices or easy credit. Indeed, he even may seek out such individuals for social comparison, information exchange, or general commiseration. Thus, to the extent that the unemployed person relies upon the sample generated by his personal experi-ence, he will be misled about the commonness of unemployment. In the same manner, employed people, who are apt to live, work, and shop near one another, are apt to err in the opposite direction.

It is important to emphasize that the people in this hypothetical example would not be compelled to rely upon biased availability criteria in estimating the frequency of unemployment. They could try to recall media presentations of data, could apply some popular rule of thumb ("When there's an energy shortage, jobs disappear"), or could employ some more appropriate "sampling procedure" ("How many people have I seen lining up outside my neighborhood unemployment office on the first of the month this year as compared with last year?"). They even could attempt to compensate for the biases distorting their samples of available data ("Hardly anyone I know is jobless, but of course, I don't get to meet many unemployed people, do I? I guess I'd better adjust my estimate upward!"). Indeed, it is quite likely that some people *would* avoid availability criteria or at least would attempt the necessary adjustments. Throughout this book, however, we present experimental evidence showing that simple, tempting, availability criteria are used in contexts in which availability and frequency are poorly correlated and are used without appropriate adjustments for the factors that bias subjective experience.

Now let us consider Example 2, about the relative prominence of Indiana natives. The Hoosier's egocentric estimate clearly contains some of the same features as in our initial example. That is, people from Indiana are disproportionately likely to know or hear about famous fellow Hoosiers. Beyond such biases in initial exposure, however, this example introduces the potential influence of additional biases in *storage*. When a national sportscaster says "Myra Swift of Grandville, Indiana and Mary Speed of Bigtown, Florida won gold medals in the Olympics yesterday," it is the accomplishment of his fellow Hoosier that the Indiana businessman is more likely to notice and to remember. Accordingly, the sample of famous people he subsequently can recall from memory will reflect biases at the "storage" stage as well as at the sampling stage.

Biases in exposure, attention, and storage can arise, of course, from many factors besides the kinship between the perceiver and the object. For instance, oddity or newsworthiness could accomplish the same end. Thus, people from all states might overestimate the number of very big, very small, very young, very pretty, or very hirsute Olympic gold medalists because such factors would bias the rater's likelihood of sampling, storing, and recalling the pertinent instances.

Example 3, about estimates of the frequency of the letter *R* in the first versus the third position, is subtler. In fact, readers who try the experiment themselves may find that they make the same incorrect assessments of relative frequency as did the original subjects. Once again, an inappropriate application of the availability criterion is the source of the difficulty. Like the subjects in Tversky's and Kahneman's (1973) demonstration, the reader probably finds that instances of words beginning with *R* are easier to generate spontaneously (at least in a casual first attempt) than are instances of words that have *R* as their third letter. But the differences in ease of generation do not reflect corresponding differences in word frequency. Any truly *random* sample of English words would reveal words beginning with $R$ to be much *less* common than words with $R$ as their third letter. The relative difficulty of generating words like "care," "street," and "derail," may give interesting hints of the storage and retrieval of one's vocabulary, but it says virtually nothing about objective word frequencies.

An analogy may be instructive here: In a quick search of the library, one would find it easier to find books by authors named Woolf than by authors named Virginia, or to find books about Australia than books by authors born in Australia. Such differences obviously would indicate little about the relative frequencies of such books in the library's collection. Instead, they would reflect the library's system for referencing books and granting access to them. By the same token, first letters apparently are more useful cues than third letters are for referencing and permitting access to the items in one's personal word collection. Once again, the use of criteria other than the subjective ease of generation (or, alternatively, recognition of relevant biases and adequate compensation) could lead people to a more accurate estimate.

### Availability of Event Relationships and of Causal Explanations

Kahneman's and Tverksy's work has been largely on the use of the availability heuristic in judgments involving the frequency or probability of individual events. Other research indicates that subjective availability may influence judgments of *relationships* between events, particularly *causal* relationships.

Jones's and Nisbett's (1972) account of the divergent causal interpretations of actors and observers—from which observers cite "dispositional" factors (traits, abilities, attitudes, etc.) to explain behaviors and outcomes that the actors themselves attribute to "situational" factors—is one case in point. For example, the actor who gives a dollar to a beggar is apt to attribute his behavior to the sad plight of the beggar, but the observer of the behavior is apt to attribute it to the actor's generosity. From the actor's perspective, it is the constantly changing features of the environment that are particularly salient or "available" as potential causes to which his behavior can be attributed. From the observer's perspective, the actor is the perceptual "figure" and the situation merely "ground," so that the actor himself provides the most available causal candidate. Indeed, by altering actors' and observers' perspectives through videotape replays, mirrors, or other methods, one can correspondingly alter the actors' and observers' causal assessments (cf. Arkin & Duval 1975; Duval & Wicklund 1972; Regan & Totten 1975; Storms 1973).

Subsequent research by a number of investigators, most notably Taylor and her associates (for example, Taylor & Fiske 1975, 1978), has demonstrated a more general point regarding availability and causal assessment. It appears that almost *any* manipulation that focuses the perceiver's attention on a potential cause, for example, on a particular participant in a social interaction, affects causal assessment. Whether the attentional manipulation is achieved by a blunt instruction about which participant to watch, subtle variations in seating arrangement, or by "solo" versus "non-solo" status of, for example, female or black participants, the person made disproportionately "available" to onlookers is seen to be a disproportionately potent causal agent. (See also McArthur & Post 1977; McArthur & Solomon 1978.)

Availability effects also may account for other biases involving perceived causality. Consider Fischhoff's (1975; Fischhoff & Beyth 1975) reports on the subjective certainty of hindsight knowledge. These reports show that outcomes often seem in retrospect to have been inevitable. This may be because the antecedents and causal scenarios that "predicted" such outcomes have far greater "after-the-fact" availability than do antecedents or scenarios that predicted alternative outcomes that did not in fact occur.

*Appropriate and Inappropriate Applications of the Availability Heuristic*

An indiscriminate use of the availability heuristic clearly can lead people into serious judgmental errors. It is important to reemphasize that in many contexts perceptual salience, memorability, and imaginability may be relatively unbiased and therefore well correlated with true frequency, probability, or even causal significance. In such cases, of course, the availability heuristic often can be a helpful and efficient tool of inference.

The same jobless individuals whose estimates of unemployment rates were distorted by the availability heuristic could make a reasonably accurate estimate of the preponderance of oak trees to maple trees in their neighborhood by using the same strategy. In estimating the frequencies of various types of trees, the individual's personal experiences and subsequent recollections would constitute generally unbiased samples. Similarly, the Indiana resident who was misled by the disproportionate availability of instances of famous fellow Hoosiers might have fared quite well if the same heuristic had been applied in estimating the success of German Olympians relative to Italian Olympians. Furthermore, the "ease of generation" criterion would have helped rather than hindered Tversky's and Kahneman's subjects if the experimental task had been to estimate the relative frequencies either of a) words beginning with *R* versus words beginning with *L*, or b) words with *R* versus *L* in the third position. In either of these cases, differences in the relative ease of generation would have reflected differences in frequency quite accurately.

The normative status of using the availability heuristic, and the pragmatic utility of using it, thus depend on the judgmental domain and context. People are not, of course, totally unaware that simple availability criteria must sometimes be discounted. For example, few people who were asked to estimate the relative number of moles versus cats in their neighborhood would conclude "there must be more cats because I've seen several of them but I've never seen a mole." Nevertheless, as this book documents, people often fail to distinguish between legitimate and superficially similar, but illegitimate, uses of the availability heuristic.

## THE REPRESENTATIVENESS HEURISTIC

The second judgmental heuristic to be introduced is one which Kahneman and Tversky (1972, 1973; Tversky & Kahneman 1974) termed the *representativeness* heuristic. This heuristic involves the application of relatively simple resemblance of "goodness of fit" criteria to problems of categorization. In making a judgment, people assess the degree to which the salient features of the object are representative of, or similar to, the features presumed to be characteristic of the category.

In the following sections we try to provide a coherent grouping of examples. It should be emphasized, however, that our classification system is neither exhaustive nor theoretically derived. We also should note that we make no attempt to specify the precise criteria by which individuals calculate the representativeness of one object or event to another.

### Judgments of the Degree to Which Outcomes Are Representative of Their Origins

People often are required to predict some outcome or judge the likelihood of some event on the basis of information about the "generating process" that produced it. On such occasions, the judgment is likely to reflect the degree to which the specified outcome represents its origin. Let us consider an example adapted from one used by Kahneman and Tversky (1972).

> Subjects are asked to assess the relative likelihood of three particular sequences of births of boys (B) and girls (G) for the next six babies born in the United States. These sequences are i) BBBBBB, ii) GGGBBB, iii) GBBGGB.

According to the conventional probability calculation, the likelihood of each of these sequences is almost identical. (Actually, the first sequence is slightly more likely than either the second or third sequence, since male births are slightly more common than female births. The latter two sequences are simply different orderings of identical, independent events.) Subjects who rely upon their intuitions and upon the representativeness criteria which guide such intuitions, are apt to regard the GBBGGB sequence as far more likely than either of the other two. In doing so, they are responding to what they know about the population of babies and about the processes of "generation," that is, that each birth is a "random" event in which the probability of "boy" and "girl" are nearly equal. Only the GBBGGB sequence is "representative" of the generating process. The GGGBBB sequence seems too "orderly" to represent a random process. The BBBBBB sequence satisfies the criteria even less: It captures neither the randomness of the birth process nor the equal sex distribution of the population from which the six births were "sampled."

The representativeness heuristic also accounts for the familiar "gamblers' fallacy." After observing a long run of "red" on a roulette wheel, people believe that "black" is now due, because the occurrence of black would make the overall sequence of events more representative of the generating process than would the occurrence of another red. In a similar vein, any researcher who has ever consulted a random number table for an unbiased ordering of events has probably felt that the result was somehow insufficiently "representative" of a chance process, that it contained suspiciously orderly sequences, suspiciously long runs, suspicious overrepresentations or underrepresentations of particular numbers early or late in the sequence, and so forth (cf. Tversky & Kahneman 1971).

## Judgments of the Degree to Which Instances Are Representative of Categories

Many everyday judgments require people to estimate the likelihood that some object or event with a given set of characteristics is an instance of some designated category or class. Typically, the judgments are made in relative terms, that is, is Event X more likely to be an instance of Class A or of Class B? Consider the following problem, which is similar in form to those in the empirical work by Kahneman and Tversky.

> The present authors have a friend who is a professor. He likes to write poetry, is rather shy, and is small in stature. Which of the following is his field: (a) Chinese studies or (b) psychology?

Those readers who quickly and confidently predicted "psychology" probably applied some version, whether sophisticated or crude, of conventional statistical canons. We congratulate these readers. We suspect, however, that many readers guessed "Chinese studies," or at least seriously considered that such a guess might be reasonable. If so, they probably were seduced by the representativeness heuristic. Specifically, they assessed the relative "goodness of fit" between the professor's personality profile and the predominant features of their stereotypes of Sinologists and psychologists. Finding the fit better for the former than for the latter, they guessed the professor's field to be Chinese studies.

In succumbing to the lure of the representativeness heuristic, what the reader likely has overlooked or not appreciated is some relevant category *base-rate* information. Let the reader who guessed "Chinese studies" now reconsider that guess in light of the relative numbers of psychologists and Sinologists in the population. Then consider the more restricted population of people likely to be friends of the authors, who themselves are psychologists. Surely *no* reader's implicit personality theory of the strength of association between academic discipline and the professor's various characteristics, that is, poetry-writing, shyness, and slightness of stature, warrants overriding such base-rate considerations.

Errors in problems of the Sinologist/psychologist variety may reflect that the judge has been led to answer the wrong question or, more specifically, to ponder the wrong conditional probability. The judge seems to be responding to the question "How likely is it that a psychologist (versus a Sinologist) would resemble the personal profile provided?" when the actual question posed is "How likely is someone resembling the personality profile to be a psychologist (versus a Sinologist)?" The representativeness heuristic leads people to give a similar answer to the two questions, since it entails consideration only of the resemblance of the two occupational stereotypes to the given personality description. The error is the failure to consider the relevant base rates or marginal probabilities, a consideration which is irrelevant to the first question but critical to the second. Although a much higher proportion of Sinologists than of psychologists may fit the profile, there would still be a much greater *absolute* number of psychologists than of Sinologists who fit it, because of the vastly greater number of psychologists than of Sinologists in the population.

*Appropriate and Inappropriate Applications of the Representativeness Heuristic*

Even more than the availability heuristic, the representativeness heuristic is a legitimate, indeed absolutely essential, cognitive tool. Countless inferential tasks, especially those requiring induction or generalization, depend on deciding what class or category of event one is observing; such judgments inevitably hinge upon assessments of resemblance or representativeness (cf. Tversky 1977). Even in our examples, the use of representativeness heuristic produced errors only because it was overapplied or misapplied while normatively important criteria were overlooked.

It leads people to recognize that an all-male or an all-white jury is more likely to reflect a biased selection procedure than will a jury with a more proportionate representation of the overall population. It also leads people to cry foul when a politician's cronies seem to enjoy a disproportionate share of good luck in their transactions with local or state agencies. Unfortunately, when people's understanding of the generating process and its implications is deficient—as when there are misconceptions about randomness—the representativeness heuristic will mislead.

In the second example, the Sinologist/psychologist problem, people are foiled mainly because important information is neglected, that is, the relevant base rates are ignored. In many circumstances, of course, such information is absent, and the representativeness heuristic has no serious contender. In other circumstances, base-rate information may have little practical significance. Sometimes the feature-matching process results in a category determination with a probability near 1.0, and when features are as powerfully diagnostic as that, there is little practical need to consider base rates. For example, in the Sinologist/psychologist problem, if the profile were extended to include the information that the person speaks Chinese, knows no statistics, and has never heard of B. F. Skinner, the relevance of base-rate frequencies would dwindle to triviality.

# References

Arkin, R., & Duval, S. (1975). Focus of attention and causal attributions of actors and observers. *Journal of Experimental Social Psychology, 11* 427–438.

Bruner, J. S. (1957). Going beyond the information given. In H. Gulber and others (Eds.), *Contemporary approaches to cognition.* Cambridge, MA: Harvard University Press.

Duval, S., & Wicklund, R. A. (1972).*A theory of objective self-awareness.* New York: Academic Press.

Fischhoff, B. (1975). Hindsight≠foresight: The effect of outcome knowledge on judgment under uncertainty. *Journal of Experimental Psychology: Human Perception and Performance, 1,* 228–299.

Fischhoff, B., & Beyth, R. (1975). "I knew it would happen"—remembered probabilities of once-future things. *Organizational Behavior and Human Performance, 13,* 1–16.

Jones, E. E., & Nisbett, R. E. (1972). The actor and the observer: Divergent perceptions of the causes of behavior. In E. E. Jones and others (Eds.), *Attribution: Perceiving the causes of behavior.* Morristown, NJ: General Learning Press.

Kahneman, D., & Tversky, A. (1972). Subjective probability: A judgment of representativeness. *Cognitive Psychology, 3,* 430–454.

Kahneman, D., & Tversky, A. (1973). On the psychology of prediction. *Psychological Review, 80,* 237–251.

Kahneman, D., & Tversky, A. (in press). Intuitive prediction: Biases and corrective procedures. *Management Science.*

McArthur, L. Z. & Post, D. (1977). Figural emphasis and person perception. *Journal of Experimental Social Psychology, 13,* 520–535.

McArthur, L. Z., & Solomon, L. K. (1978). Perceptions of an aggressive encounter as a function of the victim's salience and the perceiver's arousal. *Journal of Personality and Social Psychology, 36,* 1278–1290.

Regan, D. T., & Totten, J. (1975). Empathy and attribution: Turning observers into actors. *Journal of Personality and Social Psychology, 32,* 850–856.

Storms, M. D. (1973). Videotape and the attribution process: Reversing actors' and observers' point of view. *Journal of Personality and Social Psychology, 27,* 165–175.

Taylor, S. E., & Fiske, S. T. (1975). Point of view and perceptions of causality. *Journal of Personality and Social Psychology, 32,* 439–445.

Taylor, S. E., & Fiske, S. T. (1978). Salience, attention and attribution: Top of the head phenomena. In L. Berkowitz (Ed.), *Advances in Experimental Social Psychology* (Vol. 11). New York: Academic Press.

Tversky, A. (1977). Features of similarity. *Psychological Review, 84,* 327–352.

Tversky, A., & Kahneman, D. (1971). Belief in the law of small numbers. *Psychological Bulletin, 76,* 105–110.

Tversky, A., & Kahneman, D. (1973). Availability: A heuristic for judging frequency and probability. *Cognitive Psychology, 5,* 207–232.

Tversky, A., & Kahneman, D. (1974). Judgment under uncertainty: Heuristics and biases. *Science. 185,* 1124–1131.

Albert H. Hastorf
Hadley Cantril

# They Saw a Game—A Case Study

In this classic study of a football game between Princeton and Dartmouth, Hastorf and Cantril demonstrate one of the most fundamental ideas in all of social psychology: No two people ever "see" exactly the same event or person because each one sees it through his or her own unique cognitive filter. The authors tell us that in effect two different games were going on that day—one as seen by the Dartmouth fans and one as seen by those from Princeton. To be more technically accurate, there were probably as many different games being seen as there were people in the stands.

On a brisk Saturday afternoon, November 23, 1951, the Dartmouth football team played Princeton in Princeton's Palmer Stadium. It was the last game of the season for both teams and of rather special significance because the Princeton team had won all its games so far and one of its players, Kazmaier, was receiving All-American mention and had just appeared as the cover man on *Time* magazine, and was playing his last game.

A few minutes after the opening kick-off, it became apparent that the game was going to be a rough one. The referees were kept busy blowing their whistles and penalizing both sides. In the second quarter, Princeton's star left the game with a broken nose. In the third quarter, a Dartmouth player was taken off the field with a broken leg. Tempers flared both during and after the game. The official statistics of the game, which Princeton won, showed that Dartmouth was penalized 70 yards, Princeton 25, not counting more than a few plays in which both sides were penalized.

Needless to say, accusations soon began to fly. The game immediately became a matter of concern to players, students, coaches, and the administrative officials of the two institutions, as well as to alumni and the general public who had not seen the game but had become sensitive to the problem of big-time football through the recent exposures of subsidized players, commercialism, etc. Discussion of the game continued for several weeks.

One of the contributing factors to the extended discussion of the game was the extensive space given to it by both campus and metropolitan newspapers. An indication of the fervor with which the discussions were carried on is shown by a few excerpts from the campus dailies.

For example, on November 27 (four days after the game), the *Daily Princetonian* (Princeton's student newspaper) said:

> This observer has never seen quite such a disgusting exhibition of so-called "sport." Both teams were guilty but the blame must be laid primarily on Dartmouth's doorstep. Princeton, obviously the better team, had no reason to rough up Dartmouth. Looking at the situation rationally, we don't see why the Indians should make a deliberate attempt to cripple Dick Kazmaier or any other Princeton player. The Dartmouth psychology, however, is not rational itself.

The November 30th edition of the *Princeton Alumni Weekly* said:

> But certain memories of what occurred will not be easily erased. Into the record books will go in indelible fashion the fact that the last game of Dick Kazmaier's career was cut short by more than half when he was forced out with a broken nose and a mild concussion, sustained from a tackle that came well after he had thrown a pass.
>
> This second-period development was followed by a third-quarter outbreak of roughness that was climaxed when a Dartmouth player deliberately kicked Brad Glass in the ribs while the latter was on his back. Throughout the often unpleasant afternoon, there was undeniable evidence that the losers' tactics were the result of an actual style of play, and reports on other games they have played this season substantiate this.

Dartmouth students were "seeing" an entirely different version of the game through the editorial eyes of the *Dartmouth* (Dartmouth's undergraduate newspaper). For example, on November 27 the *Dartmouth* said:

> However, the Dartmouth-Princeton game set the stage for the other type of dirty football. A type which may be termed as an unjustifiable accusation.
>
> Dick Kazmaier was injured early in the game. Kazmaier was the star, an All-American. Other stars have been injured before, but Kazmaier had been built to represent a Princeton idol. When an idol is hurt there is only one recourse—the tag of dirty football. So what did the Tiger Coach Charley Caldwell do? He announced to the world that the Big Green had been out to extinguish the Princeton star. His purpose was achieved.
>
> After this incident, Caldwell instilled the old see-what-they-did-go-get-them attitude into his players. His talk got results. Gene Howard and Jim Miller were both injured. Both had dropped back to pass, had passed, and were standing unprotected in the backfield. Result: one bad leg and one leg broken.
>
> The game was rough and did get a bit out of hand in the third quarter.

Yet most of the roughing penalties were called against Princeton while Dartmouth received more of the illegal-use-of-the-hands variety.

On November 28 the *Dartmouth* said:

> Dick Kazmaier of Princeton admittedly is an unusually able football player. Many Dartmouth men traveled to Princeton, not expecting to win—only hoping to see an All-American in action. Dick Kazmaier was hurt in the second period, and played only a token part in the remainder of the game. For this, spectators were sorry.
>
> But there were no such feelings for Dick Kazmaier's health. Medical authorities have confirmed that as a relatively unprotected passing and running star in a contact sport, he is quite liable to injury. Also, his particular injuries—a broken nose and slight concussion—were no more serious than is experienced almost any day in any football practice, where there is no more serious stake than playing the following Saturday. Up to the Princeton game, Dartmouth players suffered about 10 known nose fractures and face injuries, not to mention several slight concussions.
>
> Did Princeton players feel so badly about losing their star? They shouldn't have. During the past undefeated campaign they stopped several individual stars by a concentrated effort, including such mainstays as Frank Hauff of Navy, Glenn Adams of Pennsylvania and Rocco Calvo of Cornell.
>
> In other words, the same brand of football condemned by the *Prince*—that of stopping the big man—is practiced quite successfully by the Tigers.

Basically, then, there was disagreement as to what had happened during the "game." Hence we took the opportunity presented by the occasion to make a "real life" study of a perceptual problem.[1]

## PROCEDURE

Two steps were involved in gathering data. The first consisted of answers to a questionnaire designed to get reactions to the game and to learn something of the climate of opinion in each institution. This questionnaire was administered a week after the game to both Dartmouth and Princeton undergraduates who were taking introductory and intermediate psychology courses.

The second step consisted of showing the same motion picture of the game to a sample of undergraduates in each school and having them check on another questionnaire, as they watched the film, any infraction of the rules they saw and whether these infractions were "mild" or "flagrant."[2] At Dart-

---

[1] We are not concerned here with the problem of guilt or responsibility for infractions, and nothing here implies any judgment as to who was to blame.

[2] The film shown was kindly loaned for the purpose of the experiment by the Dartmouth College Athletic Council. It should be pointed out that a movie of a football game follows the ball, is thus selective, and omits a good deal of the total action on the field. Also, of course, in viewing only a film of the game, the possibilities of participation as spectator are greatly limited.

mouth, members of two fraternities were asked to view the film on December 7; at Princeton, members of two undergraduate clubs saw the film early in January.

The answers to both questionnaires were carefully coded and transferred to punch cards.

## RESULTS

Table 1 shows the questions which received different replies from the two student populations on the first questionnaire.

Questions asked if the students had friends on the team, if they had ever played football themselves, if they felt they knew the rules of the game well, etc., showed no differences in either school and no relation to answers given to other questions. This is not surprising since the students in both schools come from essentially the same type of educational, economic, and ethnic background.

Summarizing the data of Tables 1 and 2, we find a marked contrast between the two student groups.

Nearly all *Princeton* students judged the game as "rough and dirty"—not one of them thought it "clean and fair." And almost nine-tenths of them thought the other side started the rough play. By and large they felt that the charges they understood were being made were true; most of them felt the charges were made in order to avoid similar situations in the future.

When Princeton students looked at the movie of the game, they saw the Dartmouth team make over twice as many infractions as their own team made. And they saw the Dartmouth team make over twice as many infractions as were seen by Dartmouth students. When Princeton students judged these infractions as "flagrant" or "mild," the ratio was about two "flagrant" to one "mild" on the Dartmouth team, and about one "flagrant" to three "mild" on the Princeton team.

As for the *Dartmouth* students, while the plurality of answers fell in the "rough and dirty" category, over one-tenth thought the game was "clean and fair" and over a third introduced their own category of "rough and fair" to describe the action. Although a third of the Dartmouth students felt that Dartmouth was to blame for starting the rough play, the majority of Dartmouth students thought both sides were to blame. By and large, Dartmouth men felt that the charges they understood were being made were not true, and most of them thought the reason for the charges was Princeton's concern for its football star.

When Dartmouth students looked at the movie of the game they saw both teams make about the same number of infractions. And they saw their own team make only half the number of infractions the Princeton students saw them make. The ratio of "flagrant" to "mild" infractions was about one to one when Dartmouth students judged the Dartmouth team, and about one

**TABLE 1.** Data from first questionnaire.

| Question | Dartmouth students (N = 163) % | Princeton students (N = 161) % |
|---|---|---|
| 1. Did you happen to see the actual game between Dartmouth and Princeton in Palmer Stadium this year? | | |
| Yes | 33 | 71 |
| No | 67 | 29 |
| 2. Have you seen a movie of the game or seen it on television? | | |
| Yes, movie | 33 | 2 |
| Yes, television | 0 | 1 |
| No, neither | 67 | 97 |
| 3. (Asked of those who answered "yes" to either or both of above questions.) From your observations of what went on at the game, do you believe the game was clean and fairly played, or that it was unnecessarily rough and dirty? | | |
| Clean and fair | 6 | 0 |
| Rough and dirty | 24 | 69 |
| Rough and fair* | 25 | 2 |
| No answer | 45 | 29 |
| 4. (Asked of those who answered "no" on both of the first questions.) From what you have heard and read about the game, do you feel it was clean and fairly played, or that it was unnecessarily rough and dirty?) | | |
| Clean and fair | 7 | 0 |
| Rough and dirty | 18 | 24 |
| Rough and fair* | 14 | 1 |
| Don't know | 6 | 4 |
| No answer | 55 | 71 |
| (Combined answers to questions 3 and 4 above) | | |
| Clean and fair | 13 | 0 |
| Rough and dirty | 42 | 93 |
| Rough and fair | 39 | 3 |
| Don't know | 6 | 4 |
| 5. From what you saw in the game or the movies, or from what you have read, which team do you feel started the rough play? | | |
| Dartmouth started it | 36 | 86 |
| Princeton started it | 2 | 0 |
| Both started it | 53 | 11 |
| Neither | 6 | 1 |
| No answer | 3 | 2 |
| 6. What is your understanding of the charges being made?** | | |
| Dartmouth tried to get Kazmaier | 71 | 47 |
| Dartmouth intentionally dirty | 52 | 44 |
| Dartmouth unnecessarily rough | 8 | 35 |
| 7. Do you feel there is any truth to these charges? | | |
| Yes | 10 | 55 |
| No | 57 | 4 |
| Partly | 29 | 35 |
| Don't know | 4 | 6 |
| 8. Why do you think the charges were made? | | |
| Injury to Princeton star | 70 | 23 |
| To prevent repetition | 2 | 46 |
| No answer | 28 | 31 |

*This answer was not included on the checklist but was written in by the percentage of students indicated.

**Replies do not add to 100% since more than one charge could be given.

**TABLE 2.** Data from second questionnaire checked while seeing film.

| | | Total number of infractions checked against | |
| | | Dartmouth team | Princeton team |
| Group | N | Mean | Mean |
| --- | --- | --- | --- |
| Dartmouth students | 48 | 4.3 | 4.4 |
| Princeton students | 49 | 9.8 | 4.2 |

"flagrant" to two "mild" when Dartmouth students judged infractions made by the Princeton team.

If should be noted that Dartmouth and Princeton students were thinking of different charges in judging their validity and in assigning reasons as to why the charges were made. It should also be noted that whether or not students were spectators of the game in the stadium made little difference in their responses.

## INTERPRETATION: THE NATURE OF A SOCIAL EVENT

It seems clear that the "game" actually was many different games and that each version of the events that transpired was just as "real" to a particular person as other versions were to other people. A consideration of the experiential phenomena that constitute a "football game" for the spectator may help us both to account for the results obtained and illustrate something of the nature of any social event.

Like any other complex social occurrence, a "football game" consists of a whole host of happenings. Many different events are occurring simultaneously. Furthermore, each happening is a link in a chain of happenings, so that one follows another in sequence. The "football game," as well as other complex social situations, consists of a whole matrix of events. In the game situation, this matrix of events consists of the actions of all the players, together with the behavior of the referees and linesmen, the action on the sidelines, in the grandstands, over the loudspeaker, etc.

Of crucial importance is the fact that an "occurrence" on the football field or in any other social situation does not become an experiential "event" unless and until some significance is given to it: an "occurrence" becomes an *event* only when the happening has significance. And a happening generally has significance only if it reactivates learned significances already registered in what we have called a person's assumptive form-world (Cantril, 1950).

Hence the particular occurrences that different people experienced in the football game were a limited series of events from the total matrix of events *potentially* available to them. People experienced those occurrences that reactivated significances they brought to the occasion; they failed to experience those occurrences which did not reactivate past significances.

In this particular study, one of the most interesting examples of this phenomenon was a telegram sent to an officer of Dartmouth College by a member of a Dartmouth alumni group in the Midwest. He had viewed the film which had been shipped to his alumni group from Princeton after its use with Princeton students, who saw, as we noted, an average of over nine infractions by Dartmouth players during the game. The alumnus, who couldn't see the infractions he had heard publicized, wired:

> Preview of Princeton movies indicates considerable cutting of important part please wire explanation and possibly air mail missing part before showing scheduled for January 25 we have splicing equipment.

The "same" sensory impingements emanating from the football field, transmitted through the visual mechanism to the brain, also obviously gave rise to different experiences in different people. The significances assumed by different happenings for different people depend in large part on the purposes people bring to the occasion and the assumptions they have of the purposes and probable behavior of other people involved.

In brief, the data here indicate that there is no such "thing" as a "game" existing "out there" in its own right which people merely "observe." The "game" "exists" for a person and is experienced by him only in so far as certain happenings have significances in terms of his purpose. Out of all the occurrences going on in the environment, a person selects those that have some significance for him from his own egocentric position in the total matrix.

Obviously in the case of a football game, the value of the experience of watching the game is enhanced if the purpose of "your" team is accomplished, that is, if the happening of the desired consequence is experienced—i.e., if your team wins. But the value attribute of the experience can, of course, be spoiled if the desire to win crowds out behavior we value and have come to call sportsmanlike.

The sharing of significances provides the links except for which a "social" event would not be experienced and would not exist for anyone.

A "football game" would be impossible except for the rules of the game which we bring to the situation and which enable us to share with others the significances of various happenings. These rules make possible a certain repeatability of events such as first downs, touchdowns, etc. If a person is unfamiliar with the rules of the game, the behavior he sees lacks repeatability and consistent significance and hence "doesn't make sense."

And only because there is the possibility of repetition is there the possibility that a happening has a significance. For example, the balls used in games are designed to give a high degree of repeatability. While a football is about the only ball used in games which is not a sphere, the shape of the modern football has apparently evolved in order to achieve a higher degree of accuracy and speed in forward passing than would be obtained with a spherical ball, thus increasing the repeatability of an important phase of the game.

The rules of a football game, like laws, rituals, customs, and mores, are registered and preserved forms of sequential significances enabling people to share the significances of occurrences. The sharing of sequential significances which have value for us provides the links that operationally make social events possible. They are analogous to he forces of attraction that hold parts of an atom together, keeping each part from following its individual, independent course.

From this point of view it is inaccurate and misleading to say that different people have different "attitudes" concerning the same "thing." For the "thing" simply is *not* the same for different people whether the "thing" is a football game, a presidential candidate, Communism, or spinach. We do not simply "react to" a happening or to some impingement from the environment in a determined way (except in behavior that has become reflexive or habitual). We behave according to what we bring to the occasion, and what each of us brings to the occasion is more or less unique. And except for these significances which we bring to the occasion, the happenings around us would be meaningless occurrences, would be "inconsequential."

From the transactional view, an attitude is not a predisposition to react in a certain way to an occurrence or stimulus "out there" that exists in its own right with certain fixed characteristics which we "color" according to our predisposition (Kilpatrick, 1952). That is, a subject does not simply "react to" an "object." An attitude would rather seem to be a complex of registered significances reactivated by some stimulus which assumes its own particular significance for us in terms of our purposes. That is, the object as experienced would not exist for us except for the reactivated aspects of the form-world which provide particular significance to the hieroglyphics of sensory impingements.

### References

Cantril, H. (1950)*The "why" of man's experience*. New York: Macmillan.

Kilpatrick, F. P. (Ed.) (1952) *Human behavior from the transactional point of view.* Hanover, N.H.: Institute for Associated Research.

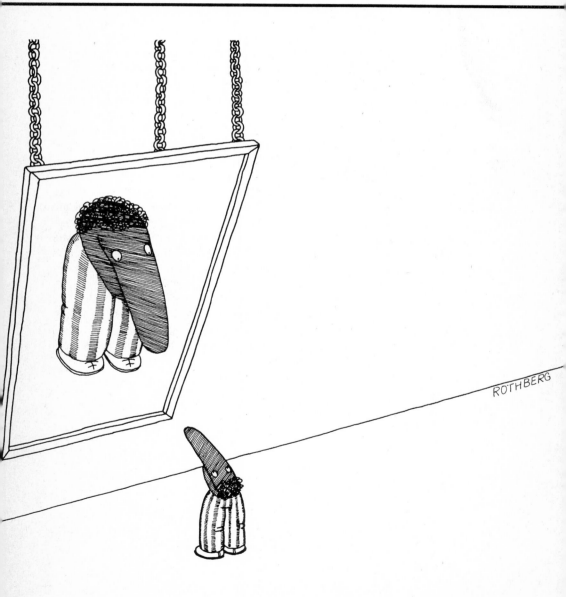

# 2

ROTHBERG

# The Self:
# Who Am I?

When we ask the question, "Who am I?," we ask about the self, the most prized
and personal possession a person can have. The study of the self has a
checkered history. At times we have rejected it as being too private and too
personal to be studied effectively, yet in recent years social psychologists have
developed a passion for learning more about who we are and how we think
about ourselves.

Jennifer Crocker, Professor of Psychology at the State University of New
York at Buffalo and a past winner of the Gordon Allport Intergroup Relations
Prize, has become one of the leading researchers in the study of the self-concept. Part of our conversation dealt with her current research concerning the
disadvantaged and stigmatized, while other topics covered ranged from the
ways in which we maintain and protect the self through a consideration of self
in relation to culture. Her comments illustrate how important the self is and
how complex it is, yet how easy it is to understand and appreciate when it is
explained clearly.

## A CONVERSATION WITH JENNIFER CROCKER

**Krupat:** *Our everyday language is so full of words that start with self: self-esteem, self-conscious, and self-image. Given our "self-centered" focus, can you tell me just what the self is?*

**Crocker:** The concept is very broad. Some would say that it refers to all the thoughts and feelings we have about ourselves, but that's a very loose definition. Other people would talk about the self as a mental representation. Someone like Hazel Markus would say that we have a representation of what we're like, what we could be like in the future, and what we've been like in the past. It's this mental representation plus an evaluation of it which constitutes the self or the self-concept.

**Krupat:** *Why is it that social psychologists seem to be interested at all in the self? It seems like it's a very individual concept rather than a social concept.*

**Crocker:** It might seem that way, but the way we think and feel about ourselves is extraordinarily influenced by our relationships with other people, and the self also has tremendous effects on how we relate to other people. It is a product of social interaction, and it influences our social interaction. There is a huge interplay, and it really is a very social or interpersonal phenomenon.

**Krupat:** *Where does the idea of self-esteem fit into this?*

**Crocker:** People think about self-esteem in different ways. One way to think about it is as a global sense of self-worth, sort of an overall self-evaluation of the form, "I am worthy of respect. I'm a worthwhile human being." There also can be domain-specific self-esteem, which is how good I am at athletics, at academics, at math, or at mechanical kinds of things.

**Krupat:** *I would assume that people must give differing weights to each specific domain, depending on what they're good at.*

**Crocker:** Right. William James said that self-esteem equals success divided by pretensions. What he was arguing is that your self-esteem depends on how good you are at what matters to you. People value certain things and devalue others. I'm not good at mechanical things, but that doesn't affect my self-esteem much at all, but I very much value academics, and how I do in that domain does affect my self-esteem a lot.

**Krupat:** *Do we value what we are good at, or do we work to get good at the things we value. Which is the chicken and which is the egg?*

**Crocker:** I think it goes both ways. Some things are very much valued by the culture and the subculture in which one grows up, and it's hard to fight your culture. This culture, for example, places a lot of importance on physical attractiveness. It's very hard to devalue that, although some people are able to do it. There also is pretty good evidence that people are able to more or less devalue certain domains. For example, when people learn that they compare badly to someone close to them, they'll often devalue that domain of achievement as a way of protecting their self-esteem and maintaining a positive view of themselves. People differ in how well they're able to do that and in what domains they do that, but they do devalue things that they don't do well in as a way of protecting their self-esteem.

**Krupat:** *It almost sounds as if life is simply a struggle to maintain, protect, and enhance self-esteem. How important is this as a human motive? Is it what makes us tick?*

**Crocker:** There certainly are people who would argue that the desire to maintain a positive view of the self is a fundamental motive. And there are a lot of different theoretical perspectives of why that might be the case. One is that low self-esteem simply feels bad. High self-esteem is associated with having positive emotions, and low self-esteem is associated with negative emotions, feeling emotional pain, or being depressed. It may also be functional or adaptive to have high self-esteem. If we think we're worthwhile, if we think we're deserving, we may aspire to do more and may make more efforts to succeed. One of the things that complicates this notion of self-esteem as a universal human motive is that the form that self-esteem takes differs widely by culture. For example, people in the United States seem to be trying constantly to enhance their levels of esteem, and they show all kinds of biases and positive illusions about the self. Those kinds of things are either much weaker or nonexistent in many Asian cultures. It truly does raise questions about how universal a motive this really is.

**Krupat:** *You mean all these self words don't exist or don't take on the same significance in other parts of the world?*

**Crocker:** Not at all. The United States has been characterized as one of the most individualistic cultures in the world. People here are motivated to realize their individual potential and to enhance themselves. Many other cultures are much less concerned with the self and are much more concerned with relationships with other people. In Japan, for example, it has been argued that people can't even think about themselves without thinking about their relationships with the groups that they belong to. Instead of wanting to enhance themselves, to express their individual uniqueness, or to realize their individual potential, people are much more oriented toward fitting in and getting along with others, submerging themselves to the group, and facilitating their relationships with others.

**Krupat:** *We have talked a little about self in relationship to nationality, but we haven't talked much about it much in relationship to matters such as race and gender.*

**Crocker:** That's one of the things that I'm especially interested in. One of the questions that's interested me is, "What are the effects of the social structure, the social hierarchy, on how people feel about themselves?" If you are in a group that's discriminated against, does that affect the way you feel about yourself? Shouldn't people who belong to groups that are discriminated against or are disadvantaged in society view themselves negatively? Amazingly, there is a good deal of evidence that members of groups that are stigmatized or subordinated do not show low self-esteem. In America, Blacks and Chicanos, for example, show self-esteem that is at least equal to and often higher than that of Whites.

**Krupat:** *How do you account for this?*

**Crocker:** There are a number of ways. One is that when people are discriminated against they learn not to value the things that they can't have. Women, for example, are seldom CEOs of big companies. Well, they may just decide that this is not really important. So one way to maintain self-esteem despite the fact that your group is doing badly is to say, "What my group doesn't get is not what really matters to me." Another way to protect self-esteem if you're in a disadvantaged or discriminated against group is to compare yourself with people that are like you. So women or Blacks might say, "The comparisons that really matter to me are the people who are like me." When you compare yourself to people who are in the same boat, then you are going to be less focused on the fact that you are disadvantaged relative to other groups. Another way self-esteem is protected if your group is discriminated against is that, when negative things happen to you, you have an explanation for why they are happening. If you don't get the job, then you suspect that discrimination might be the reason why. That provides you with an explanation that's external to yourself. It's not me; it's something about the other person or something about the situation, something about the way society is structured. It doesn't reflect my own inadequacies; it reflects the way the world is or the way the other person is. And so it doesn't lower self-esteem.

**Krupat:** *That may protect self-esteem, but if you come to believe that effort* *won't be rewarded because of the way society is, then why should you work hard?*

**Crocker:** One of the things that may be critical in terms of whether groups that are discriminated against suffer from low self-esteem is whether they believe that their society is a meritocracy, a place where people get what they deserve. Do they believe that by working hard, having the right personal qualities, exerting effort, people can get success? Maintaining self-esteem for the stigmatized or the oppressed may require at some level rejecting the notion that the world is a fair place where people who deserve it succeed and people who don't deserve it don't succeed. The data on the beliefs of Black Americans suggest that they don't believe that this is a meritocracy nearly as much as white Americans do, but they also don't entirely reject that idea either.

**Krupat:** *Let's move on to questions of how we each know the self. Where does the issue of self-awareness fit into all this?*

**Crocker:** Some of the time we are really thinking about ourselves, conscious of ourselves, and reflecting on ourselves. But some of the time we are caught up in the situation and we're really not thinking or reflecting about the self. So our attention can be basically inner-directed or it can be outer-directed.

**Krupat:** *Does that vary from situation to situation, or are some people just more self-conscious than others?*

**Crocker:** Both. There is evidence that there are chronic tendencies to be high or low in self-consciousness. And there are also clearly situations that can elicit self-awareness or direct our attention toward ourselves. The one that's most studied is being in the presence of a mirror. When we see a reflection, this draws our attention to ourselves, it makes us think about ourselves. Other kinds of situations can do that: being in front of an audience or a camera, or being in any kind of situation that makes us aware of or reflects our attention back to ourselves as an object.

**Krupat:** *When teenagers say, "I'm always so self-conscious," the term has a negative connotation. Yet when I hear you talking about self-consciousness or self-awareness, it sounds as if it can be functional rather than dysfunctional.*

**Crocker:** I think it has both functional and dysfunctional aspects to it. On the positive side, people are much more likely to behave in ways that are consistent with their attitudes when they are self-conscious than when they are not. On the other hand, self-consciousness and self-awareness can often induce negative emotions in people. One of the things that self-awareness does is to lead us to compare ourselves to our ideal standard, which we often don't live up to. That is probably the aspect of self-consciousness that teenagers are often referring to.

**Krupat:** *To what extent do we each create and shape our own self-image, and to what extent would you say this happens to us passively?*

**Crocker:** I think both processes very much occur. I know that sounds like a wishy-washy answer, but I really think that both happen. Part of it depends upon how far back you go. My self-esteem may be genetically influenced, and it is also influenced by attachment patterns that developed in early childhood. Clearly, we are somewhat passive recipients of those early influences. At another level I think people are actively engaged in maintaining, defending, or protecting their self-concept. Bill Swann argues that what people are motivated to do is to verify whatever self-concept they happen to have. He believes that people who have positive self-views want that positive self-view reinforced, but that people who have negative self-views want to get that reinforced. In fact, these people actually seek out feedback about their negative attributes to reinforce these negative views of themselves.

**Krupat:** *Interesting. I had thought in general that there is a bias toward a positive self-view.*

**Crocker:** Yes, but others have argued that this is not always the case. People very much want to have positive feedback about themselves. It feels good. But people differ in how believable they find that positive feedback. When people who start out with positive self-views get positive feedback from others, they find that information highly credible and they say, "That makes perfect sense to me." But people who start out with a negative self-view may find positive feedback difficult to accept because it is not consistent with how they see themselves. Even though they would like to believe it, they may not entirely trust it because it does not fit with what they think is true about themselves.

**Krupat:** *Up to now we have been talking about self as if there were only one "true" self, but that doesn't quite feel right to me. For instance, I would imagine that the self you might see on a first date might be a different self than you would see after six years of marriage.*

**Crocker:** That's right. Regardless of what we really think about ourselves, we don't necessarily choose to present ourselves to other people in that way. On a date you try to appear charming. On a job interview you try to appear competent and intelligent.

**Krupat:** *But still we can ask, "Which is the 'real' you?"*

**Crocker:** The problem here is that the presented self is often very sincere. It may be that a part of me really is competent. I'm just giving you that piece of me in the job interview and not revealing the incompetent me. So it's not that what I present is entirely phony; it may just be that I am choosing to present the best of me in that situation. That is the *real* me, even if it's not the *whole* me.

WILLIAM B. SWANN, JR.
J. GREGORY HIXON
CHRIS DE LA RONDE

# Embracing the Bitter "Truth": Negative Self-Concepts and Marital Commitment

In this article, Swann and his colleagues test and find support for an interesting position that he has taken concerning self-esteem. Believing that people want to find support for their existing self-concepts, Swann predicts that people will gravitate toward relationships in which their partners see them as they see themselves. Consistent with this, Swann finds that people with negative self-esteem were actually more committed to their spouses if those people thought *poorly* of them than if the spouses had a more positive opinion of them.

I flee who chases me, and chase who flees me.

Ovid, ca. 8/1925, line 36

Ovid's remarks raise eyebrows because they seem to defy a basic truth of social conduct. That is, over the years, everyone from poets and philosophers to grandmothers has noted that people love to be loved. In the last few decades, social scientists have documented this proposition so many times that it is now a bedrock assumption of most theories of social behavior (e.g., Berscheid, 1985). This is what makes Ovid's commentary so puzzling; surely, all other things being equal, rational people do not flee from loving partners in favor of indifferent ones.

Or do they? Recent theorizing has suggested that people want more than adoration from their relationship partners; they also want verification and confirmation of their self-concepts. This research suggests that there may be a grain of truth to Ovid's commentary. That is, if people with negative self-concepts truly look to their relationships for self-verification, they may shun partners who appraise them favorably and embrace those who appraise them unfavorably.

## SELF-VERIFICATION PROCESSES AND THE SEARCH FOR FEEDBACK THAT FITS

Self-verification theory (Swann, 1990) begins with the assumption that the key to successful social relations is the capacity for people to recognize how others perceive them (e.g., Cooley, 1902; Mead, 1934; Stryker, 1981). To this end, people note the reactions of others and use these reactions as a basis for inferring their own self-concepts. From this vantage point, self-concepts are cognitive distillations of past relationships.

Because self-concepts are abstracted from the reactions of others, they should allow people to predict how others will respond to them in the future. Recognizing this, people come to rely on stable self-concepts and view substantial self-concept change as a threat to intrapsychic and interpersonal functioning (for related accounts, see Aronson, 1968; Festinger, 1957; Lecky, 1945). Consider, for example, how a woman who perceives herself as socially inept might feel upon overhearing her husband characterize her as socially skilled. If she takes his comment seriously, she will probably find it thoroughly unsettling, as it challenges a long-standing belief about who she is and implies that she may not know herself after all. And if she does not know *herself*, what does she know?

Even if she lacked such existential concerns, she might still want her husband to recognize her social ineptitude for purely pragmatic or interpersonal reasons (e.g., Goffman, 1959). That is, as long as he recognizes her limitations, he will form modest expectations of her and their interactions will proceed smoothly. In contrast, should he form an inappropriately favorable impression, he might develop unrealistic expectations that she could not meet.

Both intrapsychic and interpersonal considerations may therefore motivate people to prefer self-verifying appraisals over self-discrepant ones. This reasoning leads to an unusual prediction: Although people with negative self-views may find that unfavorable evaluations frustrate their desire for praise, they may nevertheless seek such evaluations because they find them to be reassuring—particularly when they contemplate the intrapsychic and interpersonal anarchy that inappropriately favorable appraisals may bring. People with negative self-views may accordingly prefer relatively negative evaluations and relationship partners who provide such evaluations.

Although laboratory studies have shown that people with firmly held negative self-views prefer interaction partners who evaluate them unfavorably (e.g., Swann, Hixon, Stein-Seroussi, & Gilbert, 1990; Swann, Stein-Seroussi, & Giesler, in press; Swann, Wenzlaff, Krull, & Pelham, in press), no one knows whether or how this tendency influences people's choice of relationship partners outside the laboratory. This issue is not trivial, as some theorists have argued that these findings are a product of idiosyncratic features of laboratory settings and would not generalize to naturally occurring situations (e.g., Raynor & McFarlin, 1986). To address this issue, we moved outside the laboratory to examine people's reactions to appraisals from persons with whom they were involved in ongoing relationships. In particular, we focused on the extent to which married persons with negative, moderate, or positive self-concepts seemed committed to spouses who appraised them relatively favorably or unfavorably.

## SELF-VERIFICATION AT THE HORSE RANCH AND MALL

We recruited 95 married couples from a sample of patrons of a horse ranch (41 couples) and shopping mall (54 couples) in the central Texas area by offering them $5 apiece. Participants ranged in age from 19 to 78, with a mean of 32.1 years. Most participants were Caucasians (87.8%) and had at least some college education (91%). Spouses had known one another for an average of 9 years and had been married for an average of 6 years. Members of 3 couples misunderstood the instructions, and members of 6 other couples gave conflicting responses (e.g., reported having a different number of children); we accordingly deleted their data.

The experimenter seated the members of each couple at opposite ends of a long table so they could not discern one another's responses. After obtaining informed consent and assuring participants that their partners would never see their responses, the experimenter presented each participant with an identical questionnaire as part of an investigation of "the relation between personality and close relationships." In addition to the items described below, the questionnaire included items pertaining to the structure of self-knowledge, interpersonal accuracy, and related issues.

The measure of self-concepts was the short form of the Self-Attributes Questionnaire (SAQ; Pelham & Swann, 1989). The SAQ is a measure of a confederacy of five specific self-views central to self-worth: intellectual capability, physical attractiveness, athletic ability, social skills, and aptitude for arts and music. For each attribute, participants rated themselves relative to other people their own age and gender on graduated-interval scales ranging from 0 (bottom 5%) to 9 (top 5%).

After completing the self-ratings, participants filled out the principle index of partner appraisal: the sum of their ratings of their partners on the five SAQ attributes. As expected, spouses rated participants with negative self-views less favorably ($M$ = 29) than participants with moderate ($M$ = 32) or positive ($M$ = 34) self-views.

The measure of commitment focused on the participants' intentions, feelings, and actions regarding their relationships. On 9-point scales, participants responded to seven items tapping desire to remain in the relationship, plans to remain in the relationship, relationship satisfaction, time spent together, amount of talking, discussion of problems and worries, and disclosure of personal matters. Responses to these items were closely associated and were summed.

The means plotted in Table 1 suggest that people were committed to

**TABLE 1.** Average level of marital commitment by self-concept and spouse's appraisal

| Spouse's appraisal | Self-concept | | |
|---|---|---|---|
| | Negative | Moderate | Positive |
| Unfavorable | 52.4 | 52.8 | 52.0 |
| Moderate | 52.7 | 53.2 | 53.1 |
| Favorable | 43.8 | 53.8 | 58.7 |

*Note.* Higher values indicate more commitment.

spouses who verified their self-concepts. Just as participants with positive self-concepts were more committed to their relationships insofar as their spouses thought well of them, participants with negative self-concepts were more committed to the extent that their spouses thought poorly of them. Those with moderate self-concepts were not influenced by the nature of their spouses' appraisals.

## WHY PEOPLE WITH NEGATIVE SELF-VIEWS EMBRACED SPOUSES WHO DEROGATED THEM

Our most provocative finding was that people with negative self-views were most committed to spouses who appraised them unfavorably. To better understand this finding, we examined our participants' responses to several questions that they completed after the major measures. We found the following:

1. The more participants believed that their spouses' appraisals "made them feel that they really knew themselves" rather than "confused them" (summed over the five SAQ attributes), the more committed they were to the relationship.
2. There was no evidence that people were committed to partners who appraised them unfavorably because they thought such partners would help them improve themselves. In fact, participants with negative self-views were less confident that feedback from their spouses would help them improve themselves ($M = 6.56$) than were participants with moderate ($M = 7.28$) and positive ($M = 7.49$) self-views.
3. People with negative self-views were not especially committed to spouses who rated them negatively because they hoped to win their spouses over. Indeed, participants with negative self-views showed a marginally reliable tendency to be more committed to spouses to the extent that they expected their spouses' appraisals on the five SAQ attributes would worsen.
4. People with negative self-views did not commit themselves to

spouses who rated them unfavorably because they took expressions of negativity as signs of perceptiveness.

5. Self-verification was not the exclusive province of women or men.

## GENERAL DISCUSSION

In our investigation, married people with negative self-views responded in a remarkable fashion. Whereas participants with positive self-concepts displayed more commitment to spouses who evaluated them favorably than to spouses who evaluated them unfavorably, participants with negative self-views displayed more commitment to spouses who evaluated them *unfavorably* than to spouses who evaluated them favorably. Our findings therefore suggest that people embrace spouses who appraise them in a self-verifying manner, even if this means committing themselves to persons who think poorly of them. This tendency may have undesirable consequences, especially for people who want to improve their self-esteem. Such people may discover, for example, that they are unable to benefit from therapy because their spouses reinforce their negative self-concepts (for a related experiment, see Swann & Predmore, 1985).

Skeptics could, of course, note that our design was correlational and that it is thus hazardous to assume that the spouses' appraisals caused the level of commitment. Although we agree that caution is in order, we are reassured by the evidence we report that casts doubt on several alternative explanations of our effects and by the fact that recent laboratory research has yielded findings that parallel our own (see Swann, 1990, for a review). To us, a more troubling issue is the discrepancy between our findings and the voluminous literature indicating that people prefer favorable evaluations. One reason for this discrepancy may be that past researchers have typically examined participants' reactions to evaluations from complete strangers in laboratory settings. Clearly, it is one thing to express attraction for a stranger who offers an inappropriately favorable evaluation. It is quite another to pursue a relationship with such a person (e.g., Huston & Levinger, 1978), because doing so may invite the undesired intrapsychic and interpersonal consequences associated with discrepant feedback. Thus, for example, the same flattering remarks that seem harmless and pleasant when delivered by a stranger may seem disturbing and unsettling when delivered by someone who should know the person well.

Of course, some laboratory studies, including those we have conducted, *have* shown evidence of self-verification strivings. Why? Perhaps because we have focused on our participants' choice of feedback and interaction partners rather than on immediate, affective reactions to evaluations, as most past researchers have done. Recent research and theorizing (e.g., Swann, 1990; Swann et al., 1990) have suggested that when people with negative self-views first receive favorable evaluations, they are quite enamored with them; only after they have had time to compare such evaluations with their self-concepts has a preference for self-verifying evaluations emerged. Similarly, immediately after receiving unfavorable feedback, people with negative self-views report being distressed by it, yet shortly therafter they go on to seek additional unfavorable feedback (e.g., Swann, Wenzlaff, Krull, & Pelham, in press)!

This research, then, suggests that people with negative self-views are enveloped in a psychological cross fire between a desire for positive feedback and a desire for self-verifying feedback. For such persons, it seems that the warmth produced by favorable feedback is chilled by incredulity, and that the reassurance produced by negative feedback is tempered by sadness that the "truth" could not be more kind. Given this dilemma, it seems likely that people with negative self-concepts may seek unfavorable (self-verifying) evaluations in some contexts and positive appraisals in others (e.g., Swann, Hixon, & De La Ronde, 1991). When they do court unfavorable evaluations, however, it is not out of masochism, as it seems that they engage in such activities in spite of rather than because of the unhappiness that such appraisals foster.

## References

Aronson, E. (1960). A theory of cognitive dissonance: A current perspective. In L. Berkowitz (Ed.), *Advances in experimental social psychology* (Vol. 4, pp. 1–34). New York: Academic Press.

Backman, C.W., & Secord, P.F. (1962). Liking, selective interaction, and misperception in congruent interpersonal relations. *Sociometry, 25,* 321–335.

Berscheid, E. (1985). Interpersonal attraction. In G. Lindzey & E. Aronson (Eds.), *Handbook of social psychology* (Vol. 2, pp. 413–484). New York: Random House.

Cooley, C.H. (1902). *Human nature and the social order.* New York: Scribner's.

Doherty, E.G., & Secord, P.F. (1971). Change of roommate and interpersonal congruency. *Representative Research in Social Psychology, 2,* 70–75.

Festinger, L. (1957). *A theory of cognitive dissonance.* Evanston, IL: Row, Peterson.

Goffman, E. (1959). *The presentation of self in everyday life.* New York: Anchor Books.

Huston, T.L., & Levinger, G. (1978). Interpersonal attraction and relationships. *Annual Review of Psychology, 29,* 115–156.

Kenny, D.A., & Judd, C.M. (1986). Consequences of violating the independence assumption in the analysis of variance. *Psychological Bulletin, 99,* 422–431.

Lecky, P. (1945). *Self-consistency: A theory of personality.* New York: Island Press.

Mead, G.H. (1934). *Mind, self and society.* Chicago: University of Chicago Press.

Ovid. (1925). *The Loves* (Book II) (J. Lewis May, Trans.). Burgay, England: John Lane The Bodley Head. (Original work published ca. 8)

Pelham, B.W., & Swann, W.B., Jr. (1989). From self-conceptions to self-worth: On the sources and structure of global self-esteem. *Journal of Personality and Social Psychology, 57,* 672–680.

Raynor, J.O., & McFarlin, D.B. (1986). Motivation and the self-system. In R.M. Sorrentino & E.T. Higgins (Eds.), *Motivation and cognition: Foundations of social behavior* (pp. 315–349). New York: Guilford Press.

Stryker, S. (1981). *Symbolic interactionism.* Menlo Park, CA: Benjamin/Cummings.

Swann, W.B., Jr. (1990). To be adored or to be known: The interplay of self-enhancement and self-verification. In R.M. Sorrentino & E.T. Higgins (Eds.). *Motivation and cognition* (Vol. 2, pp. 408–448). New York: Guilford Press.

Swann, W.B., Jr., Hixon, J.G., & De La Ronde, C. (1991). *Dating games and marital reality*. Manuscript submitted for publication.

Swann, W. B., Jr., Hixon, J.G., Stein-Seroussi, A., & Gilbert, D.T. (1990). The fleeting gleam of praise: Behavioral reactions to self-relevant feedback. *Journal of Personality and Social Psychology, 59*, 17–26.

Swann, W.B., Jr., & Predmore, S.C. (1985). Intimates as agents of social support: Sources of consolation or despair? *Journal of Personality and Social Psychology, 49*, 1609–1617.

Swann, W.B., Jr., Stein-Seroussi, A., & Giesler, R.B. (in press). Why people self-verify. *Journal of Personality and Social Psychology.*

Swann, W.B., Jr., Wenzlaff, R.M., Krull, D.S., & Pelham, B.W. (in press). The allure of negative feedback: Self-verification strivings among depressed persons. *Journal of Abnormal Psychology.*

CLAUDE M. STEELE

# Race and the Schooling of Black Americans

Claude Steele's article from the *Atlantic Monthly* is a percep-
tive and troubling analysis of why black children are more
likely than their white counterparts to fail in school. Steele
notes the subtle and not-so-subtle ways that lead young
blacks to "disidentify" with school, to resist measuring themselves against the values and goals of the classroom. He
advocates the concept of "wise schooling," in which teachers
and classmates see value and promise in black children rather
than the opposite. Although he does not refer directly to
them, note how Steele's analysis fits very well with modern
social psychological theories about the development and
maintenance of self-esteem.

My former university offered minority students a faculty mentor to help
shepherd them into college life. As soon as I learned of the program, I
volunteered to be a mentor, but by then the school year was nearly over.
Undaunted, the program's eager staff matched me with a student on their
waiting list—an appealing nineteen-year-old black woman from Detroit, the
same age as my daughter. We met finally in a campus lunch spot just about
two weeks before the close of her freshman year. I realized quickly that I was
too late. I have heard that the best way to diagnose someone's depression is
to note how depressed you feel when you leave the person. When our lunch
was over, I felt as gray as the snowbanks that often lined the path back to my
office. My lunchtime companion was a statistic brought to life, a living
example of one of the most disturbing facts of racial life in America today: the
failure of so many black Americans to thrive in school. Before I could lift a hand
to help this student, she had decided to do what 70 percent of all black Americans
at four-year colleges do at some point in their academic careers—drop out.

I sense a certain caving-in hope of America that problems of race can be
solved. Since the sixties, when race relations held promise for the dawning of
a new era, the issue has become one whose persistence causes "problem
fatigue"—resignation to an unwanted condition of life.

This fatigue, I suspect, deadens us to the deepening crisis in the education of black Americans. One can enter any desegregated school in America, from grammar school to high school to graduate or professional school, and meet a persistent reality: blacks and whites in largely separate worlds. And if one asks a few questions or looks at a few records, another reality emerges: these worlds are not equal, either in the education taking place there or in the achievement of the students who occupy them.

As a social scientist, I know that the crisis has enough possible causes to give anyone problem fatigue. But at a personal level, perhaps because of my experience as a black in American schools, or perhaps just as the hunch of a myopic psychologist, I have long suspected a particular culprit—a culprit that can undermine black achievement as effectively as a lock on a schoolhouse door. The culprit I see is *stigma*, the endemic devaluation many blacks face in our society and schools. This status is its own condition of life, different from class, money, culture. It is capable, in the words of the late sociologist Erving Goffman, of "breaking the claim" that one's human attributes have on people. I believe that its connection to school achievement among black Americans has been vastly underappreciated.

This is a troublesome argument, touching as it does on a still unhealed part of American race relations. But it leads us to a heartening principle: if blacks are made less racially vulnerable in school, they can overcome even substantial obstacles. Before the good news, though, I must at least sketch in the bad: the worsening crisis in the education of black Americans.

Despite their socioeconomic disadvantages as a group, blacks begin school with test scores that are fairly close to the test scores of whites their age. The longer they stay in school, however, the more they fall behind; for example, by the sixth grade blacks in many school districts are two full grade levels behind whites in achievement. This pattern holds true in the middle class nearly as much as in the lower class. The record does not improve in high school. In 1980, for example, 25,500 minority students, largely black and Hispanic, entered high school in Chicago. Four years later only 9,500 graduated, and of those only 2,000 could read at grade level. The situation in other cities is comparable.

Even for blacks who make it to college, the problem doesn't go away. As I noted, 70 percent of all black students who enroll in four-year colleges drop out at some point, as compared with 45 percent of whites. At any given time nearly as many black males are incarcerated as are in college in this country. And the grades of black college students average half a letter below those of their white classmates. At one prestigious university I recently studied, only 18 percent of the graduating black students had grade averages of B or above, as compared with 64 percent of the whites. This pattern is the rule, not the exception, in even the most elite American colleges. Tragically, low grades can render a degree essentially "terminal" in the sense that they preclude further schooling.

Blacks in graduate and professional schools face a similarly worsening or stagnating fate. For example, form 1977 to 1990, though the number of Ph.D.s awarded to other minorities increased and the number awarded to whites stayed roughly the same, the number awarded to American blacks dropped from 1,116 to 828. And blacks needed more time to get those degrees.

Standing ready is a familiar set of explanations. First is societal disadvantage. Black Americans have had, and continue to have, more than their share: a history of slavery, segregation, and job ceilings; continued lack of economic opportunity; poor schools; and the related problems of broken families, drug-infested communities, and social isolation. Any of these factors—alone, in combination, or through accumulated effects—can undermine school achievement. Some analysts point also to black American culture, suggesting that, hampered by disadvantage, it doesn't sustain the values and expectations critical to education, or that it fosters learning orientations ill suited to school achievement, or that it even "opposes" mainstream achievement. These are the chestnuts, and I had always thought them adequate. Then several facts emerged that just didn't seem to fit.

For one thing, the achievement deficits occur even when black students suffer no major financial disadvantage—among middle-class students on wealthy college campuses and in graduate school among black students receiving substantial financial aid. For another thing, survey after survey shows that even poor black Americans value education highly, often more than whites. Also, as I will demonstrate, several programs have improved black school achievement without addressing culturally specific learning orientations or doing anything to remedy socioeconomic disadvantage.

Neither is the problem fully explained, as one might assume, by deficits in skill or preparation which blacks might suffer because of background disadvantages. I first doubted that such a connection existed when I saw flunk-out rates for black and white students at a large, prestigious university. Two observations surprised me. First, for both blacks and whites the level of preparation, as measured by Scholastic Aptitude Test scores, didn't make much difference in who flunked out; low scorers (with combined verbal and quantitative SATs of 800) were no more likely to flunk out than high scorers (with combined SATs of 1,200 to 1,500). The second observation was racial: whereas only two percent to 11 percent of the whites flunked out, 18 percent to 33 percent of the blacks flunked out, even at the highest levels of preparation (combined SATs of 1,400). Dinesh D'Souza has argued recently that college affirmative-action programs cause failure and high dropout rates among black students by recruiting them to levels of college work for which they are inadequately prepared. That was clearly not the case at this school; black students flunked out in large numbers even with preparation well above average.

And, sadly, this proved the rule, not the exception. From elementary school to graduate school, something depresses black achievement *at every level of preparation, even the highest.* Generally, of course, the better prepared achieve better than the less prepared, and this is about as true for blacks as for whites. But given any level of school preparation (as measured by tests and earlier grades), blacks somehow achieve less in subsequent schooling than whites (that is, have poorer grades, have lower graduation rates, and take longer to graduate), no matter how strong that preparation is. Put differently, the same achievement level requires better preparation for blacks than for whites—far better: among students with a C+ average at the university I just described, the mean American College Testing Program (ACT) score for blacks was at the 98th percentile, while for whites it was at only the 34th percentile. This pattern has been documented so broadly across so many regions of the country, and by so many investigations (literally hundreds), that it is virtually a social law in this society—as well as a racial tragedy.

Clearly, something is missing from our understanding of black under-achievement. Disadvantage contributes, yet blacks underachieve even when they have ample resources, strongly value education, and are prepared better than adequately in terms of knowledge and skills. Something else has to be involved. That something else could be of just modest importance—a barrier that simply adds its effect to that of other disadvantages—or it could be pivotal, such that were it corrected, other disadvantages would lose their effect.

That something else, I believe, has to do with the process of identifying with school. I offer a personal example:

I remember conducting experiments with my research adviser early in graduate school and awaiting the results with only modest interest. I struggled to meet deadlines. The research enterprise—the core of what one does as a social psychologist—just wasn't *me* yet. I was in school for other reasons—I wanted an advanced degree, I was vaguely ambitious for intellectual work, and being in graduate school made my parents proud of me. But as time passed, I began to like the work. I also began to grasp the value system that gave it meaning, and the faculty treated me as if they thought I might even be able to do it. Gradually I began to think of myself as a social psychologist. With this change in self-concept came a new accountability; my self-esteem was affected now by what I did as a social psychologist, something that hadn't been true before. This added a new motivation to my work; self-respect, not just parental respect, was on the line. I noticed changes in myself. I worked without deadlines. I bored friends with applications of arcane theory to their daily lives. I went to conventions. I lived and died over how experiments came out.

Before this transition one might have said that I was handicapped by my black working-class background and lack of motivation. After the transition the same observer might say that even though my background was working-class, I had special advantages: achievement-oriented parents, a small and attentive college. But these facts alone would miss the importance of the identification process I had experienced: the change in self-definition and in the activities on which I based my self-esteem. They would also miss a simple condition necessary for me to make this identification: treatment as a valued person with good prospects.

I believe that the "something else" at the root of black achievement problems is the failure of American schooling to meet this simple condition for many of its black students. Doing well in school requires a belief that school achievement can be a promising basis of self-esteem, and that belief needs constant reaffirmation even for advantaged students. Tragically, I believe, the lives of black Americans are still haunted by a specter that threatens this belief and the identification that derived from it at every level of schooling.

## THE SPECTER OF STIGMA AND RACIAL VULNERABILITY

I have a good friend, the mother of three, who spends considerable time in the public school classrooms of Seattle, where she lives. In her son's third-grade room, managed by a teacher of unimpeachable good will and competence, she noticed over many visits that the extraordinary art work of a small black boy named Jerome was ignored—or, more accurately perhaps, its significance was ignored. As a genuine art talent has a way of doing—even in the third grade—his stood out. Yet the teacher seemed hardly to notice. Moreover, Jerome's reputation, as it was passed along from one grade to the next, included only the slightest mention of his talent. Now, of course, being ignored like this could happen to anyone—such is the overload in our public schools. But my friend couldn't help wondering how the school would have responded to this talent had the artist been one of her own, middle-class white children.

Terms like "prejudice" and "racism" often miss the full scope of racial devaluation in our society, implying as they do that racial devaluation comes primarily from the strongly prejudiced, not from "good people" like Jerome's teacher. But the prevalence of racists—deplorable though racism is—misses the full extent of Jerome's burden, perhaps even the most profound part.

He faces a devaluation that grows out of our images of society and the way those images catalogue people. The catalogue need never be taught. It is implied by all we see around us: the kinds of people revered in advertising (consider the unrelenting racial advocacy of Ralph Lauren ads) and movies (black women are rarely seen as romantic partners, for example); media discussions of whether a black can be President; invitation lists to junior high school birthday parties; school curricula; literary and musical canons. These details create an image of society in which black Americans simply do not fare well. When I was a kid, we captured it with the saying "If you're white you're right, if you're yellow you're mellow, if you're brown stick around, but if you're black get back."

In ways that require no fueling from strong prejudice or stereotypes, these images expand the devaluation of black Americans. They act as mental standards against which information about blacks is evaluated: that which fits these images we accept; that which contradicts them we suspect. Had Jerome had a reading problem, which fits these images, it might have been accepted as characteristic more readily than his extraordinary art work, which contradicts them.

These images do something else as well, something especially pernicious in the classroom. They set up a jeopardy of double devaluation for blacks, a jeopardy that does not apply to whites. Like anyone, blacks risk devaluation for a particular incompetence, such as failed test or a flubbed pronunciation. But they further risk that such performances will confirm the broader, racial inferiority they are suspected of. Thus, from the first grade through graduate school, blacks have the extra fear that in the eyes of those around them their full humanity could fall with a poor answer or a mistaken stroke of the pen.

Moreover, because these images are conditioned in all of us, collectively held, they can spawn racial devaluation in all of us, not just in the strongly prejudiced. They can do this even in blacks themselves: a majority of black children recently tested said they like and prefer to play with white rather than black dolls—almost fifty years after Kenneth and Mamie Clark, conducting similar experiments, documented identical findings and so paved the way for *Brown v. Topeka Board of Education*. Thus Jerome's devaluation can come from a circle of people in his world far greater than the expressly prejudiced—a circle that apparently includes his teacher.

In ways often too subtle to be conscious but sometimes overt, I believe, blacks remain devalued in American schools, where, for example, a recent national survey shows that through high school they are still more than twice as likely as white children to receive corporal punishment, be suspended from school, or be labeled mentally retarded.

Tragically, such devaluation can seem inescapable. Sooner or later it forces on its victims two painful realizations. The first is that society is preconditioned to see the worst in them. Black students quickly learn that acceptance, if it is to be won at all, will be hard-won. The second is that even if a black student achieves exoneration in one setting—with the teacher and fellow students in one classroom, or at one level of schooling, for example—this approval will have to be rewon in the next classroom, at the next level of schooling. Of course, individual characteristics that enhance one's value in society—skills, class status, appearance, and success—can diminish the racial devaluation one faces. And sometimes the effort to prove oneself fuels achievement. But few from any group could hope to sustain so daunting and everlasting a struggle. Thus, I am afraid, too many black students are left hopeless and deeply vulnerable in America's classrooms.

## "DISIDENTIFYING" WITH SCHOOL

I believe that in significant part the crisis in black Americans' education stems from the power of this vulnerability to undercut identification with schooling, either before it happens or after it has bloomed.

Jerome is an example of the first kind. At precisely the time when he would need to see school as a viable source of self-esteem, his teachers fail to appreciate his best work. The devalued status of his race devalues him and his work in the classroom. Unable to entrust his sense of himself to this place, he resists measuring himself against its values and goals. He languishes there, held by the law, perhaps even by his parents, but not allowing achievement to affect his view of himself. This psychic alienation—the act of not caring—makes him less vulnerable to the specter of devaluation that haunts him. Bruce Hare, an educational researcher, has documented this process among fifth-grade boys in several schools in Champaign, Illinois. He found that although the black boys had considerably lower achievement-test scores than their white classmates, their overall self-esteem was just as high. This stunning imperviousness to poor academic performance was accomplished, he found, by their deemphasizing school achievement as a basis of self-esteem and giving preference to peer-group relations—a domain in which their esteem prospects were better. They went where they had to go to feel good about themselves.

But recall the young reader whose mentor I was. She had already identified with school, and wanted to be a doctor. How can racial vulnerability break so developed an achievement identity? To see, let us follow her steps onto campus: Her recruitment and admission stress her minority status perhaps more strongly than it has been stressed at any other time in her life. She is offered academic and social support services, further implying that she is "at risk" (even though, contrary to common belief, the vast majority of black college students are admitted with qualifications well above the threshold for whites). Once on campus, she enters a socially circumscribed world in which blacks—still largely separate from whites—have lower status; this is reinforced by a sidelining of minority material and interests in the curriculum and in university life. And she can sense that everywhere in this new world her skin color places her under suspicion of intellectual inferiority. All of this gives her the double vulnerability I spoke of: she risks confirming a particular incompetence, at chemistry or a foreign language, for example; but she also risks confirming the racial inferiority she is suspect of—a judgment that can feel as close at hand as a mispronounced word or an ungrammatical sentence. In reaction, usually to some modest setback, she withdraws, hiding her troubles from instructors, counselors, even other students. Quickly, I believe, a psychic defense takes over. She *disidentifies* with achievement; she changes her self-conception, her outlook and values, so that achievement is no longer so important to her self-esteem. She may continue to feel pressure to stay in school—from her parents, even from the potential advantages of a college degree. But now she is psychologically insulated from her academic life, like a disinterested visitor. Cool, unperturbed. But, like a pain-killing drug, disidentification undoes her future as it relieves her vulnerability.

The prevalence of this syndrome among black college students has been documented extensively, especially on predominantly white campuses. Summarizing this work, Jacqueline Fleming, a psychologist, writes, "The fact that black students must matriculate in an atmosphere that feels hostile arouses defensive reactions that interfere with intellectual performance. . . . They display academic demotivation and think less of their abilities. They profess losses of energy." Among a sample of blacks on one predominantly white campus, Richard Nisbett and Andrew Reaves, both psychologists, and I found that attitudes related to disidentification were more strongly predictive of grades than even academic preparation (that is, SATs and high school grades).

To make matters worse, once disidentification occurs in a school, it can spread like the common cold. Blacks who identify and try to achieve embarrass the strategy by valuing the very thing the strategy denies the value of. Thus pressure to make it a group norm can evolve quickly and become fierce. Defectors are called "oreos" or "incognegroes." One's identity as an authentic black is held hostage, made incompatible with school identification. For black students, then, pressure to disidentify with school can come from the already demoralized as well as from racial vulnerability in the setting.

Stigmatization of the sort suffered by black Americans is probably also a barrier to the school achievement of other groups in our society, such as lower-class whites, Hispanics, and women in male-dominated fields. For example, at a large midwestern university I studied women match men's achievement in the liberal arts, where they suffer no marked stigma, but underachieve compared with men (get lower grades than men with the same ACT scores) in engineering and premedical programs, where they, like blacks across the board, are more vulnerable to suspicions of inferiority.


## "WISE" SCHOOLING

"When they approach me they see . . . everything and anything except me. . . . [This] invisibility occurs because of a peculiar disposition of the eyes. . . . "

Ralph Ellison, *Invisible Man*

Erving Goffman, borrowing from gays of the 1950s, used the term "wise" to describe people who don't themselves bear the stigma of a given group but who are accepted by the group. These are people in whose eyes the full humanity of the stigmatized is visible, people in whose eyes they feel less vulnerable. If racial vulnerability undermines black school achievement, as I have argued, then this achievement should improve significantly if schooling is made "wise"—that is, made to see value and promise in black students and to act accordingly.

And yet, although racial vulnerability at school may undermine black achievement, so many other factors seem to contribute—from the debilitations of poverty to the alleged dysfunctions of black American culture—that one might expect "wiseness" in the classroom to be of little help. Fortunately, we have considerable evidence to the contrary. Wise schooling may indeed be the missing key to the schoolhouse door.

In the mid-seventies black students in Philip Uri Treisman's early calculus courses at the University of California at Berkeley consistently fell to the bottom of every class. To help, Treisman developed the Mathematics Workshop Program, which, in a surprisingly short time, reversed their fortunes, causing them to outperform their white and Asian counterparts. And although it is only a freshman program, black students who take it graduate at a rate comparable to the Berkeley average. Its central technique is group study of calculus concepts. But it is also wise; it does things that allay the racial vulnerabilities of these students. Stressing their potential to learn, it recruits them to a challenging "honors" workshop tied to their first calculus course. Building on their skills, the workshop gives difficult work, often beyond course content, to students with even modest preparation (some of their math SATs dip to the 300s). Working together, students soon understand that everyone knows something and nobody knows everything, and learning is speeded through shared understanding. The wisdom of these tactics is their subtext message: "You are valued in this program because of your academic potential—regardless of your current skill level. You have no more to fear than the next person, and since the work is difficult, success is a credit to your ability, and a setback is a reflection only of the challenge." The black students' double vulnerability around failure—the fear that they lack ability, and the dread that they will be devalued—is thus reduced. They can relax and achieve. The movie *Stand and Deliver* depicts Jaime Escalante using the same techniques of assurance and challenge to inspire advanced calculus performance in East Los Angeles Chicano high schoolers. And, explaining Xavier University's extraordinary success in producing black medical students, a spokesman said recently, "What doesn't work is saying, 'You need remedial work.' What does work is saying, 'You may be somewhat behind at this time but you're a talented person. We're going to help you advance at an accelerated rate.' "

The work of James Comer, a child psychiatrist at Yale, suggests that wiseness can minimize even the barriers of poverty. Over a fifteen-year period he transformed the two worst elementary schools in New Haven, Connecticut, into the third and fifth best in the city's thirty-three-school system without any change in the type of students—largely poor and black. His guiding belief is that learning requires a strongly accepting relationship between teacher and student. "After all," he notes, "what is the difference between scribble and a letter of the alphabet to a child? The only reason the letter is meaningful, and worth learning and remembering, is because a *meaningful* other wants him or her to learn and remember it." To build these relationships Comer focuses on the over-all school climate, shaping it not so much to transmit specific skills, or to achieve order per se, or even to improve achievement, as to establish a valuing and optimistic atmosphere in which a child can—to use his term—"identify" with learning. Responsibility for this lies with a team of ten to fifteen members, headed by the principal and made up of teachers, parents, school staff, and child-development experts (for example, psychologists or special-education teachers). The team develops a plan of specifics: teacher training, parent workshops, coordination of information about students. But at base I believe it tries to ensure that the students—vulnerable on so many counts—get treated essentially like middle-class students, with conviction about their value and promise. As this happens, their vulnerability diminishes, and with it the companion defenses of disidentification and misconduct. They achieve, and apparently identify, as their achievement gains persist into high school. Comer's genius, I believe, is to have recognized the importance of these vulnerabilities as barriers to *intellectual* development, and the corollary that schools hoping to educate such students must learn first how to make them feel valued.

These are not isolated successes. Comparable results were observed, for example, in a Comer-type program in Maryland's Prince Georges County, in the Stanford economist Henry Levin's accelerated-schools program, and in Harlem's Central Park East Elementary School, under the principalship of Deborah Meier. And research involving hundreds of programs and schools points to the same conclusion: black achievement is consistently linked to conditions of schooling that reduce racial vulnerability. These include relatively harmonious race relations among students; a commitment by teachers and schools to seeing minority-group members achieve; the instructional goal that students at all levels of preparation achieve; desegregation at the classroom as well as the school level; and a de-emphasis on ability tracking.

That erasing stigma improves black achievement is perhaps the strongest evidence that stigma is what depresses it in the first place. This is no happy realization. But it lets in a ray of hope: whatever other factors also depress black achievement—poverty, social isolation, poor preparation—they may be substantially overcome in a schooling atmosphere that reduces racial and other vulnerabilities, not through unrelenting niceness or ferocious regimentation but by wiseness, by *seeing* value and acting on it.

## WHAT MAKES SCHOOLING UNWISE

But if wise schooling is so attainable, why is racial vulnerability the rule, not the exception, in American schooling?

One factor is the basic assimilationist offer that schools make to blacks: You can be valued and rewarded in school (and society), the schools say to these students, but you must first master the culture and ways of the American mainstream, and since that mainstream (as it is represented) is essentially white, this means you must give up many particulars of being black—styles of speech and appearance, value priorities, preferences—at least in mainstream settings. This is asking a lot. But it has been the "color-blind" offer to every immigrant and minority group in our nation's history, the core of the melting-pot ideal, and so I think it strikes most of us as fair. Yet non-immigrant minorities like blacks and Native Americans have always been here, and thus are entitled, more than new immigrants, to participate in the defining images of the society projected in school. More important, their exclusion from these images denies their contributive history and presence in society. Thus, whereas immigrants can tilt toward assimilation in pursuit of the opportunities for which they came, American blacks may find it harder to assimilate. For them, the offer of acceptance in return for assimilation carries a primal insult: it asks them to join in something that has made them invisible.

Now, I must be clear. This is not a criticism of Western civilization. My concern is an omission of image-work. In his incisive essay "What America Would Be Like Without Blacks," Ralph Ellison showed black influence on American speech and language, the themes of our finest literature, and our most defining ideals of personal freedom and democracy. In *The World They Made Together,* Mechal Sobel described how African and European influences shaped the early American South in everything from housing design and land use to religious expression. The fact is that blacks are not outside the American mainstream but, in Ellison's words, have always been "one of its major tributaries." Yet if one relied on what is taught in America's schools, one would never know this. There blacks have fallen victim to a collective self-deception, a society's allowing itself to assimilate like mad from its constituent groups while representing itself to itself as if the assimilation had never happened, as if progress and good were almost exclusively Western and white. A prime influence of American society on world culture is the music of black Americans, shaping art forms from rock-and-roll to modern dance. Yet in American schools, from kindergarten through graduate school, these essentially black influences have barely peripheral status, are largely outside the canon. Thus it is not what is taught but what is *not* taught, what teachers and professors have never learned the value of, that reinforces a fundamental unwiseness in American schooling, and keeps black disidentification on full boil.

Deep in the psyche of American educators is a presumption that black students need academic remediation, or extra time with elemental curricula to overcome background deficits. This orientation guides many efforts to close the achievement gap—from grammar school tutoring to college academic-support programs—but I fear it can be unwise. Bruno Bettelheim and Karen Zelan's article "Why Children Don't Like to Read" comes to mind: apparently to satisfy the changing sensibilities of local school boards over this century, many books that children like were dropped from school reading lists; when children's reading scores also dropped, the approved texts were replaced by simpler books; and when reading scores dropped again, these were replaced by even simpler books, until eventually the children could hardly read at all, not because the material was too difficult but because they were bored stiff. So it goes, I suspect, with a great many of these remediation efforts. Moreover, because so many such programs target blacks primarily, they virtually equate black identity with substandard intellectual status, amplifying racial vulnerability. they can even undermine students' ability to gain confident from their achievement, by sharing credit for their successes while implying that their failures stem from inadequacies beyond the reach of remediation.

The psychologist Lisa Brown and I recently uncovered evidence of just how damaging this orientation may be. At a large, prestigious university we found that whereas the grades of black graduates of the 1950s improved during the students' college years until they virtually matched the school average, those of blacks who graduated in the 1980s (we chose only those with above-average entry credentials, to correct for more-liberal admissions policies in that decade) worsened, ending up considerably below the school average. The 1950s graduates faced outward discrimination in everything from housing to the classroom, whereas the 1980s graduates were supported by a phalanx of help programs. Many things may contribute to this pattern. The Jackie Robinson, "pioneer" spirit of the 1950s blacks surely helped them endure. And in a pre-affirmative-action era, they may have been seen as intellectually more deserving. But one cannot ignore the distinctive fate of the 1980s blacks: a remedial orientation put their abilities under suspicion, deflected their ambitions, distanced them from their successes, and painted them with their failures. Black students on today's campuses may experience far less overt prejudice than their 1950s counterparts but, ironically, may be more racially vulnerable.


## THE ELEMENTS OF WISENESS

For too many black students school is simply the place where, more concertedly, persistently, and authoritatively than anywhere else in society, they learn how little valued they are.

Clearly, no simple recipe can fix this, but I believe we now understand the basics of a corrective approach. Schooling must focus more on reducing the vulnerabilities that block identification with achievement. I believe that four conditions, like the legs of a stool, are fundamental.

- If what is meaningful and important to a teacher is to become meaningful and important to a student, the student must feel valued by the teacher for his or her potential and as a person. Among the more fortunate in society, this relationship is often taken for granted. But it is precisely the relationship that race can still undermine in American society. As Comer, Escalante, and Treisman have shown, when one's students bear race and class vulnerabilities, building this relationship is the first order of business—at all levels of schooling. No tactic of instruction, no matter how ingenious, can succeed without it.
- The challenge and the promise of personal fulfillment, not remediation (under whatever guise), should guide the education of these students. Their present skills should be taken into account, and they

should be moved along at a pace that is demanding but doesn't defeat them. Their ambitions should never be scaled down but should instead be guided to inspiring goals even when extraordinary dedication is called for. Frustration will be less crippling than alienation. Here psychology is everything: remediation defeats, challenge strengthens—affirming their potential, crediting them with their achievements, inspiring them.

But the first condition, I believe, cannot work without the second, and vice versa. A valuing teacher-student relationship goes nowhere without challenge, and challenge will always be resisted outside a valuing relationship. (Again, I must be careful about something: in criticizing remediation I am not opposing affirmative-action recruitment in the schools. The success of this policy, like that of school integration before it, depends, I believe, on the tactics of implementation. Where students are valued and challenged, they generally succeed.)

- Racial integration is a generally useful element in this design, if not a necessity. Segregation, whatever its purpose, draws out group differences and makes people feel more vulnerable when they inevitably cross group lines to compete in the larger society. This vulnerability, I fear, can override confidence gained in segregated schooling unless that confidence is based on strongly competitive skills and knowledge—something that segregated schooling, plagued by shortages of resources and access, has difficulty producing.

- The particulars of black life and culture—art, literature, political and social perspective, music—must be presented in the mainstream curriculum of American schooling, not consigned to special days, weeks, or even months of the year, or to special-topic courses and programs aimed essentially at blacks. Such channeling carries the disturbing message that the material is not of general value. And this does two terrible things: it wastes the power of this material to alter our images of the American mainstream—continuing to frustrate black identification with it—and it excuses in whites and others a huge ignorance of their own society. The true test of democracy, Ralph Ellison has said, is "the inclusion—not assimilation—of the black man."

Finally, If I might be allowed a word specifically to black parents, one issue is even more immediate: our children may drop out of school before the first committee meets to accelerate the curriculum. Thus, although we, along with all Americans, must strive constantly for wise schooling, I believe we cannot wait for it. We cannot yet forget our essentially heroic challenge: to foster in our children a sense of hope and entitlement to mainstream American life and schooling, even when it devalues them.

JERRY SULS
CHRISTINE A. MARCO

# William James, The Self, and the Selective Industry of the Mind

Suls and Marco review several modern theories about self in light of a classic paper written by William James over a hundred years ago. Citing a number of James's different statements about self, they help us to understand that self-esteem can result from an internal comparison with a person's ideals and goals as well as a comparison with others. In particular, Suls and Marco focus on James's idea that the mind selectively constructs a self by valuing certain activities and experiences, focusing on those domains that lead us to confirm the kind of person we want to be. The interested reader might consider the degree to which this is consistent or inconsistent with Swann's ideas about self.

William James's chapter on the self in the *Principles of Psychology* (1890/1950) set the agenda for subsequent social psychological theory and research. His observation that "a man has as many social selves as there are individuals who recognize him" (p. 294) is a cornerstone of contemporary social psychology. He also considered at length what processes contribute to "the consciousness of personal sameness." (His answer was memory.) In this article, we will examine only one portion of his essay, the section on self-seeking, or self-interest. Why do people take more interest in themselves than in others, and how is this manifested?

Our purpose is to discuss how James's thoughts about the motivated self-construction of identity are reflected in contemporary theory and research on the self. We will also identify one place where even James lapsed and will discuss one of his observations yet to be fully exploited by contemporary social and personality psychologists.

## SELF-INTEREST AND THE SELECTIVE INDUSTRY OF THE MIND

"What are our senses themselves but organs of selection?"

James, 1890/1950, p. 284

James recognized that people choose the kind of self they become: "Different characters may conceivably at the onset of life be alike possible to a man. But to make one of them actual, the rest must more or less be suppressed." This process was conceived as part of the general phenomenon of selective attention and appears throughout James's writings:

> The mind chooses to suit itself, and decides what particular sensation shall be held more real and valid than all the rest. (p. 286)

> Each has selected, out of the same mass of presented objects, those which suited his private interest and has made his experience thereby. (p. 286)

> Our thought incessantly deciding among many things of a kind, which ones for it shall be realities, here chooses one of many possible selves or characters, and forthwith reckons it no shame to fail in any of those not adopted expressly as its own. (p. 310)

The selective industry with reference to the self is reflected in two companion phenomena: (a) the selection of particular identities deemed worthy of development and promotion and (b) the perception that we are better than others on those dimensions and abilities that are personally relevant and important. Both manifestations of the "selective industry" have been examined in contemporary research. In the following section, the descendants of James's observations are described. Whether these efforts represent a direct inheritance from James or an indirect influence distilled from persons such as Mead, Cooley, Levin, and Asch who followed him cannot be easily determined, but a family resemblance is apparent.

## DEFINING THE KIND OF SELF THAT IS IMPORTANT

Areas of social psychological research on the self that reflect James's ideas include such domains as self-esteem and self-awareness. According to James's well-known formula, self-esteem = success/pretensions; that is, self-esteem is a measure of one's successes relative to one's pretensions or concerns. The notion that self-esteem is based on meeting internalized standards (or pretensions) is a major premise of Duval and Wicklund's (1972; Wicklund, 1975) theory of objective self-awareness. Duval and Wicklund argue that self-awareness involves the comparison of oneself against one's ideals and goals, which are much like the pretensions and concerns described by James. The cybernetic model of Carver and Scheier (1981) also posits that self-awareness involves checking our current self against our goals and standards. The latter model differs, however, from Duval and Wicklund by positing two distinct types of standards: private and public self-awareness (i.e., personal beliefs vs. societal standards). Finally, Higgins's (1987) self-discrepancy theory also highlights the importance of internalized standards in its contention that one's negative emotions are determined by the degree of discrepancy between one's actual behavior and the kind of inner standard one holds. Regardless of the specifics, however, these models share an emphasis on internal standards. Although contemporary perspectives place more emphasis on external sources of standards that become internalized than James did, his statement that a man has as many selves as people who recognize him is not incompatible with more recent versions of self-esteem = success/pretensions.

Another descendant of James's theories is the concept of "possible selves" developed by Markus and Nurius (1986). In fact, James used the term *possible self* in a similar sense. A possible self is a type of self-knowledge pertaining to images of one's potential, feared, or future selves. These run the gamut from the ideal self to the self we are afraid of becoming and include self-relevant manifestations of enduring goals, aspirations, motives, fears, and threats. These are not general mental constructs but specific representations that organize and energize one's actions. As for James, the possible self is a juncture between thought and action. Unlike other motivational accounts that emphasize instinctual drives, unconscious impulses, or general goals, the possible self is concerned with personalized goals and motivation. Markus makes the point that the better one is at constructing possible selves, the more vivid and specific these selves become. Consequently, one's current state can be made more similar to the desired state (and more dissimilar from the undesired or feared state). In essence, a possible self guides the recruitment of appropriate self-knowledge, the development of plans, and the search for appropriate behavioral strategies (Markus & Ruvolo, 1989).

Markus and her colleagues have provided interview data showing differences in possible selves across the life span. Further, interviews with delinquent and nondelinquent youth suggest that different possible selves are partly responsible for criminal behavior. For example, nondelinquent youth are better able to recruit and deploy possible selves to motivate themselves:

> A vivid representation of one's self in a relevant positive and desired state (e.g., "getting through school") can be used to counter the representation off the self in an undesired state (me "doing poorly in school" or me "dropping out") and to prevent the inaction that occurs when a dreaded possible self dominates the working self-concept. (Oyserman & Markus, 1988, p. x)

One difference between James and Markus is that the former emphasized the identity one desires, whereas Markus emphasizes that human action may be based as much on what one wishes to avoid as on what one desires.

## ACCENTUATING THE POSITIVE

"No wind can blow except to fill [the self's] sails."
James, 1890/1950, p. 313

The other way in which the selective industry of the mind exerts its influence is in egocentric, self-enhancing, or self-protective evaluations. James spoke of this aspect of the selective industry somewhat circumspectly but referred liberally to the German psychologist Horwicz, who noted the human tendency to feel "how much more intelligent, soulful, better is everything about us than anyone else" (James, 1890/1950, p. 326, citing H. Horwicz).

There are numerous examples of a positivistic bias in evaluating evidence relevant to self-performance (see Taylor & Brown, 1988, for a review). Greenwald (1980) perceived these biases as so pervasive that he likened the self system to a totalitarian state. One need only consider the self-serving bias in attribution, whereby people tend to make internal attributions (ability and effort) for success and external attributions (task difficulty, bad luck) for failure (Greenwald, 1980; Miller & Ross, 1975; Taylor & Brown, 1988; Zuckerman, 1979).

Self-enhancing evaluations have also been examined in the context of ability evaluation. Initial research in social psychology was concerned with how people accurately evaluate their standing on opinion and ability dimensions compared with other people (Festinger, 1954; Latané, 1966; Suls & Miller, 1977). However, more recent research indicates that sometimes there may be more motivation to think our abilities are good than to find out the truth (Goethals, 1986; Singer, 1966; Wheeler, 1966).

Several social psychological phenomena illustrate the mind's selectiveness for self-enhancement in social comparison. For example, people may compare upward in an attempt to identify with better performers (Major, Testa, & Blysma, 1990; Wheeler, 1966). They may also engage in downward comparison, first demonstrated by Hakmiller (1966) and then reviewed and systematized by Wills (1981). When self-esteem is threatened by poor performance, people frequently choose to compare with others who are less fortunate, as shown in a wide range of laboratory and field studies (Wills, 1981, 1987, 1990; Wood, Taylor, & Lichtman, 1985).

A related phenomenon is the construction or fabrication of downward comparison sources (Taylor & Lobel, 1989). Taylor, Wood, and Lichtman (1983) interviewed a sample of women with breast cancer and their husbands in order to assess the kinds of coping strategies they used to cope with the disease. A quarter of the husbands claimed they were not having as much trouble as many other men—"those animals who leave their wives" because of the cancer. Taylor et al. noted, however, that fewer than 4% of the marriages of the women in the sample broke up as a consequence of the illness. Thus, these targets, whom Taylor et al. called "mythical men," were fabricated, apparently in the interest of feeling better about one's own situation (Wood, 1989).

In addition to comparison or fabrication of specific others who are coping less well, there is evidence of self-enhancing estimates of the prevalence of desirable and undesirable attributes. Specifically, particular traits are seen as either relatively rare or prevalent in the population in a way that inflates the self. Campbell (1986), Goethals (1986; Goethals, Messick, & Allison, 1990), and Suls (Suls & Wan, 1987; Suls, Wan, & Sanders, 1988) find that people perceive their positive attributes to be uncommon in the population but their negative attributes to be very common.

The degree to which people can interpret information to be self-enhancing is sometimes truly incredible. One recent example makes this point. Affleck, Tennen, Pfeiffer, Fifield, and Rowe (1987) interviewed mothers of medically fragile infants to learn how they coped with the crisis. A large proportion of their sample mentioned downward comparisons involving infants who were smaller and sicker. However, sometimes a mother was able to infer being better off from evidence that at first thought appears to be highly negative: "I would carefully watch how other parents would react to bad news about their baby. I must have been better informed because they seemed not to be upset by the news. If you really knew what was happening you would have to be upset" (Affleck & Tennen, 1990, p. 379). In this case, the mother interpreted her greater distress as a positive sign because she felt that the more negative views she held of her child's medical status was more accurate than the views of the other parents. This example is a testament to the industry of the mind that shapes the facts in line with self-interest.

Another manifestation of the selective industry is shown in Swann's research on self-verification—behaviors and thoughts that serve to prove the validity of the person's self-concept. Swann and Read (1981) have empirically demonstrated three cognitive or behavioral routes by which people verify their self-concept. First, they selectively seek feedback from others that confirms their self-concepts. For example, in one experiment, subjects who rated themselves as either likeable or unlikable were given the opportunity to review statements about themselves. These statements were made by someone with whom they had interacted and who they were led to believe either liked or disliked them. Subjects' choices reflected a tendency to select information likely to confirm their self-concept. Subjects who thought themselves to be likable spent more time reviewing the statements when they thought the other person liked them, whereas subjects who thought themselves unlikable spent more time on the statements when they thought the other person disliked them.

Swann also found evidence of another aspect of self-verification: Subjects recalled more statements about themselves made by another person when they believed that person shared their self-concept. Finally, there is evidence for behavioral self-verification; people will actively try to prove to others the truth of their self-concepts. In one study, Swann and Read (1981) told subjects (half of whom thought of themselves as likable and half as unlikable) that a person with whom they would be having a conversation was either likely to like or likely to dislike them. Then the subjects engaged in a conversation with this person. Ratings after the conversation suggested that subjects who expected a challenge to their self-concept purposely provided a more extreme version of their usual behavior to convince the other and confirm their self-concept.

In summary, people tend to be highly selective about the identities they choose to value and try to develop. Furthermore, they tend to make selections or construct reality, cognitively or behaviorally, in a way that confirms what they want to be.

## A JAMESIAN OVERSIGHT

In one very significant way, research on self-verification diverges from other evidence for the selective industry. Swann's studies show a strong tendency for self-consistency: "People are likely to think and behave in ways that promote the survival of their self-conceptions, regardless of whether the self-conception happens to be positive or negative" (1987, p. 1039). Presumably, the reason is the need for a stable self-concept in organizing experience, predicting future events, and guiding behavior (Epstein, 1973). In contrast, evidence on consensus estimation, ability attribution, and downward social comparison suggests that people prefer self-enhancement. Currently, social psychologists are still debating which motive is dominant—self-verification or self-enhancement (Epstein, 1973; Greenwald, 1980).

James observed that people strive to find support for their self-conceptions and wish to see themselves in positive terms. However, he failed to acknowledge that the two tendencies could work at cross-purposes. If one is looking for a significant question about the self that James did not anticipate, then the self-verification versus self-enhancement debate qualifies. Of course, there is no necessary contradiction between self-enhancement and self-verification for persons with positive self-conceptions; they want positive social feedback, and it is consistent with their self-views. Persons with negative self-views pose the problem; positive feedback is inconsistent with a negative self-view (Shrauger, 1975).

James's oversight would be understandable if he had failed to acknowledge that people held negative self-views, but he himself suffered from periodic depressions, and his biographer Ralph Barton Perry spoke of James's "morbid traits," his back pains, insomnia, weakness, and digestive disorders. James was fundamentally optimistic about human nature, however, which may have made it difficult for him to understand why some people would want their worst thoughts about themselves confirmed.

## THE SOURCES OF SELF-SEEKING

What is responsible for the self-seeking selective industry of the mind? James posited that self-interest was a fundamental instinctual impulse. He wrote, "Self-seeking is the outcome of simple instinctive propensity, it is but a name for certain reflex acts" (p. 320). For James, self-seeking, whether it took a bodily, a social, or a spiritual form, was directly related to evolution, and he made much use of Darwin's ideas, as in "All minds must come, by the way of the survival of the fittest, if by no directer path, to take an intense interest in the bodies to which they are yoked" (p. 324). Hence, self-seeking developed because it encourages the survival of the species through natural selection.

Beyond a genetic evolutionary process, what are the psychological processes that make the selective industry possible? James quoted the psychologist Horwicz as saying that we prefer our own things "because we know them better" (James, 1890/1950, p. 327). This comment is reminiscent of the repeated exposure phenomenon, whereby familiarity breeds liking (Zajonc, 1968). James seemed to be satisfied that self-enhancing processes were instinctive, or built in. Contemporary researchers have looked for explanations in basic cognitive processes such as memory (Kunda & Sanitioso, 1989; Rogers, Kuiper, & Kirker, 1977), priming (Higgins, 1987), and attention (Greenwald & Pratkanis, 1984), but understanding of the processes that underlie self-enhancement is incomplete.

## CONCLUSION

James's essay on the self was based on his considerable reading, distillation, and critique of past authors mixed in with his keen observations and memorable phrases. Few essays in the psychological literature can sustain multiple readings as does "The Consciousness of Self," and no single piece has had as much influence on the psychological study of the self. Furthermore, as we have suggested, there is probably buried treasure waiting there. The philosopher R. J. Bernstein (1971) observed that James "has the power to . . . speak to us across time and space" (p. xi). George Miller (1962) wrote, "It is much easier to appreciate William James than to evaluate him, . . . but it is obvious he was, and still is, the foremost American psychologist" (pp. 77–78). Students of the self can find no better reason to read or reread him.

## References

Affleck, G., & Tennen, H. (1990). Social comparison and coping with medical disorders. In J. Suls & T. A. Wills (Eds.), *Social comparison: Contemporary theory and research* (pp. 369–393). Hillsdale, NJ: Lawrence Erlbaum.

Affleck, G., Tennen, H., Pfeiffer, C., Fifield, J., & Rowe, J. (1987). Downward comparison and coping with serious medical problems. *American Journal of Orthopsychiatry. 57,* 570–578.

Bernstein, R. J. (1971). Introduction. In W. James, *Essays in radical empiricism and a pluralistic universe* (pp. i–xi). New York: E. P. Dutton.

Campbell, J. (1986). Similarity and uniqueness: The effects of attribute type, relevance, and individual differences in self-esteem and depression. *Journal of Personality and Social Psychology, 50,* 281–294.

Carver, C. S., & Scheier, M. (1981). *Attention and self-regulation: A control-theory approach to human behavior.* New York: Springer-Verlag.

Duval, S., & Wicklund, R. (1972). *A theory of objective self-awareness.* Orlando, FL: Academic Press.

Epstein, S. (1973). The self-concept revisited, or a theory of a theory. *American Psychologist, 28,* 404–416.

Festinger, I. (1954). A theory of social comparison processes. *Human Relations, 7,* 117–140.

Goethals, A. G. (1986). Fabricating and ignoring social reality: Self-serving estimates of consensus. In J. Olson, C. P. Herman, & M. P. Zanna (Eds.), *Relative deprivation and social comparison: The Ontario Symposium* (Vol. 4). Hillsdale, NJ: Lawrence Erlbaum.

Goethals, A. G., Messick, D., & Allison, S. (1990). The uniqueness bias: Studies of constructive social comparison. In J. Suls & T. A. Wills (Eds.), *Social comparison: Contemporary theory and research* (pp. 149–176). Hillsdale, NJ: Lawrence Erlbaum.

Greenwald, A. G. (1980). The totalitarian ego: Fabrication and revision of personal history. *American Psychologist, 35,* 603–618.

Greenwald, A. G., & Pratkanis, A. R. (1984). The self. In R. S. Wyer & T. K. Srull (Eds.), *Handbook of social cognition* (Vol. 3, pp. 129–178). Hillsdale, NJ: Lawrence Erlbaum.

Hakmiller, K. (1966). Threat as a determinant of downward social comparison. *Journal of Experimental Social Psychology,* Suppl. 1, 32–39.

Hansen, R. D., & Donoghue, J. M. (1977). The power of consensus: Information derived from one's own and other's behaviors. *Journal of Personality and Social Psychology, 35,* 294–302.

Higgins, E. T. (1987). Self-discrepancy: A theory relating self and affect. *Psychological Review, 94,* 319–340.

James, W. (1950). *The principles of psychology* (Vol. 1). New York: Holt. (Original work published 1890).

Kunda, Z., & Sanitioso, R. (1989). Motivated changes in the self-concept. *Journal of Experimental Social Psychology, 25,* 272–285.

Latané, B. (Ed.). (1966). Studies in social comparison. *Journal of Experimental Social Psychology, 25,* Suppl. 1, whole issue.

Major, B., Testa, M., & Blysma, W. (in press). Responses to upward and downward social comparisons: The impact of esteem-relevance and perceived control. In J. Suls & T. A. Wills (Eds.), *Social comparison: Contemporary theory and research.* Hillsdale, NJ: Lawrence Erlbaum.

Markus, H., & Nurius, P. (1986). Possible selves. *American Psychologist, 41,* 954–969.

Markus, H., & Ruvolo, A. (1989). Possible selves: Personalized representations of goals. In L. Pervin (Ed.), *Goal concepts in personality and social psychology* (pp. 211–241). Hillsdale, NJ: Lawrence Erlbaum.

Miller, D. T., & Ross, M. (1975). Self-serving biases in the attribution of causality: Fact or fiction? *Psychological Bulletin, 82,* 213–255.

Oyserman, D., & Markus, H. (1988, August). *Possible selves and delinquency.* Paper presented at the International Congress of Psychology, Sydney, Australia.

Rogers, T. B., Kuiper, N., & Kirker, W. S. (1977). Self-reference and the encoding of personal information. *Journal of Personality and Social Psychology, 35,* 677–688.

Shrauger, J. S. (1975). Responses to evaluation as a function of initial self-perceptions. *Psychological Bulletin, 82,* 581–596.

Singer, J. E. (1966). Social comparison: Progress and issues. *Journal of Experimental Social Psychology,* Suppl. 1, 103–110.

Suls, J., & Miller, R. (Eds.). (1977). *Social comparison process: Theoretical and empirical perspectives.* Washington, DC: Hemisphere.

Suls, J., & Wan, C. K. (1987). In search of the false uniqueness phenomenon: Fear and estimates of social consensus. *Journal of Personality and Social Psychology, 52,* 211–217.

Suls, J., Wan, C., & Sanders, G. (1988). False consensus and false uniqueness in estimating the prevalence of health-relevant behaviors. *Journal of Applied Social Psychology, 18,* 66–79.

Swann, W. B., Jr. (1987). Identity negotiation: Where two roads meet. *Journal of Personality and Social Psychology, 53,* 1038–1051.

Swann, W. B., Jr., & Read, S. J. (1981). Self-verification processes: How we sustain our self-conceptions. *Journal of Experimental Social Psychology, 17,* 351–372.

Taylor, S., and Lobel, M. (1989). Social comparison activity under threat: Downward evaluation and upward contacts. *Psychological Review, 96,* 569–575.

Taylor, S., Wood, J. V., & Lichtman, R. (1983). It could be worse: Selective evaluation as a response to victimization. *Journal of Social Issues, 39,* 19–40.

Taylor, S. E., Brown, J. (1988). Illusion and well-being: A social psychological perspective on mental health. *Psychological Bulletin, 103,* 193–210.

Tesser, A. (1988). Toward a self-evaluation maintenance model of social behavior. In L. Berkowitz (Ed.), *Advances in experimental social psychology* (Vol. 21, pp. 181–227). Orlando, FL: Academic Press.

Tesser, A., & Campbell, J. (1980). Self-definition: The impact of the relative performance and similarity of others. *Social Psychology Quarterly, 43,* 341–347.

Tesser, A., Millar, M., & Moore, J. (1988). Some affective consequences of social comparison and reflection processes: The pain and pleasure of being close. *Journal of Personality and Social Psychology, 54,* 49–61.

Wheeler, I. (1966). Motivation as a determinant of upward comparison. *Journal of Experimental Social Psychology,* Suppl. 1, 27–31.

Wicklund, R. (1975). Objective self-awareness. In L. Berkowitz (Ed.), *Advances in experimental social psychology* (Vol. 8, pp. 233–275). Orlando, FL: Academic Press.

Wills, T. A. (1981). Downward comparison principles in social psychology. *Psychological Bulletin, 90,* 245–271.

Wills, T. A. (1987). Downward comparison as a coping mechanism. In C. R. Synder & C. Ford (Eds.), *Coping with negative life events: Clinical and social-psychological perspectives* (pp. 243–268). New York: Plenum.

Wills, T. A. (1990). Similarity and downward comparison. In J. Suls & T. A. Wills (Eds.), *Social comparison: Contemporary theory and research* (pp. 51–78). Hillsdale, NJ: Lawrence Erlbaum.

Wood, J. V. (1989). Theory and research concerning social comparisons of personal attributes. *Psychological Bulletin, 106,* 231–248.

Wood, J. V., Taylor, S., & Lichtman, R. (1985). Social comparison in adjustment to breast cancer. *Journal of Personality and Social Psychology, 49,* 1169–1183.

Zajonc, R. B. (1968). Attitudinal effects of mere exposure. *Journal of Personality and Social Psychology Monograph Supplement, 9,* 1–27.

Zuckerman, M. (1979). Attribution of success and failure revisited, or: The motivational bias is alive and well in attribution theory. *Journal of Personality, 47,* 245–287.

# To BIRG or to CORF, that is the question

You there, jumping up and down in the field boxes: it's those 11 mud-spattered maulers on the playing field who did all the grunt work of making it to the Super Bowl. Yet there you stand, chanting, "We're No. 1, we're No. 1." So, as the Catskills hotel owner said to tummler Buddy Hackett, since when are you a partner?

Actually, according to a report published in the Journal of Personality and Social Psychology, when we root for a team we all, in a sense, become its partners, because the team becomes an extension of our ego. Authored by psychologists Edward Hirt, of Indiana University, and Dolf Zillmann, of the University of Alabama, the article says researchers looking at fan behavior back in the 1970s and '80s found that when the team wins, we are given to BIRGing, or "basking in reflected glory." When it loses, we're prone to lying low, or CORFing—that is, "cutting off reflected failure." Their own recent study, say Hirt and Zillmann, suggests fanship can have consequences in the real world. Wars won on the playing fields of Eton, it seems, can be lost in the grandstand.

**Stuck with their team:** The two psychologists find that rooting for the team of your choice can be hazardous to your head. After a string of losses, for instance, fair-weather fans can CORF to their heart's content, but true grandstand groupies are denied that option. They're stuck with their team, in sickness and in health; it becomes part of their identity. "As a result," the article says, "the team's performance reflects directly upon the fan: team success is personal success, and team failure is personal failure." For their study, the psychologists had groups of students watch televised basketball games at the Wisconsin and Indiana campuses, then evaluate the performance of teams and players. Later they were asked to provide information about their feelings of self-esteem, on the pretext that it might affect the way they rated players.

The basic finding was that after a win, mood and self-esteem measured higher; after a loss they were "significantly" lower. The actual performance of tasks wasn't affected, although Hirt notes other studies have shown that outlook can make a difference. "Certainly," he says, "the preponderance of evidence is that rooting can be detrimental to the extent that the team loses." and apparently, there's more room to go down than to go up. "On the surface," Hurt and Zillmann write, "these findings would imply that fans are setting themselves up for a great deal of misery by committing themselves to a team."

Now they tell us. But to be sure, there are nice things about fanship, too. In becoming part of your identity, it gives you a feeling of being part of a larger group, one that shares the joys and commiserates in the griefs. "That's a good thing," Hirt says. "And maybe, after all, it outweighs the risks of losing." All right, you there in the stands sobbing in your sauerkraut: up on your feet, now, and do a wave.

David Gelman

# Social Influence: Following and Resisting

Social influence is one of the most central processes in all of social psychology. It represents to some extent the bottom line, the key end result of people interacting together. Fundamental issues of influence, such as conformity and obedience, have been with us since the beginning of time, and matters such as advertising and cult conversions are often the topics of modern discussion.

Robert Cialdini, author of the highly regarded book *Influence,* is Professor of Psychology at Arizona State University. He is one of the most innovative and highly respected voices in the field of social psychology. In our conversation, Prof. Cialdini discusses the unusual way that he has gained insights into the strategies and practices of influence and the general principles that he has derived from his experiences. I am certain that as you read this you will recognize each of these, not just as they have been used by others, but as you have used them yourselves.

## A CONVERSATION WITH
## ROBERT CIALDINI
*Arizona State University*

**Krupat:** *When we speak of social influence, the word conformity often comes up. Does the idea of conformity strike you as good, bad, or indifferent?*

**Cialdini:** Some people don't like that term because they view it only in its negative sense. I think conformity can often be quite an adaptive and even enlightened response to one's environment. It doesn't necessarily bespeak a weak-willed, wishy-washy individual who is at the mercy of the winds. In the role of an information processing efficiency expert, you may take a look at the evidence and decide that the most accurate information about how to behave comes from the behaviors of others. Conforming sometimes allows us a shortcut without having to think too hard about things in our information-over-loaded day.

**Krupat:** *For years social psychologists have been running experiments to gain a handle on the nature of influence. Based on what we know, would you say it is easy to change people?*

**Cialdini:** As social psychologists who study behavior in the laboratory, we frequently can't answer that question very well. In our laboratory procedures we eliminate all of the sources of influence in the situation except the one that we are studying. What we see very often then is change that we can't easily locate outside the antiseptic, artificial environment of the laboratory. I think we need to take a different approach and look at the prevalence and prominence of change tactics and strategies that exist in the influence professions.

**Krupat:** *When you say influence professions, I'm not quite sure whether to take you literally. Lawyers try to influence juries, teenagers try to get their* *friends to try alcohol, and college students try to get their roommates to lend them money. Aren't they all in the influence business?*

**Cialdini:** But they are not all in the influence *professions.* Only the attorney is, because there is an abiding commercial interest in getting other people to say yes to a request. That's what I mean by a profession. The economic livelihood of these people depends on the success of the influence strategies that they use. Those practitioners who use influence strategies and principles that work will flourish, and the principles themselves will remain as part of the pool of practices and procedures that are passed on to succeeding generations in the same way adaptive genes are passed on. The upshot is that, if we look across the widest range of influence professionals and we see that the same principles have risen to the surface and persisted, that's our best evidence of what the most powerful influences are in natural interaction.

**Krupat:** *Are you ever amazed that influence professionals do what they do so well even though they have never formally studied human behavior?*

**Cialdini:** It is interesting that they seem to be able to know how to do this without ever having studied social psychology. I think the reason for this is that they are beneficiaries of decades of trial and error. And to answer your earlier question as to whether it's easy to change people, my answer is yes. If one understands how the major principles of influence work and if one understands how to activate them, it's possible to change people and to change them reliably and regularly.

**Krupat:** *Even if influence professionals don't know why it works in any conceptual sense?*

**Cialdini:** It's not their job to know why it works. That's my job as a social scientist; that's what you and I do for a living. That's why we also need to go into the laboratory after we've looked to see what works powerfully and systematically in the natural environment.

**Krupat:** *But if the laboratory and the real world are both important, how can the research process best go about incorporating both?*

**Cialdini:** We need to begin with systematic observation of a phenomenon that is effective, that works on people. Then we take it to the laboratory to examine its psychological underpinnings, why it works the way it does. Then we take that new information into the natural environment to see if our new insights really represent the way the thing works in the real world. And that's the final arc in the cycle that I don't think is often enough closed by social psychologists. I once called this approach "full cycle social psychology." We seem to think that the laboratory is the standard against which we should base all our knowledge. I don't think so. The grand experiment that's going on outside is still the standard against which we should compare our results.

**Krupat:** *If I'm correct, you have observed that arena at close hand in a way that would be pretty unusual for the standard social psychologist. Can you tell me a little about that?*

**Cialdini:** I had always been a fan of the sociologists and anthropologists who used the method of participant observation, which involved a systematic immersing of the researcher into the setting to be understood. What I did was to infiltrate as many influence professions as I could possibly get access to. I would answer ads in the newspaper for sales trainees and would learn from the inside what an encyclopedia sales operator told trainees to do to get people to say yes. I did this with insurance sales, portrait photography sales, and automobile sales. I also drew on some contacts with friends of mine and managed to infiltrate some advertising agencies and a couple of charity organizations. I interviewed police bunco squad officers to see what the con artists try to do, and I even interviewed cult recruiters to see what they did that so powerfully got people to join. And across it all I looked for the commonalities, the things that occurred in parallel in each of these influence professions.

**Krupat:** *That's as fascinating as it is unusual. What did you find?*

**Cialdini:** I found six principles that had the character of universal mechanisms of influence, that seemed effective across professions, across people within those professions, across versions and varieties of techniques, and even across eras as far back as the turn of the century.

**Krupat:** *Let's take them one at a time. What's first?*

**Cialdini:** If we believe the sociologist Gouldner, there is not a single human society that does not subscribe to the principle of reciprocation, the rule that obligates people to give back to others some form of behavior that they have first received from them. That is a very powerful motivator of conduct in our culture. It applies to every single behavior, both on the positive and negative sides. We are socialized into it so thoroughly that we feel guilty taking without giving in return. So it becomes possible for people to influence us in their direction by giving us something first, by doing us a favor or a service or giving a gift. We can be made to say yes in that way, by the rules of reciprocity. The Disabled American Veterans Organization, for example, reports that when they send out a standard appeal for donations they get about an 18 percent return rate. But if they include in the envelope a little pack of individualized gummed address labels, the success rate jumps to 35 percent. It virtually doubles by adding 6 cents worth of material.

**Krupat:** *I see. You keep the labels and repay rather than stay forever in their debt.*

**Cialdini:** Right. And when a company wants you to fill out a survey, another tactic that's gaining popularity is to send you a dollar with the survey. Of course, people don't send the dollar back, but once they've kept it, they feel obligated to do something in return. So they fill out a survey that they would never had agreed to do for a dollar if they were being paid to do so after the fact.

**Krupat:** *Principle number one makes good sense. What is number two?*

**Cialdini:** Number two is scarcity. We all tend to want those things that are scarce, rare, and dwindling in their availability. You might remember the Mazda

Miata craze, where people were spending more money on a used Miata than they would have spent for a new one if it were available. But it wasn't available, so that unavailability made the car more attractive by itself. Compliance professionals have limited-time-only sales and limited-availability sales. The scarcity is just manufactured to spur interest.

**Krupat:** *What is third on the list?*

**Cialdini:** Authority is next. I think here we've seen good evidence that people who are in positions of legitimate authority, experts for example, are able to get people to comply to their requests. People tend to defer to the directives of legitimate authority, and that makes all kinds of sense because legitimately constituted authorities typically have attained their positions by virtue of greater wisdom or experience or training. However, we often fall victim to authority directives even when they make no sense at all, it seems to me, because it's such an automatic response. Advertisers will sometimes try to misuse this principle by hiring spokespeople who have an aura of authority in a particular area when there is really no authority at all. I'm thinking for example of the television commercials starring the actor Robert Young. He talks about the health consequences of Sanka decaf coffee or the pain-relieving power of Arthritis Pain Relief Formula. And the only reason he is so successful as a spokesman is that he used to play Marcus Welby, M.D., on television. But that's enough to produce persuasion in the minds of people who are not thinking, who are simply reacting to the influence.

**Krupat:** *I assume the reason that actors are no longer allowed to endorse products by saying they are doctors serves as testimony to the strength of this effect.*

**Cialdini:** I actually heard a commercial a couple of years ago where the actor began by saying, "I'm not a doctor, but I play one on TV." And then he proceeded to describe some product. That's the ultimate in mindlessness! Why should we expect that this guy who plays a doctor on TV should be more believable? But the Robert Young commercials were exceedingly effective in selling their products.

**Krupat:** *What is next on our list of strategies?*

**Cialdini:** Next is commitment. That really has to do with the principle of consistency and our tendency to want to be consistent within out attitudes, beliefs, words, and deeds. That means that, if I can get you to go on record, to take a stand in favor of some position at one point, I will be significantly more likely to get you to say yes to a request that is logically consistent with that stand at some subsequent time. The most famous consistency tactic is the foot-in-the-door technique in which a person asks a homeowner for a small favor, let's say to sign a petition favoring safe driving. Then two weeks later the homeowner is asked to put up a billboard on the lawn favoring safe driving. You find many people who will do that because they've gone on record at an earlier point as advocating safe driving and, in order to be consistent with that earlier commitment, they agree again.

**Krupat:** *I have fallen into that trap many a time. There's a problem in self-presentation, in terms of being able to say no once you've already said yes.*

**Cialdini:** You're right. Not only is there a desire on the part of people to be consistent within themselves, it is also important to be seen as consistent in the eyes of others, because consistency is a valued trait in our society. It speaks of rationality, logic, and honesty.

**Krupat:** *What's next?*

**Cialdini:** Liking is the fifth. It should come as no surprise that we prefer to say yes to the requests of the people we know and like. All you need to do is look at the wild success of the Tupperware party, which arranges for customers to buy not from a stranger across the counter, but from a friend, relative, or neighbor. When I investigated how a Tupperware party works, some of the people would say, "I really don't need any more plastic containers, but what can I do? My friend asked me."

**Krupat:** *That makes me think about a practice that cults are known to use. When potential recruits show up at a meeting, the group members huddle around them and say nice things. I recall reading that young woman said it almost felt like sorority rush.*

**Cialdini:** It's called love bombing, in which you get unqualified positive regard from all the people around you. They tell you how much they like you and respect your decision to come and see what the group is all about.

**Krupat:** *Okay, what is principle number six?*

**Cialdini:** Social validation. We frequently decide what is appropriate behavior for ourselves by examining the behavior of the people around us. The evidence here indicates that we are most likely to follow the actions of others when those others are numerous, when there are many others. I remember the wonderful experiment that Milgram and his colleagues performed where they took a research assistant, had him stand on a crowded street corner in New York City, pick a spot in the sky, and stare at it for 60 seconds to see what would happen. Not a whole lot happened when that person was by himself, but the following day five research assistants stood on that street corner and stared at that same empty spot in the sky. Within 60 seconds 84 percent of the people who had passed by had stopped to look up with them. It seems we assume that, if a lot of people are doing something, there must be value to it.

**Krupat:** *Now that we have gone through all six principles, does knowing about them make us any more likely to resist influence attempts?*

**Cialdini:** I think that's partially true. When we come upon one of these principles, we have to recognize that frequently they do steer us correctly; otherwise, we wouldn't use them as a guidepost for deciding when to comply.

What we have to decide is whether it makes sense in that particular situation to use the influence of an authority or a lot of other people or someone we know and like. I would recommend that when we encounter one or another of these principles, we should take a step back from the situation before we decide how to behave. We should analyze what it is we are being requested to do in terms of its merits, not in terms of the way that it was requested of us. Especially in the important decisions that we have to face, it's worth taking that moment out before rushing in with a decision.

Robert Cialdini

# Social Proof:
# Monkey Me, Monkey Do

In this selection, Cialdini offers us insight into the concept of
"social proof"—the idea that, if everyone else is doing it, it
must be right. Citing the dramatic example of the mass suicide of the followers of the Reverend Jim Jones in Jonestown,
Guyana, Cialdini suggests that no amount of charisma on the
part of Jones can fully account for their behavior. Instead,
Jones's isolation of the group from all outside influences
generated a herd mentality in his followers. The members of
the cult came to define reality for one another, and the perception that everyone else was willing to obey his demands
led them to this mass act of self-destruction in a way that no
physical force or personal appeal could have ever achieved.

The principle of social proof, like all other weapons of influence, works better
under some conditions than under others. Without question, when people are
uncertain, they are more likely to use others' actions to decide how they
themselves should act. In addition, there is another important working condition: similarity. The principle of social proof operates most powerfully when
we are observing the behavior of people just like us (Festinger, 1954). It is the
conduct of such people that gives us the greatest insight into what constitutes
correct behavior for ourselves. Therefore, we are more inclined to follow the
lead of a similar individual than a dissimilar one.

That is why I believe we are seeing an increasing number of average-per-
son-on-the-street testimonials on TV these days. Advertisers now know that
one successful way to sell a product to ordinary viewers (who compose the
largest potential market) is to demonstrate that other "ordinary" people like
and use it. Whether the product is a brand of soft drink or a pain reliever or a
laundry detergent, we hear volleys of praise from John or Mary Everyperson.

More compelling evidence for the importance of similarity in determining whether we will imitate another's behavior comes from scientific research.
An especially apt illustration can be found in a study done by psychologists
at Columbia University (Hornstein, Fisch, & Holmes, 1968). The researchers

placed wallets on the ground in various locations around midtown Manhattan to observe what would happen when they were found. Each wallet contained $2.00 in cash, a $26.30 check, and various information providing the name and address of the wallet's "owner." In addition to these items, the wallet also contained a letter making it evident that the wallet had been lost not once, but twice. The letter was written to the wallet's owner from a man who had found it earlier and whose intention was to return it. The finder indicated in his letter that he was happy to help and that the chance to be of service in this way had made him feel good.

It was evident to anyone who found one of these wallets that this well-intentioned individual had then lost the wallet himself on the way to the mailbox—the wallet was wrapped in an envelope addressed to the owner. The researchers wanted to know how many people finding such a wallet would follow the lead of the first finder and mail it, intact, to the original owner. Before they dropped the wallets, however, the researchers varied one feature of the letter it contained. Some of the letters were written in standard English by someone who seemed to be an average American, while the other letters were written in broken English by the first finder, who identified himself as a recently arrived foreigner. In other words, the person who initially found the wallet and had tried to return it was depicted by the letter as being either similar or dissimilar to most Americans.

The interesting question was whether the people who found the wallet and letter would be more influenced to mail the wallet if the first person who had tried to do so were similar to them. The answer was plain: Only 33 percent of the wallets were returned when the first finder was seen to be dissimilar, but 70 percent were returned when he was thought to be a similar other. These results suggest an important qualification of the principle of social proof. We will use the actions of others to decide on proper behavior for ourselves, *especially when we view those others to be similar to ourselves.*

This tendency applies not only to adults but to children as well. Health researchers have found, for example, that a school-based antismoking program had lasting effects only when it used same-age peer leaders as teachers (Murray et al., 1984). Another study found that children who saw a film depicting a child's positive visit to the dentist lowered their own dental anxieties principally when they were the same age as the child in the film (Melamed et al., 1978). I wish I had known about this second study when, a few years before it was published, I was trying to reduce a different kind of anxiety in my son, Chris.

I live in Arizona where backyard swimming pools abound. Regrettably, each year, several young children drown after falling into an unattended pool. I was determined, therefore, to teach Chris how to swim at an early age. The problem was not that he was afraid of the water; he loved it, but he would not get into the pool without wearing his inflatable inner tube, no matter how I tried to coax, talk, or shame him out of it. After getting nowhere for two months, I hired a graduate student of mine to help. Despite his background as a lifeguard and swimming instructor, he failed as I had. He couldn't persuade Chris to attempt even a stroke outside of his plastic ring.

About this time, Chris was attending a day camp that provided a number of activities to its group, including the use of a large pool, which he scrupulously avoided. One day, shortly after the graduate student incident, I went to get Chris from camp and, with my mouth agape, watched him run down the diving board and jump into the deepest part of the pool. Panicked, I began pulling off my shoes to jump in to his rescue when I saw him bob to the surface and paddle safely to the side of the pool—where I dashed, shoes in hand, to meet him.

"Chris, you can swim!" I said excitedly. "You can swim!"

"Yes," he responded casually, "I learned how today."

"This is terrific! This is just terrific," I burbled, gesturing expansively to convey my enthusiasm. "But, how come you didn't need your plastic ring today?"

Looking somewhat embarrassed because his father seemed to be raving while inexplicably soaking his socks in a small puddle and waving his shoes around, Chris explained:

"Well, I'm 3 years old, and Tommy is 3 years old. And Tommy can swim without a ring, so that means I can, too."

I could have kicked myself. Of course it would be *to little Tommy*, not to a 6'2" graduate student, that Chris would look for the most relevant information about what he could or should do. Had I been more thoughtful about solving Chris' swimming problem, I could have employed Tommy's good example earlier and, perhaps, saved myself a couple of frustrating months. I could have simply noted at the day camp that Tommy was a swimmer and then arranged with his parents for the boys to spend a weekend afternoon swimming in our pool. My guess is that Chris' plastic ring would have been abandoned by the end of the day.


## MONKEY DIE

Any factor that can spur 70 percent of New Yorkers to return a wallet, with all its contents included, must be considered impressive. Yet the outcome of the lost-wallet study offers just a hint of the immense impact that the conduct of similar others has on human behavior. More powerful examples exist in addition to this one. To my mind, the most telling illustration of this impact starts with a seemingly nonsensical statistic: After a suicide has made front-page news, airplanes—private planes, corporate jets, airliners—begin falling out of the sky at an alarming rate.

For example, it has been shown (Phillips, 1979) that immediately following certain kinds of highly publicized suicide stories, the number of people who die in commercial-airline crashes increases by 1,000 percent! Even more alarming: The increase is not limited to airplane deaths. The number of automobile fatalities shoots up as well (Phillips, 1980). What could possible be responsible?

One explanation suggests itself immediately: The same social conditions that cause some people to commit suicide cause others to die accidentally. For instance, certain individuals, the suicide-prone, may react to stressful societal events (economic downturns, rising crime rates, international tensions) by ending it all. Others will react differently to these same events; they might become angry, impatient, nervous, or distracted. To the degree that such people operate or maintain the cars and planes of our society, the vehicles will be less safe, and consequently, we will see a sharp increase in the number of automobile and air fatalities.

According to this "social conditions" interpretation, then, some of the same societal factors that cause intentional deaths also cause accidental ones, and that is why we find so strong a connection between suicide stories and fatal crashes. Another fascinating statistic indicates that this is not the correct explanation: Fatal crashes increase dramatically only in those regions where the suicide has been highly publicized. Other places, existing under similar social conditions, whose newspapers have *not* publicized the story, have shown no comparable jump in such fatalities. Furthermore, within those areas where newspaper space has been allotted, the wider the publicity given the suicide, the greater has been the rise in subsequent crashes. Thus, it is not some set of common societal events that stimulates suicides on the one hand and fatal accidents on the other. Instead, it is the publicized suicide story itself that produces the car and plane wrecks.

To explain the strong association between suicide-story publicity and subsequent crashes, a "bereavement" account has been suggested. Because, it has been argued, front-page suicides often involve well-known and respected public figures, perhaps their highly publicized deaths throw many people into states of shocked sadness. Stunned and preoccupied, these individuals become careless around cars and planes. The consequence is the sharp increase in deadly accidents involving such vehicles that we see after front-page suicide stories. Although the bereavement theory can account for the connection between the degree of publicity given a story and subsequent crash fatalities—the more people who learn of the suicide, the larger will be the number of bereaved and careless individuals—it *cannot* explain another startling fact: Newspaper stories reporting suicide victims who died alone produce an increase in the frequency of single-fatality wrecks only, whereas stories reporting suicide-plus-murder incidents produce an increase in multiple-fatality wrecks only. Simple bereavement could not cause such a pattern.

The influence of suicide stories on car and plane crashes, then, is fantastically specific. Stories of pure suicides, in which only one person dies, generate wrecks in which only one person dies; stories of suicide-murder combination, in which there are multiple deaths, generate wrecks in which there are multiple deaths. If neither "social conditions" nor "bereavement" can make sense of this bewildering array of facts, what can? There is a sociologist at the

University of California in San Diego who thinks he has found the answer. His name is David Phillips, and he points a convincing finger at something called the "Werther effect."

The story of the Werther effect is both chilling and intriguing. More than two centuries ago, the great man of German literature, Johann von Goethe, published a novel entitled *Die Leiden des jungen Werthers (The Sorrows of Young Werther)*. The book, in which the hero, named Werther, commits suicide, had a remarkable impact. Not only did it provide Goethe with immediate fame, but it also sparked a wave of emulative suicides across Europe. So powerful was this effect that authorities in several countries banned the novel.

Phillips' own work has traced the Werther effect to modern times (Phillips, 1974). His research has demonstrated that, immediately following a front-page suicide story, the suicide rate increases dramatically in those geographical areas where the story has been highly publicized. It is Phillips' argument that certain troubled people who read of another's self-inflicted death kill themselves in imitation. In a morbid illustration of the principle of social proof, these people decide how they should act on the basis of how some other troubled person has acted.

Phillips derived his evidence for the modern-day Werther effect from examining the suicide statistics in the United States between 1947 and 1968. He found that, within two months after every front-page suicide story, an average of 58 more people than usual killed themselves. In a sense, each suicide story killed 58 people who otherwise would have gone on living. Phillips also found that this tendency for suicides to beget suicides occurred principally in those parts of the country where the first suicide was highly publicized. He observed that the wider the publicity given the first suicide, the greater the number of later suicides (see Figure 1).

If the facts surrounding the Werther effect seem to you suspiciously like those surrounding the influence of suicide stories on air and traffic fatalities, the similarities have not been lost on Phillips, either. In fact, he contends that all the excess deaths following a front-page suicide incident can be explained as the same thing: copycat suicides. Upon learning of another's suicide, an uncomfortably large number of people decide that suicide is an appropriate action for themselves as well. Some of these individuals then proceed to commit the act in a straightforward, no-bones-about-it fashion, causing the suicide rate to jump.

Others, however, are less direct. For any of several reasons—to protect their reputations, to spare their families the shame and hurt, to allow their dependents to collect on insurance policies—they do not want to appear to have killed themselves. They would rather seem to have died accidentally. So, purposively but furtively, they cause the wreck of a car or a plane they are operating or are simply riding in. This can be accomplished in a variety of all-too-familiar-sounding ways. A commercial airline pilot can dip the nose of the aircraft at a crucial point of takeoff or can inexplicably land on an already

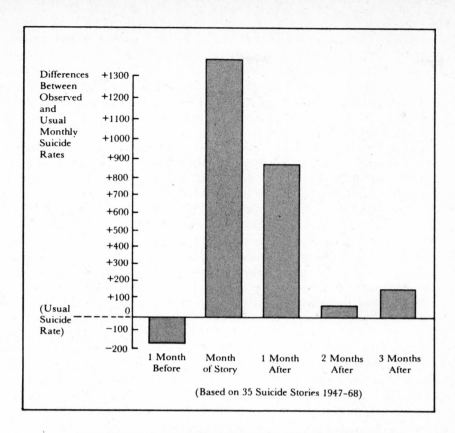

Differences Between Observed and Usual Monthly Suicide Rates

+1300
+1200
+1100
+1000
+900
+800
+700
+600
+500
+400
+300
+200
+100

(Usual Suicide Rate) 0

−100
−200

1 Month Before | Month of Story | 1 Month After | 2 Months After | 3 Months After

(Based on 35 Suicide Stories 1947–68)

FLUCTUATION IN NUMBER OF SUICIDES BEFORE, DURING,
AND AFTER MONTH OF SUICIDE STORY.

**Figure 1.** This evidence raises an important ethical issue. The suicides that follow these stories are *excess* deaths. After the initial spurt, the suicide rates do not drop below traditional levels but only return to those levels. Statistics like these might well give pause to newspaper editors inclined to sensationalize suicide accounts, as those accounts are likely to lead to the deaths of scores of people. More recent data indicate that in addition to newspaper editors, television broadcasters have cause for concern about the effects of the suicide stories they present. Whether they appear as news reports, information features, or fictional movies, these stories create an immediate cluster of self-inflicted deaths, with impressionable, imitation-prone teenagers being the most frequent victims (Bollen & Phillips, 1982; Gould & Shaffer, 1986; Phillips & Carsensen, 1986, 1988; Schmidtke & Hafner, 1988).

occupied runway against the instructions from the control tower; the driver of a car can suddenly swerve into a tree or into oncoming traffic; a passenger in an automobile or corporate jet can incapacitate the operator, causing the deadly crash; the pilot of a private plane can, despite all radio warnings, plow into another aircraft. Thus the alarming climb in crash fatalities that we find following front-page suicides is, according to Phillips, most likely due to the Werther effect secretly applied.

I consider this insight brilliant. First, it explains all of the data beautifully. If these wrecks really are hidden instances of imitative suicide, it makes sense that we would see an increase in the wrecks after suicide stories appear. It makes sense that the greatest rise in wrecks should occur after the suicide stories that have been most widely publicized and have, consequently, reached the most people. It also makes sense that the number of crashes should jump appreciably only in those geographical areas where the suicide stories were publicized. It even makes sense that single-victim suicides should lead only to single-victim crashes, whereas multiple-victim suicide incidents should lead only to multiple-victim crashes. Imitation is the key.

In addition, there is a second valuable feature of Phillips' insight. Not only does it allow us to explain the existing facts, it also allows us to predict new facts that had never been uncovered before. For example, if the abnormally frequent crashes following publicized suicides are genuinely the result of imitative rather than accidental actions, they should be more deadly as a result. That is, people trying to kill themselves will likely to arrange (with a foot on the accelerator instead of the brake, with the nose of the plane down instead of up) for the impact to be as lethal as possible. The consequence should be quick and sure death. When Phillips examined the records to check on this prediction, he found that the average number of people killed in a fatal crash of a commercial airliner is more than three times greater if the crash happened one week after a front-page suicide story than if it happened one week before. A similar phenomenon can be found in traffic statistics where there is evidence for the deadly efficiency of post-suicide-story auto crashes. Victims of fatal car wrecks that follow front-page suicide stories die four times more quickly than normal (Phillips, 1980).

Still another fascinating prediction flows from Phillips' idea. If the increase in wrecks following suicide stories truly represents a set of copycat deaths, then the imitators should be most likely to copy the suicides of people who are similar to them. The principle of social proof states that we use information about the way others have behaved to help us determine proper conduct for ourselves. As the dropped-wallet experiment showed, we are most influenced in this fashion by the actions of people who are like us.

Therefore, Phillips reasoned, if the principle of social proof is behind the phenomenon, there should be some clear similarity between the victim of the highly publicized suicide and those who cause subsequent wrecks. Realizing that the clearest test of this possibility would come from the records of automobile crashes involving a single car and a lone driver, Phillips compared the age of the suicide-story victim with the ages of the lone drivers killed in single-car crashes immediately after the story appeared in print. Once again, the predictions were strikingly accurate: When the newspaper detailed the suicide of a young person, it was young drivers who then piled their cars into trees, poles, and embankments with fatal results; but when the news story concerned an older person's suicide, older drivers died in such crashes (Phillips, 1980).

This last statistic is the clincher for me. I am left wholly convinced and, simultaneously, wholly amazed by it. Evidently, the principle of social proof is so wide-ranging and powerful that its domain extends to the fundamental decision for life or death. Phillips' findings illustrate a distressing tendency for suicide publicity to motivate certain people who are similar to the victim to kill themselves—because they now find the idea of suicide more legitimate. Truly frightening are the data indicating that many innocent people die in the bargain. A glance at the graphs documenting the undeniable increase of traffic and air fatalities following publicized suicides, especially those involving murder, is enough to cause concern for one's own safety. I have been sufficiently affected by these statistics to begin to take note of front-page suicide stories and to change my behavior in the period after their appearances. I try to be especially cautious behind the wheel of my car. I am reluctant to take extended trips requiring a lot of air travel. If I must fly during such a period, I purchase substantially more flight insurance than I normally would. Phillips has done us a service by demonstrating that the odds for survival when we travel change measurably for a time following the publication of certain kinds of front-page suicide stories. It would seem only prudent to play those odds (see Figure 2).

As if the frightening features of Phillips' suicide data weren't enough, his additional research (Phillips, 1983) brings more cause for alarm: Homicides in this country have a stimulated, copycat character after highly publicized acts of violence. Heavyweight championship prize fights that receive coverage on network evening news appear to produce measurable increases in the United States homicide rate. This analysis of heavyweight championship fights (between 1973 and 1978) is perhaps most compelling in its demonstration of the remarkably specific nature of the imitative aggression that is generated. When such a match was lost by a black fighter, the homicide rate during the following 10 days rose significantly for young black male victims but not young white males. On the other hand, when a white fighter lost a match, it was young white men, but not young black men, who were killed more frequently in the next 10 days. When these results are combined with the parallel findings in Phillips' suicide data, it is clear that widely publicized aggression has the nasty tendency to spread to similar victims, no matter whether the aggression is inflicted on the self or on another.

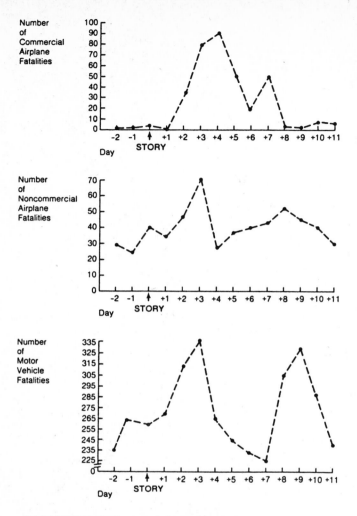

DAILY FLUCTUATION IN NUMBER OF ACCIDENT FATALITIES
BEFORE, ON, AND AFTER SUICIDE STORY DATE

**Figure 2.** As is apparent from these graphs, the greatest danger exists three to four days following the news story's publication. After a brief dropoff, there comes another peak approximately one week later. By the eleventh day, there is no hint of an effect. This pattern across various types of data indicates something noteworthy about secret suicides. Those who try to disguise their imitative self-destruction as accidents wait a few days before committing the act—perhaps to build their courage, to plan the incident, or to put their affairs in order. Whatever the reason for the regularity of this pattern, we know that travelers' safety is most severely jeopardized three to four days after a suicide-murder story and then again, but to a lesser degree, a few days later. We would be well advised, then, to take special care in our travels at these times.

## MONKEY ISLAND

Work like Phillips' helps us appreciate the awesome influence of the behavior of similar others. Once the enormity of that force is recognized, it becomes possible to understand perhaps the most spectacular act of compliance of our time—the mass suicide at Jonestown, Guyana. Certain crucial features of the event deserve review.

The People's Temple was a cultlike organization that was based in San Francisco and drew its recruits from the poor of that city. In 1977, the Reverend Jim Jones—who was the group's undisputed political, social, and spiritual leader—moved the bulk of the membership with him to a jungle settlement in Guyana, South America. There, the People's Temple existed in relative obscurity until November 18, 1978, when Congressman Leo R. Ryan of California (who had gone to Guyana to investigate the cult), three members of Ryan's fact-finding party, and a cult defector were murdered as they tried to leave Jonestown by plane. Convinced that he would be arrested and implicated in the killings and that the demise of the People's Temple would result, Jones sought to control the end of the Temple in his own way. He gathered the entire community around him and issued a call for each person's death to be done in a unified act of self-destruction.

The first response was that of a young woman who calmly approached the now famous vat of strawberry-flavored poison, administered one dose to her baby, one to herself, and then sat down in a field, where she and her child died in convulsions within four minutes. Others followed steadily in turn. Although a handful of Jonestowners escaped and a few others are reported to have resisted, the survivors claim that the great majority of the 910 people who died did so in an orderly, willful fashion.

News of the event shocked us. The broadcast media and the papers provided a barrage of reports, updates, and analyses. For days, our conversations were full of the topic, "How many have they found dead now?" "A guy who escaped said they were drinking the poison like they were hypnotized or something." "What were they doing down in South America, anyway?" "It's so hard to believe. What caused it?"

Yes, "What caused it?"—the critical question. How are we to account for this most astounding of compliant acts? Various explanations have been offered. Some have focused on the charisma of Jim Jones, a man whose style allowed him to be loved like a savior, trusted like a father, and treated like an emperor. Other explanations have pointed to the kind of people who were attracted to the People's Temple. They were mostly poor and uneducated individuals who were willing to give up their freedoms of thought and action for the safety of a place where all decisions would be made for them. Still other explanations have emphasized the quasi-religious nature of the People's Temple, in which unquestioned faith in the cult's leader was assigned highest priority.

No doubt each of these features of Jonestown has merit in explaining what happened there, but I do not find them sufficient. After all, the world abounds with cults populated by dependent people who are led by a charismatic figure. What's more, there has never been a shortage of this combination of circumstances in the past. Yet virtually nowhere do we find evidence of an event even approximating the Jonestown incident among such groups. There must be something else that was critical.

One especially revealing question gives us a clue: "If the community had remained in San Francisco, would Reverend Jones' suicide command have been obeyed?" A highly speculative question to be sure, but the expert most familiar with the People's Temple has no doubt about the answer. Louis Jolyon West, chairman of psychiatry and biobehavioral sciences at UCLA and director of its neuropsychiatric unit, is an authority on cults who had observed the People's Temple for eight years prior to the Jonestown deaths. When interviewed in the immediate aftermath, he made what strikes me as an inordinately instructive statement: "This wouldn't have happened in California. But they lived in total alienation from the rest of the world in a jungle situation in a hostile country."

Although lost in the welter of commentary following the tragedy, West's observation, together with what we know about the principle of social proof, seems to me quite important to a satisfactory understanding of the compliant suicides. To my mind, the single act in the history of the People's Temple that most contributed to the members' mindless compliance that day occurred a year earlier with the relocation of the Temple to a jungle country of unfamiliar customs and people. If we are to believe the stories of Jim Jones' malevolent genius, he realized fully the massive psychological impact such a move would have on his followers. All at once, they found themselves in a place they knew nothing about. South America, and the rain forests of Guyana, especially, were unlike anything they had experienced in San Francisco. The country—both physical and social—into which they were dropped must have seemed dreadfully uncertain.

Ah, uncertainty—the right-hand man of the principle of social proof. We have already seen that when people are uncertain, they look to the actions of others to guide their own actions. In the alien, Guyanese environment, then, Temple members were very ready to follow the lead of others. As we have also seen, it is others of a special kind whose behavior will be most unquestioningly followed: similar others. Therein lies the awful beauty of Reverend Jones' relocation strategy. In a country like Guyana, there were no similar others for a Jonestown resident but the people of Jonestown itself.

What was right for a member of the community was determined to a disproportionate degree by what other community members—influenced heavily by Jones—did and believed. When viewed in this light, the terrible orderliness, the lack of panic, the sense of calm with which these people moved to the vat of poison and to their deaths seems more comprehensible. They hadn't been hypnotized by Jones; they had been convinced—partly by him but, more importantly, by the principle of social proof—that suicide was the correct conduct. The uncertainty they surely felt upon first hearing the death command must have caused them to look around them for a definition of the appropriate response.

It is worth particular note that they found two impressive pieces of social evidence, each pointing in the same direction. The first was the initial set of their compatriots, who quickly and willingly took the poison drafts. There will always be a few such fanatically obedient individuals in any strong leader-dominated group. Whether, in this instance, they had been specially instructed beforehand to serve as examples or whether they were just naturally the most compliant with Jones' wishes is difficult to know. No matter; the psychological effect of the actions of those individuals must have been potent. If the suicides of similar others in news stories can influence total strangers to kill themselves, imagine how enormously more compelling such an act would be when performed without hesitation by one's neighbors in a place like Jonestown. The second source of social evidence came from the reactions of the crowd itself. Given the conditions, I suspect that what occurred was a large-scale instance of the pluralistic ignorance phenomenon. Each Jonestowner looked to the actions of surrounding individuals to assess the situation and—finding calmness because everyone else, too, was surreptitiously assessing rather than reacting—"learned" that patient turntaking was the correct behavior. Such misinterpreted, but nonetheless convincing, social evidence would be expected to result precisely in the ghastly composure of the assemblage that waited in the tropics of Guyana for businesslike death.

From my own perspective, most attempts to analyze the Jonestown incident have focused too much on the personal qualities of Jim Jones. Although he was without question a man of rare dynamism, the power he wielded strikes me as coming less from his remarkable personal style than from his understanding of fundamental psychological principles. His real genius as a leader was his realization of the limitations of individual leadership. No leader can hope to persuade, regularly and single-handedly, all the members of the group. A forceful leader can reasonably expect, however, to persuade some sizable proportion of group members. Then the raw information that a substantial number of group members has been convinced can, by itself, convince the rest. Thus the most influential leaders are those who know how to arrange group conditions to allow the principle of social proof to work in their favor.

It is in this that Jones appears to have been inspired. His masterstroke was the decision to move the People's Temple community from urban San Francisco to the remoteness of equatorial South America, where the conditions of uncertainty and exclusive similarity would make the principle of social proof operate for him as perhaps nowhere else. There a settlement of a thousand people, much too large to be held in persistent sway by the force of one man's personality, could be changed from a following into a *herd*. As slaughterhouse operators have long known, the mentality of a herd makes it easy to manage. Simply get some members moving in the desired direction and the others—responding not so much to the lead animal as to those immediately surrounding them—will peacefully and mechanically go along. The powers of the amazing Reverend Jones, then, are probably best understood not in terms of his dramatic personal style but in his profound knowledge of the art of social jujitsu.

# References

Bollen, K. A., & Phillips, D. P. (1982). Imitative suicides: A national study of the effects of television news stories. *American Sociological Review, 47,* 802–809.

Festinger, L. (1954). A theory of social comparison processes. *Human Relations, 7,* 117–140.

Gould, M. S., & Shaffer, D. (1986). The impact of suicide in television movies. *The New England Journal of Medicine, 315,* 690–694.

Hornstein, H. A., Fisch, E., & Holmes, M. (1968). Influence of a model's feeling about his behavior and his relevance as a comparison other on observers' helping behavior. *Journal of Personality and Social Psychology, 10,* 222–226.

Murray, D. A., Leupker, R. V., Johnson, C. A., & Mittlemark, M. B. (1984). The prevention of cigarette smoking in children: A comparison of four strategies. *Journal of Applied Social Psychology, 14,* 274–288.

Phillips, D. P. (1974). The influence of suggestion on suicide: Substantive and theoretical implications of the Werther effect. *American Sociological Review, 39,* 340–354.

Phillips, D. P. (1979). Suicide, motor vehicle fatalities, and the mass media: Evidence toward a theory of suggestion. *American Journal of Sociology, 84,* 1150–1174.

Phillips, D. P. (1980). Airplane accidents, murder, and the mass media: Towards a theory of imitation and suggestion. *Social Forces, 58,* 1001–1024.

Phillips, D. P. (1983). The impact of mass media violence on U.S. homicides. *American Sociological Review, 48,* 560–568.

Phillips, D. P., & Cartensen, L. L. (1986). Clustering of teenage suicides after television news stories about suicide. *The New England Journal of Medicine, 315,* 685–689.

Schmidtke, A., & Hafner, H. (1988). The Werther effect after television films: New evidence for an old hypothesis. *Psychological Medicine, 18,* 665–676.

Philip Meyer

# If Hitler Asked You to Electrocute a Stranger, Would You?

In this article from *Esquire*, Meyer discusses one of the most dramatic and highly debated programs of research in social psychology—Stanley Milgram's studies on obedience. Meyer offers us some insights into Milgram's interests and motivation in performing this research in which people were asked to deliver clearly painful and possibly dangerous electric shocks to another person as part of an experiment. Noting that a majority of people obeyed, Meyer prompts us to answer the question of why people acted as they did—and in doing so to analyze the powerful situational factors present and to wonder how each of us would have reacted in that situation.

In the beginning, Stanley Milgram was worried about the Nazi problem. He doesn't worry much about the Nazis anymore. He worries about you and me, and, perhaps, himself a little bit too.

Stanley Milgram is a social psychologist, and when he began his career at Yale University in 1960 he had a plan to prove, scientifically, that Germans are different. The Germans-are-different hypothesis has been used by historians, such as William L. Shirer, to explain the systematic destruction of the Jews by the Third Reich. One madman could decide to destroy the Jews and even create a master plan for getting it done. But to implement it on the scale that Hitler did meant that thousands of other people had to go along with the scheme and help to do the work. The Shirer thesis, which Milgram set out to test, is that Germans have a basic character flaw which explains the whole thing, and this flaw is a readiness to obey authority without question, no matter what outrageous acts the authority commands.

The appealing thing about this theory is that it makes those of us who are not Germans feel better about the whole business. Obviously, you and I are not Hitler, and it seems equally obvious that we would never do Hitler's dirty work for him. But now, because of Stanley Milgram, we are compelled to wonder. Milgram developed a laboratory experiment which provided a systematic way to measure obedience. His plan was to try it out in New Haven on Americans and then go to Germany and try it out on Germans. He was strongly motivated by scientific curiosity, but there was also some moral content in his decision to pursue this line of research, which was, in turn, colored by his own Jewish background. If he could show that Germans are more obedient than Americans, he could then vary the conditions of the experiment and try to find out just what it is that makes some people more obedient than others. With this understanding, the world might, conceivably, be just a little bit better.

But he never took his experiment to Germany. He never took it any farther than Bridgeport. The first finding, also the most unexpected and disturbing finding, was that we Americans are an obedient people: not blindly obedient, and not blissfully obedient, just obedient. "I found so much obedience," says Milgram softly, a little sadly, "I hardly saw the need for taking the experiment to Germany."

There is something of the theatre director in Milgram, and his technique, which he learned from one of the old masters in experimental psychology, Solomon Asch, is to stage a play with every line rehearsed, every prop carefully selected, and everybody an actor except one person. That one person is the subject of the experiment. The subject, of course, does not know he is in a play. He thinks he is in real life. The value of this technique is that the experimenter, as though he were God, can change a prop here, vary a line there, and see how the subject responds. Milgram eventually had to change a lot of the script just to get people to stop obeying. They were obeying so much, the experiment wasn't working—it was like trying to measure oven temperature with a freezer thermometer.

The experiment worked like this: If you were an innocent subject in Milgram's melodrama, you read an ad in the newspaper or received one in the mail asking for volunteers for an educational experiment. The job would take about an hour and pay $4.50. So you make an appointment and go to an old Romanesque stone structure on High Street with the imposing name of The Yale Interaction Laboratory. It looks something like a broadcasting studio. Inside, you meet a young, crew-cut man in a laboratory coat who says he is Jack Williams, the experimenter. There is another citizen, fiftyish, Irish face, an accountant, a little overweight, and very mild and harmless-looking. This other citizen seems nervous and plays with his hat while the two of you sit in chairs side by side and are told that the $4.50 checks are yours no matter what happens. Then you listen to Jack Williams explain the experiment.

It is about learning, says Jack Williams in a quiet, knowledgeable way. Science does not know much about the conditions under which people learn and this experiment is to find out about negative reinforcement. Negative reinforcement is getting punished when you do something wrong, as opposed to positive reinforcement which is getting rewarded when you do something right. The negative reinforcement in this case is electric shock. You notice a book on the table, titled, *The Teaching-Learning Process,* and you assume that this has something to do with the experiment.

Then Jack Williams takes two pieces of paper, puts them in a hat, and shakes them up. One piece of paper is supposed to say, "Teacher" and the other, "Learner." Draw one and you will see which you will be. The mild-looking accountant draws one, holds it close to his vest like a poker player, looks at it, and says, "Learner." You look at yours. It says, "Teacher." You do not know that the drawing is rigged, and both slips say "Teacher." The experimenter beckons the mild-mannered "learner."

"Want to step right in here and have a seat, please?" he says. "You can leave your coat on the back of that chair . . roll up your right sleeve, please. Now what I want to do is strap down your arms to avoid excessive movement on your part during the experiment. This electrode is connected to the shock generator in the next room.

"And this electrode paste," he says, squeezing some stuff out of a plastic bottle and putting it on the man's arm, "is to provide a good contact and to avoid a blister or burn. Are there any question snow before we go into the next room?"

You don't have any, but the strapped-in "learner" does.

"I do think I should say this," says the learner. "About two years ago, I was at the veterans' hospital . . . they detected a heart condition. Nothing serious, but as long as I'm having these shocks, how strong are they—how dangerous are they?"

Williams, the experimenter, shakes his head casually. "Oh, no," he says. "Although they may be painful, they're not dangerous. Anything else?"

Nothing else. And so you play the game. The game is for you to read a series of word pairs: for example, blue-girl, nice-day, fat-neck. When you finish the list, you read just the first word in each pair and then a multiple-choice list of four other words, including the second word of the pair. The learner, from his remote, strapped-in position, pushes one of four switches to indicate which of the four answers he thinks is the right one. If he gets it right, nothing happens and you go on to the next one. If he gets it wrong, you push a switch that buzzes and gives him an electric shock. And then you go to the next word. You start with 15 volts and increase the number of volts by 15 for each wrong answer. The control board goes from 15 volts on one end to 450 volts on the other. So that you know what you are doing, you get a test shock yourself, at 45 volts. It hurts. To further keep you aware of what you are doing to that man in there, the board has verbal descriptions of the shock levels, ranging from "Slight Shock" at the left-hand side, through "Intense Shock" in the middle, to "Danger: Severe Shock" toward the far right. Finally, at the very end, under 435- and 450-volt switches, there are three ambiguous X's. If, at any point, you hesitate, Mr. Williams calmly tells you to go on. If you still hesitate, he tells you again.

Except for some terrifying details, which will be explained in a moment, this is the experiment. The object is to find the shock level at which you disobey the experimenter and refuse to pull the switch.

When Stanley Milgram first wrote this script, he took it to fourteen Yale psychology majors and asked them what they thought would happen. He put it this way: Out of one hundred persons in the teacher's predicament, how would their break-off points be distributed along the 15-to-450-volt scale? They thought a few would break off very early, most would quit someplace in the middle and a few would go all the way to the end. The highest estimate of the number out of one hundred who would go all the way to the end was three. Milgram then informally polled some of his fellow scholars in the psychology department. They agreed that very few would go to the end. Milgram thought so too.

"I'll tell you quite frankly," he says, "before I began this experiment, before any shock generator was built, I thought that most people would break off at 'Strong Shock' or 'Very Strong Shock.' You would only get a very, very small proportion of people going out to the end of the shock generator, and they would constitute a pathological fringe."

In his pilot experiments, Milgram used Yale students as subjects. Each of them pushed the shock switches, one by one, all the way to the end of the board.

So he rewrote the script to include some protests from the learner. At first, they were mild, gentlemanly, Yalie protests, but, "it didn't seem to have as much effect as I thought it would or should," Milgram recalls. "So we had more violent protestation on the part of the person getting the shock. All of the time, of course, what we were trying to do was not to create a macabre situation, but simply to generate disobedience. And that was one of the first findings. This was not only a technical deficiency of the experiment, that we didn't get disobedience. It really was the first finding, that obedience would be much greater than we had assumed it would be and disobedience would be much more difficult than we had assumed."

As it turned out, the situation did become rather macabre. The only meaningful way to generate disobedience was to have the victim protest with great anguish, noise, and vehemence. The protests were tape-recorded so that all the teachers ordinarily would hear the same sounds and nuances, and they started with a grunt at 75 volts, proceeded through a "Hey, that really hurts," at 125 volts, got desperate with, "I can't stand the pain, don't do that," at 180 volts, reached complaints of heart trouble at 195, an agonized scream at 285, a refusal to answer at 315, and only heartrending, ominous silence after that.

Still, sixty-five percent of the subjects, twenty- to fifty-year-old American males, everyday, ordinary people, like you and me, obediently kept pushing those levers in the belief that they were shocking the mild-mannered learner, whose name was Mr. Wallace, and who was chosen for the role because of his innocent appearance, all the way up to 450 volts.

Milgram was now getting enough disobedience so that he had something he could measure. The next step was to vary the circumstances to see what would encourage or discourage obedience. There seemed very little left in the way of discouragement. The victim was already screaming at the top of his lungs and feigning a heart attack. So whatever new impediment to obedience reached the brain of the subject had to travel by some route other than the ear. Milgram thought of one.

He put the learner in the same room with the teacher. He stopped strapping the learner's hand down. He rewrote the script so that at 150 volts the learner took his hand off the shock plate and declared that he wanted out of the experiment. He rewrote the script some more so that the experimenter then told the teacher to grasp the learner's hand and physically force it down on the plate to give Mr. Wallace his unwanted electric shock.

"I had the feeling that very few people would go on at that point, if any," Milgram says. "I thought that would be the limit of obedience that you would find in the laboratory."

It wasn't.

Although seven years have now gone by, Milgram still remembers the first person to walk into the laboratory in the newly rewritten script. He was a construction worker, a very short man. "He was so small," says Milgram, "that when he sat on the chair in front of the shock generator, his feet didn't reach the floor. When the experimenter told him to push the victim's hand down and give the shock, he turned to the experiment, and he turned to the victim, his elbow went up, he fell down on the hand of the victim, his feet kind of tugged to one side, and he said, 'Like this, boss?' ZZUMPH!"

The experiment was played out to its bitter end. Milgram tried it with forty different subjects. And thirty percent of them obeyed the experimenter and kept on obeying.

"The protests of the victim were strong and vehement, he was screaming his guts out, he refused to participate, and you had to physically struggle with him in order to get his hand down on the shock generator," Milgram remembers. But twelve out of forty did it.

Milgram took his experiment out of New Haven. Not to Germany, just twenty miles down the road to Bridgeport. Maybe, he reasoned, the people obeyed because of the prestigious setting of Yale University. If they couldn't trust a center of learning that had been there for two centuries, whom could they trust? So he moved the experiment to an untrustworthy setting.

The new setting was a suite of three rooms in a run-down office building in Bridgeport. The only identification was a sign with a fictitious name: "Research Associates of Bridgeport." Questions about professional connections got only vague answers about "research for industry."

Obedience was less in Bridgeport. Forty-eight percent of the subjects stayed for the maximum shock, compared to sixty-five percent at Yale. But this was enough to prove that far more than Yale's prestige was behind the obedient behavior.

For more than seven years now, Stanley Milgram has been trying to figure out what makes ordinary American citizens so obedient. The most obvious answer—that people are mean, nasty, brutish and sadistic—won't do. The subjects who gave the shocks to Mr. Wallace to the end of the board did not enjoy it. They groaned, protested, fidgeted, argued, and in some cases, were seized by fits of nervous, agitated giggling.

"They even try to get out of it," says Milgram, "but they are somehow engaged in something from which they cannot liberate themselves. They are locked into a structure, and they do not have the skills or inner resources to disengage themselves."

Milgram, because he mistakenly had assumed that he would have trouble getting people to obey the orders to shock Mr. Wallace, went to a lot of trouble to create a realistic situation.

There was crew-cut Jack Williams and his grey laboratory coat. Not white, which might denote a medical technician, but ambiguously authoritative grey. Then there was the book on the table, and the other appurtenances of the laboratory which emitted the silent message that things were being performed here in the name of science, and were therefore great and good.

But the nicest touch of all was the shock generator. When Milgram started out, he had only a $300 grant from the Higgins Fund of Yale University. Later he got more ample support from the National Science Foundation, but in the beginning he had to create this authentic-looking machine with very scarce resources except for his own imagination. So he went to New York and roamed around the electronic shops until he found some little black switches at Lafayette Radio for a dollar apiece. He bought thirty of them. The generator was a metal box, about the size of a small foot-locker, and he drilled the thirty holes for the thirty switches himself in a Yale machine shop. But the fine detail was left to professional industrial engravers. So he ended up with a splendid-looking control panel dominated by the row of switches, each labeled with its voltage, and each having its own red light that flashed on when the switch was pulled. Other things happened when a switch was pushed. Besides the ZZUMPHing noise, a blue light labeled "voltage energizer" went on, and a needle on a dial labeled "voltage" flicked from left to right. Relays inside the box clicked. Finally, in the upper left-hand corner of the control panel was this inscription, engraved in precise block letters:

SHOCK GENERATOR TYPE ZLB
DYSON INSTRUMENT COMPANY
WALTHAM, MASS.
OUTPUT: 15 VOLTS—450 VOLTS

One day a man from the Lehigh Valley Electronics Company of Pennsylvania was passing through the laboratory, and he stopped to admire the shock generator.

"This is a very fine shock generator," he said. "But who is this Dyson

Instrument Company?" Milgram felt proud at that, since Dyson Instrument Company existed only in the recesses of his imagination.

When you consider the seeming authenticity of the situation, you can appreciate the agony some of the subjects went through. It was pure conflict. As Milgram explains to his students, "When a parent says, 'Don't strike old ladies,' you are learning two things: the content, and, also, to obey authority. This experiment creates conflicts between the two elements."

Here is a partial transcription from one of the experiments. The naive "teacher" is a heavyset, worried-looking man with prematurely grey hair. He is wearing a polo shirt. He is very polite. He has just pushed the 180-volt lever. A hidden camera is recording the performance.

**Learner** (who, from the teacher's point of view is heard but not seen, an offstage voice): Ow, I can't stand the pain. Don't do that. . . .

**Teacher** (pivoting around in his chair and shaking his head): I can't stand it. I'm not going to kill that man in there. You hear him hollering?

**Experimenter:** As I told you before, the shocks may be painful, but—

**Teacher:** But he's hollering. He can't stand it. What's going to happen to him?

**Experimenter** (his voice patient, matter-of-fact): The experiment requires that you continue, Teacher.

**Teacher:** Aaah, but, unh, I'm not going to get that man sick in there . . . know what I mean?

**Experimenter:** Whether the learner likes it or not, we must go on, through all the word pairs.

**Teacher:** I refuse to take the responsibility. He's in there hollering!

**Experimenter:** It's absolutely essential that you continue, Teacher.

**Teacher** (indicating the unused questions): There's too many left here, I mean, Geez, if he gets them wrong, there's too many of them left. I mean who's going to take the responsibility if anything happens to that gentleman?

**Experimenter:** I'm responsible for anything that happens to him. Continue please.

**Teacher:** All right. (Consults list of words.) The next one's "Slow—walk, truck, dance, music." Answer, please. (A buzzing sound indicates the learner has signaled his answer.) Wrong. A hundred and ninety-five volts. "Dance." (Zzumph!)

**Learner:** Let me out of here. My heart's bothering me! (Teacher looks at experimenter.)

**Experimenter:** Continue, please.

**Learner** (screaming): Let me out of here, you have no right to keep me here. Let me out of here, let me out, my heart's bothering me, let me out! (Teacher shakes head, pats the table nervously.)

**Teacher:** You see, he's hollering. Hear that? Gee, I don't know.

**Experimenter:** The experiment requires. . . .

**Teacher** (interrupting): I know it does, sir, but I mean—hunh! He don't know what he's getting in for. He's up to 195 volts! (Experiment continues, through 210 volts, 225 volts, 240 volts, 255 volts, 270 volts, delivered to the man in the electric chair, at which point the teacher, with evident relief, runs out of word-pair questions.)

**Experimenter:** You'll have to go back to the beginning of that page and go through them again until he's learned them all correctly.

**Teacher:** Aw, no. I'm not going to kill that man. You mean I've got to keep going up with the scale. No sir. He's hollering in there. I'm not going to give him 450 volts.

**Experimenter:** The experiment requires that you go on.

**Teacher:** I know it does, but that man is hollering in there, sir.

**Experimenter** (same matter-of-fact tone): As I said before, although the shocks may be painful. . . .

**Teacher** (interrupting): Awwww. He—he—he's yelling in there.

**Experimenter:** Start with "Blue," please, at the top of the page. Continue, please, Teacher. Just go ahead.

**Teacher** (concentrating intently on list of words in front of him, as if to shut everything else out): "Blue—boy, girl, grass, hat." (Buzz indicates answer.) Correct. "Night—day, sky, job, chair. (Buzz) Wrong. The answer is "day." Two hundred and eighty-five volts. (Zzumph!)

**Learner:** Ohhhuhhoohhh!

**Experimenter:** Continue, please.

**Teacher:** "Fat—man, lady, tub, neck." Answer, please. (Buzz) Wrong. The answer is "neck." Three hundred volts. (Zzumph!)

**Learner:** Ohhh. I absolutely refuse to answer any more. (Shouting urgently, now) Let me out of here. You can't hold me here. Get me out. Get—me—out—of—here.

**Experimenter:** Continue. The next word is "Green," please.

**Teacher:** "Green—grass, hat, ink, apple." (Nothing happens. No answering buzz. Just gloomy silence.)

**Teacher:** I don't think he is going to answer.

**Experimenter:** If the learner doesn't answer in a reasonable time, about four or five seconds, consider the answer wrong. And follow the same procedures you have been doing for wrong answers. Say "Wrong," tell him the number of volts, give him the punishment, read him the correct answer. Continue, please.

**Teacher:** "Green—grass, hat, ink, apple." Answer, please. (More silence. Teacher just sits there.)

**Experimenter:** Go on with the procedure, please, Teacher.

**Teacher:** Three hundred and fifteen volts. The answer is "ink." (Zzumph!)

**Learner:** Ohh. Ooohh.

**Teacher** (relieved to hear response): Next one.

**Learner:** I absolutely refuse to answer.

**Teacher:** You got to. You get a shock if you don't answer. (Experiment continues with learner refusing to answer, and, finally, failing even to grunt or groan. At 375 volts, the teacher stands up. Has he had enough? Will he break off the experiment? Will he disobey?)

**Teacher:** I think something's happened to that fellow in there. I don't get no answer. He was hollering at less voltage. Can't you check in and see if he's all right, please?

**Experimenter** (same detached calm): Not once we've started. Please continue, Teacher.

**Teacher** (sits down, sighs deeply): "Cool—day, shade, water, paint." Answer, please. Are you all right in there? Are you all right?

**Experimenter:** Please continue, Teacher. Continue, please. (Teacher pushes lever. Zzumph!)

**Teacher** (swiveling around in his chair): Something's happened to that man in there. (Swiveling back) Next one. "Low—dollar, necklace, moon, paint." (Turning around again) Something's happened to that man in there. You better check in on him, sir. He won't answer or nothing.

**Experimenter:** Continue. Go on, please.

**Teacher:** You accept all responsibility.

**Experimenter:** The responsibility is mine. Correct. Please go on. (Teacher returns to his list, starts running through words as rapidly as he can read them, works through to 450 volts.)

**Teacher:** That's that.

**Experimenter:** Continue using the last switch on the board, please. The four-fifty switch for each wrong answer. Continue, please.

**Teacher:** But I don't get anything!

**Experimenter:** Please continue. The next word is "White."

**Teacher:** Don't you think you should look in on him, please.

**Experimenter:** Not once we've started the experiment.

**Teacher:** But what if something has happened to the man?

**Experimenter:** The experiment requires that you continue. Go on, please.

**Teacher:** Don't the man's health mean anything?

**Experimenter:** Whether the learner likes it or not. . . .

**Teacher:** What if he's dead in there? (Gestures toward the room with the electric chair.) I mean, he told me he can't stand the shock, sir. I don't mean to be rude, but I think you should look in on him. All you have to do is look in the door. I don't get no answer, no noise. Something might have happened to the gentleman in there, sir.

**Experimenter:** We must continue. Go on, please.

**Teacher:** You mean keep giving him what? Four hundred fifty volts, what he's got now?

**Experimenter:** That's correct. Continue. The next word is "White."

**Teacher** (now at a furious pace): "White—cloud, horse, rock, house." Answer, please. The answer is "horse." Four hundred and fifty volts. (Zzumph!) Next word, "Bag—paint, music, clown, girl." The answer is

"paint." Four hundred and fifty volts. (ZZUMPH!) Next word is "short—sentence, movie."

Experimenter: Excuse me, Teacher. We'll have to discontinue the experiment.

(Enter Milgram from camera's left. He has been watching from behind
one-way glass.)

Milgram: I'd like to ask you a few questions. (Slowly, patiently, he
dehoaxes the teacher, telling him that the shocks and screams were not real.)

Teacher: You mean he wasn't getting nothing? Well, I'm glad to hear
that. I was getting upset there. I was getting ready to walk out.

(Finally, to make sure there are no hard feelings, friendly, harmless Mr.
Wallace comes out in coat and tie. Gives jovial greeting. Friendly reconciliation
takes place. Experiment ends.)*

Subjects in the experiment were not asked to give the 450-volt shock
more than three times. By that time, it seemed evident that they would go on
indefinitely. "No one," says Milgram, "who got within five shocks of the end
ever broke off. By that point, he had resolved the conflict."

Why do so many people resolve the conflict in favor of obedience?

Milgram's theory assumes that people behave in two different operating
modes as different as ice and water. He does not rely on Freud or sex or
toilet-training hang-ups for this theory. All he says is that ordinarily we
operate in a state of autonomy, which means we pretty much have and assert
control over what we do. But in certain circumstances, we operate under what
Milgram calls a state of agency (after agent, *n* . . . one who acts for or in the
place of another by authority from him; a substitute; a deputy.—*Webster's
Collegiate Dictionary*). A state of agency, to Milgram, is nothing more than a
frame of mind.

"There's nothing bad about it, there's nothing good about it," he says.
It's a natural circumstance of living with other people. . . . I think of a state of
agency as a real transformation of a person; if a person has different properties
when he's in that state, just as water can turn to ice under certain conditions
of temperature, a person can move to the state of mind that I call agency. . .
the critical thing is that you see yourself as the instrument of the execution of
another person's wishes. You do not see yourself as acting on your own. And
there's a real transformation, a real change of properties of the person."

To achieve this change, you have to be in a situation where there seems
to be a ruling authority whose commands are relevant to some legitimate
purpose; the authority's power is not unlimited.

But situations can be and have been structured to make people do
unusual things, and not just in Milgram's laboratory. The reason, says Milgram, is that no action, in and of itself, contains meaning.

*Copyright 1965 by Stanley Milgram. From the film OBEDIENCE, distributed by the New York
University film Library

"The meaning always depends on your definition of the situation. Take an action like killing another person. It sounds bad.

"But then we say the other person was about to destroy a hundred children, and the only way to stop him was to kill him. Well, that sounds good.

"Or, you take destroying your own life. It sounds very bad. Yet, in the Second World War, thousands of persons thought it was a good thing to destroy your own life. It was set in the proper context. You sipped some saki from a whistling cup, recited a few haiku. You said, 'May my death be as clean and as quick as the shattering of crystal.' And it almost seemed like a good, noble thing to do, to crash your kamikaze plane into an aircraft carrier. But the main thing was, the definition of what a kamikaze pilot was doing had been determined by the relevant authority. Now, once you are in a state of agency, you allow the authority to determine, to define what the situation is. The meaning of your action is altered."

So, for most subjects in Milgram's laboratory experiments, the act of giving Mr. Wallace his painful shock was necessary, even though unpleasant, and besides they were doing it on behalf of somebody else and it was for science. There was still strain and conflict, of course. Most people resolved it by grimly sticking to their task and obeying. But some broke out. Milgram tried varying the conditions of the experiment to see what would help break people out of their state of agency.

"The results, as seen and felt in the laboratory," he has written, "are disturbing. They raise the possibility that human nature, or more specifically the kind of character produced in American democratic society, cannot be counted on to insulate its citizens from brutality and inhumane treatment at the direction of malevolent authority. A substantial proportion of people do what they are told to do, irrespective of the content of the act and without limitations of conscience, so long as they perceive that the command comes from a legitimate authority. If, in this study, an anonymous experimenter can successfully command adults to subdue a fifty-year-old man and force on him painful electric shocks against his protest, one can only wonder what government, with its vastly greater authority and prestige, can command of its subjects."

This is a nice statement, but it falls short of summing up the full meaning of Milgram's work. It leaves some questions still unanswered.

The first question is this: Should we really be surprised and alarmed that people obey? Wouldn't it be even more alarming if they all refused to obey? Without obedience to a relevant ruling authority there could not be a civil society. And without a civil society, as Thomas Hobbes pointed out in the seventeenth century, we would live in a condition of war, "of every man against every other man," and life would be "solitary, poor, nasty, brutish and short."

In the middle of one of Stanley Milgram's lectures at C.U.N.Y. recently, some mini-skirted undergraduates started whispering and giggling in the back of the room. He told them to cut it out. Since he was the relevant authority in that time and that place, they obeyed, and most people in the room were glad that they obeyed.

This was not, of course, a conflict situation. Nothing in the coeds' social upbringing made it a matter of conscience for them to whisper and giggle. But a case can be made that in a conflict situation it is all the more important to obey. Take the case of war, for example. Would we really want a situation in which every participant in a war, direct or indirect—from front-line soldiers to the people who sell coffee and cigarettes to employees at the Concertina barbed-wire factory in Kansas—stops and consults his conscience before each action? It is asking for an awful lot of mental strain and anguish from an awful lot of people. The value of having civil order is that one can do his duty, or whatever interests him, or whatever seems to benefit him at the moment, and leave the agonizing to others. When Francis Gary Powers was being tried by a Soviet military tribunal after his U-2 spy plane was shot down, the presiding judge asked if he had thought about the possibility that his flight might have provoked a war. Powers replied with Hobbesian clarity: "The people who sent me should think of these things. My job was to carry out orders. I do not think it was my responsibility to make such decisions."

It was not his responsibility. And it is quite possible that if everyone felt responsible for each of the ultimate consequences of his own tiny contributions to complex chains of events, then society simply would not work. Milgram, fully conscious of the moral and social implications of his research, believes that people should feel responsible for their actions. If someone else had invented the experiment, and if he had been the naive subject, he feels certain that he would have been among the disobedient minority.

"There is no very good solution to this," he admits, thoughtfully. "To simply and categorically say that you won't obey authority may resolve your personal conflict, but it creates more problems for society which may be more serious in the long run. But I have no doubt that to disobey is the proper thing to do in this [the laboratory] situation. It is the only reasonable value judgment to make."

The conflict between the need to obey the relevant ruling authority and the need to follow your conscience becomes sharpest if you insist on living by an ethical system based on a rigid code—a code that seeks to answer all questions in advance of their being raised. Code ethics cannot solve the obedience problem. Stanley Milgram seems to be a situation ethicist, and situation ethics does offer a way out: When you feel conflict, you examine the situation and then make a choice among the competing evils. You may act with a presumption in favor of obedience, but reserve the possibility that you will disobey whenever obedience demands a flagrant and outrageous affront to conscience. This, by the way, is the philosophical position of many who resist the draft. In World War II, they would have fought. Vietnam is a different, an outrageously different situation.

Life can be difficult for the situation ethicist, because he does not see the world in straight lines, while the social system too often assumes such a

God-given, squared-off structure. If your moral code includes an injunction against all war, you may be deferred as a conscientious objector. If you merely oppose this particular war, you may not be deferred.

Stanley Milgram has his problems, too. He believes that in the laboratory situation, he would not have shocked Mr. Wallace. His professional critics reply that in his real-life situation he has done the equivalent. He has placed innocent and naive subjects under great emotional strain and pressure in selfish obedience to his quest for knowledge. When you raise this issue with Milgram, he has an answer ready. There is, he explains patiently, a critical difference between his naive subjects and the man in the electric chair. The man in the electric chair (in the mind of the naive subject) is helpless, strapped in. But the naive subject is free to go at any time.

Immediately after he offers this distinction, Milgram anticipates the objection.

"It's quite true," he says, "that this is almost a philosophic position, because we have learned that some people are psychologically incapable of disengaging themselves. But that doesn't relieve them of the moral responsibility."

The parallel is exquisite. "The tension problem was unexpected," says Milgram in his defense. But he went on anyway. The naive subjects didn't expect the screaming protests from the strapped-in learner. But they went on.

"I had to make a judgment," says Milgram. "I had to ask myself, was this harming the person or not? My judgment is that it was not. Even in the extreme cases, I wouldn't say that permanent damage results."

Sound familiar? "The shocks may be painful," the experimenter kept saying, "but they're not dangerous."

After the series of experiments was completed, Milgram sent a report of the results to his subjects and a questionnaire, asking whether they were glad or sorry to have been in the experiment. Eighty-three and seven-tenths percent said they were glad and only 1.3 percent were sorry; 15 percent were neither sorry nor glad. However, Milgram could not be sure at the time of the experiment that only 1.3 percent would be sorry.

Kurt Vonnegut, Jr., put one paragraph in the preface to *Mother Night,* in 1966, which pretty much says it for the people with their fingers on the shock-generator switches, for you and me, and maybe even for Milgram. "If I'd been born in Germany," Vonnegut said, "I suppose I would have *been* a Nazi, bopping Jews and gypsies and Poles around, leaving boots sticking out of snowbanks, warming myself with my sweetly virtuous insides. So it goes."

Just so. One thing that happened to Milgram back in New Haven during the days of the experiment was that he kept running into people he'd watched from behind the one-way glass. It gave him a funny feeling, seeing those people going about their everyday business in New Haven and knowing what they would do to Mr. Wallace if ordered to. Now that his research results are in and you've thought about it, you can get this funny feeling too. You don't need one-way glass. A glance in your own mirror may serve just as well.

Michael E. Patch

# The Role of Source Legitimacy in Sequential Request Strategies of Compliance

Patch's article compares two tactics for compliance—the foot-in-the-door and the door-in-the-face techniques—and asks whether each works in a variety of situations. He found that the foot-in-the-door technique, which asks for a small favor before escalating to a larger one, was successful regardless of whether the request was made for a highly legitimate cause or not. The door-the-face technique, in which a person first refuses a very large request only to be asked to comply with a more moderate one, was successful when the cause was highly legitimate; however, it did not generate as much compliance when the cause was not seen as worthy.

Two well-known strategies of sequential request offer contrasting recommendations for eliciting compliance. The foot-in-the-door technique (Dejong, 1978; Freedman & Fraser, 1966; Snyder & Cunningham, 1975) asserts that compliance with a small initial request increases the likelihood of compliance with a subsequent larger request. Freedman and Fraser suggested that this effect occurs because the individual who accedes to a small request comes to perceive himself as a person who "takes action on the things he believes in and cooperates with good causes" (p. 201). It is this perception of the self as a "doer" that thus makes compliance with a further request more likely. (See also Bem, 1972; Dejong, 1979.)

The door-in-the-face technique (Cialdini et al., 1975), by contrast, recommends the use of a large initial request, the refusal of which still increases the likelihood of compliance with a subsequent smaller request. Cialdini et al. explain this strategy in bargaining terms, arguing that the smaller request is viewed as a concession from an initial "offer." The subject then feels a pressure to reciprocate with a concession of his own, but the only means of making that reciprocation is to comply with the smaller request.

Although there is evidence for the success of both approaches, few studies have assessed their effectiveness in head-to-head comparisons. Cann, Sherman, and Elkes (1975), in a noteworthy exception, showed that the foot-in-the-door technique is more successful when a time delay is involved between requests, although both are effective when the second request immediately follows the first. However, despite this indication that there may be significant differences in the applicability of the two techniques across a wide spectrum of circumstances, little has been done to suggest specific situational parameters that might favor either technique.

A case in point, and the issue to which this article is addressed, is the matter of source legitimacy. Following Freedman and Fraser's original work, compliance studies using either the foot-in-the-door of the door-in-the-face technique generally employed "good causes." Source credibility was experimentally varied most often with respect to the size of the request (Schwarzwald, Bizman, & Ray, 1983; Schwarzwald, Ray, & Zvibel, 1979) rather than the intrinsic legitimacy of the appeal, and even in such cases (Dillard & Burgoon, 1982; Foehl & Goldman, 1983) the two strategies were not actually contrasted. Most recently, Dillard, Hunter, and Burgoon (1984) have asserted through a meta-analysis (quantitatively combining the results of several studies) that neither technique is effective unless used with prosocial appeals. More concretely, they would argue that these techniques will work for civic and environmental organizations but not for private marketing firms. As such, this conclusion would indicate that source legitimacy is not a relevant parameter for the selection of a sequential request strategy.

However, there is considerable cause for examining this conclusion more closely. For one thing, it is unsatisfactory to accept a meta-analysis in lieu of an actual manipulation of this variable. Dillard et al. themselves, having elected to omit extreme cases that did not fit the basic trend of their analysis, suggested that the effects of various appeals (in terms of intrinsic source legitimacy) needed to be investigated further. Moreover, on strictly theoretical grounds there is reason to believe that, given the basic processes through which they likely operate, the foot-in-the-door and the door-in-the-face techniques may not be equally source dependent.

If any such difference does exist, it may well follow from the fact that the foot-in-the-door technique employs action whereas the door-in-the-face technique employs refusal. The implication to be drawn from this is that the two strategies create distinctly different pressures or obligations for the individual. In the first case, taking action theoretically promotes pressure to internal consistency (Brock, 1969) because of the self-image that has been generated. But in the latter case, the pressure to comply is more normative in nature (Reingen, 1977) and, as such, must be derived from a sense of obligation to the source of the request. These possibilities then suggest the hypothesis that the foot-in-the-door technique may be less source dependent than the door-in-the-face technique in obtaining compliance in situations in which normative legitimacy is varied.

In the study to follow, the two techniques were employed in a telephone survey with the objective of getting respondents to fill out and return a lengthy questionnaire about television programming. It was predicted that both techniques would be effective as long as the source of the requests could be perceived as a matter of legitimate public interest. However, it was predicted that the foot-in-the-door technique would be superior to the door-in-the-face technique if the source ostensibly served only private interests.


## METHOD

The study was conducted by means of a telephone survey of 240 male and female subjects randomly selected from telephone directories for numerous cities in and around the San Francisco Bay area. The calls were made by three assistants, who followed prepared scripts. Numerous pilot calls were made to further insure uniform delivery, after which all data were then pooled.

There were three strategy conditions in the study: foot-in-the-door (FITD), door-in-the-face (DITF), and a control group. The requests in all these conditions concerned having the respondent supply information about his or her television viewing habits. In the FITD condition subjects were asked to follow a small request, and then, upon compliance with that request a larger moderate request was made. For the DITF condition a larger request was made first that, as expected, all subjects refused. They were then asked to perform the same moderate request made to the subjects in the FITD condition. The control group was only asked to perform the moderate request.

The subjects in each of the strategy conditions were also randomly assigned to one of two conditions of source legitimacy, thus creating a total of six experimental conditions in all. Source legitimacy was varied by having the callers represent themselves as members of one of two fictitious interest groups: (1) Parents for Good Television Programming, a nonprofit organization concerned with public interest in television programming (high legitimacy) or (2) Multi-media Programming Associates, a consulting group for commercial television interests (low legitimacy).

In order to make the telephone calls as homogeneous as possible, each subject was read the following introduction: "Hello, Mr./Mrs. _____ (Parents for Good Television Programming or Multimedia Programming Associates)." The caller then proceeded to make one of the three requests that were delivered as follows:

*Small request:* "If we could have a few minutes of your time I would like to ask you a few short questions." If the person refused to cooperate, the caller politely thanked him or her and said good-bye. If the subject agreed to cooperate, the following questions were asked: (1) "Do you own a television?" (2) "Do you watch more than ten hours of television a week?" (3) "Do you think there is too much violence on television?" (4) "Do you think your children should be allowed to watch television without supervision?"

*Moderate request:* "May we send you a 50-item questionnaire concerning your viewing habits and your opinions concerning violence on television? We will include a stamped, preaddressed envelope in which to return your questionnaire. Can we count on your cooperation?"

*Larger request.* "We would like you to keep a journal on all the programs you watch for the next two weeks. At the end of the two-week period we will send a representative to your house to discuss your viewing choices. Will you participate in our study?"

If the subject agreed to cooperate, he or she was thanked and informed that this was an initial contact only and that he or she would be contacted again and given further information.

## RESULTS AND DISCUSSION

Frequencies of compliance in the six conditions are presented in Table 1. As is evident in Table 1, both strategies promote compliance with the moderate request (i.e., exceeding the level of compliance in the control group) with the high-frequency source, but only the FITD technique is effective with the low-legitimacy source. It is also evident from the obtained patterns that the source manipulation made the greatest difference for the DITF condition, yielding compliance levels less than those of the control with low source legitimacy.

This finding in particular is in sharp contradiction to Dillard et al.'s (1984) conclusion that neither technique is effective without a prosocial appeal. Not only did the foot-in-the-door technique yield compliance without a high prosocial appeal, but the effect is surprisingly robust . . . partially because the moderate request was what Dillard et al. have labeled "low effort" in nature. That is, rather than being actual behavioral compliance, the response was only an agreement to comply at a later date. Moreover the anticipated behavior itself was relatively modest in comparison with moderate requests in other studies. Thus it is indeed possible that a "high effort" moderate request may not have allowed the study to be as sensitive to the effects of the source legitimacy variable.

More generally, although both techniques seem to operate through a system of mutual expectations that are set up by the initial request, the

**TABLE 1** Frequencies of compliance with Moderate Request

|  |  | Strategy | | |
| --- | --- | --- | --- | --- |
| Source |  | FITD | DITF | Control |
| High legitimacy | Comply | 33 | 34 | 24 |
|  | Not Comply | 7 | 6 | 16 |
| Low legitimacy | Comply | 30 | 14 | 18 |
|  | Not comply | 10 | 26 | 22 |

likelihood of compliance may be best assessed by inquiring as to what it takes to break with those expectations. It would seem for the case of the door-in-the-face technique that ultimate refusal requires only that the respondent break his or her relationship to an unfamiliar person, and any obligations he or she feels are only as strong as the normative legitimacy of that person's request. Moreover, the second request from a private source or business organization may often be viewed simply as a sales device (Mowen & Cialdini, 1980). One can thus speculate that, where adequate legitimacy is not established, reactance dynamics may often make compliance even more unlikely. For the case of the foot-in-the-door technique, however, refusal necessitates a break with a self-image made salient by prior action. Presumably, this need for personal consistency often transcends the extent of legitimacy or social responsibility behind the original action.

As indicated at the outset, the main concrete difference between the two strategies for obtaining compliance is that the FITD technique follows from action whereas the DITF technique follows from refusal. Beyond this fact, however, considerable speculation still remains as to the processes that are set in motion by each. The precise nature of the self-perception process, for example—despite several versions in the literature (Dejong, 1979; Harris, 1972; Pendleton & Batson, 1979; Zuckerman, Lazzano, & Waldgeir, 1979)—are not yet entirely clear. The matter of how and when source legitimacy is perceived also leaves much unanswered. For the case of the door-in-the-face technique such perceptions may, as Mowen and Cialdini (1980) have suggested, be mediated through characteristics of the second request irrespective of whether private or public interests are served. If, as they argue, the perception of a legitimate concession in the second request can facilitate this technique in a business context, the bases (normative or otherwise) for any sense of obligation in the subject must be explored more fully in subsequent manipulations of source legitimacy. As for the foot-in-the-door effect in this regard, it is still necessary to learn (as a cognitive dissonance or self-justification explanation might suggest) whether taking a requested action, as opposed to refusing one, affects the perception of source legitimacy. Although this kind of inquiry was not practical in the context of the method employed in this study, such information is needed to further explain the apparent greater generality and source independence of the foot-in-the-door technique.

## References

Bem, D. J. (1972). Self-perception theory. In L. Burkowitz (Ed.), *Advances in experimental social psychology: Vol. 6.* New York: Academic Press.

Brock, T. C. (1969). On interpreting effects of transgression upon compliance. *Psychological Bulletin, 72,* 138–145.

Cann, A., Sherman, S. J., & Elkes, R. (1975). Effects of initial request size and timing of a second request on compliance: The foot-in-the-door and the door-in-the-face. *Journal of Personality and Social Psychology, 32,* 774–782.

Cialdini, R. B., Vincent, J. E., Lewis, S. K., Catalan, J., Wheeler, D., & Darby, B. L.

(1975). A reciprocal concessions procedure for inducing compliance: the door-in-the-face technique. *Journal of Personality and Social Psychology, 31,* 206–215.

Dejong, W. (1979). An examination of self-perception mediation of the foot-in-the-door effect. *Journal of Personality and Social Psychology, 37*(12), 2221–2239.

Dillard, J. P., & Burgoon, M. (1982). An appraisal of two sequential request strategies for eliciting compliance. *Communication, 11,* 40–57.

Dillard, J. P., Hunter, J. E., & Burgoon, M. (1984). Sequential request persuasive strategies: Meta-analysis of foot-in-the-door and door-in-the-face. *Human Communication Research, 10*(4), 461–488.

Foehl, J., & Goldman, M. (1983). Increasing altruistic behavior by using compliance techniques. *Journal of Social Psychology, 119*(1), 21–29.

Freedman, J. L., & Fraser, S. C. (1966). Compliance without pressure: The foot-in-the-door technique. *Journal of Personality and Social Psychology, 4,* 195–202.

Harris, M. B. (1972). The effects of performing one altruistic act on the likelihood of performing another. *Journal of Social Psychology, 88,* 65–73.

Mowen, J. C., & Cialdini, R. B. (1980). On implementing the door-in-the-face compliance technique in a business context. *Journal of Marketing Research, 17*(2), 253–258.

Pendleton, M. G., & Batson, C. D. (1979). Self-presentation and the door-in-the-face technique for inducing compliance. *Personality and Social Psychology Bulletin, 5,* 77–81.

Reingen, P. H. (1977). Inducing compliance via door-in-the-face and legitimization of paltry contributions. *Psychological Reports, 41,* 924.

Schwarzwald, J., Bizman, A., & Ray, M. (1983). The foot-in-the-door paradigm: Effects of second request size on donation probability and donor generosity. *Personality and Social Psychology Bulletin, 9,* 443–450.

Schwarzwald, J., Ray, M., & Zvibel, M. (1979). The application of the door-in-the-face technique when established customs exist. *Journal of Applied Social Psychology, 9,* 576–586.

Snyder, M., & Cunningham, M. R. (1975). To comply or not comply: Testing the self-perception explanation of the "foot in the door" phenomenon. *Journal of Personality and Social Psychology, 31,* 64–67.

Zuckerman, M., Lazzano, M., & Waldgeir, D. (1979). Undermining effects of foot-in-the-door with extrinsic rewards. *Journal of Applied Social Psychology, 9,* 292–296.

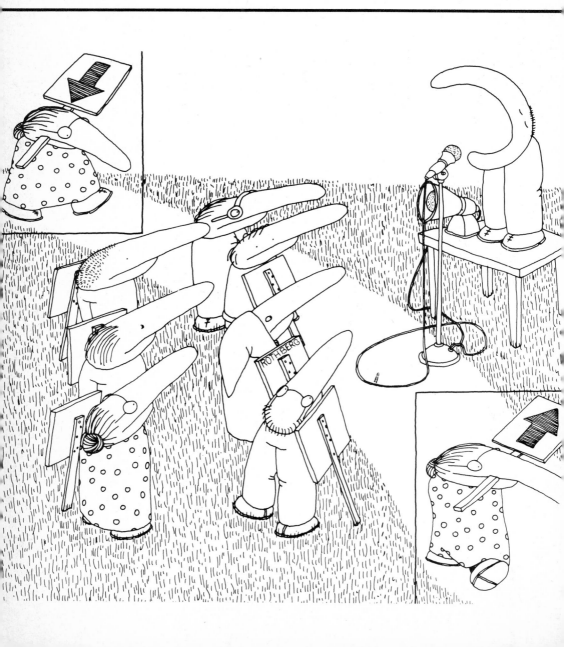

# 4

# Attitudes: Feeling, Believing, and Behaving

To the extent that people have popular images of social psychologists, we are sometimes thought to be attitude pollsters or experts in persuasion. While social psychology involves a great deal more than this, the measurement and change of attitudes has been one of the central interests of the field from its early development to the current day.

Richard Petty, who is Professor of Psychology at Ohio State University, carries a well-deserved reputation as one of the leading names in the field of attitudes and attitude change. He is the former editor of the *Personality and Social Psychology Bulletin* and, along with his colleague John Cacioppo, has developed the Elaboration Likelihood Model, one of the most influential theories in social psychology today. In our conversation, we discussed the many ways in which the study of attitude change has advanced and changed in recent years. Having now clarified many conceptual and theoretical issues, Prof. Petty believes that attitude researchers are now on the verge of making major contributions to important issues, such as drug abuse and AIDS.

## A CONVERSATION WITH RICHARD PETTY
*Ohio State University*

**Krupat:** *Let's begin at the beginning. Can you tell me what an attitude is and why it is that social psychologists seem to find this concept so important and interesting?*

**Petty:** The most common perspective today would be that attitudes refer to people's general evaluations of objects, issues, and people. There are a variety of sources that these general evaluations come from. They can be based on your emotions or specific information or beliefs or past behavioral experiences. The reason I think attitudes are important is that a good amount of evidence shows that these general evaluations are one of the most critical determinants of our behavior. So when people talk about social problems of the day, whether it's heart disease and cholesterol, AIDS, or drug abuse, one of the critical things we must do is to influence and modify people's attitudes. Most of our major social problems turn out to be problems of attitudes. For example, people think that they don't like low-fat food. They say it's not good tasting, or they are afraid to try it. So the first step in any kind of public education campaign is to look at what people's attitudes are and attempt to modify them so that behavior will follow.

**Krupat:** *But couldn't someone say, "Why bother with attitudes? Why not get right to the matter of interest and just get people to comply, to change their behavior without worrying about attitudes?"*

**Petty:** According to most attitude theorists, change through compliance is only temporary. Compliance occurs because of people's responses to particular aspects of some situation. The factors that produce compliance in one situation might not be present in another situation. On the other hand, people carry their attitudes with them from one situation to the next. So producing an internalized change in attitudes is the best way of influencing behavior across situations.

**Krupat:** *It's very interesting that you've been giving examples from a lot of very important social areas, such as AIDS and various kinds of health issues. Aren't attitude researchers often thought of as laboratory-type theoreticians rather than applied problem solvers?*

**Petty:** This has varied over the course of history to some extent. If you go back to Kurt Lewin, one of the founders of social psychology, he was trying to modify people's attitudes about eating generally disliked, but surplus, foods during World War II, and Carl Hovland's group was studying the morale of the troops during that war. Understanding attitudes and persuasion turned out to be more complex than it initially seemed, however, and lots of conflicting findings were produced. For example, expert sources were sometimes good for persuasion and sometimes they weren't. Sometimes variables influenced attitudes initially, but the effects were very short lived. These problems almost killed the field. It's only recently by going back to the lab and trying to get more control over things that we are getting a handle on what's happening. Now we may finally be ready to reemerge and apply what we know. I think we have learned enough about when things work and why that it's time again to start looking at important problems in the real world.

**Krupat:** *You said that we are now just beginning to master the complexity of attitude change and to learn just when things work and why. When do things work, and why?*

**Petty:** That's a big question, isn't it?

**Krupat:** *Agreed. Too big and too general, but let's start out at that level if you don't mind, and then we can get more specific as we go along.*

**Petty:** Let me offer a sort of abstract answer in terms of what we've learned over the past 20 years that we didn't know before. In some ways, the whole approach to the field of attitudes and persuasion has changed. If you went back 15 to 20 years ago, we had all these competing theories, each trying to explain all phenomena all the time. And, of course, what happened was that it turned out that one theory worked here, but maybe it didn't work there. One of the biggest advances of the past 10 years or so is the recognition that different processes work in different situations. For example, in our own work on the Elaboration Likelihood Model, we find that classical conditioning is a very important mechanism, but it is especially effective in situations where people are relatively unmotivated or unable to think about the stimuli presented to them.

**Krupat:** *Let me interrupt you midstream, if I may. The model that you and John Cacioppo have developed—the Elaboration Likelihood Model (ELM)—is one of the most important in the field. Yet I am certain that some people aren't familiar with it. Maybe you could describe it for us.*

**Petty:** Sure. The basic idea is that sometimes people like to and are able to think before they make decisions and sometimes decisions are made without much thought. So we have this continuum of thinking from very high levels of thought where careful deliberation occurs before forming a judgement or decision, which we refer to as the central route, to very little thought, consideration, and elaboration, which we refer to as the peripheral route. The basic postulate of the model is that different attitude change processes work at different points along this continuum. Simple processes like classical conditioning or mere exposure work best when people are unmotivated or unable to think. But they don't work so well when people are motivated to think. Other variables, like a person's mood, work by different processes at different points along this continuum. If you're in a good mood and you're not really motivated to think about something, you'll generally like anything that's associated with that good mood. But if you are highly motivated to think, mood doesn't work that way. Instead, mood influences the nature of the thoughts that come to mind. So mood can work in a thoughtful way or a less thoughtful way.

**Krupat:** *I follow you. But why does it matter whether we change someone's attitude as the result of high or low levels of thoughtfulness or, as you would say, by the central or peripheral route?*

**Petty:** The reason we care whether you are at one end of the continuum or the other is that, although you can be effective at changing a person's attitude at any point along the continuum using the appropriate process, the attitude changes resulting from careful and deliberative thinking tend to last longer and to be more resistant to counterpressures. That, for example, is important in the drug abuse field. For example, you could bring in celebrities or high-status figures to say "Don't use drugs" and you would get the kids to say "We don't like drugs." But the first time their attitudes were challenged, they would have no defense. Their attitudes wouldn't be very resistant to countervailing forces, even though it looked as though the researchers were successful. One of the lessons of a model like the ELM is that the amount of attitude change isn't necessarily the critical thing, it's the strength of the change. Some procedures produce strong attitudes—ones that will persist over time, resist counterforces, and be predictive and directive of behavior. But other attitude changes which look exactly the same on an attitude change scale don't have those qualities.

**Krupat:** *Before I interrupted you to explain the ELM, we were on the verge of getting from the larger, more abstract issues into specific questions about what works and why. Let's get back to that.*

**Petty:** When you think about a theory like the ELM, there are a couple of kinds of variables that are highlighted. One very powerful consideration is that there are individual differences in the extent to which people like to think about issues. John Cacioppo and I have investigated this in our work on the "need for cognition." High-need-for-cognition people generally like to think, and they tend to form strong attitudes that persist over time and are predictive of behavior.

**Krupat:** *But if I were just facing an audience and I couldn't measure their need for cognition, how would I use that information?*

**Petty:** In a case like that you could take one step back. We know that there are some correlates of the need for cognition, like education level. Or, if you picking jurors for a trial, you could ask them a few questions related to the need for cognition scale to get a sense of whether you would need to use a central or a peripheral strategy. But if you knew absolutely nothing about your audience and wanted to induce central route change, what you'd want to do is to build some things into your message itself. I think the most powerful is self-relevance. If you can make people think that a message is relevant to themselves, they will naturally process it. We've demonstrated this in the lab by varying whether the consequences of the message are likely to affect the message recipients or not, like whether a tuition increase is for their university or some other university. One of my favorite studies on self-relevance simply varied the use of a pronoun. All the arguments were exactly the same, but, instead of having a detached third-person message that read, "*Students* will benefit by having an improved library," the message simply said, "*You* will benefit." And it showed the same kinds of effects that we got with more dramatic manipulations just by changing the pronouns and invoking the self-concept.

**Krupat:** *That sounds like a wonderful strategy. Are there others that work as well?*

**Petty:** Another thing that we found you can do quite easily is to use rhetorical questions. For one reason or another, people have learned that when they are asked questions they have to pay attention because they might have to give an answer. So simply by framing an argument in a way that says, "Wouldn't this be great if we did such-and-such?" people think about it more than if you just say, "It would be great if we did such-and-such."

**Krupat:** *As I listen to you, I am trying to integrate some of the newer thinking on attitudes with some classic approaches. For instance, the old communications model tried to understand attitude change by asking "who says what to whom?" Would I be correct to say that you are taking things like this and trying to go one step beyond?*

**Petty:** That's the idea. We still need to deal with source variables, the question of who, and message variables, the question of what, and so forth. But we think about these variables in different ways now. Before, people would just take a long list of variables like expertise or attractiveness and say that these qualities are good for persuasion. You would think an expert source would be good for persuasion, right? But we now have research that shows that sometimes expert sources actually have the opposite effect. Now we recognize that some source variables can work by a simple peripheral process or they can motivate you to think. If an expert motivates you to think but presents weak arguments, your thinking will lead to greater rejection of the message.

**Krupat:** *But what happens when we try to export our knowledge to decision makers and policy developers? How do they feel about conditional statements that offer complex advice such as "If X then Y?"*

**Petty:** In the abstract it sounds complicated, but practically, if you are allowed to have control over the situation, you can move groups into the high-elaboration set by invoking self-relevance. As I mentioned, simple things can work, such as just changing the pronouns or including rhetorical questions. You might be able to assess what the level of interest is and use different persuasion strategies, depending on the nature of your audience. It means that you don't go in and mindlessly say, "Here's my message. I'm going to give it this way regardless." Once you get some sense of your audience, you can change your message to fit them.

**Krupat:** *Are you finding these days that people in "the real world" are still skeptical about the findings and advice of academic researchers?*

**Petty:** Just with the number of phone calls that come from advertising agencies, law firms, and government panels, I think it's certainly not the case anymore. They are becoming more aware of what's going on. For example, more and more I see commercials and messages that you think were taken right out of the professional journals.

**Krupat:** *It seems to me that social psychologists are using their knowledge not so much to sell commercial products as to promote ideas and behaviors that most people value. Is that a direction you think we should be going?*

**Petty:** Yes. When people talk about the drug problem, there is a growing recognition that it isn't just the supply of drugs that we need to affect, but also the demand for drugs. When you start talking about demand, you're talking about changing individuals and their attitudes. AIDS is also in large part a problem of attitudes. More and more social psychologists are getting involved in working with AIDS task forces. There's always resistance of some people who think, "This is common sense. We know what we are doing." But as people see the success rates you get from using laboratory-based persuasion techniques appropriately (as with Project DARE), their attitudes are definitely changing.

Stuart Oskamp

# Attitudes and Opinions

In this selection, Oskamp poses a very basic but important question: Why study attitudes? He offers several different answers concerning their importance, noting that "attitude" can be considered a shorthand term to summarize many behaviors and explain the consistency between what people believe and feel and what they do. In the course of this discussion, Oskamp also defines the attitudes concept and discusses the different ways in which the various elements of attitudes (thinking, feeling, and doing) have been conceptualized and interrelated.

Attitude. It's the current buzzword. It's also one of the most important factors of success, according to more than 1,000 top- and middle-level executives of 13 major American corporations. . . . Your attitude can make or break your career.

—Allan Cox, 1983, p. 11.

What are laws but the expressions of the opinion of some class which has power over the rest of the community? By what was the world ever governed but by the opinion of some person or persons? By what else can it ever be governed?

—Thomas B. Macaulay, 1830.

As these quotations illustrate, attitudes and opinions are important. They can help people, they can hurt people, they have influenced the course of history. Novelists and poets describe them, historians weigh and assess them, average citizens explain people's behavior in terms of their attitudes, politicians attempt to understand and shape public opinion. Consequently social psychologists, too, have long had a great interest in attitudes and opinions and have devised many ways of studying them.

## WHY STUDY ATTITUDES?

One long-standing controversy has been whether to study attitudes or behavior. This debate goes back to the early years of social psychology, when it was just beginning to be differentiated from other areas of psychology and sociology. For instance, the well-known sociologist Read Bain (1928, p. 940) wrote, "The development of sociology as a natural science has been hindered by . . . too much attention to subjective factors, such as . . . attitudes." Behaviorists, following the lead of psychologists such as B. F. Skinner (1957), have generally tried to avoid use of "mentalistic concepts" like attitude, and to study observable behavior instead.

However, the majority view among social psychologists was best expressed in a landmark handbook chapter by Gordon Allport, one of the founders of the field, who stressed the central importance of attitudes. In 1935 he wrote:

> The concept of attitude is probably the most distinctive and indispensable concept in contemporary American social psychology. . . . This useful, one might almost say peaceful, concept has been so widely adopted that it has virtually established itself as the keystone in the edifice of American social psychology. (1935, p. 798)

Though there have been some periods since then when research in other areas of social psychology, such as small-group dynamics, has somewhat overshadowed the amount of work on attitudes, by and large the study of attitudes and related topics has remained dominant (McGuire, 1985). Herbert Kelman, who succeeded Allport as a professor at Harvard, has written: "In the years since publication of Allport's paper, attitudes have, if anything, become even more central in social psychology" (1974, p. 310). Recent reviews of the field agree that the high interest in attitude research seems likely to continue in the foreseeable future (Cooper & Croyle, 1984; Chaiken & Stangor, 1987; Tesser & Shaffer, 1990).

Nonscientists, as well as scientists, frequently use the concept of attitude in their descriptions and explanations of human behavior. For instance, "She has a very good attitude toward her work." Or, "His suspicious attitude made me want to avoid him." In everyday conversation we often speak of a person's attitude as the cause of his actions toward another person or an object; e.g., "Her hostile attitude was shown in everything she did." Similarly, in his 1935 review, Allport concluded that the concept of attitudes was "bearing most of the descriptive and explanatory burdens of social psychology" (Allport, 1935, p. 804).

Why is attitude such a popular and useful concept? We can point to several reasons:

1. "Attitude" is a *shorthand* term. A single attitude (e.g., love for one's family) can summarize many different behaviors (spending time with them, kissing them, comforting them, agreeing with them, doing things for them).

2. An attitude can be considered the *cause* of a person's behavior toward another person or an object.
3. The concept of attitude helps to explain the *consistency* of a person's behavior, since a single attitude may underlie many different actions. (In turn, Allport says, the consistency of individual behavior helps to explain the stability of society.)
4. Attitudes are *important in their own right,* regardless of their relation to a person's behavior. Your attitudes toward various individuals, institutions, and social issues (e.g., a political party, the church, capital punishment, the President of the United States) reflect the way you perceive the world around you, and they are worth studying for their own sake.
5. The concept of attitude is relatively *neutral and acceptable* to many theoretical schools of thought. For instance, it bridges the controversy between heredity and environment, since both instinct and learning can be involved in the formation of attitudes. It is broad enough to include the operation of unconscious determinants and the dynamic interplay of conflicting motives, which have been stressed by Freud and other psychoanalysts. At the same time it provides a topic of common interest to theorists as diverse as phenomenologists, behaviorists, and cognitive psychologists.
6. Attitude is an *interdisciplinary* concept. Not just psychologists but also sociologists, political scientists, communication researchers, and anthropologists all study attitudes. In particular, the subarea of public opinion—the shared attitudes of many members of a society—is of great interest to students of politics, public affairs, and communication.

Yet, in spite of the popularity and apparent utility of the concept of attitude to lay people and scientists alike, some theorists have challenged the value of the concept. Some of the critical issues in this debate are definitional, and they are discussed later in this chapter. Other chapters analyze other aspects of the debate, as will be outlined a little later on.


## DEFINITIONS OF "ATTITUDE"

So far we have been using the term "attitude" without defining it. Since it is a common term in the English language, every reader will probably have a notion of its meaning. Unfortunately, however, there may be relatively little overlap between your notion and that of other readers. Indeed, there has sometimes been little overlap between the definitions of "attitude" suggested by different social scientists.

Originally the term "attitude" referred to a person's bodily position or posture, and it is still sometimes used in this way—for instance, "He sat slumped in an attitude of dejection." There is a marvelous example in Gilbert and Sullivan's operetta, *H.M.S. Pinafore*, in which the proper stance for a British tar is described (Gilbert, 1932, p. 31):

> His foot should stamp and his throat should growl,
> His hair should twirl and his face should scowl;
> His eyes should flash and his breast protrude,
> And this should be his customary attitude.

In social science, however, the term has come to mean a "posture of the mind," rather than of the body. In his careful review, Allport cited many definitions with varying emphases and concluded with a comprehensive definition of his own which has been widely adopted. The aspects stressed in the various definitions include attitude as a mental set or disposition, attitude as a readiness to respond, the psychological basis of attitudes, their permanence, their learned nature, and their evaluative character.

The central feature of all these definitions of attitude, according to Allport, is the idea of **readiness for response**. That is, an attitude is not behavior, not something that a person does; rather it is a preparation for behavior, a predisposition to respond in a particular way to the attitude object. The term **attitude object** is used to include things, people, places, ideas, actions, or situations, either singular or plural. For instance, it could be a group of people (e.g., teenagers), an inanimate object (e.g., the city park), an action (e.g., drinking beer), an abstract concept (e.g., civil rights), or an idea linking several concepts (e.g., rights of teenagers to drink beer in the city park).

Another point to note is the **motivating** or driving force of attitudes. That is, attitudes are not just a passive result of past experience. Instead they have two active functions, described by Allport as "exerting a directive or dynamic influence." "Dynamic" indicates that they impel or motivate behavior: i.e., they can be what behaviorists or psychoanalysts call "drives." "Directive" indicates that attitudes guide the form and manner of behavior into particular channels, encouraging some actions and deterring others.

The **relatively enduring** nature of attitudes is also important. This stability was illustrated by a study during the height of the Vietnam War when the feelings of college students were being hammered by dramatic and highly publicized events such as antiwar protests, U.S. troops crossing the Vietnam border to invade neutral Cambodia, and American National Guardsmen killing and injuring some students on two U.S. college campuses. For three years in a row Thistlethwaite (1974) measured many different attitudes of men enrolled at 25 American universities, and he found quite small average effects of even these dramatic events on the relevant social attitudes of the students. In other research, even over periods as long as *20 years*, people's values and vocational interests have been shown to have a high degree of stability, though other kinds of attitudes are apt to display greater fluctuations (Kelly, 1955).

In recent years the **evaluative** aspect of attitudes has been increasingly stressed. That is, an attitude is now generally seen as a disposition to respond *in a favorable or unfavorable manner* to given objects. For example, in many studies the evaluative dimension of Osgood's Semantic Differential (Osgood, Suci, & Tannenbaum, 1957) is used *alone,* without other dimensions, as the sole measure of attitudes. This emphasis is clearly shown in Bem's simple definition: "Attitudes are likes and dislikes" (1970, p. 14). Though this statement is an oversimplification, it emphasizes the central importance of the evaluative aspect of attitudes.

Since all of these aspects of attitudes are important, a comprehensive definition of the concept will be used in this book. A useful example of such a comprehensive definition of attitude is offered by Fishbein and Ajzen (1975; p. 6); "a learned predisposition to respond in a consistently favorable or unfavorable manner with respect to a given object."

## THEORETICAL VIEWS ON ATTITUDE COMPONENTS

### Tri-Componential Viewpoint

There are two main theoretical viewpoints about the essential nature of attitudes. The older one, called the **tri-componential viewpoint,** holds that an attitude is a single entity but that is has three aspects or components, as follows (see Figure 1):

1. A **cognitive** component, consisting of the ideas and beliefs which the attitude-holder has about the attitude object. For example, let us take Martians as an attitude object (you can substitute any other group if you wish). Examples of the cognitive component of an attitude would be:

   "Martians look strange—they have green skins and antennae coming out of their foreheads."

   "Martians can read your thoughts."

2. An **affective (emotional)** component.This refers to the feelings and emotions one has toward the object. For instance:

   "Martians make me feel uncomfortable—I hate to think of them reading my mind."

   "I don't like Martians."

3. A **behavioral** component, consisting of one's action tendencies toward the object. For example:

   "If I saw a Martian, I'd run away as fast as I could."

   "I certainly wouldn't let one into my club nor allow my daughter to marry one."

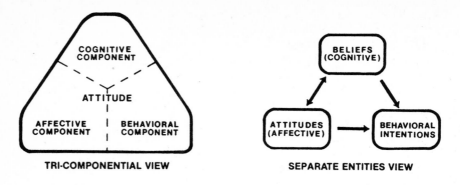

**Figure 1.** Two viewpoints on components of attitudes.

This conceptual distinction between thoughts, feelings, and actions as separate but interrelated parts of an attitude has a long history in philosophy. Though the term "attitude" was first used by Herbert Spencer in 1862 (Allport, 1985), the thought-emotion-behavior distinction is essentially identical with one made by Plato, who used the terminology of cognition, affection, and conation.

However, honored as this tripartite division is in tradition, and clear as it seems conceptually, there is still an important question about its *empirical* validity and usefulness. The view of attitudes as having separate cognitive, affective, and behavioral components raises the question of consistency between these components. This view requires a relatively high (but not perfect) degree of consistency. If there is little or no consistency among them, there is no reason to consider the three components as aspects of the same concept (attitude); instead they would have to be viewed as entirely independent entities. On the other hand, if they are perfectly correlated, they cannot be separate components; in this case they would merely be different names for the same thing.

McGuire (1969, p. 157) concluded, after surveying the literature, that the three components have proven to be so highly intercorrelated that "theorists who insist on distinguishing them should bear the burden of proving that the distinction is worthwhile." However, an opposite conclusion was reached by Krech, Crutchfield, and Ballachey (1962), who favor the tripartite view. On the basis of their review of the literature, they stated that there is only a "moderately high" relationship between the three components (typically, a correlation coefficient of about +.5); and they even cited evidence from one study showing a relationship as low as $r = +.2$ or +.3 between the cognitive and behavioral components. More recent studies have confirmed the view that there is generally a moderately strong relationship among the three components (Bagozzi, Tybout, Craig, & Sternthal, 1979; Breckler, 1984).

## Separate Entities Viewpoint

The newer theoretical view of attitudes is that the three components described above are distinct, **separate entities** which may or may not be related, depending on the particular situation (see Figure 1). This viewpoint has been strongly advocated by Fishbein and Ajzen (1975). They suggest that the term "attitude" be reserved solely for the affective dimension, indicating evaluation or favorability toward an object. The cognitive dimension they label as "beliefs," which they define as indicating a person's subjective probability that an object has a particular characteristic (for example, how sure the person feels that "This book is interesting," or that "Smoking marijuana is no more dangerous than drinking alcohol"). The behavioral dimension they refer to as "behavioral intentions," defined as indicated a person's subjective probability that (s)he will perform a particular behavior toward an object (e.g., "I intend to read this book," or "I am going to write my congressperson about legalization of marijuana").

Fishbein and Ajzen point out that a person usually has various beliefs about the same object and that these beliefs are not necessarily related. For instance, if someone believes, "This book is interesting," that person may or may not also believe that "This book is attractively printed" or that "This book is inexpensive." The same situation also holds true for behavioral intentions. "I intend to read this book," does not imply "I am going to buy this book" nor even "I am going to study this book carefully." By contrast, these authors say, all measures of a person's *affect* toward a particular object should be highly related. "I like this book" *does* imply "I enjoy reading it," and such responses should be quite consistent with the same person's answers to an attitude scale evaluating the book.

A final point about the separate entities viewpoint is that there is no necessary congruence among beliefs, attitudes, and behavioral intentions, which the tri-componential viewpoint would consider all aspects of the same attitude. "I like this book" (attitude) does *not* necessarily imply "This book is inexpensive" (belief), nor does it imply "I am going to buy this book" (behavioral intention). Thus these distinctions provide a justification for treating the three concepts as entirely separate entities. This viewpoint seems to have both theoretical and empirical advantages over the older tripartite view of attitude components, and it is the viewpoint endorsed by this text.

The conflicting findings mentioned above about the varying degrees of relationship among the three attitude "components" in different studies give support to the separate entities viewpoint because it does not require a necessary connection among these concepts but does allow for a strong relationship under certain specified conditions. Fishbein and Ajzen (1972) point out that most attitude scales are made up of several items stating various beliefs and/or intentions about the attitude object. However, many beliefs or intentions will not make satisfactory items for such a scale. Examples include beliefs which are so widely agreed upon that they are not held differentially by people with different attitudes ("President Bush is a Republican"); or statements whose evaluative significance is ambiguous (e.g., "As a national leader, President Bush's performance was about average"—disagreement here might indicate either a high or a low evaluation of Bush). Thus, it is only when an "attitude scale" has been carefully constructed from several well-chosen belief or intention items that we should expect it to correlate highly with other standard attitude measures. And in any case there will always be many possible items about particular beliefs and/or behavioral intentions which will not correlate highly with such a scale (e.g., "I believe President Bush is the Messiah," or "I am going to write President Bush a letter").

## References

Allport, G. W. (1935). Attitudes. In C. Murchison (Ed.), *A handbook of social psychology* (pp. 798–844). Worcester, MA: Clark University Press.

Bagozzi, R. P., Tybout, A. M., Craig, C. S., & Sternthal, B. (1979). The construct validity of the tripartite classification of attitudes. *Journal of Marketing Research, 16,* 88–95.

Bain, R. (1928). An attitude on attitude research. *American Journal of Sociology, 33,* 940–957.

Bem, D. J. (1970). *Beliefs, attitudes, and human affairs.* Belmont, CA: Brooks/Cole.

Breckler, S. J. (1984). Empirical validation of affect, behavior, and cognition as distinct components of attitude. *Journal of Personality and Social Psychology, 47,* 1191–1205.

Chaiken, S., & Stangor, C. (1987). Attitudes and attitude change. *Annual Review of Psychology, 38,* 575–630.

Cooper, J., & Croyle, R. T. (1984). Attitudes and attitude change. *Annual Review of Psychology, 35,* 395–426.

Cox, A. (1983, October). The business of attitudes. *United,* p. 11.

Fishbein, M., & Ajzen, I. (1972). Attitudes and opinions. *Annual Review of Psychology, 23,* 487–544.

Fishbein, M., & Ajzen, I. (1975). *Belief, attitude, intention, and behavior: An introduction to theory and research.* Reading, MA: Addison-Wesley.

Gilbert, W. S. (1932). *The best known works of W. S. Gilbert.* New York: Illustrated Editions.

Kelman, H. C. (1974). Attitudes are alive and well and gainfully employed in the sphere of action. *American Psychologist, 29,* 310–324.

Krech, D., Crutchfield, R., & Ballachey, E. (1962). *Individual in society.* New York: McGraw-Hill.

Macaulay, T. B. (1830). *Southey's colloquies.* (Cited in G. Seldes (Compiler), *The great quotations.* New York: Pocket Books, 1967, p. 706.)

McGuire, W. J. (1969). The nature of attitudes and attitude change. In G. Lindzey & E. Aronson (Eds.), *The handbook of social psychology* (2nd ed., Vol. 3, pp. 136–314). Reading, MA: Addison-Wesley.

McGuire, W. J. (1985). Attitudes and attitude change. In G. Lindzey & E. Aronson (Eds.), *The handbook of social psychology* (3rd ed., Vol. 2, pp. 233–346). New York: Random House.

Osgood, C. E., Suci, G. J., & Tannenbaum, P. H. (1957). *The measurement of meaning.* Urbana: University of Illinois Press.

Skinner, B. F. (1957). *Verbal behavior.* New York: Appleton-Century-Crofts.

Tesser, A., & Shaffer, D. R. (1990). Attitudes and attitude change. *Annual Review of Psychology, 41,* 479–523.

Thistlethwaite, D. L. (1974). Impact of disruptive external events on student attitudes. *Journal of Personality and Social Psychology, 30,* 228–242.

Richard E. Petty
John T. Cacioppo
David Schumann

# Central and Peripheral Routes to Advertising Effectiveness: The Moderating Role of Involvement

This article is one of many discussing and testing the Elaboration Likelihood Model that was discussed in the conversation with Richard Petty. In this research, those students who heard that the product they were reading about would be test marketed in their city (high involvement) were most affected by the quality of the arguments offered. However, those who were low in involvement were more affected by the prominence of the endorser (a sports celebrity vs. an average citizen). These findings lend support for the existence of two routes of persuasion—central and peripheral.

Over the past three decades, a large number of studies have examined how consumers' evaluations of issues, candidates, and products are affected by media advertisements. Research on the methods by which consumers' attitudes are formed and changed has accelerated at a pace such that Kassarjian and Kassarjian were led to the conclusion that "attitudes clearly have become the central focus of consumer behavior research" (1979, p. 3). Not only are there a large number of empirical studies on consumer attitude formation and change, but there are also a large number of different theories of persuasion vying for the attention of the discipline (see Engle and Blackwell 1982; Kassarjian 1982).

In our recent reviews of the many approaches to attitude change employed in social and consumer psychology, we have suggested that—even though the different theories of persuasion possess different terminologies, postulates, underlying motives, and particular "effects" that they specialize in explaining—these theories emphasize one of two distinct routes to attitude change (Petty and Cacioppo 1981, 1983). One, called the *central route*, views attitude change as resulting from a person's diligent consideration of information that s/he feels is central to the true merits of a particular attitudinal position. Attitude changes induced via the central route are postulated to be relatively enduring and predictive of behavior (Cialdini, Petty, and Cacioppo 1981; Petty and Cacioppo 1980).

A second group of theoretical approaches to persuasion emphasizes a more *peripheral route* to attitude change. Attitude changes that occur via the peripheral route do not occur because an individual has personally considered the pros and cons of the issue, but because the attitude issue or object is associated with positive or negative cues—or because the person makes a simple inference about the merits of the advocated position based on various simple cues in the persuasion context. For example, rather than diligently considering the issue-relevant arguments, a person may accept an advocacy simply because it was presented during a pleasant lunch or because the source is an expert. Similarly, a person may reject an advocacy simply because the position presented appears to be too extreme. These cues (e.g., good food, expert sources, extreme positions) and inferences (e.g., "If an expert says it, it must be true") may shape attitudes or allow a person to decide what attitudinal position to adopt without the need for engaging in any extensive thought about issue- or product-relevant arguments.

The accumulated research on persuasion clearly indicates that neither the central nor the peripheral approach alone can account for the diversity of attitude-change results observed. Thus, a general framework for understanding attitude change must consider that in some situations people are avid seeks and manipulators of information, and in others they are best described as "cognitive misers" who eschew any difficult intellectual activity (Burnkrant 1976; McGuire 1969). An important question for consumer researchers then is: when will consumers actively seek and process product-relevant information, and when will they be more cursory in their analysis of ads? Recent research in consumer behavior and social psychology has focused on the concept of "involvement" as an important moderator of the amount and type of information processing elicited by a persuasive communication (see Burnkrant and Sawyer 1983; Petty and Cacioppo 1981, 1983). One major goal of the experiment reported in this paper was to test the hypothesis that under "high involvement," attitudes in response to an advertisement would be affected via the central route, but that under "low involvement," attitudes would be affected via the peripheral route.

## INVOLVEMENT AND ATTITUDE CHANGE

### Methods of Studying Involvement

Although there are many specific definitions of involvement within both social and consumer psychology, there is considerable agreement that high involvement messages have greater personal relevance and consequences or elicit more personal connections than low involvement messages (Engel and

Blackwell 1982; Krugman 1965; Petty and Cacioppo 1979; Sherif and Hovland 1961). Various strategies have been employed in studying involvement.

A preferred procedure for studying involvement would be to hold recipient, message, and medium characteristics constant and randomly assign participants to high and low involvement groups. Apsler and Sears (1968) employed an ingenious method to manipulate involvement: some participants were led to believe that a persuasive proposal had personal implications for them (an advocated change in university regulations would take effect while the student participants were still in school), while others were led to believe that it did not (i.e., the change would not take effect until after the students had graduated). A variation of this procedure was developed by Wright (1973, 1974) to manipulate involvement in an advertising study. Participants in the high involvement group were told that they would subsequently be asked to evaluate the product in an advertisement they were about to see, and were given some additional background information. Participants in the low involvement group did not expect to evaluate the product and were given no background information. The background information provided to the high involvement subjects explained the relevance of their product decisions to "their families, their own time and effort, and their personal finances" (Wright 1973, p. 56). However, it is somewhat unclear to what extent this background information made certain product-relevant arguments salient or suggested appropriate dimensions of product evaluation for high but not low involvement subjects.

In the present experiment, participants in both the high and low involvement groups were told that they would be evaluating advertisements for products, but subjects in the high involvement group were led to believe that the experimental advertised product would soon be available in their local area, and that after viewing a variety of advertisements they would be allowed to choose one brand from the experimental product category to take home as a gift. Low involvement participants were led to believe that the experimental advertised product would not be available in their local area in the near future, and that after viewing the ads they would be allowed to take home one brand from a category of products other than the experimental category.

## Theories of Involvement

In addition to the methodological differences that have plagued the involvement concept, another area of disagreement concerns the effects on persuasion that involvement is expected to have. Perhaps the dominant notion in social psychology stems from the Sherifs' social judgment theory (Sherif et al. 1965). Their notion is that on any given issue, highly involved persons exhibit more negative evaluations of a communication because high involvement is associated with an extended "latitude of rejection." Thus, incoming messages on involving topics are thought to have an enhanced probability of being rejected because they are more likely to fall within the unacceptable range of a person's implicit attitude continuum. Krugman (1965) has proposed an alternative view that has achieved considerable recognition among consumer researchers. According to this view, increasing involvement does not increase resistance to persuasion, but instead shifts the sequence of communication impact. Krugman argues that under high involvement, a communication is likely to affect cognitions, then attitudes, and then behaviors, whereas under low involvement, a communication is more likely to affect cognitions, then behaviors, then attitudes (see also Ray et al. 1973).

As noted earlier, a focal goal of this study is to assess the viability of a third view of the effects of involvement on consumer response to advertisements. This view stems from our Elaboration Likelihood Model (ELM) of attitude change (Petty and Cacioppo 1981). The basic tenet of the ELM is that different methods of inducing persuasion may work best depending on whether the elaboration likelihood of the communication situation (i.e., the probability of message- or issue-relevant thought occurring) is high or low. When the elaboration likelihood is high, the central route to persuasion should be particularly effective, but when the elaboration likelihood is low, the peripheral route should be better. The ELM contends that as an issue or product increases in personal relevance or consequences, it becomes more important and adaptive to forming a reasoned and veridical opinion. Thus, people are more motivated to devote the cognitive effort required to evaluate the true merits of an issue or product when involvement is high rather than low. If increased involvement increases one's propensity to think about the true merits of an issue or product, then manipulations that require extensive issue- or product-relevant thought in order to be effective should have a greater impact under high rather than low involvement conditions. On the other hand, manipulations that allow a person to evaluate an issue or product without engaging in extensive issue- or product-relevant thinking should have a greater impact under low rather than high involvement.

Research in social psychology has supported the view that different variables affect persuasion under high and low involvement conditions. For example, the quality of the arguments contained in a message has had a greater impact on persuasion under conditions of high rather than low involvement (Petty and Cacioppo 1979; Petty, Cacioppo, and Heesacker 1981). On the other hand, peripheral cues such as the expertise or attractiveness of a message source (Chaiken 1980; Petty, Cacioppo, and Goldman 1981; Rhine and Severance 1970) have had a greater impact on persuasion under conditions of low rather than high involvement. In sum, under high involvement conditions people appear to exert the cognitive effort required to evaluate the issue-relevant arguments presented, and their attitudes are a function of this information-processing activity (central route). Under low involvement conditions, attitudes appear to be affected by simple acceptance and rejection cues in the persuasion context and are less affected by argument quality (peripheral route). Although the accumulated research in social psychology is quite consistent with the ELM, it is not yet clear whether or not the ELM predictions would hold when involvement concerns a product (such as toothpaste) rather than an issue (such as capital punishment), and when the persuasive message is an advertisement rather than a speech or editorial.

## CENTRAL AND PERIPHERAL ROUTES TO ADVERTISING EFFECTIVENESS

One important implication of the ELM for advertising messages is that different kinds of appeals may be most effective for different audiences. For example, a person who is about to purchase a new refrigerator (high involvement) may scrutinize the product-relevant information presented in an advertisement. If this information is perceived to be cogent and persuasive, favorable attitudes will result, but if this information is weak and specious, unfavorable attitudes will result (central route). On the other hand, a person who is not considering purchasing a new refrigerator at the moment (low involvement) will not expend the effort required to think about the product-relevant arguments in the ad, but may instead focus on the attractiveness, credibility, or prestige of the product's endorser (peripheral route). Some evidence in consumer psychology is consistent with this reasoning. For example, Wright (1973, 1974) exposed people to an advertisement for a soybean product under high and low involvement conditions (see earlier description) and measured the number of source comments (derogations) and message comments (counterarguments) generated after exposure. Although Wright (1974) predicted that involvement would increase both kinds of comments, he found that more message comments were made under high rather than low involvement, but that more source comments were made under low involvement conditions. This finding, of course, is consistent with the ELM.

In an initial attempt to provide a specific test of the utility of the ELM for understanding the effectiveness of advertising messages (Petty and Cacioppo 1980), we conducted a study in which three variables were manipulated: (1) the personal relevance of a shampoo ad (high involvement subjects were led to believe that the product would be available in their local area, whereas low involvement subjects were not); (2) the quality of the arguments contained in the ad; and (3) the physical attractiveness of the endorsers of the shampoo. Consistent with the ELM predictions, the quality of the arguments contained in the advertisement had a greater impact on attitudes when the product was of high rather than low relevance. Contrary to expectations, however, the attractiveness of the endorsers was equally important under both the high and low involvement conditions. In retrospect, in addition to serving as a peripheral cue under low involvement, the physical appearance of the product endorsers (especially their hair) may have served as persuasive visual testimony for the product's effectiveness. Thus, under high involvement conditions, the physical attractiveness of the endorsers may have served as a cogent product-relevant argument.

The present study was a conceptual replication of previous work (Petty and Cacioppo 1980), except that we employed a peripheral cue that could not be construed as a product-relevant argument. In the current study, participants were randomly assigned to high and low involvement conditions and viewed one of four different ads for a fictitious new product, "Edge disposable razors." The ad was presented in magazine format and was embedded in an advertising booklet along with 11 other ads. Two features of the Edge ad were manipulated: the quality of the arguments in support of Edge (strong or weak), and the celebrity status of the featured endorsers of Edge (celebrity or average citizen). It is important to note that preliminary testing revealed that for most people, the celebrity status of the endorsers was irrelevant to an evaluation of the true merits of a disposable razor, but that because the celebrity endorsers were liked more than the average citizens, they could still serve as a positive peripheral cue.

We had two major hypotheses. First, we expected the quality of the arguments presented in the ad to have a greater impact on product attitudes under high rather than low involvement conditions. Second, we expected the celebrity status of the product endorsers to have a greater impact on product attitudes under low rather than high involvement conditions. If these hypotheses were supported, it would provide the first evidence to understanding the effects of involvement on attitudinal responses to advertisements.

## METHOD

### Subjects and Design

A total of 160 male and female undergraduates at the University of Missouri–Columbia participated in the experiment to earn credit in an introductory psychology course; 20 subjects were randomly assigned to each of the cells in a 2 (involvement: high or low) × 2 (argument quality: strong or weak) × 2 (cue: celebrity or noncelebrity status) factorial design. Subjects participated in groups of three to 15 in a very large classroom. The subjects were isolated from each other so that they could complete the experiment independently, and subjects in a single session participated in different experimental conditions.

### Procedure

Two booklets were prepared for the study. The first contained the advertising stimuli and the second contained the dependent measures. The first page of the advertising booklet explained that the study concerned the evaluation of magazine and newspaper ads and that the psychology department was cooperating with the journalism school in this endeavor. The first page also contained part of the involvement manipulation (see below). It was explained that each ad in the booklet was preceded by an introductory statement that told a little about the advertisement that followed (e.g., "The _____ company of Paris, France has just opened an American office in New York City. This élite men's clothing company originally sold clothing only in Europe, but is now in the process of attempting to enter the American market. The ad on the next page is one that they will be testing soon in Tampa, Florida before running the ads in other major cities that will eventually carry their products"). The instructions told subjects to continue through the booklet at their own pace and to raise their hands when finished. The ad booklet contained 10 real magazine ads for both relatively familiar (e.g., Aquafresh toothpaste) and unfamiliar (e.g., Riopan antacid) products, and two bogus ads. The sixth ad in each booklet was the crucial fictitious ad for Edge razors (the nature of the other bogus ad was varied but is irrelevant to the present study). When subjects had completed perusing their ad booklets, they were given a questionnaire booklet to complete. Upon completion of the questionnaire, the subjects were thoroughly debriefed, thanked for their participation, and dismissed.

*Independent Variables*

*Involvement.* Involvement was embedded in two places in the ad booklet. First, the cover page offered subjects a free gift for participation in the experiment. Subjects were either informed that they would be allowed to choose a particular brand of disposable razor (high involvement with the fictitious Edge ad) or that they would be allowed to choose a brand of toothpaste (low involvement with Edge). A toothpaste ad did appear in the ad booklet, but it was the same ad for all subjects. To bolster the involvement manipulation, the page that introduced the Edge ad also differed in the high and low involvement conditions. High involvement subjects were told that the advertisement and product would soon be test-marketed in medium-sized cities throughout the Midwest, including their own city (Columbia, Missouri); low involvement subjects were told that the advertisement and product were being test-marketed only on the East Coast. Thus high involvement subjects were not only led to believe that they would soon have to make a decision about the product class, they were also led to believe that the product would be available in their area in the near future. Low involvement subjects, on the other hand, did not expect to make a decision about razors (but did expect to make one about toothpaste), and were led to believe that Edge razors would not be available for purchase in their area in the forseeable future.

*Argument quality.* A variety of arguments for disposable razors were pretested for potency on a sample of undergraduates. In the strong arguments ad, the razor was characterized as "scientifically designed," and the following five statements were made about the product:

- New advanced honing method creates unsurpassed sharpness
- Special chemically formulated coating eliminates nicks and cuts and prevents rusting

- Handle is tapered and ribbed to prevent slipping
- In direct comparison tests, the Edge blade gave twice as many close shaves as its nearest competitor
- Unique angle placement of the blade provides the smoothest shave possible

In the weak arguments version of the ad, the razor was characterized as "designed for beauty," and the following five statements were made about the product:

- Floats in water with a minimum of rust
- Comes in various sizes, shapes, and colors
- Designed with the bathroom in mind
- In direct comparison tests, the Edge blade gave no more nicks or cuts than its competition
- Can only be used once but will be memorable

*Peripheral cue.* In the "famous endorser" conditions, the headline accompanying the advertisement read "Professional Athletes Agree: Until you try new Edge disposable razors you'll never know what a really close shave is." In addition, the ad featured the pictures of two well-known, well-liked golf (male) and tennis (female) celebrities. In the "nonfamous endorser" conditions, the headline read "Bakersfield, California Agrees: _____," and the ad featured pictures of average looking people who were unfamiliar to the subjects. The average citizens in the ad were middle-aged and characterized as coming from California to minimize perceptions of similarity to the subjects (Missouri college students). Figure 1 depicts two of the four Edge ads used in the present study.

*Dependent Measures*

On the first page of the dependent variable booklet, subjects were asked to try to list all of the product categories for which they saw advertisements, and to try to recall the brand name of the product in that category. On the next page, subjects were given descriptions of the 12 product categories and were asked to select the correct brand name from among seven choices provided. Although we had no specific hypotheses about brand recall and recognition, these measures were included because of their practical importance and for purposes of comparison with the attitude data.

Next, subjects responded to some questions about one of the legitimate ads in the booklet; this was followed by the crucial questions about Edge razors. The questions about Edge were placed relatively early in the booklet to avoid subject fatigue and boredom and to maximize the effectiveness of the manipulations. Subjects were first asked to rate, on a four-point scale, how likely it would be that they would purchase Edge disposable razors "the next

## PROFESSIONAL ATHLETES AGREE

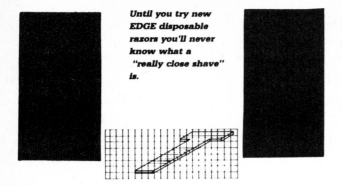

*Until you try new EDGE disposable razors you'll never know what a "really close shave" is.*

**Figure 1**
EXAMPLE MOCK ADS

- **Scientifically Designed**
- New advanced honing method creates unsurpassed sharpness
- Special chemically formulated coating eliminates nicks and cuts and prevents rusting
- Handle is tapered and ribbed to prevent slipping
- In direct comparison tests the EDGE blade gave twice as many close shaves as its nearest competitor.
- Unique angle placement of the blade provides the smoothest shave possible

### GET THE EDGE DIFFERENCE!

Note: Panel above shows celebrity endorser ad for Edge razors employing the strong arguments. Panel below shows average citizen endorser ad for Edge razors employing the weak arguments. Pictures of celebrities and citizens have been blacked out to preserve propriety and anonymity.

## BAKERSFIELD, CALIFORNIA AGREES

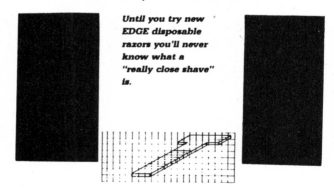

*Until you try new EDGE disposable razors you'll never know what a "really close shave" is.*

- **Designed for Beauty**
- Floats in water with a minimum of rust
- Comes in various sizes, shapes, and colors
- Designed with the bathroom in mind
- In direct comparison tests the EDGE blade gave no more nicks or cuts than its competition
- Can only be used once but will be memorable.

### GET THE EDGE DIFFERENCE!

time you needed a product of this nature." The description for each scale value were: 1 = "I definitely would not buy it," 2 = "I might or might not buy it," 3 = "I would probably buy it," and 4 = "I would definitely buy it." Following this measure of purchase intentions, subjects were asked to rate their overall impression of the product on three nine-point semantic differential scales anchored at −4 and +4 (bad–good, unsatisfactory–satisfactory, and unfavorable–favorable). Since the intercorrelations among these measures were very high, responses were averaged to assess a general positive or negative attitude toward the product.

Several questions were asked to check on the experimental manipulations, and subjects were asked to try to list as many of the attributes mentioned in the ad about Edge razors as they could recall. Following the questions about Edge were several questions about some of the other products and ads in the booklet. As a check on the involvement manipulation, the very last questions in the booklet asked subjects to recall the free gift they had been told to expect.

## RESULTS

### Manipulation Checks

In response to the last question in the dependent variable booklet asking subjects what gift they had been told to expect, 92.5 percent of the subjects in the high involvement conditions correctly recalled that they were to select a brand of disposable razor. In the low involvement conditions, none of the subjects indicated a razor and 78 percent correctly recalled that they were to select a brand of toothpaste. Thus, subjects presumably realized what product they were soon to make a decision about as they examined the ad booklet.

To assess the effectiveness of the endorser manipulation, two questions were asked. First, subjects were asked if they recognized the people in the ad for the disposable razor. When the famous athletes were employed, 94 percent indicated "yes," whereas when the average citizens were employed, 96 percent indicated "no." In addition, subjects were asked to rate the extent to which they liked the people depicted in the ad on an 11-point scale, where 1 indicated "liked very little" and 11 indicated "liked very much." An analysis of this measure revealed that the famous endorsers were liked more ($M$ = 6.06) than the average citizens ($M$ = 3.64); on average, women reported liking the endorsers more ($M$ = 5.32) than did men ($M$ = 4.44).

As a check on the argument-persuasiveness manipulation, two questions were asked. The first required respondents to "rate the reasons as described in the advertisement for using EDGE" on an 11-point scale anchored by "unpersuasive" and "persuasive"; the second question asked them to rate the reasons on an 11-point scale anchored by "weak reasons" and "strong reasons." In short, all of the variables were manipulated successfully. The tendency for females to be more positive in their ratings of both endorsers and the arguments in the ads is generally consistent with previous psychological

**TABLE** Means and Standard Deviations for Each Experimental Cell on the Attitude Index

| | Low involvement | | High involvement | |
| --- | --- | --- | --- | --- |
| | Weak arguments | Strong arguments | Weak arguments | Strong arguments |
| Citizen endorser | −.12 (1.81) | .98 (1.52) | −1.10 (1.66) | 1.98 (1.25) |
| Celebrity endorser | 1.21 (2.28) | 1.85 (1.59) | −1.36 (1.65) | 1.80 (1.07) |

NOTE: Attitude scores represent the average rating of the product on three nine-point semantic differential scales anchored at −4 and +4 (bad–good, unsatisfactory–satisfactory, and unfavorable–favorable). Standard deviations are in parentheses

research portraying women as more concerned with social harmony than men (Eagly 1978). Importantly, these sex differences did not lead to any significant gender effects on the crucial measures of attitude and purchase intention.

*Attitudes and Purchase Intentions*

The Table presents the means and standard deviations for each cell on the attitude index. A number of interesting main effects emerged. First, involved subjects were somewhat more skeptical of the product ($M$ = 0.31) than were less involved subjects ($M$ = 0.99). Second, subjects liked the product significantly more when the ad contained cogent arguments ($M$ = 1.65) than when the arguments were specious ($M$ = −0.35). Third, subjects tended to like the product more when it was endorsed by the famous athletes ($M$ = 0.86) than by the average citizens of Bakersfield, California ($M$ = 0.41).

Each of these main effects must be qualified and interpreted. First, the nature of the product endorser had a significant impact on product attitudes only under low involvement but not under high involvement (see top panel of Figure 2). On the other hand, although argument quality had an impact on product attitudes under both low involvement and high involvement, the impact of argument quality on attitudes was significantly greater under high rather than low involvement (see bottom panel of Figure 2).

Two significant effects emerged from the question asking subjects to rate their likelihood of purchasing Edge disposable razors the next time they needed a product of this nature. Subjects said that they would be more likely to buy the product when the arguments presented were strong ($M$ = 2.23) rather than weak ($M$ = 1.68). Additionally, argument quality was a more important determinant of purchase intentions under high rather than low involvement.

The correlation between attitudes and purchase intentions for low involvement subjects was 0.36; and for high involvement subjects it was 0.59. Although both correlations are significantly different from zero it is interesting to note that

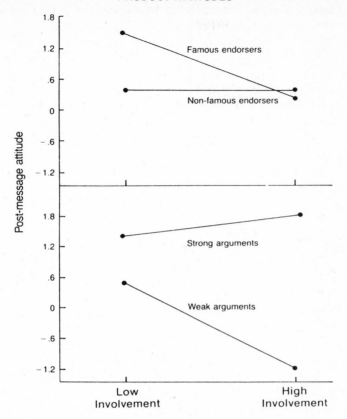

PRODUCT ATTITUDES

NOTE: Top panel shows interactive effect of involvement and endorser status on attitudes toward Edge razors. Bottom panel shows interactive effect of involvement and argument quality on attitudes toward Edge razors.

**Figure 2.** Product Attitudes.

the low involvement correlation is considerably smaller than the high involvement correlation. The fact that the argument quality manipulation affected behavioral intentions while the endorser manipulation did not (although it did affect attitudes)—and the fact that attitudes were better predictors of behavioral intentions under high rather than low involvement—provide some support for the ELM view that attitudes formed via the central route will be more predictive of behavior than attitudes formed via the peripheral route.

*Recall and Recognition Measures*

Subjects were asked to list all of the products for which they saw ads and all of the brand names they encountered. Following this, all subjects were told that they had seen an advertisement for a disposable razor and were asked to select the correct brand name from a list of seven (Gillette, Wilkinson, Schick, Edge, Bic, Schaffer, and Remington).

The involvement manipulation had a significant impact on free recall of the product category, with more high involvement subjects (81 percent) recalling the product category than low involvement subjects (64 percent). Additionally, exposure to the famous endorser increased recall of the product category under low involvement conditions (from 52 percent to 75 percent), but had no effect on product category recall under high involvement (80 versus 82 percent).

Involvement affected free recall of the brand name of the product, increasing it from 42 percent in the low involvement conditions to 60 percent in the high involvement conditions. There was also an effect for gender on this measure, with males showing greater brand name recall (61 percent) than females (39 percent). The endorser manipulation had a marginally significant effect on brand name recall, with the famous endorsers tending to enhance recall over average citizens from 43 to 58 percent.

On the measure of brand name recognition, an interaction pattern emerged. Under low involvement, the use of famous endorsers reduced brand name recognition from 85 to 70 percent, but under high involvement, the use of famous endorsers improved brand name recognition from 77 to 87 percent.

To summarize the recall and recognition data thus far, it appears that increasing involvement with the product enhanced recall not only of the product category, but also of the brand name of the specific product advertised. The effects of the endorser manipulation were more complex and depended on the level of involvement. In general, under low involvement a positive endorser led to increased recall of the product category but reduced brand name recognition. Thus, people may be more likely to notice the products in low involvement ads when they feature prominent personalities, but because of the enhanced attention accorded the people in the ads and the general lack of interest in assessing the merits of the product (due to low involvement), reductions in brand recognition may occur. This finding is similar to the results of studies on the use of sexually oriented material in ads for low involvement products—the sexual material enhances recognition of the ad, but not the brand name of the product (e.g., Chestnut, LaChance, and Lubitz 1977; Steadman 1969). Under high involvement, however, the use of prominent personalities enhanced brand name recognition. When people are more interested in the product category, they may be more motivated to assess what brand the liked personalities are endorsing. The manipulation of argument quality had no effect on recall of the product category, brand name recall, or brand name recognition.

A final recall measure assessed how many of the specific arguments for Edge razors the subjects could spontaneously recall after they had examined the entire ad booklet. Overall, subjects were able to correctly reproduce only

1.75 of the five arguments presented. This was not affected by any of the experimental manipulations.

Clearly, the manipulations produced a very different pattern of effects on the recall and recognition measures than on the attitude and purchase intention measures. In addition, the recall and recognition measures were uncorrelated with attitudes or intentions toward Edge razors. This finding is consistent with a growing body of research indicating that simple recall or recognition of information presented about an attitude object is not predictive of attitude formation and change (e.g., Cacioppo and Petty 1979; Greenwald 1968; Insko, Lind, and LaTour 1976).

The present data also argue against using measures of brand name recall or recognition as the sole indicants of advertising effectiveness. For example, in the present study, enhancing involvement led to a significant improvement in brand name recall, but increasing involvement led to a decrement in attitude toward the brand when the arguments presented were weak.

## DISCUSSION

As we noted earlier, previous research on attitude formation and change has tended to characterize the persuasion process as resulting either from a thoughtful (though not necessarily rational) consideration of issue-relevant arguments and product-relevant attributes (central route), or from associating the attitude object with various positive and negative cues and operating with simple decision rules (peripheral route). Over the past decade, investigators in both social psychology and consumer behavior have tended to emphasize the former process over the latter. Consider the recent comments of Fishbein and Ajzen (1981, p. 359):

> The general neglect of the information contained in a message . . . is probably the most serious problem in communication and persuasion research. We are convinced that the persuasiveness of a communication can be increased much more easily and dramatically by paying careful attention to its content . . . than by manipulation of credibility, attractivenes . . . or any of the other myriad factors that have caught the fancy of investigators in the area of communication and persuasion.

The present study suggests that, although the informational content of an advertisement may be the most important determinant of product attitudes under some circumstances, in other circumstances such noncontent manipulations as the celebrity status (likeability) or credibility of the product endorsers may be even more important. Specifically, we have shown that when an advertisement concerned a product of low involvement, the celebrity status of the product endorsers was a very potent determinant of attitudes about the product. When the advertisement concerned a product of high involvement, however, the celebrity status of the product endorsers had no effect on attitudes, but the cogency of the information about the product contained in the ad was a powerful determinant of product evaluations. These data clearly suggest that it would be inappropriate for social and consumer researchers to overemphasize the influence of issue-relevant arguments or product-relevant attributes and ignore the role of peripheral cues. Each type of attitudinal influence occurs in some instances, and the level of personal involvement with an issue or product appears to be one determinant of which type of persuasion occurs.

According to the Elaboration Likelihood Model, personal relevance is thought to be only one determinant of the route to persuasion. Personal relevance is thought to increase a person's motivation for engaging in a diligent consideration of the issue- or product-relevant information presented in order to form a veridical opinion. Just as different situations may induce different motivations to think, different people may typically employ different styles of information processing, and some people will enjoy thinking more than others (Cacioppo and Petty 1982, forthcoming). However, a diligent consideration of issue- or product-relevant information requires not only the motivation to think, but also the ability to process the information. Thus situational variables (e.g., distraction; Petty, Wells, and Brock 1976) and individual difference variables (e.g., prior knowledge; Cacioppo and Petty 1980) may also be important moderators of the route to persuasion. In the present study, subjects' ability to think about the product was held at a high level across experimental conditions—that is, the messages were easy to understand, the presentation was self-paced, and so on. Thus the primary determinant of the route to persuasion was motivational in nature.

It is important to note that although our "peripheral" manipulation was a source variable presented visually and our "central" manipulation was a message variable presented verbally, neither the source/message nor the visual/verbal dichotomy is isomorphic with the central/peripheral one. Thus a source variable may induce persuasion via the central route, and a message variable may serve as a peripheral cue. For example, in one study described previously (Petty and Cacioppo 1980), we observed that a physically attractive message endorser might serve as a cogent product-relevant argument for a beauty product. In another study (Petty and Cacioppo, forthcoming), we found that the mere number of message arguments presented may activate a simple decision rule (the more the better) under low involvement, but not under high involvement, where argument quality is more important than number. Similarly, a "central" manipulation may be presented visually—e.g., depicting a kitten in an advertisement for facial tissue to convey the product-relevant attribute "softness" (Mitchell and Olson 1981)—and a "peripheral" manipulation may be presented verbally—e.g., providing a verbal description of a message source as an expert or as likeable (Chaiken 1980; Petty, Cacioppo, and Goldman 1981). The critical feature of the central route to persuasion is that an attitude change is based on a diligent consideration of information that a person feels is central to the true merits of an issue or product. This information may be conveyed visually, verbally, or in source or message characteristics. In the peripheral route, attitudes change because of the presence of simple positive or negative cues, or because of the invocation of simple decision rules which obviate the need for thinking about issue-relevant arguments. Stimuli that serve as peripheral cues or that invoke simple decision rules may be presented visually or verbally, or may be part of source or message characteristics.

In sum, the present study has provided support for the view that different features of an advertisement may be more or less effective, depending upon a person's involvement with it. Under conditions of low involvement, peripheral cues are more important than issue-relevant argumentation, but under high involvement, the opposite is true. The realization that independent variables may have different effects, depending on the level of personal relevance of a message, may provide some insight into the conflicting pattern of results that is said to characterize much attitude research. It may well be that attitude effects can be arranged on a continuum, depending on the elaboration likelihood of the particular persuasion situation. This continuum would be anchored at one end by the peripheral route and at the other end by the central route to persuasion. Furthermore, these two routes may be characterized by quite different antecedents and consequents. If so, future work could be aimed at uncovering the various moderators of the route to persuasion and at tracking the various consequents of the two different routes.

## References

Ajzen, Icek and Martin Fishbein (1980). *Understanding Attitudes and Predicting Social Behavior*. Englewood Cliffs, NJ: Prentice-Hall.

Apsler, Robert and David O. Sears (1968). Warning, Personal Involvement, and Attitude Change. *Journal of Personality and Social Psychology*, 9 (June), 162–166.

Burnkrant, Robert E. (1976). A Motivational Model of Information Processing Intensity. *Journal of Consumer Research*, 3 (June), 21–30.

———and Alan G. Sawyer (1983). Effects of Involvement and Message Content on Information Processing Intensity, in *Information Processing Research in Advertising*. Richard Harris, ed. Hillsdale, NJ: Lawrence Erlbaum.

Cacioppo, John T. and Richard E. Petty (1979). Effects of Message Repetition and Position on Cognitive Responses, Recall, and Persuasion. *Journal of Personality and Social Psychology*, 37 (January), 97–109.

——— and Richard E. Petty (1980). Sex Differences in Influenceability: Toward Specifying the Underlying Processes. *Personality and Social Psychology Bulletin*, 6 (December), 651–656.

———and Richard E. Petty (1982). The Need for Cognition. *Journal of personality and Social Psychology*, 42 (January), 116–131.

———and Richard E. Petty (forthcoming). The Need for Cognition: Relationships to Social Influence and Self Influence, *Social Perception in Clinical and Counseling Psychology*. Richard P. McGlynn, James E. Maddux, Cal D. Stoltenberg, and John H. Harvey, eds. Lubbock, TX: Texas Tech Press.

Chaiken, Shelly (1980). Heuristic Versus Systematic Information Processing and the Use of Source Versus Message Cues in Persuasion. *Journal of Personality and Social Psychology*, 39 (November), 752–766.

Chestnut, Robert W., Charles C. LaChance, and Amy Lubitz (1977). The Decorative Female Model: Sexual Stimuli and the Recognition of Advertisements. *Journal of Advertising Research*, 6, 11–14.

Cialdini, Robert B., Richard E. Petty, and John T. Cacioppo (1981). Attitude and Attitude Change. *Annual Review of Psychology*, 32, 357–404.

Eagly, Alice H. (1978). Sex Differences in Influenceability. *Psychological Bulletin*, 85 (January), 86–116.

Engel, James F. and Roger D. Blackwell (1982). *Consumer Behavior*, Hinsdale, IL: Dryden Press.

Fishbein, Martin and Icek Ajzen (1981). Acceptance, Yielding, and Impact: Cognitive Processes in Persuasion. *Cognitive Responses in Persuasion*, Richard E. Petty, Thomas Ostrom, and Timothy C. Brock, eds. Hillsdale, NJ: Lawrence Erlbaum, 339–359.

Greenwald, Anthony G. (1968). Cognitive Learning, Cognitive Response to Persuasion, and Attitude Change. *Psychological Foundations of Attitudes*, eds. Anthony G. Greenwald, Timothy C. Brock, and Thomas Ostrom, New York: Academic Press, 147–170.

———, Irving Janis, and Harold Kelley (1953). *Communication and Persuasion*, New Haven, CT: Yale University Press.

Insko, Chester A., E. Allen Lind, and Stephen LaTour (1976). Persuasion, Recall, and Thoughts. *Representative Research in Social Psychology*, 7, 66–78.

Kassarjian, Harold H. (1982). Consumer Psychology. *Annual Review of Psychology*, 33, 619–649.

——— and Waltraud M. Kassarjian (1979). Attitudes under Low Commitment Conditions. *Attitude Research Plays for High Stakes*, eds. John C. Maloney and Bernard Silverman, Chicago: American Marketing Association, 3–15.

Krugman, Herbert E. (1965). The Impact of Television Advertising: Learning without Involvement. *Public Opinion Quarterly*, 29 (Fall), 349–356.

——— (1967). The Measurement of Advertising Involvement. *Public Opinion Quarterly*, 30 (Winter), 853–596.

McGuire, William J. (1969). The Nature of Attitudes and Attitude Change. *The Handbook of Social Psychology*, Vol. 3, Gardner Lindzey and Elliot Aronson, eds. Reading, MA: Addison-Wesley, 136–314.

Mitchell, Andrew A. and Jerry C. Olson (1981). Are Product Attribute Beliefs the Only Mediator of Advertising Effects on Brand Attitude? *Journal of Marketing Research*, 18 (August), 318–332.

Petty, Richard E. and John T. Cacioppo (1979). Issue Involvement Can Increase or Decrease Persuasion by Enhancing Message-Relevant Cognitive Responses. *Journal of Personality and Social Psychology*, 37 (October), 1915–1926.

——— and John T. Cacioppo (1980). Effects of Issue Involvement on Attitudes in an Advertising Context. *Proceedings of the Division 23 Program*, Gerald G. Gorn and Marvin E. Goldberg, eds. Montreal, Canada: American Psychological Association, 75–79.

——— and John T. Cacioppo (1981). *Attitudes and Persuasion: Classic and Contemporary Approaches*, Dubuque, IA: William C. Brown.

——— and John T. Cacioppo (1983). Central and Peripheral Routes to Persuasion: Application to Advertising. *Advertising and Consumer Psychology*, Larry Percy and Arch Woodside, eds. Lexington, MA: Lexington Books, 3–23.

——— and John T. Cacioppo (forthcoming). The Effects of Involvement on Responses to Argument Quantity and Quality: Central and Peripheral Routes to Persuasion. *Journal of Personality and Social Psychology*.

———, John T. Cacioppo, and Rachel Goldman (1981). Personal Involvement as a Determinant of Argument-Based persuasion. *Journal of Personality and Social Psychology*, 41 (November), 847–855.

———, John T. Cacioppo, and Martin Heesacker (1981). The Use of Rhetorical Questions in Persuasion: A Cognitive Response Analysis. *Journal of Personality and Social Psychology*, 40 (March), 432–440.

———, Gary L. Wells, and Timothy C. Brock (1976). Distraction Can Enhance or Reduce Yielding to Propaganda: Thought Disruption Versus Effort Justification. *Journal of Personality and Social Psychology*, 34 (November), 874–884.

Ray, Michael L., Alan G. Sawyer, Michael L. Rothschild, Roger M. Heeler, Edward C. Strong and Jerome B. Reed (1973). Marketing Communication and the Hierarchy of Effects. *New Models for Mass Communication Research*, Vol. 2, Peter Clarke, ed. Beverly Hills, CA: Sage Publications, 147–176.

Rhine, Ramon, and Laurence J. Severance (1970). Ego-Involvement, Discrepancy, Source Credibility, and Attitude Change. *Journal of Personality and Social Psychology*, 16 (October), 175–190.

Sherif, Muzifer and Carl I. Hovland (1961). *Social Judgment*, New Haven: Yale University Press.

Sherif, Carolyn W., Muzifer Sherif, and Roger E. Nebersall (1965). *Attitude and Attitude Change*, Philadelphia: Saunders.

Steadman, Major (1969). How Sexy Illustrations Affect Brand Recall. *Journal of Advertising Research*, 9 (1), 15–19.

Wright, Peter L. (1973). The Cognitive Processes Mediating Acceptance of Advertising. *Journal of Marketing Research*, 10, (February), 53–62.

———(1974). Analyzing Media Effects on Advertising Responses. *Public Opinion Quarterly*, 38 (Summer), 192–205.

Anthony Pratkanis
Elliot Aronson

# The Fear Appeal

This selection asks an important and basic question about
attitude change: Do fear tactics work? Reviewing the literature in this area, the authors tell us that the answer is "it
depends"—on the nature of the audience and what the message contains. In particular, they point out that in order to
bring positive results a fear campaign must offer specific
recommendations that are perceived as both effective and
doable. You might consider, as the authors do, what these
findings say about the likely effectiveness of an antidrug
campaign whose main message is "Just say no."

In 1741, in the small New England town of Enfield, Jonathan Edwards delivered a sermon entitled "Sinners in the Hands of an Angry God." In this
sermon, he preached:

> Thus it is that natural men are held in the hand of God, over the pit of hell;
> they have deserved the fiery pit, and are already sentenced to it . . . the
> devil is waiting for them, hell is gaping for them, the flames gather and
> flash about them, and would fain lay hold on them, and swallow them up.
> . . . In short, they have no refuge, nothing to take hold of; all that preserves
> them every moment is the mere arbitrary will and uncovenanted, un-
> obliged forbearance of an incensed God.

Eyewitness accounts indicate that the sermon left the congregation
"breathing of distress and weeping." The records show that thousands gave
over their lives to Christ as part of the Great Awakening of eighteenth-century
America.

Two centuries later, in 1932, Adolf Hitler inspired his fellow countrymen
and women with the words:

> The streets of our country are in turmoil. The universities are filled with
> students rebelling and rioting. Communists are seeking to destroy our
> country. Russia is threatening us with her might, and the Republic is in

danger. Yes—danger from within and without. We need law and order! Without it our nation cannot survive.

Millions of Germans gladly embraced Hitler's Nationalist Socialist party.

Although the goals of Edwards and Hitler were quite different, their method was the same—instilling fear. Both Edwards and Hitler threatened their audiences with dire consequences if, of course, a certain course of action was not followed.

Ministers and politicians are not the only ones who arouse fear in order to motivate and persuade. Life insurance agents use fear to induce purchase of their policies; parents use fear to persuade their children to come home early from a date; and physicians use fear to insure that patients adopt and maintain a prescribed medical regimen. Sometimes these fear appeals are based on legitimate concerns—smoking does cause cancer; "unsafe sex" increases one's chance of contracting AIDS; failure to brush and floss can lead to painful tooth decay. But often fear appeals are based on dark, irrational fears—fears stemming from racial prejudice or the notion that there is a communist under every bed. At times a regime instills fear by terrorizing its own citizens, as in Hitler's Germany, Stalin's Soviet Union, Argentina of the junta, Hussein's Iraq, and at countless other times and places. Fear appeals are powerful because they channel our thoughts away from careful consideration of the issue at hand and toward plans for ridding ourselves of the fear. When illegitimate fears are used, the message promotes deception—not to mention the cruelty of the fear itself. It behooves us to look closely at just when and how fear appeals are effective.

Not all fear appeals are successful in obtaining their objectives. For the past few years, public service announcements have alerted viewers to the dangers of drug abuse and cigarette use and have frightened Americans about the possibility of contracting AIDS. Opponents of the nuclear arms race have often painted a graphic picture of nuclear winter. Yet drug abuse and cigarette smoking remain *high,* the practice of safe sex *low,* and the possibility of world annihilation through the use of nuclear weapons ever present. Just what are the factors that make a fear-arousing appeal more or less effective?

Let's begin with a seemingly simple question: Suppose you wish to arouse fear in the hearts of your audience as a way of inducing opinion change. Would it be more effective to arouse just a little fear, or should you try to scare the hell out of them?

For example, if your goal is to convince people to drive more carefully, would it be more effective to show them gory technicolor films of the broken and bloody bodies of highway accident victims, or would it be more effective if you soft-pedaled your communication—showing crumpled fenders,discussing increased insurance rates due to careless driving, and pointing out the possibility that people who drive carelessly may have their driver's licenses suspended?

Common sense argues on both sides of this street. On the one hand, it suggests that a good scare will motivate people to action; on the other hand, it argues that too much fear can be debilitating—that is, it might interfere with a person's ability to pay attention to the message, to comprehend it, and to act upon it. We have all believed, at one time or another, that it only happens to the other guy, it can't happen to me. Thus people continue to drive at very high speeds and to insist on driving after they've had a few drinks, even though they should know better. Perhaps this is because the possible negative consequences of these actions are so great that we try not to think about them. Thus, if a communication arouses extreme fear, we tend *not* to pay close attention to it.

What does the evidence tell us? Experimental data overwhelmingly suggest that all other things being equal, the more frightened a person is by a communication, the more likely he or she is to take positive preventive action.

The most prolific researchers in this area have been Howard Leventhal and his associates. In one experiment, they tried to induce people to stop smoking and obtain chest X-rays. Some subjects were exposed to a low-fear treatment: They were simply presented with a recommendation to stop smoking and get their chests X-rayed. Others were subjected to moderate fear. They were shown a film depicting a young man whose chest X-rays revealed he had lung cancer. The people subjected to the high-fear condition saw the same film the "moderate-fear" people saw—and, in addition, they were treated to a vivid, gory color film of a lung cancer operation. The results showed that those people who were most frightened were also most eager to stop smoking and most likely to sign up for chest X-rays.

Is this true for all people? It is not. There is good reason why common sense can lead us to believe that a great deal of fear leads to inaction: It does—for certain people, under certain conditions.

What Leventhal and his colleagues discovered is that the people who had a reasonably good opinion of themselves (high self-esteem) were the ones most likely to be moved by high degrees of fear arousal. People with low opinions of themselves were the least likely to take immediate action when confronted with a communication arousing a great deal of fear—but (and here is the interesting part) after a delay, they behaved very much like the subjects with high self-esteem. People who have a low opinion of themselves may have difficulty coping with threats to themselves. A high-fear communication overwhelms them and makes them feel like crawling into bed and pulling the covers up over their heads. Low or moderate fear is something they can more easily deal with at the moment they experience it. But, given time—that is, if it is not essential they act immediately—they will be more likely to act if the message truly scared the hell out of them.

Subsequent research by Leventhal and his colleagues lends support to this analysis. In one study, subjects were shown films of serious automobile accidents. Some subjects watched the films on a large screen from up close; others watched them from far away on a much smaller screen. Among those subjects with high or moderate self-esteem, those who saw the films on the large screen were much more likely to take subsequent protective action than were those who saw the films on the small screen. Subjects with low self-esteem were more likely to take action when they saw the films on a small screen; those who saw the films on a large screen reported a great deal of fatigue and stated they had great difficulty even thinking of themselves as victims of automobile accidents.

It should be relatively easy to make people with high self-esteem behave like people with low self-esteem. We can overwhelm them by making them feel there is nothing they can do to prevent or ameliorate a threatening situation. Much research has shown that if recipients of a fear appeal perceive that there is no way to cope effectively with the threat, they are not likely to respond to the appeal but will just bury their heads in the sand—even those who have high self-esteem. Franklin D. Roosevelt knew the debilitating effect of extreme fear and sought to counteract it when he announced in his first inaugural address, "The only thing we have to fear is fear itself."

Conversely, suppose you wanted to reduce the automobile accident rate or to help people give up smoking, and you were faced with low self-esteem people. How would you proceed? if you were to construct a message containing clear, specific, and optimistic instructions, it might increase the feeling among the members of your audience that they could confront their fears and cope with the danger.

These speculations have been confirmed; experiments by Howard Leventhal and his colleagues show that fear-arousing messages containing specific instructions about how, when, and where to take action are much more effective than recommendations that omit such instructions. For example, a campaign conducted on a college campus urging students to get tetanus shots included specific instructions about where and when they were available. The campaign materials included a map showing the location of the student health service and a suggestion that each student set aside a convenient time to stop by.

The results showed high-fear appeals to be more effective than low-fear appeals in producing favorable *attitudes* toward tetanus shots among the students, and they also increased the students' stated intentions to get the shots. The highly specific instructions about how to get the shots did not affect these opinions and intentions, but the instructions did have a big effect on the *actual behavior*: Of those subjects who were instructed about how to proceed, 28% actually got the tetanus shots; but of those who received no specific instructions, only 3% got them. In a control group exposed only to the instructions, with no fear-arousing message, no one got the shots. Thus specific instructions alone were not enough to produce action—fear was a necessary component for action in such situations.

Very similar results were obtained in Leventhal's cigarette experiment. Leventhal found that a high-fear communication produced a much greater *intention* to stop smoking. Unless it was accompanied by recommendations for specific behavior, however, it produced little results. Similarly, specific instructions (buy a magazine instead of a pack of cigarettes, drink plenty of water when you have the urge to smoke, and so on) without a fear-arousing communication were relatively ineffective. The combination of fear arousal and specific instructions produced the best results; the students in this condition were smoking less four months after they were subjected to the experimental procedure.

In sum, a fear appear is most effective when (1) it *scares* the hell out of people, (2) it offers a *specific recommendation* for overcoming the fear-arousing threat, (3) the recommended action is perceived as effective for reducing the threat, and (4) the message recipient believes that he or she *can* perform the recommended action.

This is exactly what Jonathan Edwards and Adolf Hitler offered their listeners. Both men described rising menaces—sin or communism—that, if allowed free rein, would devastate the soul or the national spirit. Each man offered a specific remedy for the crisis—commitment to Christ or joining the Nazi party. These courses of action were easy enough to perform—one needed only to answer the altar call or to vote for a Nazi candidate.

In contrast, fear appeals to increase nuclear disarmament or to decrease drug abuse rarely incorporate all four components of a successful fear appeal. We have all been alerted to the dread of nuclear winter and the personal and social destruction of drug abuse. However, there have been few specific recommendations for removing these threats that have been generally perceived as *effective* and *doable*.

Two counterexamples of effective anti-nuclear arms appeals will make our point. First, during the 1950s and early 1960s, many people purchased and installed "nuclear fallout shelters" in their homes. The reason: Fear of nuclear war was high and the installation of a home fallout shelter, at the time, appeared to be an effective, doable response.

Second, during the 1964 presidential campaign, Lyndon Johnson, in a series of television ads, was able to sway voters by portraying his opponent, Barry Goldwater, as a supported of the use of nuclear weapons. One controversial ad featured a young girl counting to ten as she pulled petals from a daisy. A moment later, the television screen filled with the mushroom cloud of a nuclear bomb. Johnson's appeal was successful because it linked the fear of nuclear war to Goldwater and then proposed a vote for Johnson as a specific, doable way to avoid this threat.

Or consider the recent campaign to reduce the incidence of drug abuse by telling kids to "just say no." Although many children and teenagers are probably frightened by the drug scene, "just saying no" is not perceived as an effective and doable response. Imagine yourself as a teenager whose friends are pressuring you to try cocaine. Just saying no is likely to result in even more pressure—"Come on, just one try. What are you? A fraidy-cat?" Such pressure is not easy to resist.

The drug problem, given its scope and complexity, will require more than just a cleverly worded advertisement to solve. However, we can design our appeals so that they are more effective. For example, recently a teacher asked her elementary school class to come up with specific ways to say no when their friends pressure them to use drugs. The students produced a book of "ways to say no"—for example, walking away, calling the dealer the fraidy-cat, offering the friend an alternative to doing drugs. Such an approach has the advantage of "self-selling" the class not to use drugs and also provides a list of specific ways that children will perceive as effective for dealing with peer pressure; such a list can then be illustrated on television or role-played in the schools. But in the final analysis, for our fear appeals to work, we need to offer our children a more effective and doable solution to life's problems than the advice to "just say no."

But there is a broader question: Should fear appeals be used at all? Given the power of fear to motivate and direct our thoughts, there is much potential for abuse. Illegitimate fears can always be invented for any given propaganda purpose. As persuaders, it is our responsibility, if we decide to use a fear appeal, to insure that the fear we instill is, at least, legitimate and that it serves to alert the target to potential dangers as opposed to obscuring the issue with emotion. As targets of such appeals, we owe it to ourselves to first ask, "How legitimate is this fear?" before taking the propagandist's bait.

Tori DeAngelis

# Cognitive Dissonance Theory Alive and Well

In this brief article, DeAngelis discusses one of the most highly researched and influential theories in social psychology—cognitive dissonance—through the eyes of one of its most influential thinkers, Elliot Aronson. the theory of cognitive dissonance, which says that people are motivated to change their attitudes or behavior when they hold two psychologically inconsistent thoughts, has become less popular among social psychologists today. Yet Aronson tries to demonstrate that it is alive, well, and still important.

Although it fell out of fashion in the 1970s and early 1980s, the theory of cognitive dissonance is alive and well, Elliot Aronson told attendees at the Western Psychological Association (WPA) annual convention. In fact, several modern subtheories calling themselves by other names can and probably should be subsumed under its heading, he said.

Aronson, WPA president, described in his presidential address the history of the theory from its conception by his mentor, the late Leon Festinger. He also discussed applied research on the theory he and his graduate students are conducting that holds promise for curbing negative social behavior like wasting water and spreading the AIDS virus.

The original theory, described by Festinger in his 1957 book, *A Theory of cognitive Dissonance*, presented a new, more subtle way of looking at human behavior, said Aronson. It posits that if people hold two psychologically inconsistent thoughts, they will experience dissonance. Since dissonance is unpleasant, they will try to reduce it, much as they would drives like hunger or thirst, said Aronson.

The 1970s saw the expansion of the theory into other fields and its popularization in the media, said Aronson. The theory made its way into the *New York Times, Newsweek, Playboy,* "and alas, the *National Enquirer,*" he said.

For several reasons, the theory started waning around the same time it was being hyped in the media, Aronson said. For one, public officials in that era regularly deceived the public about important events, such as Vietnam and Watergate. Since conducting cognitive dissonance experiments requires some deception of subjects, for researchers "it became distasteful to do anything in which Nixon was engaging," said Aronson.

For another, experiments using the theory "caused subjects some discomfort," and those who objected to such tactics won out. Third, cognitive psychology was booming and social psychologists began to incorporate their findings into the cognitive literature, which began a trend toward separating the theory from its roots. Finally, the theory simply "became unpopular, like last year's hemline," said Aronson.

Since then, a lot of studies have entered the literature that make remarkably similar claims to those noted in Festinger's original theory, said Aronson.

For instance, Charlie Lord, Mark Lepper and Lee Ross proposed in the 1979 abstract to their cognition experiment that "people who hold strong opinions on complex social issues are likely to examine relevant empirical evidence in a biased manner," said Aronson.

"What I find titillating is that the . . . abstract could have been written in 1957—and the experiment could have been performed in 1957 and performed in Festinger's book," he said.

Aronson said he singled out the team "precisely because they are such irreproachably good scholars." Their work is "an illustration of what happens when artificial barriers are erected and related theories get insulated from each other," he said.

Some researchers are asserting in a variety of mini-theories that "it might be interesting to combine cognition and motivation"—Festinger's precise proposal 32 years ago, said Aronson.

Aronson and some of his graduate students recently took to task one of these new theories—Joel Cooper's and Russ Fazio's "new look dissonance theory." The theory holds that dissonance occurs only when there are aversive consequences. Cooper and Fazio state what they see as a limiting condition to cognitive dissonance theory—"that dissonance is aroused only when someone acts with personal responsibility to bring about an unwanted event," said Aronson.

In the first of two experiments, Aronson and graduate students Carrie Fried and Jeff Stone conducted a two-by-two experiment examining whether they could influence subjects' views about using condoms. They had some of the subjects make a videotape on safe sex for high school students, while other rehearsed the argument without making a tape. Some of the subjects were asked 15 minutes before their presentation to think about times they found it difficult to use condoms.

The team predicted that the subjects who made the tape *and* were made aware of their behavior would reduce their discomfort by vowing to use condoms, which is in fact what they found, said Aronson.

The study partially confirmed that Cooper and Fazio were wrong, that aversive consequences *aren't* necessarily an aspect of dissonance, he said.

However, the experiment wasn't ideal, since the team couldn't follow the students into their bedrooms to see if they were using condoms, said Aronson. So he and graduate students Ruth Thibodeau and Chris Dickerson did another study.

In it, the team "intercepted women at the field house on their way to the shower," said Aronson. They asked some to sign a flyer saying they advocated conserving water, and others to respond to a water conservation awareness "survey," which included the idea that too much showering can be wasteful.

"The results were really clear," said Aronson. The students who had advocated taking shorter showers on the flyer *and* were made aware of their past negative behaviors reduced their shower time to 3½ minutes—"that's a short shower!" he said.

But as in the other experiment, there were overwhelmingly positive consequences implied if they conserved water, he said.

Cognitive dissonance theory successfully challenged theories of the time, said Aronson. One was reinforcement theory, which contends that people like the things for which they're rewarded and shun those for which they're punished. Social psychology "was dominated by a loose application" of that theory, he said.

Cognitive dissonance exposed the limitations of that theory "and in some cases, showed it was flat-out wrong," said Aronson. For instance, reinforcement theory suggests that if you reward people for saying something they don't believe in, they might become attached to the statement through secondary reinforcement, said Aronson. But Festinger's and Carlsmith's forced compliance experiment "exploded that simplistic notion by showing that you believe lies only if you are *under*-rewarded for telling them," said Aronson.

Cognitive dissonance also shot down the notion of catharsis in psycho-analytic theory, which held that if you feel hostility toward someone and express those feelings, you'll release pent up anger and feel better about the person as a result.

Dissonance theory showed that if people hurt someone with whom they are angry, they will try to justify their actions by denigrating the person. This in turn makes them feel more hostility toward the person, "which opens the door for still further aggression," he said.

Festinger successfully melded cognition and motivation in the theory, and "sounded the clarion call for taking cognition seriously in social psychology," said Aronson.

In 1962, Aronson and others modified Festinger's original theory. They discovered that the theory made the most sense when the person's self-concept was engaged, said Aronson.

Their modification held that if people's self-concept was challenged—which for most people, meant thinking of themselves as stable and predictable, competent and morally good—they would try to retain that sense of self, even if they compromised their integrity in the process, said Aronson.

In telling the story of the theory's development, Aronson recalled his first encounters with Festinger, who taught at Stanford while Aronson was a graduate student there. Festinger was, said Aronson, a "genius," but one reputed to be an "aggressive, harsh, even devastating individual," who could use his "rapier-like wit . . . to cut up and devour tender young graduate students like me for breakfast."

When Aronson asked Festinger for something to read to prepare him for Festinger's graduate seminar, Festinger glared at him, grunted, and gave Aronson his only copy of the draft of *A Theory of Cognitive Dissonance,* which had just been sent to the publisher. Despite this introduction, Aronson read the book in one sitting. "I was knocked out! It was the most exciting thing I had ever read in psychology," he recalled.

Aronson said he hoped in trying to show that dissonance theory has had the last laugh he was not "starting to sound like the worst kind of smarty-pants, or worse . . . like an old curmudgeon."

Ultimately, "When we build this way, we add continuity to the field," said Aronson. Beginning from a single grand theory "will also generate richer hypotheses," he said. "That's what creative synthesis is all about."

# 5

# Groups: Working with Others

As social beings we cannot avoid being a part of many groups. The family is the most basic, but every time you play on a team, attend a class, hang around with your friends, or work on a committee, you become part of a group. Groups work to find a cure for AIDS, groups try to figure how to cut the national deficit, and groups aim to win the Super Bowl and the World Cup. Just about every medical advance in recent years is the product of a group effort, but it was also a group decision that sent the astronauts on the Challenger shuttle to their deaths. Groups are critical to our existence, yet there is a great deal that we do not understand about them.

James Davis, Professor of Psychology at the University of Illinois at Urbana-Champaign, is one of the world's leading experts on decision making in small groups. He has devoted a lifetime to this field, and his findings have been influential in shaping policies, especially those governing jury trials. In our conversation we touched on several issues concerning group performance and group decision making and discussed the relative importance of basic and applied research in the area of small groups.

## A CONVERSATION WITH JAMES DAVIS
*University of Illinois*
*at Urbana-Champaign*

**Krupat:** *If our topic is groups, let's start by asking you the most basic of questions: What is one?*

**Davis:** That depends on who you're talking to, but, as far as I'm concerned, a group is no more than a set of people. It's that simple.

**Krupat:** *Are there any requirements other than being able to identify them as a set? Do they have to interact together or care about each other—anything of that sort?*

**Davis:** Not necessarily. Researchers use the term in different ways, and one hears the phrase, "But that's not a *real* group." People who say that have some idea that the people have some sort of relationship with each other or they've known each other for a certain period of time. There may be such groups, but there are many transitory groups of great importance. For example, the criminal jury is a group of enormous importance that consists of strangers, together for a limited time, who will never see each other again. Yet they'll make enormously important decisions.

**Krupat:** *When we talk about a term such as "committee," is this just another word for group, or is this different or special in some way?*

**Davis:** The word committee carries with it a little bit of extra baggage. Usually when we say committee we're referring to a task-oriented group that has been brought together to serve some particular kind of purpose, like a budget committee in an organization or a promotion committee in a university. Still, this needs to be defined further because the budget committee does something quite different from the Christmas party committee.

**Krupat:** *If you take a look at almost any textbook in social psychology, from the earliest to the most recent, you will find a great deal of interest in groups and group phenomena. Why is the study and understanding of groups so important to us?*

**Davis:** If one is interested in the behavior of the individual, that's fine. But like all the primates, human beings tend to congregate, and if there is more than one person, you automatically have a group. So a group by definition is the social part of social psychology. And naturally it is the place we go to look for behavior.

**Krupat:** *Once people form groups, do they serve us well? For instance, are groups more efficient than individuals—are two heads better than one?*

**Davis:** Sometimes two heads are better than one, sometimes they're worse. It depends on the task and the experience of the people involved. Obviously some tasks, like carrying a large log someplace, can only be performed by several people, yet trying to run a relay with everybody holding the baton at the same time is ridiculous. These are extreme examples, but it's easy to show that six people working on a word puzzle or a calculus problem typically are less creative, less able, and generally perform more poorly in the same period of time than the same number of people would be if they worked apart. Now this flies in the face of a lot of educational doctrine. But alas, the data are very, very clear. For other kinds of tasks, however, when you can break up the problem, groups work well. You add those columns of figures, I add this column, somebody does something else, and then we can put it together. So, it depends on the nature of the task whether the per unit time efficiency of the set of people is better or worse than if they were alone. Of course there are also nonperformance factors. People like being in groups, and if it's a long, difficult problem, although it may be inefficient to do so, people may simply enjoy being together enough that they keep working on the problem. Whereas if they were alone, they would abandon the task altogether.

**Krupat:** *Some of your comments about group inefficiency fly in the face of common wisdom. How is it that myths about groups persist in spite of the findings of research?*

**Davis:** I can't think of any question that's a better example of it than the "groups versus individuals" question that you've raised. Take for example brainstorming groups. There are consulting firms that will tell your organization, for a suitable fee of course, how to do a better job at brainstorming. There's a whole set of rules for brainstorming: people should freely interact, they should try to bolster each other's opinions, etcetera, but it doesn't work. If people cost money and time is money, then it's a losing proposition. People are better off working alone. However, that is not attractive. It does not fit our notions of fair play, democracy, and goodness. Consequently, writers of textbooks and magazine articles and peddlers of services don't like that or don't believe it.

**Krupat:** *But why don't these kinds of groups generate better solutions? What are the factors that make group performance sometimes less good?*

**Davis:** In a group it's easy to imagine that, if you're talking, you're distracting me and I can't think very well. It's very hard to work that calculus problem if a lot of noise is going on around me and if I'm supposed to listen to you at the same time. In addition, there are individual differences in the world. Some people are better than others at the problem. But if it's a truly group problem, then presumably everybody has some input. You could structure the group so that only the best people would work on the problem, and then you can expect a superior solution. In fact, we could construct a group over a protracted period of time that probably would do better. But many important decisions are made by people who don't know each other very well, who are not particularly organized, and who certainly don't know who the best people are.

**Krupat:** *Right now I'm on a committee and we are having a terrible time ever reaching a consensus. Can you tell me something about group decision making?*

**Davis:** Well, that's what keeps me in business. In every group, where it's a collective act that's the object of our concern, there has to be agreement, some sort of group decision or solution. Most freely interacting groups who get together do not have formal rules or a constitution, but rather the social norms that people bring to the group with them help organize discussion and lead to a decision. When our department advisory committee reaches a decision, it doesn't mean that everybody agrees. But we all understand the norms of comportment, and to get the job done the minority will acquiesce to the majority, with more important decisions requiring larger majorities. That seems to be true for juries, promotion committees, and many other kinds of groups. Some groups have formal decision rules, such as a simple majority or a strong majority like two-thirds or four-fifths, and sometimes they might even take a vote. Other times, there is implied pressure from the majority to the minority to simply yield, not because they're spineless wretches, but because it's the democratic and civilized thing to do. Incidentally, under certain circumstances, minorities can be very influential.

**Krupat:** *Are there some instances where a group just cannot come to a decision?*

**Davis:** There are issues, of course, where people are so violently in disagreement that some members won't acquiesce and consensus is not possible. On a jury that requires a vote of guilty or not guilty, there's no room for compromise. You either are convinced beyond a reasonable doubt that the person is guilty, or you're obligated to say not guilty even if you're not convinced that they're innocent. With a civil jury, however, damage awards may be an issue. I may agree to an award, but disagree with the group on the amount—but I am willing to compromise. Consensus processes are fascinating, and there are a lot of techniques and mechanisms for managing discussion and criteria for reaching a decision that can themselves influence the outcome.

**Krupat:** *Such as?*

**Davis:** We have just concluded some experiments on mock juries indicating that the mere order in which you take up issues on the agenda can determine the outcome. We would like to think that things like criminal justice are administered in an orderly way and that you do not influence the outcome, for example, depending on which direction you happen to take a straw vote. But it turns out that the order in which members express their preference in a straw poll can make a difference in the outcome. If it just happens that five guilty votes precede you and you're sort of undecided, it seems that a significant proportion of people will change their position to guilty, having responded not guilty initially. Wily old senators in Washington and experienced committee members have known about procedural influences for a long time.

**Krupat:** *One issue relating to groups and their performance that hasn't come up yet is the matter of group size. Is there an ideal size that a group should be to accomplish its goals?*

**Davis:** I suspect you've already guessed—that depends on the task and the context. A good example again comes from the criminal justice system. In the mid-70s, the Supreme Court decided that there was nothing in the constitution that forbid legislation from setting aside a criminal jury of less than 12 and, similarly in other decisions, a less than unanimity rule. Suddenly people became very interested in group size and group decision rules, asking, "Do these simple features have any effect?" On the face of it, the size of the group determines the resources they bring to the problem. If one person doesn't know the answer, somebody else might. Or somebody on a jury can recall an item of testimony that somebody else cannot. That's part of the appeal of groups. Intuitively, you can also see that with very large groups there's some coordination problems. Clearly, 50 people trying to discuss the details of the criminal case to arrive at a verdict is going to be very different than 6 people. Fifty people may have better recall of testimony, but 6 people may be better to get the job done. So the question has to be: given a particular task demand, what is the optimal size?

**Krupat:** *So how do you decide?*

**Davis:** It comes down to questions like how many distractions there are or what kind of interpersonal coordination problems there may be. The actual question you raised becomes basically an engineering problem. And, although the court decisions are somewhat more complex than I have implied here, that's what has been going on in the criminal justice system for some time now. It is the case that probably 12 is a pretty good size across the board, and, at least for *my* taste, 6, which is the minimum size that the courts have decided to allow, is inadequate for certain conditions.

**Krupat:** *You are someone who has dedicated his career to the understanding of groups. How did you become so interested in this area in the first place?*

**Davis:** Well, by accident. When I went to graduate school, I had no intention of studying small groups, and I certainly wasn't interested in constructing mathematical models of their interaction and performance. As a graduate student, I found that problems of small group behavior kept popping up in conversation and in things I read. And in the end I read some very stimulating papers about group performance that intrigued me. Later it came to me that in society at large, small groups actually engage in problems of some importance to us all. For example, besides juries, we're studying public school boards right now. Some months ago I was watching the news and a local school board member was being interviewed by a reporter. He said, "We have all these graphs and tables, but you know, I don't understand a damn bit of it. I just plan to go with my gut feeling." This guy had more data than almost any school board member will typically have, and he didn't understand it. He wanted to do a good job, make a good decision, but he couldn't understand what was in front of him, so he was going to vote intuitively about a matter of substantial local importance. And he's not alone. Having watched him on TV, I thought, "My word, we haven't the faintest idea how these kinds of groups go about their work. There may be, and indeed there are, some very simple techniques applicable to both groups and individuals to improve performance."

**Krupat:** *Having done a good deal of research in the laboratory as well as the real world, to what extent do you believe we ought to be directing our energies toward basic issues versus applied problems?*

**Davis:** For a lot of research, it's hard to draw the line between practical and applied versus basic and fundamental, and I don't think this matters a great deal most of the time. But there is a problem which does matter. You have to come up with the money to fund research, and Congress contains people who are no better off than our jury member or our school board member when it comes to understanding why we're concerned with getting as fundamental an answer as possible. The sad part is we're probably going to waste billions in the months and years ahead by looking for answers to problems that are too shallow in conception. A good example in my mind comes with regard to the polio vaccines. When I was young, polio was a terrible disease, and one would see friends not only die but become paralyzed for the rest of their lives. So the search for a polio cure or a vaccine to prevent it was extremely important. We all know Sabin and Salk, and their accomplishments should not be diminished. But the truly important result that led to a vaccine didn't come from these perfecters of the vaccine. The real issue was growing the polio virus in the test tube among the tissue. Three Harvard biochemists did that. They earned a Nobel prize, but few know their names. In psychology there are lots of things like that. They are not quite so dramatic, but it's the same kind of thing. We would like to know how people can recall information under certain conditions, because that's what leads to inefficiency in the group coming together. It's very hard to explain to people why this is so important. Still, if you think about it, most scientists would rather discover something basic than something very applied, for the simple reason that they will go down in history books as having done something truly important. We must encourage *both* basic and applied research.

Mitchell Lee Marks

# The Question of Quality Circles

Marks discusses quality circles, in which groups of workers get together on a regular basis to analyze work-related problems and propose solutions. Some people have attributed their widespread use in Japan as a major reason for that country's industrial success and have employed them as a cure-all for the problems of U.S. industry. Others have said that this form of group involvement only treats the symptoms, but misses the underlying problems. Marks reviews the arguments on both sides, noting the potential value of quality circles and offering suggestions for how and when to use group participation.

Blue Cross of Washington and Alaska reports that more efficient employee procedures have saved $430,000 in less than three years, improved service to customers and increased communication between departments. A better method for checking coating thickness of floppy disks has saved $100,000 for the Verbatim Corporation in Sunnyvale, California. Sales agents at Hertz Rent a Car in Oklahoma City now get information about car availability 27 seconds faster using computers rather than microfiche.

Neither industrial engineers nor human factors analysts developed these innovations. Rather, they came directly from the workers themselves—sales agents, clerks and factory workers participating in Quality Circles (QC's, as they are often called), an employee-participation technique popularized in Japan and now widely applied in the United States.

Many business people, management experts and organizational psychologists dispute the savings claimed by QC adherents and say that QC's fail more often than they work. These critics describe the technique as management snake oil, a quick fix too often aimed at generating short-term profits rather than addressing the real problems underlying poor productivity, quality and employee morale.

A major reason for these sharp differences of opinion is that until recently the benefits of QC's have been studied and touted chiefly by people with a vested interest in QC success: managers whose bonuses and career advancement are at stake and consultants looking for ways to impress and sell new clients. There have been few rigorously collected data on how QC's affect the attitudes and productivity of employees and the effectiveness and financial performance of their organizations.

Several such evaluations have been made in the last few years. Before examining what they found, it will be useful to look at how QC's work and the reasons—aside from any accomplishments—for their tremendous growth in popularity.

Although QC programs vary from site to site, most share a basic format: Small groups of people who perform similar work meet voluntarily on a regular basis, usually once a week, to analyze work-related problems and propose solutions to them. QC's are usually led by the supervisor or manager of the work unit in which they are located. Members receive training in problem solving, quality control and group dynamics to help them function well.

Discussions are limited to issues directly related to the quantity or quality of work, such as paperwork and material waste, machine maintenance, cooperation between departments and productivity. Pay, benefits, hiring or promotion decisions and factors restricted by labor-relations contracts are out of bounds. Members of QC's have no power to implement ideas directly. Instead, they present them to the person in charge of the operation involved, usually a middle-level manager, who is free to accept or reject the recommendations.

The QC process draws substantially upon psychological theory and research for its rationale. The technique, consistent with the work of theorists such as Abraham Maslow, assumes that employees become more motivated if jobs meet their need for growth. Proponents claim that QC's accomplish this by giving workers opportunities to identify and solve real problems, make presentations to company management and operate successfully in groups. They also contend that QC's offer the advantages of group decision-making— advantages that include, according to psychologist Norman R. F. Maier of the University of Michigan, higher-quality decisions and increased commitment to implementing them.

QC's are a major part of a broader current movement toward greater employee participation in decision-making. Robert E. Cole, a sociologist at the University of Michigan and former director of that school's Center for Japanese Studies, notes, "In the early 1970s there were extensive discussions in America . . . about the need to 'humanize work' and raise the quality of work life. By increasing employee participation in workplace decisions, increasing job variety, and making more effective use of worker potential, it was argued, not only would the quality of work life be enhanced, but organizational efficiency and worker productivity would be improved."

Cole recalls, "Japan scared the pants off U.S. business in the 1970s. People were desperately looking for something to try." The media, as well as many academics, attributed Japan's success in the late 1970s to its superior approach to management, and QC's were seen as the easiest part of the Japanese approach to implement. QC programs were accessible, well packaged and aggressively marketed by management consultants. Additionally, American business leaders saw them as a low-risk method for increasing worker involvement without changing the organization. Finally, QC usage also became a fad. Many managers jumped on the bandwagon simply because the technique symbolized modern management.

QC proponents argue that their technique is much more than a fad, that it is part of a trend that is permanently changing managerial assumptions and practices in the United States. Donald Dewar, president of Quality Circle Institute, the largest QC consulting firm in the United States, insists, "You don't have quality control without quality circles. Of all the participative management techniques, this is the first time it went below supervisory levels and down to the people who actually do the work. Many managers have been surprised that people could learn the problem-solving techniques. It is changing not only the quality of work, but also how managers regard their people."

Many American management scholars and practitioners, including executives who refuse to use QC's in their organizations, view these claims with caution. They contend that the technique is a poor fit with American management styles. Tai K. Oh, a management professor at California State University at Fullerton and a consultant to businesses in the United States on Japanese management techniques, says that QC programs have failed in more than 60 percent of the American organizations in which they have been tried.

At the core of these failures are the very reasons that QC programs are so popular in this country: their availability as easy-to-implement packages and the perception by many managers that the technique is a simple way to solve a firm's personnel problems. Oh likens the effects of QC's to those of aspirin or Valium: They treat symptoms and provide some immediate relief but don't touch the underlying issues of management-employee tensions, lack of respect and underutilization of workers that cause the problems in the first place.

Three recent studies provide some light to supplement the heat of the debate over the value of QC's. In one of them, psychologists Philip H. Mirvis and James F. Grady, sociologist Edward J. Hackett and I examined the claims that QC's improve participants' quality of work life and job performance. Specifically, we studied whether QC's actually increase decision-making opportunities, change employees' attitudes toward their work by convincing them that their jobs are challenging and satisfy their needs for growth. We also examined whether participating in a QC program improves productivity and lessens absenteeism.

We conducted our study in the manufacturing department of a decentralized manufacturing firm that was about to start a QC program. About half of the machine operators eligible for the program chose to participate. Working independently of the program, we developed an employee-attitude survey and administered it twice to all the machine operators, immediately before the program started and 20 months later. We also collected raw data directly from company records to assess any changes in employee behavior during the QC program. We used these data to compare rates of productivity and attendance for a 30-month period, starting six months before the QC program began.

Looking first at employee attitudes, we found that participation in the QC had a strong impact only in work-life areas directly related to QC activity—decision-making opportunities, group communication, and opportunities and skills needed for advancement. Participation did not, however, contrary to the usual claims of QC proponents, affect worker attitudes toward communication through the entire organization, job challenge, personal responsibility for getting work done and overall job satisfaction.

We also found, unexpectedly, that being in a QC did not make machine operators more satisfied with any facets of their work situation, even those directly related to their QC work. Their ratings of the quality of their work life didn't change during the 30-month period. I suspect that this was due to factors separate from the QC program. During the 20 months between the two surveys, the division we studied was merged with a much larger division and the local economy experienced a severe recession. Rumors abounded about cutbacks and layoffs; these, combined with the poor economic news, could well have depressed the operators' outlook on work and life in general.

This interpretation is strengthened by the fact that the work satisfaction of machine operators who did not participate in the QC program decreased during the same 20-month period. Perhaps taking part in QC's provided satisfaction and social support that lessened some of the stress and negative feelings produced by the rumors and the bad economic news.

Unlike the mixed nature of these attitudinal findings, our analysis of the behavioral data is quite positive: Participation in QC's raised machine operators' productivity and reduced absenteeism. Before the program started, the participants and nonparticipants had similar records of productivity, percentage of paid hours actually spent on production, quality, efficiency and monthly attendance. Over the course of the QC program, participants showed steady increases in each of these areas while nonparticipants stayed about the same.

In another study, a professor of organizational behavior, James W. Dean Jr. of Pennsylvania State University, examined why employees chose to join QC programs in the electronic equipment division of a large manufacturing corporation and how their participation affected job satisfaction. He interviewed and administered questionnaires to members of 15 QC's in both the engineering and assembly functions and to a group of similar employees who were not QC members. The QC program had been in place for two years when he did his research.

Dean found several factors that distinguish QC participants from nonparticipants. Those who join QC's want greater involvement at work and believe that a QC will address this need. They also believe that the QC process can really change things by improving their jobs and the overall organization. Factors such as age, tenure and wanting a break from work did not affect the decision to participate.

Dean concluded that employees who join a QC see it as a way to accomplish real change at work and usually choose problems that are likely to be successfully solved and implemented. Workers are satisfied by the experience if they see a direct link between QC activities and organizational change and if their QC has capable and productive people.

Commenting on this last point, Dean suggests that QC successes, both in terms of employee satisfaction and effective problem solving, can be increased through appropriate training. In his observations of QC programs, however, he finds that "training is largely pro forma in most applications and not taken very seriously. Most people who go through training are bored to death because much of what is covered does not relate to their personal work situation. Training should be differentiated for engineers, blue-collar or clerical workers and others."

Dean attributes the training problem to the fact that most QC's use the very detailed problem-solving model originally adopted by Lockheed in the early 1970s. Unfortunately, as Dean sees it, most problems addressed by QC's do not require that approach. "It is like using a tank to kill a fly," he says.

In a third study, a team from the University of Southern California (USC) Center for Effective Organizations focused on the factors that influence QC success. Organizational behaviorist Susan A. Mohrman and psychologists Edward E. Lawler III and Gerald E. Ledford Jr. studied QC's in nine separate units of a large conglomerate, using interviews, questionnaires and company data such as internal reports, newsletters and training material. The nine units varied greatly in the amount of training provided, membership criteria and use of rewards.

The researchers found that most QC's that succeed in changing the organization share several characteristics. They include sufficient training of members and direct efforts to improve group process dynamics; access to useful information inside and outside the organization; accurate record-keeping, including the establishment of measurable goals for the QC; and creation of QC's from intact work teams. However, while such QC's usually prompt some technical changes in an organization, the researchers found little evidence that they change corporate culture or improve individual work satisfaction and productivity.

The USC team also found reason to doubt the extent of the financial savings claimed for QC's. Mohrman cautions that while changes proposed by QC's often seem likely to save a great deal of money, "In many cases, the change is not implemented well, is not implemented at all, or is implemented and just does not save the money projected."

This is largely because the people who propose the changes are usually not the ones who actually implement them. The workers who do may resist the change because they do not understand the need for it or because they give priority to their regular work responsibilities. Moreover, since recognition and rewards are given only to people who develop the ideas, those who must implement them have little incentive to do so.

The USC team identified several other problems that limit QC success. One is resistance by middle-level managers, who have no direct involvement until they are called upon to approve or implement a QC suggestion. Many are uncomfortable with getting ideas from subordinates and either reject them out of hand or respond slowly and unenthusiastically.

Either response may discourage QC participants; they may feel that the program is a waste of time or a management trick and eventually stop meeting. Other QC's become victims of their own success. Having successfully dealt with key issues, they have no major problems left to solve and disband. Sometimes, as QC's become less productive, the company scales down the resources provided for their activities. Participants become less enthusiastic, begin to meet less often and finally stop completely.

Despite these problems, Mohrman, Lawler and Ledford conclude that QC's can be valuable under the right conditions. They recommend three effective ways to use them. First, QC's may operate as group suggestion programs to improve communications and raise employee consciousness about quality and productivity. Second, QC's may be used for special projects when organizations must deal with temporary or critical issues, such as introducing a new technology, retooling for a new product line or solving a major quality problem. Third, QC's may help in making the transition toward more participative management systems. This can take place when a company, recognizing limitations of the QC approach, moves on to make the basic managerial and organizational changes needed to create a more participative organization.

Taken together, the three studies verify that QC's may have a positive impact on organizations and employees. But they do not support the larger claims of some PC proponents that the technique routinely improves employee productivity, morale and growth as well as overall organizational effectiveness. QC's can improve employee productivity and have a limited impact on morale and work satisfaction but only when programs are backed by sufficient training and genuine management commitment to them.

As Mohrman points out, the QC technique "does not take the huge financial commitment of some other programs and does rally people, but it clearly is not the stable long-term organizational change that some people make it out to be. The technique does not go far enough, it is not strong enough to promote real organizational change. For that, you need to go further and rethink the design of jobs, decision making processes, and organizational structures."

Clearly, much more research is needed to evaluate QC's accurately. We should compare, for example, how well they work in various kinds of organizations and why they work better in some than in others. In Japan, a government-sponsored association oversees QC activity. A similar industry-sponsored organization in the United States could support the necessary studies and at the same time promote a national commitment to quality and to participative management.

Bill Courtwright, a corporate manager of QC's for Hughes Aircraft, has no doubts about why QC's have grown so rapidly: "It is a spiritual reason—people want to work together. They are more effective as a team. It increases their knowledge. It increases their dignity. If handled properly, with a serious commitment on the part of management, then quality circles can do nothing but succeed."

However, as the many failed QC programs show, that's an awfully big "if." Implementing some of the suggestions made by the researchers mentioned in this article, as changed and supplemented by future research, could help QC's remove the "fad" label and more fully live up to the claims made by their advocates. They might then clearly improve the design and management of organizations, help make American companies more competitive and enhance the quality of their employees' work life.

Stephen G. Harkins
Jeffrey M. Jackson

# The Role of Evaluation in Eliminating Social Loafing

Harkins and Jackson's research concerns social loafing—a finding that on many tasks people will put out less effort when working with others than they do when alone. It has been argued that this occurs in group efforts because people will loaf when their individual contributions cannot be identified and they cannot receive blame or praise for their efforts. Harkins and Jackson find that to overcome social loafing the individual's output must be identifiable, but in addition group members must also feel that their output can be evaluated against those of their fellow group members.

For a variety of tasks it has been found that participants when working alone put out greater effort than when working with others, an effect that has been termed "social loafing" (Latané, Williams, & Harkins, 1979). This effect has been demonstrated on tasks requiring physical effort (e.g., rope-pulling: Ingham, Levinger, Graves, & Peckham, 1974; shouting: Latané et al., 1979; pumping air: Kerr & Bruun, 1981) and cognitive effort (evaluating essays: Petty, Harkins, & Williams, 1980; brainstorming and vigilance: Harkins & Petty, 1982) by females as well as males (Harkins, Latané, & Williams, 1980). Using Steiner's (1972) typology, some of these tasks have been maximizing (requiring the participant to produce as much as possible: e.g., rope-pulling, pumping air), whereas others have been optimizing (requiring the participant to achieve some criterion performance: e.g., evaluating essays, vigilance); but on the "group" trials of all of these tasks, individual outputs have been pooled to arrive at a group product.

Williams, Harkins, and Latané (1981) have suggested that loafing arises at least in part from the fact that when the participants' outputs are pooled, individual outputs are lost in the crowd, submerged in the total, and are separately unrecoverable by the experimenter. Because participants can receive neither credit nor blame for their individual performances, they loaf. Williams et al. (1981) tested this notion in two experiments in which shouting was used as the effortful activity. In Experiment I, participants performed alone and together and, consistent with previous research (Latané et al., 1979), produced less noise when performing together than when performing alone. However, in phase two of the experiment, after having donned individual microphones, which they were told allowed monitoring of individual outputs even when they performed in groups, participants produce as much noise in groups as when alone. Experiment I was replicated in a second experiment in which a between-groups design was used. In a condition that replicated previous loafing experiments, participants performed alone and together, and were thus identifiable only when they performed alone (social-loafing replication). In a second condition, participants performed alone and together but wore individual microphones and were identifiable at all times, replicating phase two of Experiment I (always identifiable). Finally in a new condition, participants performed alone and together, but were told that interest centered on the group totals and so individual performances would be summed and compared to their group performances (never identifiable). As in phase one of Experiment I, in the social-loafing replication in which participants were identifiable only when alone, they put out greater effort when shouting alone than when shouting together. When always identifiable, participants put out as much effort when shouting together as when alone, replicating phase two of Experiment I. Finally when never identifiable, participants put out as little effort when shouting alone as when shouting together.

The results of these studies are consistent with the notion that identifiability of individual effort is a critical factor in social loafing. When individual outputs were always identifiable, people exerted consistently high levels of effort; and when outputs were never identifiable, they exerted consistently low levels. However, in this research, what has been termed identifiability has actually involved more than identifiability alone. Participants in these experiments have all worked on the same tasks; thus when their performances were identifiable, they could also be directly compared to the performances of the other participants. Identifiability alone may not be sufficient to eliminate loafing. Motivation may come from the participant's knowledge that his or her performance can be compared to the performances of other participants. The opportunity for comparison may lead the participants to believe that their performance can be evaluated, and this potential for evaluation may motivate performance. In the present research, we attempted to test this notion by manipulating identifiability and evaluation potential separately to allow an assessment of their independent effects.

We used a brainstorming task in which groups of four participants were asked to generate as many uses as they could for an object. These uses were written on slips of paper that were deposited in a box that was either divided into four compartments so that each participant's uses were collected separately (individually identifiable) or not divided so that each participant's uses were combined with those of the other group members (pooled). Crossed with this identifiability manipulation was a manipulation of evaluation potential.

Participants were told that we were interested in the number of uses that could be generated for a range of objects. Some of these objects were difficult to generate uses for and some were easy, and as a result their outputs could be compared only to the outputs of participants who had the same object. By then telling participants that they had the same object as or different objects from the others we were able to manipulate evaluation potential. Of course, everyone was actually generating uses for the same object.

We hypothesized that social loafing would be eliminated only when individual outputs were identifiable and could be compared because only then could evaluation take place. When outputs were pooled or were identifiable but not comparable, evaluation was not possible, which was expected to lead to loafing.

## METHOD

### Participants

One hundred sixty male and female participants took part in this research as a means of fulfilling an introductory psychology course requirement. The participants were run in groups of four that were randomly assigned to one of four conditions comprising a 2 (Individually Identifiable outputs vs. Pooled outputs) × 2 (Comparability vs. No Comparability) factorial.

### Procedure

When the participants arrived, they were seated at a table with partitions that prevented them from seeing one another and were informed that we were studying the performance of individuals and groups on a task called brainstorming. They would be given the name of an object and their task would be to generate as many uses as they could for this object.

Participants in the identifiable conditions read the following: "We are interested in the number of uses generated for this (these) object(s) by each of you. So, at the end of the experimental session, we will count the number of uses generated by each of you individually and determine how many you generated." If the group was in the pooled condition, members read these instructions: "We are interested in the total number of uses generated for this (these) object(s) by your group. So, at the end of the experimental session we will count the total number of uses generated by your group and determine how many the four of you generated." All then read that they should not be concerned about the quality of their uses, but should make sure that each use was a possible use for the object.

Comparability was manipulated by informing participants that the object for which they would be generating uses was the same as or different from the object the others were to be given. All participants were told that we were interested in the number of uses that could be generated for a range of objects and that because some of these objects were easy and some were difficult to generate uses for, the number of uses they generated was comparable only to the number generated by others working on the same object.

In the comparability condition, after having read the previous instructions, the participants read that each of the members of their group would be presented with this particular object and they were to generate as many uses for this object as they could. In the no comparability condition the participants read that each of the members of their group would be presented with a different object and they were to generate as many uses for this object as they could.

After having read their respective instructions, participants selected an envelope that contained the name of their particular object and were given a number of slips of paper on which they were to write their uses. The envelopes were presented in a manner consistent with the participants' previous instructions. Thus if the participants were in the comparability condition, each participant selected one of a number of envelopes after having been told that each envelope contained a different object. All participants actually generated uses for the same object, a knife.

After the participants selected their envelopes, they were asked to remove their object slips, memorize their object name, fold their object slips three times, and slide them down the tubes in front of them, which extended into a box. The top of the box was then removed, and the participants were shown either that the box was divided into four compartments, allowing us to determine exactly how many uses each of them individually generated (individually identifiable), or that there were no dividers, allowing us to determine only how many total uses the group generated (pooled).

The participants were told to write one use per slip, to fold it, and to slide it down the tube. They were then asked to don headsets, to begin writing when the music started, and to continue until they were stopped. The music (Beethoven's Fifth Symphony) served as a masking noise so that participants could not hear the others sliding their uses down the tubes. The participants were given 12 minutes to list uses, a length of time that previous research suggested would be more than ample (Harkins & Petty, 1982), and were then asked to respond to a set of questions on anchored 11-point scales. Among these measures were manipulation checks for identifiability (To what extent do you believe the experimenter could tell exactly how many uses you individually generated on this task?) and comparability (To what extent do you feel that your performance can be directly compared to that of the other participants who are present now?) Also included were measures of how much effort the participants thought they expended on the task, how unusual they thought their uses were, how much pressure to perform there was, how competitive they felt, and to what extent they felt that their uses represented a unique contribution unlikely to be duplicated by other participants. After completing the questionnaire, participants were debriefed and dismissed.

Unknown to the subjects, each of the envelopes contained exactly 100 slips of paper. By counting the number of slips left by each person, we arrived at the number of uses generated by each person even in the pooled conditions.

## RESULTS

### Manipulation Checks

Participants whose uses were pooled reported that the experimenter was less able to determine exactly how well they performed, M = 6.2, than participants whose uses were individually identifiable, M = 7.6. Participants in the comparability condition felt that their performances were more comparable to those of the others in their group, M = 6.7, than participants in the no comparability condition who had been told that each person in their group had been given a different object, M = 5.9.

### Uses

Analysis of the uses data revealed that consistent with previous research on social loafing, participants whose uses were individually identifiable generated more uses, M = 22.3, than those whose uses were pooled, M = 19.6. In addition, there was a main effect for comparability such that participants for whom there was comparability generated more uses, M = 22.4, than those whose uses were not comparable, M = 19.5.

However, these main effects must be viewed in light of the significant Identifiability × Comparability interaction. When the participants' outputs were identifiable and comparable to those of the others in their group, they produced more uses, M = 24.9, than were produced in any of the other three conditions. In the pooled/comparability condition, participants generated no more uses, M = 19.8, than participants in the pooled/no comparability condition, M = 19.3. When individual outputs were identifiable, but not directly comparable to the outputs of the others in their group, the participants generated no mores uses, M = 19.7, than participants in the pooled conditions.

## DISCUSSION

Williams et al. (1981) suggested that social loafing arises from the fact that when participants "work together," individual outputs are not identifiable, and because participants can receive neither credit nor blame for their performances, they loaf. In the current research we argued that more than identifiability alone may be required to eliminate loafing. In the Williams et al. (1981) research when the participants' individual outputs could be monitored, not only were their outputs identifiable, but these outputs could be monitored, not only were their outputs identifiable, but these outputs could be compared to those of the other performers. This potential for evaluation, which was absent when outputs were pooled, could motivate performance. To test this notion we orthogonally manipulated identifiability and comparability. Replicating previous research using this brainstorming task (Harkins & Petty, 1982), we found that when outputs were identifiable participants generated more uses than when their outputs were pooled. However, this difference emerged *only* when participants believed that their outputs could be compared to their co-workers' performances. When participants believed that their individual performances were not comparable and thus could not be evaluated, there was no difference in the number of uses generated by participants whose outputs were identifiable and those whose outputs were pooled.

Superficially, it may appear that these findings and results from other loafing research are at variance with what one might expect on the basis of social facilitation research. After all, "social psychological theory holds that, at least for simple well-learned tasks involving dominant responses, the presence of others, whether as coactors or spectators, should facilitate performance (Latané et al., 1979, p. 823)." Pulling ropes, shouting, clapping, and generating uses for an ordinary object are all easily accomplished, but using these tasks loafing researchers have found that people working individually put out more, not less, effort than people working together. However, we would like to argue that the findings from loafing and facilitation are consistent.

Two explanations, mere presence (Zajonc, 1980) and learned drive (Cottrell, 1972), have been used most often to account for facilitation effects. Mere presence cannot account for loafing effects given that—in all published loafing studies save one (Kerr & Bruun, 1981)—the number of people present for both individual and group trials has actually been held *constant*. However, it appears that learned drive can. Cottrell (1972) has suggested that the presence of others is often associated with evaluation and/or competition and it is this association that leads to increased drive and enhanced performance on simple tasks. In facilitation research, when participants work together (coact), their outputs can be evaluated (compared) and they work harder than participants working alone. In social loafing research, when participants work together, their outputs are pooled and evaluation is not possible, leading to loafing. In both cases, evaluation potential is central. In social facilitation, working together enhances evaluation potential; in social loafing, working together reduces it.

This analysis suggests that evaluation potential plays a central role in both facilitation and loafing effects, but what is necessary for evaluation to take place? We would suggest that two pieces of information must be known: the participant's individual output and a standard against which this output can be compared. The necessity for a standard can be satisfied in a number of ways. For example, in the present research the standard of comparison was the number of uses generated by the other participants. When this standard was not available either because each person in the group had a different object or because outputs were pooled, performance dropped. Norms generated from the performances of previous participants could also provide a standard. If the task were optimizing (requiring some criterion performance,

Steiner, 1972) rather than maximizing (requiring as much as effort as possible), the criterion could serve as the standard. Whatever the standard, we would argue that the standard—as well as the participant's output—must be known for evaluation to be possible, but known by whom?

In loafing research the role of the experimenter as evaluator has been emphasized. For example, Harkins et al. (1980) write: "The results (social loafing) are easily explained by a minimizing strategy where participants are motivated to work only as hard as necessary to gain credit for a good performance or to avoid blame for a bad one. Whenever the experimenter was unable to monitor individual outputs directly, performers sloughed off" (p. 464). However, the experimenter is only one of three potential sources of evaluation in loafing research. When outputs are pooled, participants may also feel that they cannot evaluate their own output, nor can their output be evaluated by their fellow participants. In our experiment, when individual outputs were identifiable and comparable within a group, each of these sources could evaluate an individual's performance. Social facilitation researchers have employed each of these sources in their explanations of coaction effects (e.g., experimenter evaluation: Seta, Paulus, & Schkade, 1976; coactor evaluation: Klinger, 1969; self-evaluation: Sanders, Baron, & Moore, 1978). However, although the potential for evaluation by each of these sources could motivate performance, clear evidence of their independent contributions is lacking.

The same is true of the evaluation conditions of loafing research. In some loafing research the fact that everyone would see scores after the performance was mentioned (e.g., Ingham et al., 1974; Latané et al., 1979), whereas in other research (e.g., Harkins, et al., 1980; Kerr & Bruun, 1981; Harkins & Petty, 1982), nothing was said about to whom performance scores would be made available. By manipulating to whom information about the individual outputs and standard is made available, it will be possible to determine how each of these sources of evaluation functions independently and in concert to motivate performance in group performance settings.

## References

Cottrell, N. (1972). Social facilitation. In C. McClintock (Ed.), *Experimental social psychology*. New York: Holt, Rinehart & Winston.

Harkins, S., Latané, B., & Williams, K. (1980). Social loafing: Allocating effort or taking it easy? *Journal of Experimental Social Psychology, 16*, 457–465.

Harkins, S., & Petty, R. (1982). Effects of task difficulty and task uniqueness on social loafing. *Journal of Personality and Social Psychology, 43*, 1214–1229.

Ingham, A., Levinger, G., Graves, J., & Peckham, V. (1974). The Ringelmann effect: Studies of group size and group performance. *Journal of Experimental Social Psychology, 10*, 371–384.

Kerr, N., & Bruun, S. (1981). Ringelmann revisited: Alternative explanations for the social loafing effect. *Personality and Social Psychology Bulletin, 7*, 224–231.

Kirk, R. (1982). *Experimental design*. Belmont, CA: Wadsworth.

Klinger, E. (1969). Feedback effects and social facilitation of vigilance performance: Mere coaction versus potential evaluation. *Psychonomic Science, 14,* 161–162.

Latané, B., Williams, K., & Harkins, S. (1979). Many hands make light the work: The causes and consequences of social loafing. *Journal of Personality and Social Psychology, 37,* 823–832.

Petty, R., Harkins, S., & Williams, K. (1980). The effects of group diffusion of cognitive effort on attitudes: An information-processing view. *Journal of Personality and Social Psychology, 38,* 81–92.

Sanders, G., Baron, R., & Moore, D. (1978). Distraction and social comparison as mediators of social facilitation effects. *Journal of Experimental Social Psychology, 14,* 291–303.

Seta, J., Paulus, P., & Schkade, J. (1976). Effects of group size and proximity under cooperative and competitive conditions. *Journal of Personality and Social Psychology, 34,* 47–53.

Steiner, I. (1972). *Group process and productivity.* New York: Academic Press.

Williams, K., Harkins, S., & Latané, B. (1981). Identifiability as a deterrent to social loafing: Two cheering experiments. *Journal of Personality and Social Psychology, 40,* 303–311.

Zajonc, R. (1980). Compresence. In P. Paulus (Ed.), *Psychology of group influence.* Hillsdale, NJ: Lawrence Erlbaum.

Gregory Moorhead
Richard Ference
Chris P. Neck

# Group Decision Fiascoes Continue: Space Shuttle Challenger and a Revised Groupthink Framework

In this article, the authors review the events surrounding the tragic decision to launch the space shuttle Challenger. Moorhead and his colleagues assert that the decision-making process demonstrates *groupthink*, a phenomenon wherein cohesive groups become so concerned with their own process that they lose sight of the true requirements of their task. The authors review the events in light of this concept, suggesting that the groupthink concept needs to be expanded to consider time pressures, which were surely present in the Challenger situation, as well as the kind of leadership patterns that exist in a group.

In 1972, a new dimension was added to our understanding of group decision making with the proposal of the groupthink hypothesis by Janis (1972). Janis coined the term "groupthink" to refer to "a mode of thinking that people engage in when they are deeply involved in a cohesive in-group, when the members' striving for unanimity override their motivation to realistically appraise alternative courses of action" (Janis, 1972, p. 8). The hypothesis was supported by his hindsight analysis of several political-military fiascoes and successes that are differentiated by the occurrence or non-occurrence of antecedent conditions, groupthink symptoms, and decision making defects.

In a subsequent volume, Janis further explicates the theory and adds an analysis of the Watergate transcripts and various published memoirs and accounts of principals involved, concluding that the Watergate cover-up decision also was a result of groupthink (Janis, 1983). Both volumes propose prescriptions for preventing the occurrence of groupthink, many of which have appeared in popular press, in books on executive decision making, and in management textbooks. Multiple advocacy decision-making procedures have been adopted at the executive levels in many organizations, including the executive branch of the government. One would think that by 1986, 13 years after the publication of a popular book, that its prescriptions might be well ingrained in our management and decision-making styles. Unfortunately, it has not happened.

On January 28, 1986, the space shuttle Challenger was launched from Kennedy Space Center. The temperature that morning was in the mid-20's, well below the previous low temperatures at which the shuttle engines had been tested. Seventy-three seconds after launch, the Challenger exploded, killing all seven astronauts aboard, and becoming the worst disaster in space flight history. The catastrophe shocked the nation, crippled the American space program, and is destined to be remembered as the most tragic national event since the assassination of John F. Kennedy in 1963.

The Presidential Commission that investigated the accident pointed to a flawed decision-making process as a primary contributory cause. The decision was made the night before the launch in the Level I Flight Readiness Review meeting. Due to the work of the Presidential Commission, information concerning that meeting is available for analysis as a group decision possibly susceptible to groupthink.

In this paper, we report the results of our analysis of the Level I Flight Readiness Review meeting as a decision-making situation that displays evidence of groupthink. We review the antecedent conditions, the groupthink symptoms, and the possible decision-making defects, as suggested by Janis (1983). In addition, we take the next and more important step by going beyond the development of another example of groupthink to make recommendations for renewed inquiry into group decision-making processes.

## THEORY AND EVIDENCE

The meeting(s) took place throughout the day and evening from 12:36 pm (EST), January 27, 1986 following the decision to not launch the Challenger due to high crosswinds at the launch site. Discussions continued through about 12:00 midnight (EST) via teleconferencing and Telefax systems connecting the Kennedy Space Center in Florida, Morton Thiokol (MTI) in Utah, Johnson Space Center in Houston, and the Marshall Space Flight Center. The Level I Flight Readiness Review is the highest level of review prior to launch. It comprises the highest level of management at the three space centers and at MTI, the private supplier of the solid rocket booster engines.

To briefly state the situation, the MTI engineers recommended not to launch if temperatures of the O-ring seals on the rocket were below 53 degrees Fahrenheit, which was the lowest temperature of any previous flight. Laurence B. Mulloy, manager of the Solid Rocket Booster Project at Marshall Space Flight Center, states:

The bottom line of that, though, initially was that Thiokol engineering, Bob Lund, who is the Vice President and Director and Engineering, who is here today, recommended that 51-L [the Challenger] not be launched if the O-ring temperatures predicted at launch time would be lower than any previous launch, and that was 53 degrees. (*Report of the Presidential Commission on the Space Shuttle Accident*, 1986, p. 91–92).

This recommendation was made at 8:45 pm, January 27, 1986 (*Report of the Presidential Commission on the Space Shuttle Accident*, 1986). Through the ensuing discussions the decision to launch was made.

### Antecedent Conditions

The three primary antecedent conditions for the development of groupthink are: a highly cohesive group, leader preference for a certain decision, and insulation of the group from qualified outside opinions. These conditions existed in this situation.

*Cohesive Group.* The people who made the decision to launch had worked together for many years. They were familiar with each other and had grown through the ranks of the space program. A high degree of *esprit de corps* existed between the members.

*Leader Preference.* Two top level managers actively promoted their pro-launch opinions in the face of opposition. The commission report states that several managers at space centers and MTI pushed for launch, regardless of the low temperatures.

*Insulation from Experts.* MTI engineers made their recommendations relatively early in the evening. The top level decision-making group knew of their objections but did not meet with them directly to review their data and concerns. As Roger Boisjoly, a Thiokol engineer, states in his remarks to the Presidential Commission:

and the bottom line was that the engineering people would not recommend a launch below 53 degrees Fahrenheit. . . . From this point on, management formulated the points to base their decision on. There was never one comment in favor, as I have said, of launching by any engineer or other nonmanagement person. . . . I was not even asked to participate in giving any input to the final decision charts (*Report of the Presidential Commission on the Space Shuttle Accident*, 1986, p. 91–92).

This testimonial indicates that the top decision-making team was insulated from the engineers who possessed the expertise regarding the functioning of the equipment.

### Groupthink Symptoms

Janis identified eight symptoms of groupthink. They are presented here along with evidence from the *Report of the Presidential Commission on the Space Shuttle Accident* (1986).

*Invulnerability.* When groupthink occurs, most or all of the members of the decision-making group have an illusion of invulnerability that reassures them in the face of obvious dangers. This illusion leads the group to become overly optimistic and willing to take extraordinary risks. It may also cause them to ignore clear warnings of danger.

The solid rocket joint problem that destroyed Challenger was discussed often at flight readiness review meetings prior to flight. However, Commission member Richard Feynman concluded from the testimony that a mentality of overconfidence existed due to the extraordinary record of success of space flights. Every time we send one up it is successful. Involved members may seem to think that on the next one we can lower our standards or take more risks because it always works (*Time*, 1986).

The invulnerability illusion may have built up over time as a result of NASA's own spectacular history. NASA had not lost an astronaut since 1967 when a flash fire in the capsule of Apollo 1 killed three. Since that time NASA had a string of 55 successful missions. They had put a man on the moon, built and launched Skylab and the shuttle, and retrieved defective satellites from orbit. In the minds of most Americans and apparently their own, they could do no wrong.

*Rationalization.* Victims of groupthink collectively construct rationalizations that discount warnings and other forms of negative feedback. If these signals were taken seriously when presented, the group members would be forced to reconsider their assumptions each time they re-commit themselves to their past decisions.

In the Level I flight readiness meeting when the Challenger was given final launch approval, MTI engineers presented evidence that the joint would fail. Their argument was based on the fact that in the coldest previous launch (air temperature 30 degrees) the joint in question experienced serious erosion and that no data existed as to how the joint would perform at colder temperatures. Flight center officials put forth numerous technical rationalizations faulting MTI's analysis. One of these rationalizations was that the engineer's data were inconclusive. As Mr. Boisjoly emphasized to the Commission:

> I was asked, yes, at that point in time I was asked to quantify my concerns, and I said I couldn't. I couldn't quantify it. I had no data to quantify it, but I did say I knew that it was away from goodness in the current data base. Someone on the net commented that we had soot blow-by on SRM-22 [Flight 61-A, October, 1985] which was launched at 75 degrees. I don't remember who made the comment, but that is where the first comment

came in about the disparity between my conclusion and the observed data because SRM-22 [Flight 61-A, October 1985] had blow-by at essentially a room temperature launch. I then said that SRM-15 [Flight 51-C, January, 1985] had much more blow-by indication and that it was indeed telling us that lower temperature was a factor. I was asked again for data to support my claim, and I said I have none other than what is being presented (*Report of the Presidential Commission on the Space Shuttle Accident*, 1986, p. 89).

Discussions became twisted (compared to previous meetings) and no one detected it. Under normal conditions, MTI would have to prove the shuttle boosters readiness for launch, instead they found themselves being forced to prove that the boosters were unsafe. Boisjoly's testimony supports this description of the discussion:

This was a meeting where the determination was to launch, and it was up to us to prove beyond a shadow of a doubt that it was not safe to do so. This is in total reverse to what the position usually is in a preflight conversation or a flight readiness review. It is usually exactly the opposite of that. (*Report of the Presidential Commission on the Space Shuttle Accident*, 1986, p. 93).

*Morality.* Group members often believe, without question, in the inherent morality of their position. They tend to ignore the ethical or moral consequences of their decision.

In the Challenger case, this point was raised by a very high level MTI manager, Allan J. McDonald, who tried to stop the launch and said that he would not want to have to defend the decision to launch. He stated to the Commission:

I made the statement that if we're wrong and something goes wrong on this flight, I wouldn't want to have to be the person to stand up in front of board in inquiry and say that I went ahead and told them to go ahead and fly this thing outside what the motor was qualified to. (*Report of the Presidential Commission on the Space Shuttle Accident*, 1986, p. 95).

Some members did not hear this statement because it occurred during a break. Three top officials who did hear it ignored it.

*Stereotyped Views of Others.* Victims of groupthink often have a stereotyped view of the opposition of anyone with a competing opinion. They feel that the opposition is too stupid or too weak to understand or deal effectively with the problem.

Two of the top three NASA officials responsible for the launch displayed this attitude. They felt that they completely understood the nature of the joint problem and never seriously considered the objections raised by the MTI engineers. In fact they denigrated and badgered the opposition and their information and opinions.

*Pressure on Dissent.* Group members often apply direct pressure to anyone who questions the validity of these arguments supporting a decision or position favored by the majority. These same two officials pressured MTI to change its position after MTI originally recommended that the launch not take place. These two officials pressured MTI personnel to prove that it was not safe to launch, rather than to prove the opposite. As mentioned earlier, this was a total reversal of normal preflight procedures. It was this pressure that top MTI management was responding to when they overruled their engineering staff and recommended launch. As the Commission report states:

> At approximately 11 p.m. Eastern Standard Time, the Thiokol/NASA teleconference resumed, the Thiokol management stating that they had reassessed the problem, that the temperature effects were a concern, but that the data was admittedly inconclusive (p. 96).

This seems to indicate the NASA's pressure on these Thiokol officials forced them to change their recommendation from delay to execution of the launch.

*Self-Censorship.* Group members tend to censor themselves when they have opinions or ideas that deviate from the apparent group consensus. Janis feels that this reflects each member's inclination to minimize to himself or herself the importance of his or her own doubts and counter-arguments.

The most obvious evidence of self-censorship occurred when a vice president of MTI, who had previously presented information against launch, bowed to pressure from NASA and accepted their rationalizations for launch. He then wrote these up and presented them to NASA as the reasons that MTI had changed its recommendation to launch.

*Illusion of Unanimity.* Group members falling victim to groupthink share an illusion of unanimity concerning judgments made by members speaking in favor of the majority view. This symptom is caused in part by the preceding one and is aided by the false assumption that any participant who remains silent is in agreement with the majority opinion. The group leader and other members support each other by playing up points of convergence in their thinking at the expense of fully exploring points of divergence that might reveal unsettling problems.

No participant from NASA ever openly agreed with or even took sides with MTI in the discussion. The silence from NASA was probably amplified by the fact that the meeting was a teleconference linking the participants at three different locations. Obviously, body language which might have been evidenced by dissenters was not visible to others who might also have held a dissenting opinion. Thus, silence meant agreement.

*Mindguarding.* Certain group members assume the role of guarding the minds of others in the group. They attempt to shield the group from adverse information that might destroy the majority view of the facts regarding the appropriateness of the decision.

The top management at Marshall knew that the rocket casings had been ordered redesigned to correct a flaw 5 months previous to this launch. This information and other technical details concerning the history of the joint problem was withheld at the meeting.

## Decision-Making Defects

The result of the antecedent conditions and the symptoms of groupthink is a defective decision-making process. Janis discusses several defects in decision making that can result.

*Few Alternatives.* The group considers only a few alternatives, often only two. No initial survey of all possible alternatives occurs. The Flight Readiness Review team had a launch/no-launch decision to make. These were the only two alternatives considered. Other possible alternatives might have been to delay the launch for further testing, or to delay until the temperatures reached an appropriate level.

*No Re-Examination of Alternatives.* The group fails to re-examine alternatives that may have been initially discarded based on early unfavorable information. Top NASA officials spent time and effort defending and strengthening their position, rather than examining the MTI position.

*Rejecting Expert Opinions.* Members make little or no attempt to seek outside experts opinions. NASA did not seek out other experts who might have some expertise in this area. They assumed that they had all the information.

*Rejecting Negative Information.* Members tend to focus on supportive information and ignore any data or information that might cast a negative light on their preferred alternative. MTI representatives repeatedly tried to point out errors in the rationale the NASA officials were using to justify the launch. Even after the decision was made, the argument continued until a NASA official told the MTI representative that it was no longer his concern.

*No Contingency Plans.* Members spend little time discussing the possible consequences of the decision and, therefore, fail to develop contingency plans. There is no documented evidence in the Rogers Commission Report of any discussion of the possible consequences of an incorrect decision.

*Summary of the Evidence*

The major categories and key elements of the groupthink hypothesis have been presented (albeit somewhat briefly) along with evidence from the discussions prior to the launching of the Challenger, as reported in the President's Commission to investigate the accident. The antecedent conditions were present in the decision-making group, even though the group was in several physical locations. The leaders had a preferred solution and engaged in behaviors designed to promote it rather than critically appraise alternatives. These behaviors were evidence of most of the symptoms leading to a defective decision-making process.

## DISCUSSION

This situation provides another example of decision making in which the group fell victim to the groupthink syndrome, as have so many previous groups. It illustrates the situation characteristics, the symptoms of group think, and decision-making defects as described by Janis. This situation, however, also illustrates several other aspects of situations that are critical to the development of groupthink that need to be included in a revised formulation of the groupthink model. First, the element of time in influencing the development of groupthink has not received adequate attention. In the decision to launch the space shuttle Challenger, time was a crucial part of the decision-making process. The launch had been delayed once, and the window for another launch was fast closing. The leaders of the decision team were concerned about public and congressional perceptions of the entire space shuttle program and its continued funding and may have felt that further delays of the launch could seriously impact future funding. With the space window fast closing, the decision team was faced with a launch now or seriously damage the program decision. One top level manager's response to Thiokol's initial recommendation to postpone the launch indicates the presence of time pressure:

> With this LCC (Launch Commit Criteria), i.e., do not launch with a temperature greater [sic] than 53 degrees, we may not be able to launch until next April. We need to consider this carefully before we jump to any conclusions. *(Report of the Presidential Commission on the Space Shuttle Accident,* 1986, p. 96).

Time pressure could have played a role in the group choosing to agree and to self-censor their comments. We propose that in certain situations when there is pressure to make a decision quickly, the elements may combine to foster the development of groupthink.

The second revision needs to be in the role of the leadership of the decision-making group. In the space shuttle Challenger incident, the leader-

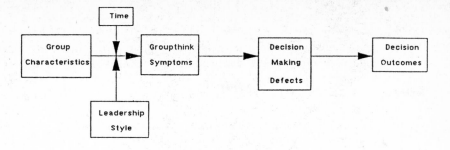

**Figure 1** Revised groupthink framework.

ship of the group varied from a shared type of leadership to a very clear leader in the situation. This may indicate that the leadership role needs to be clearly defined and a style that demands open disclosure of information, points of opposition, complaints, and dissension. We propose the leadership style is a crucial variable that moderates the relationship between the group character- istics and the development of the symptoms. Janis (1983) is a primary form of evidence to support the inclusion of leadership style in the enhanced model. His account of why the *same* group succumbed to groupthink in one decision (Bay of Pigs) and not in another (Cuban Missile Crisis) supports the depiction of leadership style as a moderator variable. In these decisions, the only condition that changed was the leadership style of the President. In other words, the element that seemed to distinguish why groupthink occurred in the Bay of Pigs decision and not in the Cuban Missile Crisis situation is the president's change in his behavior.

These two variables, time and leadership style, are proposed as moder- ators of the impact of the group characteristics on groupthink symptoms. This relationship is portrayed graphically in Fig. 1. In effect, we propose that the groupthink symptoms result from the group characteristics, as proposed by Janis, but only in the presence of the moderator variables of time and certain leadership styles.

Time, as an important element in the model, is relatively straightfor- ward. When a decision must be made within a very short time frame, pressure on members to agree, to avoid time-consuming arguments and reports from outside experts, and to self-censor themselves may increase. These pressures inevitably cause group members to seek agreement. In Janis's original model, time was included indirectly as a function of the antecedent condition, group cohesion. Janis (1983) argued that time pressures can adversely affect decision quality in two ways. First, it affects the decision makers' mental efficiency and judgment, interfering with their ability to concentrate on complicated discus- sions, to absorb new information, and to use imagination to anticipate the future consequences of alternative courses of action. Second, time pressure is a source of stress that will have the effect of inducing a policy-making group to become more cohesive and more likely to engage in groupthink.

Leadership style is shown to be a moderator because of the importance it plays in either promoting or avoiding the development of the symptoms of the groupthink. The leader, even though she or he may not promote a preferred solution, may allow or even assist the group seeking agreement by not forcing the group to critically appraise all alternative courses of action. The focus of this leadership variable is on the degree to which the leader allows or promotes discussion and evaluation of alternatives. It is not a matter of simply not making known a preferred solution; the issue is one of stimulation of critical thinking among the group.

*Impact on Prescriptions for Prevention*

The revised model suggests that more specific prescriptions for prevention of groupthink can be made. First, group members need to be aware of the impact that a short decision time frame has on decision processes. When a decision must be made quickly, there will be more pressure to agree, i.e., discouragement of dissent, self-censorship, avoidance of expert opinion, and assumptions about unanimity. The type of leadership suggested here is not one that sits back and simply does not make known her or his preferred solution. This type of leader must be one that requires all members to speak up with concerns, questions, and new information. The leader must know what some of these concerns are and which members are likely to have serious doubts so that the people with concerns can be called upon to voice them. This type of group leadership does not simply assign the role of devil's advocate and step out of the way. This leader actually plays the role or makes sure that others do. A leader with the required style to avoid groupthink is not a laissez faire leader or non-involved participative leader. This leader is active in directing the activities of the group but does not make known a preferred solution. The group still must develop and evaluate alternative courses of action, but under the direct influence of a strong, demanding leader who forces critical appraisal of all alternatives.

Finally, a combination of the two variables suggests that the leader needs to help members to avoid the problems created by the time element. For example, the leader may be able to alter an externally imposed time frame for the decision by negotiating an extension or even paying late fees, if necessary. If an extension is not possible, the leader may need to help the group eliminate the effects of time on the decision processes. This can be done by forcing attention to issues rather than time, encouraging dissension and confrontation, and scheduling special sessions to hear reports from outside experts that challenge prevailing views within the group.

Janis presents, in both editions of his book, several recommendations for preventing the occurrence of groupthink. These recommendations focus on the inclusion of outside experts in the decision-making process, all members taking the role of devil's advocate and critically appraising all alternative courses of action, and the leader not expressing a preferred solution. The revised groupthink framework suggests several new prescriptions that may be helpful in preventing further decision fiascoes similar to the decision to launch the space shuttle Challenger.

## References

*Time*. Fixing NASA. June 9, 1986.

Janis, I. L. (1983) *Victims of groupthink*. Boston: Houghton Mifflin.

Janis, I. L. (1983) *Groupthink* (2nd ed., revised). Boston: Houghton Mifflin.

*Report of the Presidential Commission on the Space Shuttle Accident*. Washington, D.C.: July 1986.

# 6

# Attraction: Liking and Loving Others

Few topics generate the curiosity and interest that interpersonal attraction and relationships do. Why are we attracted to some people more than others? How do relationships form? Why do some last, while others fade away or break up unpleasantly? These and other questions have fascinated poets, novelists, and song writers, but can they be studied and explained by social psychologists?

In our conversation, Ellen Berscheid, Professor of Psychology at the University of Minnesota, answers that question with a resounding *yes*. Prof. Berscheid is one of the most respected social psychological researchers in this area. Her pioneering work in attraction, love, and relationships has led to important discoveries that have not only advanced our conceptual understanding of these issues, but have been utilized widely by practitioners in the field—marriage counselors and therapists of all sorts. In our conversation, we talked about several issues, including the degree of choice people have (or don't really have) in selecting partners and the many ways in which the term love has been used and misused.

## A CONVERSATION WITH ELLEN BERSCHEID
*University of Minnesota*

**Krupat:** *Before we start talking about relationships, let's start out at the beginning with attraction. What is attraction and how does it come about?*

**Berscheid:** Social psychologists started out defining attraction as affiliation. They looked at who was associating with whom and then simply assumed that, if you interacted with someone frequently, you probably liked that person. Of course, we know now that you cannot equate those two things. We interact with a great many people that we do not like. So one of the first steps is to differentiate between attraction and affiliation.

**Krupat:** *Well then, if attraction is more than simple affiliation, what is it?*

**Berscheid:** Attraction has been defined as a predisposition to respond to a particular person in a favorable way. What this implies is that we will attribute to the other person favorable properties, traits, and characteristics. We will want to interact with them, to help and not hurt them, and so on.

**Krupat:** *And what factors bring it about?*

**Berscheid:** If I had to list the determinants of attraction in order of their importance, I would say that the major principle is familiarity. And under familiarity you can put subprinciples such as proximity and similarity, both of which are associated with familiarity.

**Krupat:** *How do these work?*

**Berscheid:** Nature sorts us out by putting similar people together in time and place. Without any effort on our part, most of the people we are likely to meet are similar to ourselves. If you should meet a dissimilar person and you have a choice about pursuing a relationship with him or her, probably you won't. We actually prefer those who are similar. Familiarity appears to be a fundamental, wired-in principle of attraction. Familiar people are safe. We know how to deal with them, we know how to anticipate what they want, and we expect that they will like us. When you interact with dissimilar people, it's always an uncertain situation and may even be dangerous. So familiarity is probably the principle that underlies almost all of the subprinciples of attraction.

**Krupat:** *And what about proximity? How important is that in determining whom you will be attracted to?*

**Berscheid:** Physical proximity probably accounts for a lion's share of the cases.

**Krupat:** *Why? Is it simply that someone from Boston isn't very likely to fall in love with a person from Missouri if their paths never cross?*

**Berscheid:** That's right. But some people overlook the power of proximity and similarity. You have people who write into the lovelorn columns and complain that they can't find a partner. It often turns out that they're physically isolated from other people and they don't meet many others, or they are associating with people who are very dissimilar to themselves. Consider, for example, those adults who spend all their time with children or a young adult whose time is spent with old people.

**Krupat:** *It's not hard to see what you are saying, but these are hardly the answers that the average person would give about the determinants of attraction.*

**Berscheid:** The explanations they come up with are often quite different from those a social psychologist will list. Invariably, they will mention the personality traits or other attributes of the person—for instance, their sense of humor, intelligence, and so on. I think in dating or marital relationships people especially want to put some kind of strong personal choice interpretation on it, so they look to the attributes of the other person that seemed to influence their choice. One of the things they leave out, of course, are all the environmental variables that are so potent in determining who pairs off with whom. Perhaps the most misleading thing about the attraction literature is that it seems to assume choice. We sometimes talk as if people have an infinite range of choice, that all of us have a sort of smorgasbord where we go through life picking out relationship partners from a large array of alternatives. Some of us have few alternatives or have to work hard to develop alternatives. We have, I suspect, much less choice in choosing our relationship partners than we like to think.

**Krupat:** *But within that realm of choice, however narrow it is, how do people select partners? How much does physical attractiveness play a role?*

**Berscheid:** When Elaine Hatfield and I started out with the matching hypothesis of physical attractiveness, we thought that similarity would rule here too. We thought that people would prefer to interact with those who were approximately of their own social desirability, including people of their own physical attractiveness level. Over the years, it's become very apparent that that is not so, that everybody wants to pair off with the most physically attractive person. But what happens is that the most physically attractive people tend to pair off with each other because they also want the most attractive partners. So they take themselves out of contention, and then it just sorts itself like that all the way down. It is matching—people of similar physical attractiveness are more likely to pair off—but the matching is not due to preference.

**Krupat:** *I see. So you get the same result, but for a different reason. But once people pair off, where does love come into the picture?*

**Berscheid:** One of the reasons that I don't even like to talk about the love literature is because it is so confusing and diffuse. People use the term so loosely.

**Krupat:** *I agree. If I say that I love my wife and I love my mother and I love my children and I love watching television, it seems that I am robbing the term of any significance.*

**Berscheid:** Absolutely, and that's precisely the problem, because, when you say you love watching television, you're expressing a preference for that kind of activity. You are saying that you would choose to do that kind of activity over many others. Very often, when you say that you love somebody, just as you would say that you love this ice cream, all you really mean is that you have a positive appraisal of the ice cream or the person or whatever.

**Krupat:** *How about love for people rather than objects or activities? What does it mean to say that I love my wife versus I love my children or my mother?*

**Berscheid:** With your mother what you're probably saying is that you care about her and her welfare and that you enjoy being with her. So it may be you're saying that you enjoy being with this person as a companion, that you care about her and you would gladly help her. In other words, there's altruistic love involved there. And often, when people say I love my wife, that's also what it means. But sometimes people will say—and you'll hear it in a therapy setting—I love my wife, but I'm not in love with her and maybe I ought to get a divorce. What they mean there is that they are no longer sexually attracted. They no longer feel sexual desire, and perhaps they also don't experience other intense positive emotions in the relationship. Their heart no longer beats faster when the person comes back after separation, for example. So people use the word love in many different ways. And I think that investigators, themselves, have not gotten their terminology clear.

**Krupat:** *Even when people talk about their love for another person, do they always show their love or even mean what they say?*

**Berscheid:** There are strong social pressures to say that you love your mother or you love your kids. If you look at the relationship as an outside observer, it may be that this father avoids his kid every chance he gets. When he does interact with him, he's aloof and has nothing but negative things to say. In other words, by anyone's standards, that is not a loving relationship. But, if you ask the man, he will say "Oh, yes. I love my kids."

**Krupat:** *So being in a relationship or expressing love may not mean that love and affection truly exist there.*

**Berscheid:** This is a major point I'd like to make. You cannot equate loving and liking or disliking and hating with having a relationship with somebody, even a long-term relationship. Ordinarily, it is the case that we do like and love family members. But it is not always the case. In fact, rather frequently we may dislike, certainly momentarily, people with whom we are in long-term and family relationships. Experts in violence say that the family is the most violent institution in this society. So we can't assume that, just because it's a long-term relationship, it's a loving relationship.

**Krupat:** *Listening to what you are saying, it is not so surprising that relationships don't last and that many marriages fail.*

**Berscheid:** People just tend to take a lot of relationships for granted and say, "Yes, of course I love this person." That is why sometimes it's so disappointing, and even tragic, when something happens and that individual really needs the other person to be loving and they're not. The relationship gets tested and it fails.

**Krupat:** *Let me change our focus somewhat, if I may. You and others in the field have done many experimental laboratory studies, and also a good deal of real-life work on marriage, divorce, etcetera. To what extent do you personally feel that it's important that we, as social psychologists, become involved in both laboratory and applied issues?*

**Berscheid:** There's no question—it's essential. In an article I'm writing now on the progress we have made in the interpersonal relationships area, I'm trying to show that, if you get into applied problems, if you get into the front lines of relationships and look at the problems there, the kinds of questions you encounter will highlight the basic research that needs to be done. Similarly, basic research in areas such as social cognition is unlikely to progress further unless we get into the front line because there are too many things that change between social cognition as it occurs with strangers in the laboratory and social cognition as it occurs in an ongoing long-term relationship. So anybody who tries to make an either/or out of basic and applied research is, at least in this area, really sadly mistaken.

**Krupat:** *Having talked about the back-and-forth between lab and field, let me ask you about a different kind of connection. In your research, have you ever begun with or come back to poets or novelists for inspiration or for hypotheses worth testing? Is that a back-and-forth that people who study relationships do and find worthwhile?*

**Berscheid:** I think some do. But I don't. Probably the reason for that with many psychologists is that we're human; there is much give and take between one's own experiences and what one finds puzzling and wants to figure out. When

I was zeroing in on the area of love, I think early on I read everything I could get my hands on—philosophers, poets, and so forth. But it was so disappointing I stopped looking for any enlightenment there, and I was much more likely to read in other areas of psychology. I found George Mandler's theory of human cognition much more enlightening about love and hate and joy and disappointment than anything a poet or novelist had to say.

**Krupat:** *As we both know, some people have criticized work in this area, saying that social scientists should stay away from emotions, love, and relationships. Can I assume that you have few misgivings about doing so?*

**Berscheid:** If you were to look at all the things in this world that should be studied, you would come up with this one at the top of your list. From the very beginning, relationships influence the quality and character of our lives. Relationships can kill us or they can contribute to our physical health, never mind about all of their psychological functions, including their effects on our mental health and happiness. There is nothing in our lives more important than our relationships with other people. And I think that social psychologists have amply demonstrated that interpersonal attraction and love can be studied successfully in a systematic way.

Keith E. Davis

# Near and Dear: Friendship and Love Compared

In this article Davis distinguishes two critical sorts of human relationships—friendship and love. According to his research, friendship is characterized by enjoyment, acceptance, trust, respect, mutual assistance, confiding, understanding, and spontaneity. Love has all of these in addition to two other clusters: 1) a preoccupation with one's partner, sexual desire, and feeling that theirs is a special and unique commitment; and 2) a desire to give unselfishly to the other and to be his or her advocate. Davis finds, however, that in addition to a greater depth of caring among lovers, love relationships also carry a potential for more distress, conflict, and criticism.

Love and friendship are the warp and woof of the social fabric. They not only bind society together but provide essential emotional sustenance, buffering us against stress and preserving physical and mental health. When those ties are severed, the loss can precipitate illness and even suicide in some people.

While we readily distinguish between friends and lovers in everyday life and value each differently, psychologists have not provided a systematic answer to how these two essential relationships differ.

My colleague Michael J. Todd and I developed a list of what we believe are characteristics central to friendship and romantic love. We then tested our model against the experiences and expectations of about 250 college students and community members, both single and married.

We found that love and friendship are alike in many ways, but that some crucial differences make love relationships both more rewarding and more volatile. Some 19 centuries ago, Seneca observed, "Friendship always benefits; love sometimes injures." Love relationships fared far better than that in our own studies, but there's an element of truth to the observation.

## THE FABRIC OF FRIENDSHIP

The original profile of friendship we developed included these essential characteristics beyond the fact that two people participate in a reciprocal relationship as equals:

- ENJOYMENT: They enjoy each other's company most of the time, although there may be temporary states of anger, disappointment or mutual annoyance. ("I find whatever we do more enjoyable when Jim and I do it together." "He has the ability to make me laugh.")
- ACCEPTANCE: They accept one another as they are, without trying to change or make the other into a new or different person. ("She's not always on me to do things that I don't want to do." "He appreciates my style.")
- TRUST: They share mutual trust in the sense that each assumes that the other will act in light of his or her friend's best interest. ("Even when he is bugging me, I know that it's for my own good." "I just know that I can count on her; whatever she says, she will do." "He would never intentionally hurt me—except in a fit of extreme anger.")
- RESPECT: They respect each other in the sense of assuming that each exercises good judgment in making life choices. ("She doesn't give advice unless asked, but then it is always good." "He will usually do what's right.")
- MUTUAL ASSISTANCE: They are inclined to assist and support one another and, specifically, they can count on each other in times of need, trouble or personal distress. ("I feel like doing things that she needs to have done.")
- CONFIDING: They share experiences and feelings with each other. ("He tells me things that no one else knows about him.")
- UNDERSTANDING: They have a sense of what is important to each and why the friend does what he or she does. In such cases, friends are not routinely puzzled or mystified by each other's behavior. ("I know what makes her tick." "I can usually figure out what's wrong when he's troubled or moody.")
- SPONTANEITY: Each feels free to be himself or herself in the relationship rather than feeling required to play a role, wear a mask or inhibit revealing personal traits. ("I feel completely comfortable around him.")

## THE TAPESTRY OF LOVE

We assumed that romantic relationships would share all the same characteristics as friendship but that they would have additional and unique ones. We identified two broad categories unique to love relationships:

*The Passion Cluster*

This consists of three characteristics—fascination, exclusiveness and sexual desire:

- FASCINATION: Lovers tend to pay attention to the other person even when they should be involved in other activities. They are preoccupied with the other person and tend to think about, look at, want to talk to or merely be with the other. ("I would go to bed thinking about what we would do together, dream about it and wake up ready to be with him again." "I have trouble concentrating; she just seems to be in my head no matter what I'm doing.") A person worthy of this kind of attention is worthy of devotion. Thus, fascination provides one basis for idealizing the other, a phenomenon so often noted in romantic love.
- EXCLUSIVENESS: Lovers have a special relationship that precludes having the same relationship with a third party. ("What we have is different than I've ever had with anyone else." "We're committed to each other.") Thus, a romantic love relationship is given priority over other relationships in one's life.
- SEXUAL DESIRE: Lovers want physical intimacy with the partner, wanting to touch and be touched and to engage in sexual intercourse. They may not always act on the desire, even when both members of the couple share it, since it may be overridden by moral, religious or practical considerations (for example, fear of pregnancy or of getting caught.)

*The Caring Cluster*

This has two components: giving the utmost and being a champion/advocate.

- GIVING THE UTMOST: Lovers care enough to give the utmost when the other is in need, sometimes to the point of extreme self-sacrifice. One of the best-known literary examples is in O. Henry's short story *The Gift of the Magi*, in which a man pawns his favorite pocket watch to buy his beloved a set of combs for her beautiful hair, while she cuts and sells her hair to buy him a gold chain for his watch. Each gives something priceless to make the other happy.
- BEING A CHAMPION/ADVOCATE: The depth of lovers' caring shows up also in an active championing of each other's interests and in a positive attempt to make sure that the partner succeeds. "I realize that whatever my parents said that was critical of him just made me all the more determined to defend him.")

Overall, what we found in our first two studies largely confirmed our model of the ways in which love and friendship are similar and different, but there were some surprises. The studies generally supported our expectation that the typical best friendship would share many characteristics with spouse/lover relationships. The levels of acceptance, trust, and respect were virtually identical. Also quite similar were the levels of confiding, understanding, spontaneity and mutual assistance. And generally, the level of success (happiness and satisfaction with the relationship) in these two relationships was seen as similar.

Also, as expected, components of the passion cluster differentiated spouses and lovers from best friends, showing up in much more fascination and exclusiveness among spouses and lovers. (In the first two studies we did not examine sexual desire as part of the passion cluster for fear of losing research subjects, a precaution we later found to be unnecessary.)

The data ran counter to our expectations in three areas: First, we had anticipated that spouses and lovers would be more willing than best friends to give the utmost when needed and to be a champion or advocate of the other's interests. But to our surprise, only the give-utmost scale showed the expected difference. Furthermore, the difference between spouses or lovers and best friends was much smaller than in the case of the passion cluster. But the frequency with which this topic was expressed in our interviews, and the fact that other investigators such as Zick Rubin of Brandeis University and Loren Steck of the University of California at Los Angeles have emphasized the same distinction as a central aspect of romantic love, make us inclined to take it seriously as an area of difference between friendship and love.

A second surprise came in an area in which we expected few differences between best friends and lovers: enjoyment of each other's company. We had asked subjects to rate their agreement with the statement, "I enjoy doing things with [name of lover or best friend] more than doing them with others." We found lovers more likely than friends to endorse the statement. This finding may reflect the greater range of human needs that can be met in the typical love relationship.

A third unanticipated finding was that best friendships were seen as more stable than spouse/lover relationships. The lower levels of stability among spouses and lovers seemed to reflect a greater concern about the possibility of the relationship' breaking up, particularly among the unmarried lovers.

If the kinds of characteristics that we have identified as central to love and best-friendship are valid, then less intense and less special types of friendship should differ from love relationships in an even greater range of characteristics. So we then looked at close rather than best friends of the same sex as compared to lover/spouse relationships.

We found that with the exception of acceptance, trust, spontaneity and stability, spouses and lovers were higher on all characteristics than were close friends of the same sex. A similar pattern held for the contrast with close friends of the opposite sex. Only trust and stability were not significantly higher among the spouses and lovers.

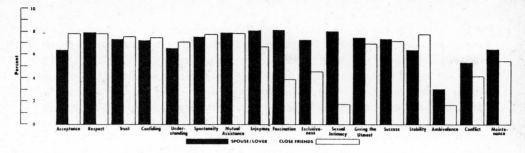

**Figure 1.** Close friends and lovers compared.

Looking at our data on best friends and close friends, we found one very surprising fact: Although the majority of best friends were of the same gender, 27 percent of our subjects listed a member of the opposite sex as a best friend (and explicitly indicated that the relationship was not romantic). Further, 56 percent of the men in the sample nominated at least one woman as a close friend, and 44 percent of the women nominated at least one man as a close friend. Thus, while same-sex friendships tend to predominate, many of our subjects were reaching outside of their own gender for friendship.

Are the typical close friendships with people of the same sex different in any respect from opposite-sex close friendships? Our findings suggest that they are. Same-sex friendships are marked by greater sharing (both of personal confidences and practical assistance), a greater sense of stability and a greater willingness to give the utmost.

So far we have discussed only the positive aspects of friendship and love. But what about the negative aspects? Do friendship and love have different potentials for destructiveness, possessiveness, ambivalence and conflict? It seemed to us that clear-cut differences should follow from the fascination and exclusiveness characteristics of love relationships.

A person entering into a love relationship makes a commitment to the other person that normally involves giving up other similar relationships. Being a lover or spouse also involves a closer coordination of everyday activities and giving the partner priority over other people. These kinds of commitments can leave many lovers and spouses confused about whether they have made the right choice, puzzled by still feeling attracted to someone they have left or perplexed by attraction to someone new. For all these reasons, love relationships provide an excellent breeding ground for ambivalence and conflict.

Harriet Braiker and Harold Kelley of UCLA identified ambivalence, conflict and "maintenance" (discussing the relationship and trying to work out problems in it) as three areas in which recently married couples reported changes over the course of their courtships. We used their scales in the third of our study series to determine whether people would report higher levels of all three characteristics in their spouse/lover relationships than in their close, same-sex friendships. The third study also gave us an opportunity to ask explicitly about sexual desire and sexual intimacy.

We found that spouse/lover relationships elicit higher levels of passion and a somewhat greater depth of caring; they are higher in fascination, exclusiveness, sexual intimacy, enjoyment and giving-the-utmost than are close friendships. But we also found higher levels of ambivalence, conflict and maintenance activities than in close friendships.

The major surprise in these data was that the level of acceptance was significantly lower among spouses and lovers than among friends. Marilyn Rands of Wheaton College and George Levinger of the University of Massachusetts also found spouses and lovers readier to criticize their partners than their friends.

Two other aspects of our work merit some discussion: how our findings relate to those of other psychologists studying personal relationships and how individuals deal with borderline cases of friendship.

Paul Wright of the University of North Dakota, working with Paula Bergloff, has recently found that love relationships differ from friendships in four areas: Love relationships are more exclusive, more intense in emotional expression and more permanent than friendships and are viewed as more dominated by social rules and expectations.

The tendency of Wright and Bergloff's lovers to see their relationships as under the influence of social rules and expectations may well explain the Rands and Levinger findings that lovers are more critical of each other as well as our finding (in our third study) that they were less accepting and tolerant of each other.

Our findings concerning romantic love are quite similar to Dorothy Tennov's concept of "limerence," or romantic passion. Many of her 12 central features directly parallel ones we have also identified as central to love. But she has stressed some features of love that we may not have sufficiently emphasized. Among these are an acute longing for reciprocation (wanting the love object to love you) and having one's mood depend on reciprocation. Tennov's work appears to characterize aptly the emotional intensity of some romantic relationships, especially in their early phases and particularly for some people.

Studies by two other researchers indicate that some people do not seek or want traditional romantic love. The work of John Alan Lee of the University of Toronto suggests that some people do not experience romantic love. That of Mary K. Roberts of the Kaiser Permanente Health Care Plan in Denver indicates that some men and women are looking for companionship rather than romantic relationships with their life partners.

Indeed, Roberts found that when she asked people to imagine what kinds of feelings and thoughts other men and women have just after they have completed sexual intercourse, they answered according to their own particular friendship or romantic orientations. People with a romantic orientation report more thoughts of euphoria, well-being and intensity—the kinds of thoughts suggested by our analysis of love and by those of Tennov and others.

Naturally enough, the people we interviewed sometimes described friendship or love relationships that did not completely and fully fit our profiles. These were the relationships that occasionally puzzled them or made them uneasy. We found that in about one-third of cases of best or close friendships, people reported violations of their basic expectations of friendship. These ranged from minor infringements, such as using one's personal items without asking, to serious offenses such as "betraying the friendship by repeating things told in confidence," "trying to seduce my wife" or "her total lack of trust for anyone." Not surprisingly, violations were associated with lower ratings on many of the friendship characteristics and were consistently linked with lower ratings of acceptance, respect and trust.

Some of the people we interviewed had no qualms about classifying someone as a friend even though they knew that the relationship was limited, qualified or inconsistent with our categories. Some examples are: "Susie is my best friend, but I have to watch her because she will bend the truth to get her way." Others, in response to the question, "Are there things that you cannot talk about?" mentioned topics they had learned to avoid because differences were too great and discussions proved unprofitable.

If the findings of this research and of others cited are valid, then the typical love relationships will differ from even very good friendships in having higher levels of fascination, exclusiveness and sexual desire (the passion cluster), a greater depth of caring about the other person (which would be manifest in a willingness to give the utmost when needed) and a greater potential for enjoyment and other positive emotions. Love relationships will also have, however, a greater potential for distress, ambivalence, conflict and mutual criticism.

One clear implication of these differences is that love relationships tend to have a greater impact on both the satisfaction and frustration of the person's basic human needs. It may be important, then, to acknowledge these differences in emotional significance as researchers study the mental and physical health implications of having—and of losing—lovers and close friends.

Rubin has recently reminded us that "the most illuminating writing about close relationships has come from storytellers and playwrights, not from psychologists and sociologists." We hope that the characteristics used in our prototypes of friendship and love reach far enough toward the specific reality of everyday relationships to do justice to them. We also hope that we have provided important distinctions that can enhance psychological studies and understanding.

Caryl E. Rusbult
Dennis J. Johnson
Gregory D. Morrow

# Impact of Couple Patterns of Problem Solving on Distress and Nondistress in Dating Relationships

Having proposed a model of the ways in which couples solve problems, Rusbult and her colleagues test the model using a sample of dating couples at the University of Kentucky. They found that a major difference between those couples that function effectively and those that do not has to do with the extent to which each reacts to problems in a destructive fashion. That is, the bad things that partners do to one another rather than the good seem to have a greater role in determining whether the relationship goes well or not. Readers should check the details of these findings and ask whether they hold true in their own personal relationships.

What determines whether a relationship will function successfully? Are certain couple patterns of problem solving more promotive of healthy functioning than others? One of the most important goals in the study of close relationships is to understand how couples react to inevitable, perhaps reparable, periodic decline and to identify the patterns of response that produce the most favorable consequences. Unfortunately, despite the abundance of theory and research devoted to understanding the development and deterioration of relationships (Altman & Taylor, 1973; Johnson, 1982; Lee, 1984; Levinger, 1979; Murstein, 1970; Rusbult, 1983), people still know relatively little about the form and effectiveness of various patterns of couple problem solving.

The classic model for identifying what "works" in relationships is to compare the behavior of partners in nondistressed relationships with comparable behavior in distressed relationships (Billings, 1979; Birchler, Weiss, & Vincent, 1975; Fiore & Swensen, 1977; Frederickson, 1977; Gottman, 1979; Gottman et al., 1976; Margolin & Wampold, 1981; Nettles & Loevinger, 1983;

Schaap, 1984). This approach to the study of relationships is predicated on the assumption that the problem-solving behavior of nondistressed couples, in comparison with that of distressed couples, is reflective of healthy functioning. Unfortunately, very little of the prior work on distress/nondistress in close relationships is based on a larger, more comprehensive theory of problem solving.

According to Kelley (1979; Kelley et al, 1983), in formulating a comprehensive theory of relationships, one should take into consideration not only the behaviors of the individual partners but also, and more importantly, the interdependence of the partners, or the impact of their joint behaviors on their relationship (Kelley & Thibault, 1978). In addition, Kelley suggested that one take into consideration the types of attributions that the partners form about one another's dispositions. Accordingly, the theory of problem solving that we advance deals with three important components of close relationships: First, it addresses the simple effects of each individual's problem-solving responses on the quality of the relationship; second, it addresses the more complex effects of various interdependent patterns of problem-solving responses on relationship quality; and third, it enables one to explore the impact of partner perceptions of one another's problem-solving responses on relationship functioning. Our goal in developing such a theory is to understand the effects of each of these variables on the couple; that is, we use as the unit of analysis the relationship itself, rather than the individual partners. In our theory we use an extant typology of problem solving in close relationships with demonstrated utility: the exit–voice–loyalty–neglect typology (Rusbult & Zembrodt, 1983). This typology is a useful means of characterizing couple problem solving in that it is an abstract and comprehensive model that specifies the dimensions on which a variety of responses differ from one another.

## THE EXIT–VOICE–LOYALTY–NEGLECT TYPOLOGY

The Rusbult and Zembrodt (1983) typology is based loosely on the writings of Hirschman (1970), who discussed three characteristic reactions to decline in economic domains; (a) *exit*, actively destroying the relationship; (b) *voice*, actively and constructively attempting to improve conditions; and (c) *loyalty*, passively but optimistically waiting for conditions to improve. To assess the comprehensiveness of this model, Rusbult and Zembrodt (1983) carried out a multidimensional scaling analysis of couple problem-solving responses. They found that Hirschman's three categories characterize behaviors in romantic involvements, and also identified a fourth important response: *neglect*, passively allowing one's relationship to deteriorate. The following are examples of behaviors representative of each category of response:

> *Exit*—separating, moving out of a joint residence, actively [physically] abusing one's partner, getting a divorce;

*Voice*—discussing problems, compromising, seeking help from a friend or therapist, suggesting solutions, changing oneself or one's partner;

*Loyalty*—waiting and hoping that things will improve, supporting the partner in the face of criticism, praying for improvement;

*Neglect*—ignoring the partner or spending less time together, refusing to discuss problems, treating the partner badly [insulting], criticizing the partner for things unrelated to the real problem, just letting things fall apart.

As is shown in Figure 1, the four responses differ from one another along two dimensions: Voice and loyalty are *constructive* responses, wherein the individual attempts to revive or maintain the relationship, whereas exit and neglect are relatively more *destructive*.

Previous researchers have demonstrated that the four responses are influenced by a variety of relationship- and individual-level variables. Unfortunately, none of this research answers the question "What 'works' in relationships?" If the typology is to serve as a useful model of problem solving, the adaptive value of the four responses must be empirically established.

## A MODEL OF PROBLEM SOLVING IN DISTRESSED RELATIONSHIPS

What implications does the prior work on distressed and nondistressed relationships have for understanding the functional value of exit, voice, loyalty, and neglect responses? First, previous researchers have demonstrated that partners in distressed couples react more positively and less negatively

**Figure 1.** Exit, voice, loyalty, and neglect: a typology of problem-solving responses in close relationships.

to problems: Billings (1979) found that in comparison with nondistressed couples, distressed couples exhibit more negative and fewer positive problem-solving acts (e.g., more hostile-dominant, rejecting, and coercive-attacking behaviors, and fewer friendly-dominant behaviors). In the light of the consistency of these findings, we predict that couple distress will be greater to the degree that partners exhibit higher levels of the destructive problem-solving responses and lower levels of the constructive responses. We should find that distress is greater in relationships in which couples respond to problems in an abusive manner, threatening to end their relationships (i.e., exiting), or by refusing to discuss problems, ignoring the partner, spending less time together, and so on (i.e., engaging in neglect). In contrast, distress should be lower to the extent that partners compromise, suggest solutions to problems, and talk things over (i.e., voice), or quietly but optimistically wait for things to improve (i.e., remain loyal).

Previous researchers have also demonstrated that interdependent patterns of response may distinguish between well- and poorly functioning couples. In the language of interdependence theory (Kelley & Thibault, 1978), distressed couples appear to engage in fewer relationship "transformations" of the problem situation, and thus react to destructive actions from partners with destructive responses in return. Thus we predict that couples will evince greater distress to the degree that partners reciprocate negative problem-solving responses, reacting to exit and neglect from partners with higher levels of exit and neglect in return.

Previous researchers have also demonstrated that partners in well- and poorly functioning couples may perceive one another's behaviors quite differently. Some research has shown that distress is a function not so much of how partners intend their behaviors as it is a function of how they experience one another's behaviors (Gottman, 1979; Gottman et al., 1976; Markman, 1979, 1981). Thus the prediction advanced earlier about individual response tendencies may also apply to *perceptions* of partner behaviors; partners in distressed couples may *receive* one another's response more negatively, attributing to one another greater tendencies toward exit and neglect and lesser tendencies toward voice and loyalty.

Lastly, in light of prior work on the differences in problem-solving responses of men and women, we expected to uncover some gender differences in response style. On the basis of previous research, we can characterize the behavior of women, in relation to that of men as showing greater direct communication, a more contactful and less controlling style, greater emphasis on maintenance behavior, a desire to confront and discuss problems and feelings, lesser tendencies toward conflict-avoidance, a greater desire for affectional behaviors and a lesser emphasis on instrumental behaviors, and higher levels of intimate self-disclosure (Hawkins, Weisberg, & Ray, 1980; Kelley et al., 1978; Kitson & Sussman, 1982; Morgan, 1976; Rubin, Hill, Peplau, & Dunkel-Schetter, 1980). Given the woman's generally greater affiliative/communal orientation, we predicted that in comparison with men, women will evince greater tendencies to respond constructively and lesser tendencies to respond destructively to relationship problems.

As a preliminary test of the current model, we obtained information, from both members of dating couples, regarding (a) self-reports of response tendencies; (b) perceptions of partner's response tenencies; (c) reports of probable reactions to exit, voice, loyalty, and neglect from partner (i.e., interdependent patterns); and (d) reported satisfaction with and commitment to relationship, liking and loving for partner, and perceived effectiveness of own and partner's pattern of problem-solving. Furthermore, in light of the Gottman et al. (1976) argument that high-conflict situations may be a better means of evaluating the adaptive value of problem-solving responses, we examined interdependent patterns of response for both mild and serious relationship problems.

## METHOD

### Respondents

The respondents were 68 dating couples from the University of Kentucky. One member of each couple completed the questionnaire during an on-campus research session in partial fulfillment of the requirements for introductory psychology, and was asked to take a packet of materials to his or her partner. This packet included an identical questionnaire (coded with the same number as on that of the first partner's), a cover explaining the purpose of the study, and a stamped return envelope. In the cover letter we asked that individuals complete and return their questionnaires without showing them to their partners, and we assured them that their partners would not be privy to their responses.

The respondents were approximately 20 years old, 21 for male subjects (range = 17 to 36) and 19 for female subjects (range = 17 to 26), had been involved with one another for about 18 months (range = 2 to 66 months), spent about 3 or 4 evenings a week together (range = 1 to 7), and were in one another's company for about 37 hours per week (range = 2 to 110). Seventy-eight percent reported that they were dating regularly, 12% were engaged to be married, and 10% reported that they were dating casually. Eighty-two percent reported that neither partner dated others, 5% reported that one partner dated others and the other partner did not, and 13% reported that both partners dated other persons as well. Ninety-eight percent of the respondents were white.

### Questionnaires

In addition to the demographic information mentioned earlier, each questionnaire also enabled us to assess the following:

*Self-reported responses and perceptions of partner's responses.* Each respondent completed a 28-item scale in order to measure his or her own self-reported tendencies to engage in exit, voice, loyalty, and neglect. Each of the seven items designed to measure each response category was a 9-point Likert-type scale (1 = *never do this*; 9 = *always do this*). Items from the four response categories were randomly ordered in the questionnaire. The verbatim items were as follows:

*Exit*—"When I'm unhappy with my partner, I consider breaking up," "When I'm angry at my partner, I talk to him/her about breaking up," "When we have serious problems in our relationship, I take action to end the relationship," "When I'm irritated with my partner, I think about ending our relationship," "When we have problems, I discuss ending our relationship," "When things are going really poorly between us, I do things to drive my partner away," and "When I'm dissatisfied with our relationship, I consider dating other people."

*Voice*—"When my partner says or does things I don't like, I talk to him/her about what's upsetting me," "When my partner and I have problems, I discuss things with him/her," "When I am unhappy with my partner, I tell him/her what's bothering me," "When things aren't going well between us, I suggest changing things in the relationship in order to solve the problem," "When my partner and I are angry with one another, I suggest a compromise solution," "When we've had an argument, I work things out with my partner right away," and "When we have serious problems in our relationship, I consider getting advice from someone else (friends, parents, minister, or counselor)."

*Loyalty*—"When we have problems in our relationship, I patiently wait for things to improve," "When I'm upset about something in our relationship, I wait awhile before saying anything to see if things will improve on their own," "When my partner hurts me, I say nothing and simply forgive him/her," "When my partner and I are angry with each other, I give things some time to cool off on their own rather than take action," "When there are things about my partner that I don't like, I accept his/her faults and weaknesses and don't try to change him/her," "When my partner is inconsiderate, I give him/her the benefit of the doubt and forget about it," and "When we have troubles, no matter how bad things get I am loyal to my partner."

*Neglect*—"When I'm upset with my partner I sulk rather than confront the issue," "When I'm really bothered about something my partner has done, I criticize him/her for things that are unrelated to the real problem," "When I'm upset with my partner, I ignore him/her for awhile," "When I'm really angry, I treat my partner badly (for example, by ignoring him/her or saying cruel things)," "When we have a problem in our relationship, I ignore the whole thing and forget about it," "When I'm angry at my partner, I spend less time with him/her (for example, I spend more time with my friend, watch a lot of television, work longer hours, etc.)," and "When my partner and I have problems, I refuse to talk to him/her about it."

We assessed individuals' perceptions of their partners' problem-solving responses, using the same items, reworded to describe partner's rather than own response tendencies (e.g., "When I say or do things my partner doesn't like, he/she talks to me about what's upsetting him/her").

*Interdependent patterns of response.* Twenty open-ended items were designed to enable us to assess response tendencies in reaction to partner's exit, voice, loyalty, and neglect. Respondents wrote brief (one-sentence) responses to statements of the form "If we had a minor problem in our relationship and my partner wanted to ignore it, I would probably . . . ." These responses were coded for exit, voice, loyalty, and neglect content (e.g., 0 = *no exit*, 1 = *some exit*) by two judges naive to each couple's distress level.

> *Exit*—"If my partner was irritated by something I had done and started dating someone else, I would probably . . . ."; "If we had a minor problem in our relationship and my partner thought about ending our relationship, I would probably . . . .";
>
> *Voice*—"If my partner was irritated by something I had done and wanted to have a heart-to-heart talk about it, I would probably . . . ."; "If we had a minor problem in our relationship and my partner wanted to talk it over, I would probably . . . .";
>
> *Loyalty*—"If my partner was annoyed by one of my personal habits and graciously tried to live with it rather than trying to change me, I would probably . . . ."; "If my partner was irritated by something I had done and just waited patiently for it to pass away, I would probably . . . .";
>
> *Neglect*—"If we had a minor problem in our relationship and my partner wanted to ignore, I would probably . . . ."; "If my partner was annoyed by one of my personal habits and started to treat me badly (ignoring me or saying cruel things), I would probably . . . .";

On the basis of these data, we calculated six dependent measures for each response: response to mild problems (e.g., total voice for the 12 mild-problem statements), response to severe problems (e.g., total loyalty for the eight severe problems), and response to exit, voice, loyalty, and neglect from partner (e.g., total neglect in response to the five partner-voice problems). The response to mild and severe problem measures were used as additional measures of individual response tendencies.

*Distress measures.* The questionnaire also included Rubin's (1973) liking and loving instrument, a set of 18 items to which respondents indicated degree of disagreement/agreement on a 9-point Likert-type scales (1 = *don't agree at all*, 9 = *agree completely*). Using Rusbult's (1983) items, we measured satisfaction with and commitment to maintain relationships. Five 9-point Likert-type scales enabled us to measure each construct (e.g., for satisfaction, "To what extent are you satisfied with your current relationship?" and "How does your relationship compare to other people's?"; for commitment, "To what extent are you committed to maintaining your relationship?" and "For how much longer do you want your relationship with your partner to last?"). In addition, we assessed participants' perceptions of the effectiveness of their own and their partners' problem-solving styles, using eight 9-point Likert-type scales. The items with which we assessed perceived effectiveness of participants' own behaviors were "Do you think that *your* method of solving problems works?" "Do you think that *you* respond to problems in your relationship in a healthy manner?"; "Does *your* method of solving problems make you feel good afterwards?"; and "Does the way in which *you* react to periods of dissatisfaction make your relationship stronger?" We used the same items, reworded appropriately, to assess participants' perceptions of the effectiveness of their partners' problem-solving behaviors (e.g., "Do you think that *your partner's* method of solving problems works?")

*Socially desirable responding.* Respondents also completed the Marlow-Crowne (Crowne & Marlow, 1964) instrument, designed to enable us to assess tendencies to describe oneself in a socially desirable manner.

## RESULTS

### Validity of Exit, Voice, Loyalty, and Neglect Measures

To assess the validity of our measures of problem solving, we calculated the correlation between respondents' descriptions of their own tendencies to react to problems with exit, voice, loyalty, and neglect, and partners' descriptions of the individual's tendencies. These analyses provided fairly good evidence of convergence: The correlations were .53 for exit, .34 for voice, .30 for loyalty, and .42 for neglect. Also, the relation between self-reported tendencies toward exit, voice, loyalty, and neglect and the total coded measure of each response tendency (mild plus severe) from the open-ended items were significant for exit (.48), voice (.35), loyalty (.28), and neglect (.39).

### Distress Measure

We calculated a total score for each respondent by summing his or her reported satisfaction, commitment, liking, loving, and perceived effectiveness of own and partner's problem-solving style (each measure first scaled from 1 to 9). Then we calculated a single distress score for each couple by summing male and female partners' reported distress. This composite score captures the feelings of both partners, and should be a valid means of assessing couple distress/nondistress.

### Relation Between Problem-Solving Responses and Distress/Nondistress

*Impact of individual responses.* In the regression models in which we used measures of self-reported response tendencies and measures of responses to both mild and severe problems, both exit and neglect were consistently negatively predictive of couple distress/nondistress. Thus the prediction that destructive tendencies would be deleterious to couple functioning was strongly supported. However, although the tendency to voice in reaction to mild problems was associated with nondistress, voice did not contribute to the prediction of distress/nondistress for models in which we used the measures of self-reported tendencies or responses to severe problems. Furthermore, there was no evidence that loyalty responses contributed to the prediction of couple functioning.

To further examine the power of each mode of response in predicting couple functioning, we performed additional analyses in which we regressed the three measures of each response onto overall couple nondistress. These analyses revealed that the exit, voice, and neglect measures significantly improved the prediction of nondistress beyond that accounted for loyalty; for the weakest improvement (voice). Also, both the exit and voice measures improved the prediction of nondistress beyond that accounted for by voice; for the weakest improvement (neglect). Lastly, the exit measures improved the prediction of nondistress beyond that accounted for by neglect.

*Impact of perceptions of partner responses.* As predicted, the multiple regression analysis demonstrated that perceptions of partners' tendencies toward exit, voice, and neglect contributed significantly, and perceptions of loyalty contributed marginally, to the prediction of nondistress. Thus there is some evidence that perceptions of partner voice (and perhaps loyalty) do contribute to our understanding of couple functioning, though the analyses of individual response tendencies revealed only weak evidence of such effects.

*Impact of interdependent patterns of response.* According to our model, couple distress will be greater to the degree that persons react to destructive responses from partners with destructive responses in return. Using data from the open-ended measures of interdependent responses to test this prediction, we found that nondistress was negatively associated with tendencies to respond to partner's exit with exit and neglect (though the latter coefficient was only marginally significant), and with tendencies to respond to partner's neglect with exit and neglect. But tendencies to react with voice and loyalty to partner's exit were also significantly related to nondistress, as were voice reactions in response to partner's neglect. In general, then, we find that couple distress is associated not only with tendencies to reciprocate destructive responses, but also with failure to respond constructively to destructive partner responses.

### Gender Differences

*Gender differences in the relationships between problem-solving responses and couple distress/nondistress.* To determine whether the aforementioned relations between problem-solving responses and couple distress/nondistress hold for both male and female subjects, we performed hierarchical regression analyses. First, we found that female subjects' tendencies to engage in exit exerted a more deleterious impact on couple functioning than did male subjects' exit tendencies. Second, female subjects' tendencies to engage in neglect were more destructive to the relationship in terms of their responses to severe problems. Thus the destructive behaviors of female partners (exit, and perhaps neglect) appear to be particularly deleterious to couple functioning.

*Gender differences in mean level of problem-solving responses.* To assess gender differences in response tendencies, we performed four two-factor multivariate analyses of variance. The results of these analyses are summarized in Table 1. As predicted, females engaged in higher levels of voice than did their male partners. Lastly, as predicted, female subjects evinced somewhat lower neglect scores than did male subjects.

**Table 1**  Gender differences in Tendencies to Engage in Exit, Voice, Loyalty, and Neglect

| Subject responses | Men | Women |
| --- | --- | --- |
| Exit | | |
| Self-reported responses | 17.26 | 18.86 |
| Responses to mild problems | 1.84 | 1.56 |
| Responses to severe problems | 1.87 | 2.03 |
| Voice | | |
| Self-reported responses | 41.74 | 45.22 |
| Responses to mild problems | 15.69 | 17.70 |
| Responses to severe problems | 11.23 | 11.92 |
| Loyalty | | |
| Self-reported responses | 37.26 | 37.13 |
| Responses to mild problems | 5.07 | 6.11 |
| Responses to severe problems | 3.67 | 5.17 |
| Neglect | | |
| Self-reported responses | 23.50 | 22.63 |
| Responses to mild problems | 5.35 | 4.08 |
| Responses to severe problems | 1.94 | 1.35 |

# DISCUSSION

The results of this study provide good support for the predictions advanced in our model. First, we found that couples evince poorer functioning to the extent that partners report that they engage in higher levels of destructive responses (i.e., exit and neglect). However, there was no evidence of any link between couple functioning and tendencies to respond to problems with loyalty, and only weak evidence that voice affects couple functioning (voice contributed significantly to predicting nondistress only for mild problems). Thus it appears that the destructive problem-solving responses may be more powerful determinants of couple functioning than are the constructive responses. It is not so much the good, constructive things that partners do or do not do for one another that determines whether a relationship "works" as it is the destructive things that they do or not do in reaction to problems. Why might this be so? We entertain three possible explanations: First, the constructive responses may be more congruent with individuals' schemata for close relationships. If individuals expect their partners to behave well, the constructive responses may be taken for granted; constructive behavior, being the norm, gains one no benefits. Second, there may be an affective asymmetry in the impact of the various responses, destructive responses producing far more negative affect than constructive responses produce positive affect. Third, the response may be differentially salient; destructive responses may simply be more cognitively salient than their constructive counterparts. These speculations remain to be further explored.

Second, we found that couples evince greater health to the degree that partners attribute to one another greater constructive and lesser destructive problem-solving style. Thus in a result that is consistent with the work of Gottman and his colleagues (Gottman, 1979; Gottman et al., 1976; Markman, 1979, 1981), we find that the actual impact of partners' actions is critical in determining how well the relationship functions. Interestingly, the perception that one's partner engages in voice and is loyal (though the loyalty effect was only marginal) contributes to couple functioning, whereas other measures of loyalist tendencies bear no significant relation to couple health, and voice contributes to couple functioning only in response to mild problems.

Third, we found that certain interdependent patterns of couple response distinguish between well- and poorly functioning couples. In accordance with predictions, tendencies to behave destructively (with exit or neglect) in reaction to destructive problem-solving behaviors from partners (exit or neglect) were especially powerful in enabling us to predict level of distress/nondistress (though the impact of neglect in response to partner's exit was only marginal). In addition, distress is greater to the degree that individuals react to partners' exit and neglect with voice, and react to partners' exit with loyalty. However, the models wherein we attempted to predict couple distress/nondistress on the basis of reactions to partners' voice and loyalty were only marginally predictive of overall couple functioning (though tendencies to voice in response to partners' loyalty were, individually, significantly predictive of nondistress). Together, these findings suggest that a critical issue in solving problems in relationships may be the manner in which individuals react to destructive responses from their partners: Distress is greater to the extent that partners react destructively and fail to react constructively when their partners behave in ways that might be destructive to their relationship. Reactions when partners are behaving well (i.e., constructively) are not as effectively predictive of couple health.

Lastly, we found some support for hypotheses regarding gender differences in problem solving. In comparison with their male partners, female subjects were more likely to engage in voice and loyalty, and were somewhat less likely to engage in neglect (the latter effect was weak and inconsistently observed, however). The result of sex role socialization may be to teach women to attend more closely to the social-emotional domain, encouraging them to behave in ways that should promote healthy functioning in relationships. In contrast, men learn to attend to the instrumental domain, and are more likely to ignore or not wish to attend to interpersonal matters (i.e., engage in neglect). It is interesting to note that those behaviors at which women excelled—voice and loyalty—have much less impact on the functioning of the relationship; though women are very "good" at engaging in constructive responses, these response tendencies have very little impact on the quality of their relationships.

We found some evidence of gender differences in the aforementioned relations between problem-solving responses and couple functioning. Specifically, though we advanced no predictions in this regard, we found that the female subjects' tendencies to engage in exit are more damaging to the relationship than were their partners' exit tendencies. Also, there was a weak tendency for the female subjects' neglect tendencies to be more deleterious to the health of the relationship. Why are the women's destructive responses, particularly exit, more harmful to the relationship than are those of the male subjects? This may be due to absolute differences between men and women in mean level of each form of problem solving. Recall that in comparison with women, men are less likely to attempt to solve problems through the constructive reactions of voice and loyalty, and are somewhat more likely to engage in neglect. When his female partner engages in destructive behaviors—exit or neglect—the man is thus somewhat less likely than his partner would be under similar circumstances to help matters by engaging in voice or loyalty or by avoiding neglect. Under such circumstances, then, we may observe a pattern whereby the woman's destructive behaviors are not compensated for by adaptive partner reactions, and thus exert a strongly destructive effect on the couple's functioning. Also, it may be, because the woman generally shows greater tendencies toward constructive responding, that when she does behave destructively, it is a sign of serious trouble. However, this line of reasoning is clearly speculative, and remains to be further explored.

Before concluding, we note some of the strengths and weaknesses of this work. The most critical weakness concerns the validity of our measures. Specifically, our measure of couple distress is based entirely on self-reported feelings regarding partners and relationships. In the classic studies of distress/nondistress, distressed and nondistressed couples differ in terms of both counseling status and in terms of standard measures of marital satisfaction (cf. Billings, 1979; Birchler et al., 1975; Gottman et al., 1976). The critical question in assessing the validity of our measure of distress is "What defines healthy functioning?" Is the critical issue how the partners feel about one another? If so, several of our distress component measures (i.e., liking, love, satisfaction) have been shown to be essential components of partners' affective reactions to one another (cf. Rubin, 1973; Rusbult, 1983). Is the critical issue whether the relationship persists? If so, the commitment component of our distress measure has been shown to be powerfully predictive of long-term stability in relationships (cf. Rusbult, 1983). Thus we feel that our distress measure is a valid one. Furthermore, if our couple distress measure was not as sensitive as it could have been, the strength and consistency of our findings suggest that these effects are especially powerful and robust. Nevertheless, it would be fruitful to replicate this work, using a sample of married couples and using the traditional means of differentiating between distressed and nondistressed couples: counseling status.

A second drawback concerns the validity of our exit, voice, loyalty, and neglect measures. These measures were based entirely on verbal report: responses to Likert-type scales or responses to open-ended statements. It is possible that verbal reports bear little relation to actual problem-solving behaviors. However, two aspects of our findings are comforting in this regard: First, the various measures of individual response tendencies were significantly correlated with one another. Second, the fact that we obtained a relatively complicated, yet consistent, pattern of results—wherein constructive responses were not always positively related to couple functioning and destructive responses were not always negatively related to couple functioning—suggests that our findings do not result from artifacts of self-report such as positive response bias.

Our work has several strengths that render it particularly noteworthy. First, we used multiple modes of measurement in assessing tendencies toward exit, voice, loyalty, and neglect: self-reported tendencies, partner reports of tendencies, and relatively more behavioral measures obtained from responses to open-ended questions. The fact that we obtained similar patterns of findings across the several modes of measurement suggests that our findings should be regarded as relatively more dependable. Second, we have developed and obtained support for a model of problem solving in close relationships that is a relatively complex one, addressing the effects of individual response tendencies, partner perceptions of one anothers' response tendencies, and interdependent patterns of couple responding.

One final issue concerns causal ordering: We must ask whether the couple patterns of problem solving observed herein cause level of couple distress, or whether level of distress causes the observed patterns of problem solving. Given that we are assessing the relation between an attribute variable—couple distress/nondistress—and various problem-solving behaviors, we cannot be certain of direction of causality. The only way to determine which of these causal orderings is the more valid account is to carry out a longitudinal investigation of dating or married couples: to follow newly formed couples, charting the development of their relationships as well as changes in patterns of individual and couple problem solving (cf. Markman, 1981). We are at present carrying to such an investigation.

Our work contributes to the understanding of couple problem solving by demonstrating first, that whether a couple functions effectively appears to have much to do with tendencies to (or not to) react to relationship problems in a destructive fashion. It is the bad things that individual partners do rather than the good things that they do not do that distinguishes between well- and poorly functioning couples. Second, partners' perceptions of one another's problem-solving styles are also predictive of level of couple health; relationships benefit from individual perceptions that their partners engage in high levels of voice and loyalty and low levels of exit and neglect. Third, interdependent patterns of response are effectively predictive of nondistress. In more distressed relationships, when partners engage in exit or neglect, individuals tend to respond with high levels of destructive behaviors and low levels of constructive behaviors in return. Thus it is the way in which partners react during difficult times rather than the way they behave when things are going well that determines whether a relationship "works." Lastly, we observed some gender differences in problem-solving style: In comparison with men, women are more likely to evince voice and loyalty and may be somewhat less likely to engage in neglectful responses. These findings contribute to the understanding of behavior in close relationships by identifying several variables that appear to be critical in determining whether a relationship functions successfully. These results extend the domain to which one can apply the exit–voice–loyalty–neglect typology of responses to periodic decline in close relationships, and demonstrate that this typology is a useful means of portraying what "works" in close relationships.

# References

Altman, I., & Taylor, D. A. (1973). *Social penetration: The development of interpersonal relationships.* New York: Holt, Rinehart & Winston.

Billings, A. (1979). Conflict resolution in distressed and nondistressed married couples. *Journal of Consulting and Clinical Psychology, 47,* 368–376.

Birchler, G. R., Weiss, R. L., & Vincent, J. P. (1975). Multimethod analysis of social reinforcement exchange between maritally distressed and nondistressed spouse and stranger dyads. *Journal of Personality and Social Psychology, 31,* 349–360.

Cohen, J., & Cohen, P. (1975). *Applied multiple regression/correlation analysis for the behavioral sciences.* Hillsdale, NJ: Erlbaum.

Crowne, D., & Marlowe, D. (1964). *The approval motive.* New York: Wiley.

Fiore, A., & Swensen, C. H. (1977). Analysis of love relationships in functional and dysfunctional marriages. *Psychological Reports, 40,* 707–714.

Frederickson, C. G. (1977). Life stress and marital conflict: A pilot study. *Journal of Marriage and Family Counseling, 3,* 41–47.

Gottman, J. (1979). *Experimental investigation of marital interaction.* New York: Academic Press.

Gottman, J. M., Notarius, C., Markman, H., Bank, S., Yoppi, B., & Rubin, M. E. (1976). Behavior exchange theory and marital decision making. *Journal of Personality and Social Psychology, 34,* 14–23.

Hagistad, G. O., & Smyer, M. A. (1982). Dissolving long-term relationships: Patterns of divorcing in middle age. In S. Duck (Ed.), *Personal relationships 4: Dissolving personal relationships* (pp. 155–188). London: Academic Press.

Hawkins, J. L., Weisberg, C., & Ray, D. W. (1980). Spouse differences in communication and style: Preference, perception, behavior. *Journal of Marriage and the Family, 42,* 585–593.

Hill, C. T., Rubin, Z., & Peplau, L. A. (1976). Breakups before marriage: The end of 103 affairs. *Journal of Social Issues, 32*(1), 147–168.

Hirschman, A. O. (1970). *Exit, voice, and loyalty: Responses to decline in firms, organizations, and states.* Cambridge, MA: Harvard University Press.

Johnson, M. P. (1982). Social and cognitive features of the dissolution of commitment to relationships. In S. Duck (Ed.), *Personal relationships 4: Dissolving personal relationships* (pp. 51–73). London: Academic Press.

Kelley, H. H. (1979). *Personal relationships: Their structures and processes.* Hillsdale, NJ: Erlbaum.

Kelley, H. H., Berscheid, E., Christensen, A., Harvey, J. H., Huston, T. L., Levinger, G., McClintock, E., Peplau, L. A., & Peterson, D. R. (1983). Analyzing close relationships. In H. H. Kelley, E. Berscheid, A. Christensen, J. H. Harvey, T. L. Huston, G. Levinger, E. McClintock, L. A. Peplau, & D. R. Peterson (Eds.), *Close relationships* (pp. 20–67). San Francisco: W. H. Freeman.

Kelley, H. H., Cunningham, J. D., Grisham, J. A., Lefebvre, L. M., Sink, C. R., & Yablon, G. (1978). Sex differences in comments during conflict within close heterosexual pairs. *Sex Roles, 4,* 473–492.

Kelley, H. H., & Thibault, J. W. (1978). *Interpersonal relations: A theory of interdependence.* New York: Wiley.

Kitson, G. C., & Sussman, M. B. (1982). Marital complaints, demographic characteristics, and symptoms of mental distress in divorce. *Journal of Marriage and the Family, 44,* 87–101.

Lee, L. (1984). Sequences in separation: A framework for investigating endings of the personal (romantic) relationship. *Journal of Social and Personal Relationships, 1,* 49–73.

Levinger, G. (1979). A social exchange view on the dissolution of pair relationships. In R. L. Burgess & T. L. Huston (Eds.), *Social exchange in developing relationships* (pp. 169–193). New York: Academic Press.

Margolin, G., & Wampold, B. E. (1981). Sequential analysis of conflict and accord in distressed and nondistressed marital partners. *Journal of Counseling and Clinical Psychology, 49,* 554–567.

Markman, H. J. (1979). Application of a behavioral model of marriage in predicting relationship satisfaction of couples planning marriage. *Journal of Consulting and Clinical Psychology, 47,* 743–749.

Markman, H. J. (1981). Prediction of marital distress: A 5-year follow-up. *Journal of Consulting and Clinical Psychology, 49,* 760–762.

Morgan, B. (1976). Intimacy of disclosure topic and sex differences in self-disclosure. *Sex Roles, 2,* 161–166.

Murstein, B. I. (1970). Stimulus–value–role: A theory of marital choice. *Journal of Marriage and the Family, 32,* 465–481.

Nettles, E. J., & Loevinger, J. (1983). Sex role expectations and ego level in relation to problem marriages. *Journal of Personality and Social Psychology, 45,* 676–687.

Rubin, Z. (1973). *Liking and loving.* New York: Holt, Rinehart & Winston.

Rubin, Z., Hill, C. T., Peplau, L. A., & Dunkel-Schetter, C. (1980). Self-disclosure in dating couples: Sex roles and the ethic of openness. *Journal of Marriage and the Family, 42,* 305–317.

Rusbult, C. E. (1983). A longitudinal test of the investment model: The development (and deterioration) of satisfaction and commitment in heterosexual involvements. *Journal of Personality and Social Psychology, 45,* 101–117.

Rusbult, C. E., & Zembrodt, I. M. (1983). Responses to dissatisfaction in romantic involvements: A multidimensional scaling analysis. *Journal of Experimental Social Psychology, 19,* 274–293.

Schaap, C. (1984). A comparison of the interaction of distressed and non-distressed married couples in a laboratory situation: Literature survey, methodological issues, and an empirical investigation. In K. Hahlweg & N. S. Jacobson (Eds.), *Marital interaction: Analysis and modification* (pp. 133–158). New York: Guilford.

Linda L. Carli
Roseanne Ganley
Amy Pierce-Otay

# Similarity and Satisfaction in Roommate Relationships

In the first of two studies of college roommates, the authors found that the more similar that roommates were in personality and physical attractiveness, the more satisfied they were with one another. In a second study, however, they found that the more attractive that people saw themselves in comparison to their roommate, the more they believed that their roommate interfered with their social lives and was not a help in meeting people. In short, the more attractive partner generally was less satisfied and saw fewer benefits in the relationship. Once again, you are invited to compare these findings with your own experiences and to consider the role of physical attractiveness in attraction and relationships.

Most studies of friendship and similarity have focused either on the effects of similarity on reactions to strangers or on the degree of similarity between friends in existing relationships. A few have examined the effect of value similarity on friendship development in randomly assigned college dorm- or roommates (Berg, 1984; Hill & Stull, 1981; Newcomb, 1961). In the present research, we used this approach to examine the effects of similarity in attractiveness and personality on friendship development in college freshmen.

## SIMILARITY IN PHYSICAL ATTRACTIVENESS BETWEEN FRIENDS

Attractive people are considered to be more intelligent and likeable than those who are less attractive (Byrne, London, & Reeves, 1968; Curran & Lippold, 1975; Dion, Berscheid, & Walster, 1972; Walster, Aronson, Abrahams, & Rottmann, 1966). However, even though physical attractiveness appears to be valued, people do not always prefer relationships with very attractive individuals (Berscheid, Dion, Walster, & Walster, 1971; Folkes, 1982; Shanteau & Nagy, 1979). Moreover, in existing relationships, including friendships, partners tend to be similar in attractiveness (Cash & Derlega, 1978; McKillip & Riedel, 1983; Murstein & Christy, 1976; Price & Vandenberg, 1979; White, 1980), suggesting that people may prefer similar rather than highly attractive partners.

One explanation for the inconsistency in findings is that relationships can be considered a social exchange in which attractiveness is one important commodity; if one partner is highly attractive, the other must compensate him or her with some other desirable characteristic or risk rejection (Berscheid et al., 1971). Consequently, in selecting friends and romantic partners, people may balance a desire for an attractive partner against the risk of possible rejection. In fact, people are more likely to prefer a similar over a more attractive partner when the possibility of rejection is high (Huston, 1973; Shanteau & Nagy, 1979). Although Berscheid's social exchange model (Berscheid et al., 1971) was developed with romantic relationships in mind, it may also apply to friendships; highly attractive friends may be considered desirable but risky, because they may be perceived as less committed to the relationship.

Why might people desire attractive friends? Having an attractive friend would probably not enhance one's status the way having an attractive romantic partner does (Bar-Tal & Saxe, 1976). However, such friends may bring other benefits: a wider social circle and more opportunities to meet potential romantic partners. Adolescents and young adults, in particular, may find a physically attractive friend desirable because they are concerned with establishing friendships and romantic relationships (Parker & Gottman, 1989; Reisman, 1981) and physical attractiveness is an important determinant of popularity (Cavior & Dokecki, 1973). Whereas a physically attractive friend may bring benefits, such as increased popularity, he or she may also evoke feelings of envy in the less attractive friend (see Salovey & Rodin, 1986). Nevertheless, advantages of having a friend who is more attractive than oneself may outweigh those associated with having a friend who is less attractive. A less attractive friend may even be considered a social handicap. Consequently, people, particularly attractive people, may be more satisfied with friends who are similar to themselves in physical attractiveness than with those who are dissimilar.

## SIMILARITY IN PERSONALITY

Friends tend to be similar in personality, as well as appearance (Duck & Craig, 1978; Izard, 1960, 1963). Research on the effects of similarity in personality on attraction has revealed that people prefer strangers who have personalities similar to their own (Byrne, Griffitt, & Stefaniak, 1967; Griffitt, 1966). Perceived similarity produces good feelings (Prisbell & Andersen, 1980), which may lead to attraction if these feelings become associated with the other person (Byrne, 1969; Byrne et al., 1967).

Similarity of personality may be of particular importance to adolescents and young adults. This stage of development is a time of identity formation, a time of trying a variety of roles, establishing relationships, forming commitments (Erikson, 1968; Marcia, 1980), and becoming autonomous from parents (Steinberg & Silverberg, 1986). Consequently, at this time, self-definition is an important function of friendship (Parker & Gottman, 1989; Rubin, 1985). Young adults engage in social comparison to determine how similar they are to their peers, something that facilitates identity formation (Dickens & Perlman, 1981; Parker & Gottman, 1989). Similarity of personality should, therefore, be important to adolescents and young adults.

During this stage of development individuals experience major life changes, such as moving away from home and continuing their education; because of these changes, they are particularly motivated to find friends who are similar to themselves and who have similar concerns and uncertainties (Reisman, 1981). In addition, friendships during late adolescence are evaluated according to how committed friends are to each other, how much they contribute emotionally to the relationship (Dickens & Perlman, 1981), the extent to which they self-disclose (Parker & Gottman, 1989), and their loyalty, helpfulness, and dependability (Kon, 1981; Parker & Gottman, 1989). It is likely, therefore, that similarity in personality dimensions involving interpersonal skills, commitment to work or education, and dependability would be most important to satisfaction with friendships among young adults.

Unfortunately, it is not clear from previous findings whether people actually do prefer similar friends (Duck, 1977). In research in which subjects are asked to evaluate a stranger, they may report a preference for similarity because they are given no other information about the stranger with which to make a judgment. In real life they would have far more information at their disposal, so that information about personality would be less salient. Nor does the fact that friends tend to be similar necessarily imply such a preference. Friends tend to be similar across a wide variety of characteristics, such as marital status, ethnic background, and age (Verbrugge, 1977). People tend to meet friends in contexts that expose them to similar others—for example, in neighborhoods, at work or school, or through family or friends (Feld, 1982; Verbrugge, 1977). Therefore, similarity in friendships may be due to the greater proximity of similar individuals (Cohen, 1977; Feld, 1982; Verbrugge, 1977).

To test whether similarity is causally related to satisfaction with friendships and not simply the result of greater proximity of similar others, it would be necessary to randomly assign friends to each other and then test whether similar pairs are more satisfied than dissimilar pairs. Our subjects were pairs of freshman college roommates, assigned to each other at random. We hypothesized (a) that similarity in attractiveness and personality would result in greater satisfaction with the friendship and (b) that this effect would be most likely to occur for the more attractive partner in each pair.

Our personality scale consisted of items from the California Personality Inventory (CPI), which measures a variety of personality characteristics falling into four dimensions of personality: *interpersonal adequacy*, which includes measures of poise, leadership, self-acceptance, and sociability and reflects an individual's social skills; *character*, which includes measures of maturity, tolerance, self-control, and responsibility and reflects how reliable a person is; *achievement potential*, which reflects an individual's competitiveness and potential to achieve, and *intellectual and interest modes*, which includes measures of psychological-mindedness and flexibility and reflects an individual's general interests. We hypothesized that similarity in interpersonal adequacy and character would be predictive of satisfaction with the friendship, as these factors correspond most to those that adolescents and young adults find important to friendships.

## STUDY 1

*Method*

### Subjects

The subjects were 30 pairs of second-semester freshman roommates at a small liberal arts college. Half of the pairs were male and half were female. All subjects had been randomly assigned a same-sex roommate, with the exception that students who smoked were never paired with nonsmokers. All the pairs had been living together approximately 6 months, since the beginning of their freshman year, and were going to be selecting roommates for the following year within 2 weeks after participating in the study.

### Procedure

Experimenters recruited subjects by approaching them in their dormitories and asking that they volunteer for a study on roommate relationships. All students agreed to participate. Each subject completed the questionnaire independent of his or her roommate.

*Questionnaire items.* The questionnaire began with 42 statements taken from the CPI reflecting the four dimensions of personality measured by the scale: interpersonal adequacy, character, achievement potential, and intellectual and interest modes. Subjects indicated whether they agreed or disagreed with each statement on a 9-point scale with endpoints (1) *disagree completely* and (9) *agree completely*.

The last three items on the questionnaire were measures of the quality of the roommate relationship. Subjects indicated how satisfied they were with their relationship with their roommates and how satisfied they thought their roommates were on a 9-point scales with endpoints (1) *completely dissatisfied* and (9) *completely satisfied.* They also indicated whether they were requesting the same roommates for the following year.

*Physical attractiveness ratings.* One male and one female judge independently rated each subject's attractiveness on a 7-point scale, higher scores indicating greater attractiveness. Ratings were based on photographs of students in a freshmen register. Judges were not told the hypotheses or that subjects were roommates.

## Results

The absolute value of the difference between the responses of roommates was computed for each personality item and for the attractiveness ratings. Pearson correlation coefficients revealed no relation between roommates in personality or attractiveness, which was expected because roommate assignments had been made randomly. Pairs were similar, however, in their ratings of how satisfied they were, how satisfied they felt their roommates were and whether they intended to live together the next year. The results provided support for the hypothesis. Similarity in personality and similarity in attractiveness were direct predictors of how satisfied subjects were with their roommates, how satisfied they felt their roommates were, and whether they planned to have the same roommates the next year.

If there are fewer benefits of having friends who are less attractive than oneself than of having friends who are more attractive, the relation between similarity in attractiveness and subjects' ratings of their own satisfaction may be more likely to occur for the more attractive roommate in each pair. To test this, correlations between similarity in attractiveness and subjects' own satisfaction were computed separately for the more and the less attractive member of each pair. The correlation was significant for the more, but not for the less attractive members. This same pattern of results was obtained for subjects' ratings of their desire to have the same roommates the next year. Similarity in attractiveness was marginally associated with the desire to keep the same roommate for the more attractive member of each pair, but not for the less attractive member.

Finally, to test whether satisfaction in friendships may depend more on particular personality characteristics than on others, separate analyses were conducted on the four dimensions of personality assessed by the CPI. In support of the third hypothesis, similarity in two of them, interpersonal adequacy and, marginally, character, predicted satisfaction; similarity in achievement potential and intellectual and interest modes did not.

## Discussion

The results support the hypotheses that similarity in attractiveness and personality leads to greater satisfaction with roommate relationships. Similar roommates were more satisfied, felt their roommates were more satisfied, and were more likely to want the same roommates the next year. Because subjects were assigned to each other at random, we conclude that dissimilarity can cause dissatisfaction and the dissolution of friendships.

The results suggest that, in friendships, similarity in attractiveness may be more important to the more attractive partner. Perhaps such a partner may view his or her less attractive friend as a social handicap, whereas the less attractive partner may perceive the relationship as yielding both negative consequences, such as envy, and positive consequences, such as greater social opportunities.

The attractiveness of one's roommate may be particularly important to college freshmen because they, and other groups who have experienced a major life transition, must form a new social network (Reisman, 1981). Having a socially desirable roommate may help. We therefore hypothesized that the more attractive freshmen perceived themselves to be relative to their roommates, the more problems they would report (such as that their roommates interfered with their social life) and the less they would report either that they were envious of their roommates or that their roommates helped them to meet other people.

In Study 1, roommates were more satisfied when they were similar in two dimensions of personality: interpersonal adequacy and character. The importance of similarity in interpersonal adequacy and character in our sample probably reflects the particular concerns of college freshmen: forming new intimate friends, developing an informal social life, adapting to their new workload, and adjusting to living independently with other young adults. Students who are similar in interpersonal adequacy and character would probably have similar social lives and study habits. We hypothesized that perceived similarity in these areas, as well as other areas that might directly affect the interaction of roommates, would be predictive of satisfaction. Besides social life and study habits, areas of greatest concern to roommates include the way problems are solved, neatness, and the degree of closeness in the relationship (Roby, Zelin, & Chechile, 1977), suggesting that similarity in emotional expression and neatness would also be predictive of satisfaction. In addition, we hypothesized that the more similar students perceived themselves to be to their roommates in personality, the more they would report having similar habits and engaging in activities with their roommates.


## STUDY 2

*Method*

### Subjects

The subjects were 67 first-semester freshmen at a small liberal arts college. Each had been living on campus with the same randomly assigned roommate since the beginning of his or her freshman year, approximately 4 months. Only one member of each roommate pair was selected to participate.

### Procedure

Subjects were contacted in their classes or by telephone and asked to complete a questionnaire on college life. All who were contacted agreed to participate and completed the questionnaire independent of their roommates.

*Self-ratings.* Subjects rated themselves on 26 9-point bipolar scales, including *unemotional—emotional, disorganized—organized,* and *socially skill—socially awkward.* They also rated how physically attractive they felt they were on a 9-point scale with endpoints (1) *unattractive* and (9) *attractive.* Finally, they indicated how much time they spent each week in 12 activities, including watching television, studying, going to parties, talking with friends, and participating in college organizations.

*Roommate ratings.* After completing the self-ratings, subjects were given the same questionnaire items with which to rate their roommates. They were also given the list of activities again and asked to indicate the extent to which they engaged in them with their roommates on a 5-point scale with endpoints (1) *I never do this with my roommate* and (5) *I always do this with my roommate.* Finally, eight items were included to assess how often subjects experienced particular problems or benefits in their relationship with their roommates. On 9-point scales with endpoints (1) *never occurs* and (9) *always occurs,* subjects indicated how often they felt envious of their roommates, felt that their roommates helped them to meet other people, wished they could be like their roommates, wished that their friendship could be more exclusive, worried that their roommates would end the relationship, felt that their roommates interfered with their social life, felt that their other friends would not like their roommates, and thought about ending their relationship with their roommates.

*Satisfaction items.* Subjects completed three 9-point scales measuring satisfaction. They indicated how satisfied they were with their relationship, with endpoints (1) *very dissatisfied* and (9) *very satisfied*; how much they liked their roommates, with endpoints (1) *dislike a great deal* and (9) *like a great deal*; and to what extent they were friends, with endpoints (1) *not at all* and (9) *we are best friends.*

### Results

*Similarity in attractiveness and personality.* To test the first hypothesis, each subject's attractiveness rating was subtracted from that of his or her roommate. Pearson correlation coefficients were computed to determine whether these differences were associated with subjects' judgments of problems and benefits in the relationship. The results provide support for the first hypothesis. The more attractive subjects considered themselves to be, relative to their roommates, the more they reported feeling that their roommates interfered with their social life, that other friends would not like their roommates, and that they thought about ending their relationship with their roommates. The more relatively attractive they considered their roommates to be, the more they felt envious of them, felt that their roommates helped them to meet people, and wished they could be more like their roommates.

For the measure of physical attractiveness, each personality item, and each activity, the absolute value of the difference between subjects' self-ratings and their ratings of their roommates was computed. As predicted, satisfaction was associated with similarity in social skills, responsibility, orderliness, and emotional expressiveness. Similarity in independence also predicted satisfaction.

Overall measures of similarity in personality and activities were computed by averaging the absolute value of the difference scores for all the personality variables and all the activities, respectively. The results replicate the effects of similarity on satisfaction found in the first study; similarity in attractiveness or personality was predictive of satisfaction, liking, and friendship. In addition, in support of the third hypothesis, similarity in personality, but not attractiveness, directly predicted perceived similarity in activities and subjects' reports of how often they shared activities with their roommates.

## GENERAL DISCUSSION

The results of both studies, taken together, suggest that similarity in attractiveness may affect friendships in much the same way as it affects romantic relationships. The more attractive friend may perceive fewer benefits to the relationship and may feel less satisfied with it. Moreover, although less attractive friends may perceive benefits to a friendship with someone more attractive, this does not necessarily mean that they will be more satisfied with such a relationship; on the contrary, for them, similarity in attractiveness is positively, though not significantly, associated with satisfaction. This is probably so because the less attractive friend may experience not only social benefits to the relationship but envy and possibly other negative consequences. For example, less attractive individuals may feel uncomfortable or awkward when interacting with their more attractive friends. Because of the dissatisfaction of the more attractive member and the ambivalence of the less attractive member, dissimilarity in attractiveness may put friendships at risk.

The present studies reveal that similarity in the personalities of friends can lead to more satisfying and enduring relationships. As suggested by Byrne (1969), people who have similar characters may find each other's company highly reinforcing, which may help to maintain the relationship. This may be especially true of individuals in new and unfamiliar circumstances, such as college freshmen. Moreover, our results indicate that similarity in personality leads roommates to engage in similar activities and to participate in them together. In the second study, shared activity was associated with satisfaction with the relationship and in general, it may help to maintain friendships.

It is likely that proximity does play a part in creating friendships between individuals who are similar in attractiveness and personality. However, the results of the present studies suggest that people may also select friends who are similar to themselves. Similarity may be of particular importance to college freshmen. College encourages a developmental moratorium, a transitional stage between adolescence and adulthood during which late adolescents can try out different roles, identities, and commitments (Erikson, 1968; Marcia, 1980; Waterman, 1982). The developmental objectives of late adolescence—gaining an autonomous sense of self, forming intimate relationships with romantic partners, and establishing educational and career goals (Erikson, 1968; Marcia, 1980)—can all be facilitated through friendship formation. By evaluating the differences and similarities between themselves and others, late adolescents can gain self-definition (Gottman & Mettetal, 1986; Parker & Gottman, 1989).

Friendships with similar, as opposed to dissimilar, others may help late adolescents to set reasonable career expectations (Reisman, 1981) and provide a better basis for social comparison in new and uncertain circumstances (Suls & Miller, 1977). A similar friend may also provide them with better opportunities to meet desirable potential mates and expand their own circles of friends, because such a friend is likely to have similar (and therefore compatible) friends of his or her own. Finally, at this stage of life in particular, during which late adolescents are breaking away from family and old social connections but have not yet acquired a complete sense of identity, relationships with similar others can provide them with a measure of autonomy (Rubin, 1985). Similar friends may, therefore, help late adolescents to judge their abilities and achievement potential, expand their social network, and discover who they are.

## References

Bar-Tal, D., & Saxe, L. (1976). Perceptions of similarly and dissimilarly attractive couples and individuals. *Journal of Personality and Social Psychology, 33*, 772–781.

Berg, J. H. (1984). Development of friendship between roommates. *Journal of Personality and Social Psychology, 46*, 346–356.

Berscheid, E., Dion, K., Walster, E., & Walster, G. W. (1971). Physical attractiveness and dating choice: A test of the matching hypothesis. *Journal of Experimental Social Psychology, 7*, 173–189.

Byrne, D. (1969). Attitudes and attraction. In L. Berkowitz (Ed.), *Advances in experimental social psychology* (Vol. 4, pp. 35–89). Orlando, FL: Academic Press.

Byrne, D., Griffitt, W., & Stefaniak, D. (1967). Attraction and similarity of personality characteristics. *Journal of Personality and Social Psychology, 5*, 82–90.

Byrne, D., London, O., & Reeves, K. (1968). The effects of physical attractiveness, sex, and attitude similarity on interpersonal attraction. *Journal of Personality, 36*, 259–271.

Cash, T. F., & Derlega, V. J. (1978). The matching hypothesis: Physical attractiveness among same-sexed friends. *Personality and Social Psychology Bulletin, 4*, 240–243.

Cavior, N., & Dokecki, P. R. (1973). Physical attractiveness, perceived attitude similarity, and academic achievement as contributors to interpersonal attraction among adolescents. *Developmental Psychology, 9*, 44–54.

Cohen, J. (1977). Sources of peer homogeneity. *Sociology of Education, 50*, 227–241.

Curran, J. P., & Lippold, S. (1975). The effects of physical attraction and attitude similarity on attraction in dating dyads. *Journal of Personality, 43*, 528–539.

Dickens, W. J., & Perlman, D. (1981). Friendship over the life-cycle. In S. Duck & R. Gilmour (Eds.), *Personal relationships 2: Developing personal relationships*. Orlando, FL: Academic Press.

Dion, K., Berscheid, E., & Walster, E. (1972). What is beautiful is good. *Journal of Personality and Social Psychology, 24*, 285–290.

Duck, S. W. (1977). *The study of acquaintance*. Westmead, England: Saxon House, Teakfield Ltd.

Duck, S. W., & Craig, G. (1978). Personality similarity and the development of friendship. *British Journal of Social and Clinical Psychology, 17*, 237–242.

Erikson, E. H. (1968). *Identity: Youth and crisis*. New York: Norton.

Feld, S. L. (1982). Social structural determinants of similarity among associates. *American Sociological Review, 47*, 797–801.

Folkes, V. S. (1982). Forming relationships and the matching hypothesis. *Personality and Social Psychology Bulletin, 8*, 631–636.

Gottman, J. M., & Mettetal, G. W. (1986). Speculation about social and affective development: Friendship and acquaintanceship through adolescence. In M. Gottman & J. M. Parker (Eds.), *Conversations of friends: Speculations on affective development*. New York: Cambridge University Press.

Griffitt, W. B. (1966). Interpersonal attraction as a function of self-concept and personality similarity-dissimilarity. *Journal of Personality and Social Psychology, 4*, 581–584.

Hill, C. T., & Stull, D. E. (1981). Sex differences in effects of social and value similarity in same-sex friendships. *Journal of Personality and Social Psychology, 41*, 488–502.

Huston, T. L. (1973). Ambiguity of acceptance, social desirability, and dating choice. *Journal of Experimental Social Psychology, 9*, 32–42.

Izard, C. (1960). Personality similarity and friendship. *Journal of Abnormal and Social Psychology, 61*, 47–51.

Izard, C. (1963). Personality similarity and friendship: A follow-up study. *Journal of Abnormal and Social Psychology, 66*, 598–600.

Kon, I. S. (1981). Adolescent friendships: Some unanswered questions for future research. In S. Duck & R. Gilmour (Eds.), *Personal relationships 2: Developing personal relationships*. Orlando, FL: Academic Press.

Marcia, J. E. (1980). Identity in adolescence. In J. Adelson (Ed.), *Handbook of adolescent psychology*. New York: Wiley.

McKillip, J. M., & Riedel, S. L. (1983). external validity of matching on physical attractiveness for same and opposite sex couples. *Journal of Applied Social Psychology, 13*, 328–337.

Murstein, B. I., & Christy, P. (1976). Physical attractiveness and marriage adjustment in middle aged couples. *Journal of Personality and Social Psychology, 34*, 537–542.

Newcomb, T. M. (1961). *The acquaintance process*. New York: Holt, Rinehart & Winston.

Parker, J. G., & Gottman, J. M. (1989). Social and emotional development in a relational context: Friendship interaction from early childhood to adolescence. In T. J. Berndt & G. W. Ladd (Eds.), *Peer relationships in child development*. New York: Wiley.

Price, R. A., & Vandenberg, S. G. (1979). Matching for physical attractiveness in married couples. *Personality and social Psychology Bulletin, 5*, 398–400.

Prisbell, M., & Andersen, J. F. (1980). The importance of perceived homophily, level of uncertainty, feeling good, safety, and self-disclosure in interpersonal relationships. *Communication Quarterly, 28,* 22–33.

Reisman, J. M. (1981). Adult friendships. In S. Duck & R. Gilmour (Eds.), *Personal relationships 2: Developing personal relationships.* Orlando, FL: Academic Press.

Roby, T., Zelin, M., & Chechile, R. (1977). matching roommates by an optimal indirect technique. *Journal of Applied Psychology, 62,* 70–75.

Rubin, L. B. (1985). *Just friends: The role of friendship in our lives.* New York: Harper & Row.

Salovey, P., & Rodin, J. (1984). The differentiation of social-comparison jealousy and romantic jealousy. *Journal of Personality and Social Psychology, 50,* 1100–1112.

Shanteau, J., & Nagy, G. F. (1979). Probability of acceptance in dating choice. *Journal of Personality and Social Psychology, 37,* 522–533.

Steinberg, L., & Silverberg, S. B. (1986). The vicissitudes of autonomy in early adolescence. *Child Development, 57,* 841–851.

Suls, J., & Miller, R. L. (1977). *Social comparison processes.* Washington, DC: Hemisphere.

Verbrugge, L. M. (1977). The structure of adult friendship choices. *Social Forces, 56,* 576–597.

Walster, E., Aronson, V., Abrahams, D., & Rottmann, L. (1966). Importance of physical attractiveness in dating behavior. *Journal of Personality and Social Psychology, 39,* 508–516.

Waterman, A. S. (1982). Identity development from adolescence to adulthood: An extension of theory and a review of research. *Developmental Psychology, 18,* 341–358.

White, G. L. (1980). Physical attractiveness and courtship process. *Journal of Personality and Social Psychology, 39,* 660–668.

# 7

# Helping: Whether and When to Give Aid

Questions about when and why people help have always set off great debate and speculation. We can cite dramatic examples of people who risked their lives for the sake of strangers, at the same time recounting acts of apparent callousness where witnesses to a crime failed to offer any assistance to the victim. In ways that are rarely scientific or systematic, we all seek answers to what motivates helping and what sets it off.

Daniel Batson, Professor of Psychology at the University of Kansas, is a social psychologist who has studied helping behavior for over two decades, trying to identify and disentangle the complex motives that lead people to act on another person's behalf. In his recent book, *The Altruism Question,* he reviews his own careful research and that of others, making a strong case for the relationship between empathy, altruism, and helping. In our conversation he deals with some of these same basic issues, noting his discoveries in this field and tracing the evolution of his own interest in it.

## A CONVERSATION WITH DANIEL BATSON
*University of Kansas*

**Krupat:** *Let me begin by asking you a question that sounds simple, but probably has no simple answer: Why do people help one another?*

**Batson:** That's been a question that has intrigued philosophers for centuries because it raises the possibility that maybe people are capable of caring for something beyond just their own interests. Obviously, there are lots of reasons, but the thing that's particularly intriguing about the fact that people do help others is the possibility that maybe we're more social than we thought.

**Krupat:** *In what sense?*

**Batson:** Clearly, helping is a social behavior—it's doing something for someone else. But it goes beyond that because it suggests or at least raises the possibility that there is a social or a prosocial motive, where one person actually has the other person's welfare as the goal. To try to sort out motives for helping is a delicate operation because there are a lot of subtle benefits that one can get from helping someone else. So the philosophical debates swing back and forth: Is it because helpers really are trying to benefit themselves, or is there somewhere within us a capacity to care about the other as an ultimate goal—not as a means for something else, but as an end in itself?

**Krupat:** *For example?*

**Batson:** Anytime you see a dramatic, wonderful example like the rescuing of Jews in Nazi Europe or the fellow who dove into the icy Potomac to rescue a plane crash victim, you look at it and you say, "Gee, that's remarkable." But still, from Mother Teresa on down, it's possible to say, "Yes, but they do get benefits." That's part of the logical confusion. Simply to say that a person does get benefits from helping another doesn't rule out the possibility that getting those benefits was not the person's ultimate goal. It's a tricky issue, but I actually think that it's one of those problems where the experimental methods of social psychology are ideally suited—so far as I know, *uniquely* suited–to providing an answer.

**Krupat:** *Now, if I'm correct, you have some very strong feelings about what the answer is to this.*

**Batson:** When I started out doing research on helping behavior, I shared with most social psychologists the belief that people were always egoistic—self-interested. I took that as a given, relatively uncritically. But, working with a graduate student here at Kansas, Jay Coke, doing some research on empathy and helping, I was surprised by what we found. People seemed to be much more caring about the welfare of the other person than I, at least, would have expected. So that got us thinking that maybe there is more to this than we had imagined, and also thinking about how we could tease the possible motives apart.

**Krupat:** *Now one word that I don't think either one of us has used—and certainly we ought to introduce into the rest of the equation—is the term altruism. When you talk about helping behavior, where does altruism fit? Is it a special kind of helping?*

**Batson:** I think of helping as a *behavior*. Conceptually, it's important to distinguish that from the motive that promotes the behavior. I think of altruism as a *motive*. Altruism is a motivational state with the ultimate goal of increasing another's welfare. By ultimate goal here, I don't mean something cosmic, but just what the person is after in the situation. I juxtapose altruism with egoism, which is a motivational state with the ultimate goal of increasing one's own welfare. There are a whole range of possible helping motives, egoistic and altruistic. Both types of motives can operate at the same time. It's not an either/or. The fact that they can be mixed together simply makes it a more complicated problem.

**Krupat:** *Then where is the problem? Why do people have such a hard time accepting that altruistic motives could be driving social behaviors?*

**Batson:** Historically, and this goes back to the philosophical tradition, we have taken a very strong stand. The strong stand is that altruistic motivation as I've defined it does not exist. It's like a unicorn, something that you can imagine, but just doesn't happen to be part of the real world. The dominant position in Western thought is one of universal egoism, that anytime you see somebody doing something nice for somebody, ultimately they're doing it for themselves. That's a view within philosophy that we've gotten from Thomas Hobbes and his descendants. Within psychology, it comes to us in part from the Darwinian tradition, especially as interpreted by Freud. Reinforcement theory and behaviorism have also contributed. In part, psychologists' belief in universal egoism comes from a very fundamental insight that Freud had about our enormous capacity for ulterior or unconscious motives. We may think that we're doing something because we care about somebody else, but in fact we may be doing it for self-benefits of which we may not even be aware. What has happened historically, both within psychology and society at large, is that this has turned into a basic assumption that whatever we do, that there has to be some self-benefit.

Krupat: *So what I'm hearing you say is that, at a minimum, your goal has been to establish firmly that people are at least capable of altruistic motivation. Is that right?*

Batson: Not establish—find out. If we're not capable of altruism, then we don't need to worry about ways to promote it. We don't spend a lot of time worrying about trying to help people fly without airplanes because doing so is not within our physical repertoire. If altruism is within our psychological repertoire, if at least some people some of the time get invested in the welfare of others in much the same way they get invested in their own, then this changes our conception of human nature; then we humans are more social than we have thought.

Krupat: *Would I be correct in saying that you believe that helping and altruism are not only real, but that they are useful or necessary in helping us survive as a species?*

Batson: When you ask in what ways altruistic impulses could actually promote genetic survival, I think about mammalian species. At least within many mammalian species, the young live in a very vulnerable state for some period of time. Obviously, if the parents didn't give a rip about the needs or the welfare of their offspring, these species would quickly die out.

Krupat: *Okay, then to what extent is it built in and to what extent is it learned?*

Batson: I don't know the answer to that one. It may be hardwired, it may be learned, or it may be a mixture of the two. In my research the factor that I have tended to focus on in looking for altruistic motives is an empathic emotional response, a sort of feeling of compassion, sympathy, or tenderness. And in my more metaphorical moments, I tend to think of this empathy as an emotional umbilical cord, perhaps like the parental reaction to the child, which involves a very strong sense of attachment and an emotional feeling of concern for the child. It may be that the empathic emotions that we're looking at in the behavior of one undergraduate responding to the need of another or to the need of someone in society whom they have never met may be extensions of that parental impulse. It's just speculation, of course, but I think it is worth considering.

Krupat: *And I assume that, as you've pursued this empathic response further in your research, it doesn't disappear with closer scrutiny.*

Batson: No, it has not seemed to. There's always the danger of jumping too quickly to a flattering interpretation of human behavior based on altruistic motives. So it becomes a job of trying to be very, very careful and thinking as hard as we can about plausible self-benefits or egoistic motives that could hide behind and motivate helping evoked by empathic feelings. We have to take every plausible egoistic alternative seriously.

**Krupat:** *Now, you were saying that empathy and altruism do not disappear even when you study them critically and carefully. Yet in one of your more poetic moments, you describe the concern for others as "a fragile flower easily crushed by self-concern," suggesting that it needs to be carefully nurtured in order to survive. Can you recommend ways in which we can encourage and promote altruistic motives?*

**Batson:** To the degree that we have assumed that all human motivation is exclusively egoistic, when you ask, "How do I raise my son or daughter so that he or she is a kind, caring person?," what's likely to come to mind is that we need to reinforce these behaviors, praise our children when they do nice things, punish them when they do not, try to teach them the basic norms of reciprocity, sharing and fairness, and principles such as these. Pursuing this strategy, we haven't even entertained the possibility that there may be other sources of prosocial motivation, of motivation for helping, such as empathic feelings. If there are other sources, then maybe we need to think about trying to inculcate those as well, maybe we need to ask what we might do to increase our capacity to feel these empathic emotions for a wider range of individuals.

**Krupat:** *Such as?*

**Batson:** Such as giving children experiences of feeling these emotions. In fact, they get a fair number. A lot of children's fairy tales, the Disney sorts of movies, and things like that are designed, at least in part, to generate these kinds of feelings. But we may need to have children read these stories and watch these films in a context where they can recognize these feelings; we may need to help them label their feelings to understand what's going on. We don't tend to see teaching emotional sensitivity as integral to developing a caring individual.

**Krupat:** *I can see how we need to do this one-on-one, parent to child. But are there other things we can do on a larger scale?*

**Batson:** In terms of social organization, it may be that there are certain community configurations—mainly stability in the community and contact with neighbors—that increase the likelihood of these kinds of emotional reactions. So the research on empathy and altruism carries implications for how one organizes society. If we assume that, in fact, everybody's only out for themselves and the only way that you're going to have them help other people is to make it worth their while, that leads to a strategy like introducing good samaritan laws—people get paid if they help a stranger or punished if they don't. But that strategy is dramatically different from one that says,"No, we've got some other resources that we can employ. If the structure of the community is of a particular type, people can actually care for one another." Now another alternative is to say, "OK, then let's encourage that as well; let's beat every drum. Let's try to reinforce the child and punish and so forth, and at the same time let's encourage the emotional reactions and caring." But that may backfire.

**Krupat:** *Is there something wrong with* not *putting all your eggs in one basket?*

**Batson:** It may be that the two things—shaping prosocial behavior with rewards and punishments and encouraging empathy and altruism—at least under certain circumstances—work against each other. To the degree that you make salient the self-benefits and the sort of self-gratification reasons for caring for somebody else, you may undermine the ability to care for them as an end in itself, just as extrinsic rewards have been found to undermine intrinsic actions in other areas of human behavior. So, what we may be doing with our current strategy is inadvertently undermining that altruistic motivation that does exist. Back to the fragile flower.

**Krupat:** *Up till now, we have been talking about other people's motives. At this point, I'd like to change from the motives of others to your own motivation. Some people take a topic, study if for a few years, and get tired of it. You've been at the business of studying altruism and helping for many years now. Can you tell me a little bit about how you came to be interested and how it is that you remain interested?*

**Batson:** When I left college, I went to theological seminary, planning to be a minister. After a few years, it was clear to me that I wasn't cut out for that; I really enjoyed research. I applied to graduate school at Princeton to work with Harry Schroeder, whom I had worked with before. Well, between the spring when I applied and the fall when I matriculated, Harry left Princeton. That placed me in an awkward situation; I think the rest of the faculty at Princeton was a bit appalled at having this seminarian. That's not the normal route into psychology. So I was casting about for somebody to work with and I met John Darley who had recently come to Princeton. Through him I came to find out that you could take behavioral measures on something as complex as helping behavior. To think that one could study ethical issues in a scientific way was a real eye-opener for me and an exciting possibility. So, in the initial work that we did, we actually used seminary students as subjects in a study looking at some situational variables, but also looking at different dimensions of personal religion and the way that these related to a person's helpfulness.

**Krupat:** *That sounds like a good start. What has kept you going?*

**Batson:** When I was being considered for a position here at Kansas and came for an interview, I gave a talk about my dissertation work, which was an attributional analysis of how people help, focused on the cognitive factors in helping. In the audience was Fritz Heider, the originator of many attribution notions and emeritus professor at Kansas at that time. After my talk, I had a chance to sit down with Fritz and ask him what he thought. He was extremely nice. He said that the talk was very interesting, but then he added, "It seems to me that you're taking a matter of the heart and trying to turn it into a matter of the head." I really didn't know what to do with his comment. Basically I let it drop because within social psychology at that time people were studying helping behavior by looking at situational factors in a cognitive framework. But later, when Jay Coke and I collected our data and it looked like helping was much more a matter of the heart than I had imagined, I remembered the comment. I think now I have at least some understanding of what Fritz Heider was talking about: Feeling and desire. When I began to think about prosocial emotion and motivation, it was like coming out of the woods into a clearing, and there was this huge landscape ahead—much bigger than I had imagined. People looking at my research over the years have said, "My God, how can you possibly stay at one thing this long?," implying that I ought to move on. But I've been pleased that so far it has stayed interesting, and so far, at least, I feel like I'm still learning. The question of the existence of altruism is wonderfully complex and, I believe, fundamentally important.

R. Lance Shotland

# When Bystanders Just Stand By

Citing the tragic murder of Kitty Genovese in New York City well over 25 years ago, Shotland reviews some of the factors that make bystanders more or less likely to help a person in need. In particular, he cites the factor of ambiguity, noting that incidents are not always as easy to interpret during the time they are occurring as they are after the fact. On the positive side, he points to occasions where people spontaneously rush in to stop a crime and catch the offender. After reading this, you might consider ways in which we might increase helping among bystanders.

Twenty-one years ago, Kitty Genovese was brutally murdered as her cries in the night went unanswered by 38 of her neighbors. That infamous incident riveted public attention on just how helpless and alone crime victims may be without the support of their fellow citizens.

In fact, bystanders often do play a crucial role in preventing street crimes when they serve as extended "eyes and ears" of the police. Arrests occur more frequently when bystanders are present than when they are not. More than three-fourths of all arrests result from reports by bystanders or victims, while relatively few come from police surveillance alone. In more than half of all criminal cases, bystanders are present when the police arrive. These citizens may be important information sources, potential witnesses and influences on the victim's decision to report the crime.

Bystanders can also help control crime directly. In some cases, they leap in and rescue crime victims, or even form spontaneous vigilante groups that catch and punish offenders. Yet at other times they are peculiarly passive, neither calling the police nor intervening directly. What accounts for these differences?

The death of Kitty Genovese intrigued the press, the public and social psychologists, all of whom wondered how 38 people could do so little. In 1968, psychologists John Darley and Bibb Latané started a torrent of research by discovering experimentally that a person is less likely to help someone in trouble when other bystanders are present.

As Latané and Steven Nida have noted, by 1981 some 56 experiments had tested and extended this observation. These studies examined the reactions of unwitting subjects who witnessed a staged emergency—either alone or in the presence of actors instructed to ignore the incident. In 48 of the studies, bystanders helped less when someone else was present. People who were alone helped 75 percent of the time, while those with another person helped just 53 percent of the time. After close to 20 years of research, the evidence indicates that "the bystander effect," as it has come to be called, holds for all types of emergencies, medical or criminal.

The effect occurs, the studies show, because witnesses diffuse responsibility ("Only one person needs to call the police, and certainly someone else will") and because they look at the behavior of other bystanders to determine what is happening ("If no one else is helping, does this person really need help?"). As a result, membership in a group of bystanders lowers each person's likelihood of intervening.

This phenomenon does not completely explain the behavior of bystanders, however. In the Genovese murder, for example, even if each bystander's probability of helping had dropped appreciably, with 38 witnesses we would expect several people to attempt to help. Other factors must be involved.

When the witnesses in the Genovese case were asked why they did not intervene, they said, "Frankly, we were afraid," or "You don't realize the danger," or "I didn't want to get involved," and even, "I was tired." In other words, in deciding whether to help, they considered the cost to themselves. When direct intervention might lead to physical harm, retaliation from the criminal or days in court testifying, consideration of such costs is understandable. However, the deterrent effects of other costs, such as intervention time, are more surprising. Some of my own work indicates that if helping is likely to take approximately 90 rather than 30 to 40 seconds, the rate is cut in half.

Ambiguity also lowers the intervention rate. In a simulated rape, many more bystanders intervene if they glimpse a struggle than if they only hear the incident. In a simulated accidental electrocution, researchers Russell Clark and Larry Wood found that more people intervene if they see a victim being "electrocuted" than if they see and hear only the flashes and sounds of a presumed victim's electrocution.

At times, people misinterpret rare events such as crimes even if they see them. A young woman recently told me about an incident in which she had intervened. She and her friends had met three young men in a bar. After some friendly conversation, the young men left, and the women left shortly afterwards. From a distance, the woman saw her recent acquaintances in the parking lot and thought they were simply horsing around. It wasn't until she reached her car, which was closer to the scene, that she realized the young men were being assaulted in a robbery attempt.

Even if they interpret the situation correctly, bystanders may still be unsure about what they are seeing. People who see a crime, an accident or other unlikely event may wonder, "Did it really happen?" and freeze while they try to figure it out. Latané and Darley were the first to observe that if people are going to intervene, most do it in the first few seconds after they notice the emergency.

Certain types of crime, such as a man's attack on a woman, have unique features that may particularly invite misinterpretation and inhibit intervention. One Genovese witness said, "We thought it was a lovers' quarrel." Bystanders frequently reach similar conclusions when a man attacks a woman. Nine years after the Genovese incident, this story was carried by the Associated Press:

"A 20-year-old woman who works for the Trenton [New Jersey] Police Department was raped yesterday in full view of about 25 employees of a nearby roofing company who watched intently but did not answer her screams for help. [One witness explained]. 'Two people did that up there about a year ago but it was mutual. We thought, well, if we went up there, it might turn out to be her boyfriend or something like that.'"

Some of my own research conducted with Gretchen Straw, a former graduate student, shows that bystanders behave very differently if they assume a quarreling man and woman are related rather than strangers. For example, bystanders who witnessed a violent staged fight between a man and a woman and heard the woman shout, "Get away from me, I don't know you!" gave help 65 percent of the time. But those who saw the fight and heard the woman scream, "Get away from me, I don't know why I ever married you!" only helped 19 percent of the time.

People interpret fights between married people and between strangers quite differently. In our study, the nonresponsive bystanders who heard the "married" woman scream said they were reluctant to help because they weren't sure their help was wanted. They also viewed the "married" woman as much less severely injured than was the woman attacked by the "stranger," despite the fact that the two fights were staged identically. Hence, a woman seen as being attacked by a stranger is perceived as needing help more than is one fighting with a spouse. Furthermore, people expect the husband to stay and fight if they intervene, while they expect a stranger to flee. This makes intervention with fighting strangers seem safer and less costly. Unfortunately, if bystanders see a man and a woman fighting, they will usually assume that the combatants know each other.

What role do individual characteristics play in bystander behavior? Researchers have identified only a few personality factors that differentiate helpers from nonhelpers. Psychologist Louis Penner and his colleagues at the University of South Florida have found that people with relatively high scores for "sociopathy" on a personality test (although not clinically sociopaths) are less likely to help and are less bothered by others' distress than are people with low scores. On the other side of the coin, Shalom Schwartz and his colleagues at the Hebrew University in Jerusalem have shown that people who have a sense of moral obligation to the victim are more likely to help than those who do not.

Psychologist John Wilson of Cleveland State University and his colleagues have found that those concerned with achieving a sense of security are less likely to help than those who feel secure but need to build their sense of self-esteem.

These personality characteristics, combined with all the situational factors described earlier, go a long way in explaining the behavior of bystanders. But there are other factors as well. Consider those rare individuals who intervene directly when a crime is in progress:

Psychologists Ted Huston of the University of Texas at Austin and Gilbert Geis of the University of California at Irvine and their colleagues, who interviewed 32 of these people, found them to be quite different from the ordinary person. Active interveners were very self-assured and felt certain they could handle the situation by themselves. Further, they were likely to have specialized training in police work, first aid or lifesaving, and almost all were male. These people were more likely to have been victimized themselves and to have witnessed more crime in the prior 10 years than were people in general.

From other research, we know that when direct interveners were asked why they did not seek help, they answered that "there wasn't enough time" and boasted that they could "handle the situation." In addition, many either had training in physical defense or boxing or possessed—and were willing to use—a knife.

Not everyone is born or trained to be a hero. Some bystanders help indirectly, by reporting the incident to authorities and/or providing information concerning the crime. Unlike those who leap into the fray, these people do not feel competent to intervene. A typical comment: "I couldn't do anything myself so I went to get help." Such people may also see the potential cost of intervention—injury or death—as too high. A bungled rescue attempt may not help the victim and may harm the rescuer.

Even indirect intervention calls for a quick response. Otherwise the criminal act may be over and the attacker gone. But sometimes the crime happens too suddenly for anyone to comprehend and react in time. The *New York Daily News* reported an example a few years ago.

"A plumber was shot dead on a sunny Brooklyn street last weekend in full view of about 50 of his friends and neighbors. But not a single witness has come forward to tell the police exactly what happened. Treglia was about to get into his truck when a car pulled up alongside him. A man in the car shot him four times and drove off, leaving him dead in the street."

The bystanders were willing to cooperate with the police, but there were no firsthand accounts. Almost every piece of information was based on what the bystanders had heard from others. The police found this hard to believe, but they did not interpret the behavior as a fearful coverup of mob murder. The bystanders' reactions are understandable if you look closely at how the situation probably developed:

The incident itself must have been over in seconds. Bystanders had no reason to look at the victim until they heard the shots. It would only have taken a second or two to realize that the man was shot, but by then, where was the gunman? Eyewitness testimony would have been impossible for most people. The great majority would not have seen the man fall, or been certain that shots were fired, or known their source. After talking to their neighbors, however, bystanders could have pieced the event together and told the police what they collectively knew.

Another response, a rare one, is spontaneous vigilantism, in which bystanders not only apprehend a criminal but mete out punishment themselves. For example, *The Washington Post* reported:

"... in the fashion of a Mack Sennett comedy, 29 cab drivers from the L&M Private Car Service and the No-Wait Car Service chased three men who had robbed and stolen one of No-Wait's taxis. Alerted over radio by their dispatcher, the cab drivers chased the suspects from 162nd Street and Amsterdam Avenue through two boroughs, finally cornering their prey in the Bronx. There, they collared two of the suspects, beat them and held them until the police arrived. Both were admitted to Fordham Hospital. One of the drivers, a Vietnam veteran, said after the incident, 'We've got to stick together.'"

Research shows that spontaneous vigilantism happens only in response to certain types of crimes under definable conditions: First, the crimes generate strong identification with the victim (as in the case of the taxi drivers), leaving community members with a strong sense of their own vulnerability. Second, the crimes are particularly threatening to the local community's standards; bystanders would be especially motivated to prevent any recurrence. Third, bystanders are certain (even if sometimes mistaken) both about the nature of the crime and the identity of the criminal. Although people who resort to spontaneous vigilantism usually do not witness the incident directly, the details seem unambiguous because they are interpreted unambiguously to them by someone they view as credible. Fourth, spontaneous vigilantism usually occurs in neighborhoods that are socially and ethnically homogeneous, factors that enhance communication and trust as well as identification with the victim. Poor areas with high crime rates also breed vigilantes motivated by frustration with crime and by the apparent ineffectiveness of the legal system in deterring it.

When vigilantes join together to take illegal action, each person's share of the responsibility is proportionately lessened. Thus, unlike its usual effects in fostering inaction in bystander groups, the diffusion of responsibility in a vigilante group leads to action.

Bystanders can prevent crime by their very presence on the streets. Interviews with convicted felons confirm that, when planning a crime, they view every bystander as a potential intervener and take steps to avoid being seen by potential witnesses. For example, they avoid heavily traveled commercial districts and favor sparsely used residential streets where potential victims often park. Similarly, victimization on subways is highest when there are few riders, and crime rates are higher in areas that offer the greatest possibilities for concealment.

If bystanders decrease the likelihood of crime, then keeping pedestrians on the street should help to reduce it. Unfortunately, people who fear crime are likely to stay behind locked doors and avoid the streets. The greater their fears, the more they stay off the streets, thereby increasing the risks for those who do venture out.

The prevalence of crime in a community can be viewed as the result of a delicate balance between criminals' fear of bystander intervention and possible arrest and bystanders' fear of criminal victimization. To maintain social control effectively, the balance must strongly favor the citizenry. If fear of crime gains ascendance in a neighborhood, residents lose control of criminals, who then rule the streets.

Districts in which social control has been lost need not remain this way. A major item on the public agenda should be developing strategies to help community members exert social control, thus returning the streets to law-abiding citizens.

Samuel P. Oliner
Pearl M. Oliner

# The Altruistic Personality:
# Concern into Action

This selection by Oliner and Oliner is based on extensive research done in Germany investigating those factors that led some Germans to help save the lives of Jews during World War II. Although many people *felt* they should help, the authors found that those who actually helped did so for several different reasons. They note three different kinds of motivation: an empathic orientation by which the people were able to identify with the plight of the victims; a feeling that helping was expected of them by others whose opinions they valued; or a belief that the persecution of the Jews was a moral violation and a need to act out of principle in order to save them.

My parents were loving and kind. I learned from them to be helpful and considerate. There was a Jewish family living in our apartment building, but I hardly noticed when they left. Later, when I was working in the hospital as a doctor, a Jewish man was brought to the emergency room by his wife. I knew that he would die unless he was treated immediately. But we were not allowed to treat Jews; they could only be treated at the Jewish hospital. I could do nothing.

These are the words of a German nonrescuer, a kind and compassionate woman predisposed by sentiment and the ethics of her profession to help a dangerously ill man but who nonetheless did not do so. Thus, it is clearly not enough—in explaining rescuers' activities—to cite sentiments of caring and compassion. Several nonrescuers shared similar tendencies.

Rescuers' attachments to others and their inclusive view of humanity influenced their interpretations of events and situations and may have inclined them toward benevolent behavior. But the step from inclination to action is a large one. To understand what actually aroused rescuers to act on behalf of Jews, submerging or overriding fundamental considerations regarding their own and their families' survival, we must examine yet another motivational source.

It took a catalyst to translate predisposition into action—an external event that challenged rescuers' highest values. However, such actions were not the consequence of objective external events but rather of the subjective meanings rescuers conferred on them. Rescuers and nonrescuers interpreted the demands on themselves differently. Faced with the same knowledge, observation of needs, or requests, only rescuers felt compelled to help.

Based on theoretical proposals developed by Janusz Reykowski, we were able to discern three kinds of catalysts that generally aroused a response. They were able to serve as catalysts because they were congruent with the ways rescuers characteristically made important life decisions. Rescuers who were characteristically *empathically* oriented responded to an external event that aroused or heightened their empathy. Rescuers who were characteristically *normocentrically* oriented responded to an external even which they interpreted as a normative demand of a highly valued social group. Rescuers who characteristically behaved according to their own overarching *principles,* in the main autonomously derived, were moved to respond by an external event which they interpreted as violating these principles.

As the illustrative profiles of individual rescuers and their situations reveal, the altruistic act of rescue was not a radical departure from previous ways of responding but an extension of characteristic forms of relating to others.

An empathic orientation is centered on the needs of another, on that individual's possible fate. It emerges out of a direct connection with the distressed other. Compassion, sympathy, and pity are its characteristic expressions. The reactions may be emotional or cognitive; frequently they contain elements of both. An empathic reaction aroused more than a third (37 percent) of rescuers to their first helping act.

The impact of a direct encounter with a distressed Jew was sometimes overpowering. Consider, for example, the following episode related by a Polish woman, then approximately thirty-five years of age:

> In 1942, I was on my way home from town and was almost near home when M. came out of the bushes. I looked at him, in striped camp clothing, his head bare, shod in clogs. He might have been about thirty or thirty-two years old. And he begged me, his hands joined like for a prayer—that he had escaped from Majdanek and could I help him? He joined his hands in this way, knelt down in front of me, and said: "You are like the Virgin Mary." It still makes me cry. "If I get through and reach Warsaw, I will never forget you."
>
> Well, how could one not have helped such a man? So I took him home, and I fed him because he was hungry. I heated the water so that he could have a bath. Maybe I should not mention this, but I brushed him, rinsed him, gave him a towel to dry himself. Then I dressed him in my husband's underwear, a shirt, and a tie. I had to do it for him because I wasn't sure if

he could do it himself. He was shivering, poor soul, and I was shivering too, with emotion. I am very sensitive and emotional.

Despite the striped clothes and the shaven head, the stranger emerged as a human being, the vital connection perhaps being made by his prayerlike gesture. Overcoming what may have been some feelings of aversion and modesty, the respondent took him home to take care of his most basic needs. The interaction terminated quickly. The rescuer gave the man about ten zloty (less than a dollar), and he went on his way.

In the case of "Stanislaus" empathic motivations were central and consistent.

Stanislaus was born in 1920 to a poor Polish Roman Catholic family. His mother had come to Warsaw from the countryside, where she worked as a domestic and part-time midwife. His father, who had some high school education, was disabled by an accident when Stanislaus was eight years old and lived on a pension thereafter. He had one brother, four years older than himself. He graduated from high school in 1939 but was unable to resume his studies until after the war, when he completed a degree in the diplomatic-consular department of the Academy of Political Science. During the war, he and his family lived near the Warsaw Ghetto. His helping activities continued over several years:

> The gallery of people changed all the time—it comprised several tens of people. Some obtained help in the form of a bowl of soup, others came for temporary shelter during the roundups. Still others, whom I had never met before, came and stayed with us until some other hideout was found.

One of the most noteworthy clues to Stanislaus' motivation is his recollection of details regarding almost all the individuals he helped—details not only of their physical appearance but also their psychological condition. He makes few references to himself; sentences that begin with "I" quickly change to focus on others. "I had my friends" in the ghetto, he says, and then begins to describe what life in the ghetto was like from the point of view of those who were there. Stanislaus thus appears particularly capable of centering on others' needs.

Understanding others, taking their perspective, and anticipating their futures may have left Stanislaus little psychological room to consider his own needs. He speaks little of his own wartime deprivations or even his mother's. His understanding of how others felt left him with the feeling of "no choice" regarding his response:

> Human compassion. When someone comes and says "I escaped from the camp," what is the alternative? One alternative is to push him out and close the door—the other is to pull him into the house and say, "Sit down, relax,

wash up. You will be as hungry as we are because we have only this bread.".

Caring for others and respect in its universal sense were both taught by his mother explicitly and by example. "I learned to respect the world from my mother," he said. His mother modeled caring behaviors in many ways. His childhood and adolescence were spent in a household filled with his mother's relatives, who sought her support as they looked for work or studied in the big city. His mother herself worked as a maid and midwife occasionally to earn the money necessary to provide for the boys' education. Stanislaus credits her with initiating his wartime helping activities.

Unlike an empathic reaction, a normocentric reaction is not rooted in a direct connection with the victim, but rather in a feeling of obligation to a social reference group with whom the actor identifies and whose explicit and implicit rules he feels obliged to obey. The social group, rather than the victim him- or herself, motivates the behavior. The actor perceives the social group as imposing norms for behavior, and for these rescuers, inaction was considered a violation of the group's code of proper conduct. Feelings of obligation or duty are frequently coupled with anticipation of guilt or shame if one fails to act. For their first helping act, the majority of rescuers (52 percent) responded to a normocentric expectation.

In some cases, a normocentric response was activated when a person of authority representing the salient social group simply asked the rescuer to help. In the following episode, a very religious German woman, the wife of a parish minister, himself a member of the Bekennende Kirche, responded to a joint request by her husband and a prestigious intermediary:

> I was called to the parish office by my husband. I was then expecting my eighth child. The wife of Professor T. was there and said she had come on account of two Jews who appeared to her as poor animals escaping from the hunt. Could they come that very afternoon to stay with me? I said yes, but with a heavy heart because of the expected child. K. came at midday— she was a bundle of nerves. They stayed for three weeks. I was afraid.

Asked for the main reasons why she became involved, she said: "One cannot refuse someone who is concerned about the fate of others." The "someone" she was concerned about was not the Jews but her husband and the professor's wife.

Requests came from various authoritative sources whom rescuers felt obliged to obey: political groups, family members or friends. Frequently, they came from resistance groups. For example, a Polish member of PLAN (Polska Ludowa Akcja Niepodleglosciowa, Polish National Independence Action) found himself cooperating with Jewish resistance organizations. Asked why he did it, he responded:

It was not a personal, individual activity—I had orders from the organization. In helping these people, I was helping myself since it weakened the Germans. It was an act of cooperation, military cooperation.

In general, normocentric motivations were more conducive to group actions than to strictly individual undertakings. Although such motivations could lead to extraordinary sacrifices, they were usually less likely to result in close personal relationships with the victims. For rescuers like "Dirk," an internalized normocentrically motivated Dutch rescuer, help was more often perceived as a matter of "duty" rather than sympathy or affection.

It's not because I have an altruistic personality. It's because I am an obedient Christian. I know that is the reason why I did it. I know it. The Lord wants you to do good work. What good is it to say you love your neighbor if you don't help them. There was never any question about it. The Lord wanted us to rescue those people and we did it. We could not let those people go to their doom.

A principled motivation, like a normative one, is rooted in an indirect connection with the victim. The indirect connection, however, does not come about through a social group with whom the actor identifies but is rather mediated by a set of overarching axioms, largely autonomously derived. People with this orientation interpreted the persecution of Jews as a violation of moral precepts, and the main goal of their rescue behavior was to reaffirm and act on their principles. Even when their actions might prove futile, individuals tended to believe that the principles were kept alive as long as there were people who reaffirmed them by their deeds. Somewhat more than a tenth (11 percent) of rescuers were aroused to action by principles.

Rescuers, like most people, had multiple values, any one of which might assume supremacy at a given moment. For some rescuers, however, certain values became central principles around which they characteristically interpreted events and organized their lives. For these people, their principles were fundamental canons of belief whose violation was accompanied by strong moral indignation. They felt compelled to act more out of a sense of these principles than empathy for the victims.

These rescuers most frequently highlighted two kinds of moral principles—the principle of justice (the right of innocent people to be free from persecution) and the principle of care (the obligation to help the needy). Those motivated by the principle of justice tended to exhibit different emotional characteristics than did those who were motivated by the principle of care. They usually had more impersonal relationships with those they assisted and reserved strong emotions (anger and hate) for those who violated the principle of justice they held dear. Rescuers motivated primarily by care, on the other hand, usually focused on the subjective states and reactions of the victims. Kindness toward the victim was the dominant theme, while hate and indignation toward the violators were most transitory. In some cases the rescuer was even ready to extend help to the enemy if he was in pain or danger.

High independence from external opinions and evaluations is the major characteristic of people who share this orientation. Hence, they are more likely to act alone and on their own initiative. If other people are involved, it is mostly for instrumental reasons rather than for psychological support or guidance.

The capacity for such independent action has also been noted in individuals characterized by internalized norms. But principles differ in their origins from internalized norms. While internalized norms can be traced directly back to particular authoritative social groups, those who have a principled motivation appear to a great extent to develop their principles on the basis of their own intellectual and moral efforts. Normocentrically motivated persons refer repeatedly to certain groups or categories of people who espouse the same norms: religious groups, professional groups, friends, or family. Such references are rarely made by people with a principled motivation. To the extent that relationships are mentioned, they are presented as deliberately chosen on the basis of support for the principles to which the subject was previously committed. Adherence to the principles appears to play the primary role in determining the association. Among normocentrically oriented persons, it is the other way around—the reference group with which one is associated appears to be the source of values. As one representative of rescuers who had a principled motivation, we offer "Suzanne," who emphasizes the principles of justice.

Suzanne's reason for helping was simple: "All men are equal and are born free and equal by right." Pressed by the interviewer to add other reasons, she replied, "There is no other." This is a fundamental conception of the principle of justice—universal in character, it extends to all persons. For Suzanne this principle was rooted in an intellectual world view that made infractions immediately obvious. Fascism, Nazism, and totalitarianism by their very nature violated the principle. "Consequently," she explained, "I am against all dictatorial systems." The Pétain regime was a dictatorship; she recognized its implications immediately and reacted immediately.

Personal relationships played no part in Suzanne's helping activities. Over three years, in various ways, she helped several hundred people, including over a hundred children, all of whom [were] previously unknown to her. In all these cases she initiated helping and actively sought out people to help. She worked independently and was not connected with any resistance group. She did not seem to seek nor need any external reinforcement for her activity; the opinions of others apparently did not interest her. When asked what her neighbors who had found out about her activities felt, she replied, "Don't know." She was remarkably consistent in her action from the moment she made the decision until the end of the war. Stable and sustained task orientation, the impersonal context of helping, independence from external opinions or reinforcement, and engagement in action as long as injustice persisted—all testify to a principled motivation, as did her scores on the personality scales.

How did Suzanne develop into such a person? She describes her family as "very close and very united." Unity came from a convergence of values shared by both parents as well as her brother, twelve years her senior. Both mother and father emphasized above all being a responsible person. It was a value she learned well; "I always finish a task I commit myself to," she said. Her father particularly emphasized the need "to take care of one's neighbor and the duty to be an example to others." She credits her brother with having "taught me to practice and to live a good life." Her brother was a much-decorated hero of the resistance.

The variation in motivations leading to rescue behavior highlights the important point that the paths to virtue are neither uniform nor standardized. Rather, they represent alternative pathways through which individuals are equipped and disposed to interpret events of moral significance. Different rescuers found different meanings in what was happening to Jews, but once their plight was understood through the prism of the individual's orientation, the necessity to act became compelling.

Most commonly, rescuers were normocentrically oriented. Thus, they were aroused to act by external authorities whose values and standards they had internalized to varying degrees. The majority of rescuers (52 percent) perceived helping Jews as a means of expressing and strengthening their affiliations with their social groups. Those whose group norms were only weakly internalized depended on overt pressure from some authoritative group member to initiate and sustain their activity. (This suggests the potential power authoritative social groups might have galvanized in the service of rescue had more of them chosen to do so.) Those who had internalized their group norms deeply did not require such external pressure.

The empathic orientation was the next most common. An empathic reaction was characteristic of more than a third (37 percent) of rescuers. They had a particular capacity to focus on others' needs and to be moved by their distress. While visible cues were necessary for some, for others merely knowing that others were suffering was sufficient to arouse them. Principled motivations largely autonomously derived were the least common type of motivation. Only 11 percent of rescuers were aroused to action by principles alone.

While in many cases, the motivation appeared to be similar over a number of different helping acts, in several others the motivation for the first helping act was not necessarily the same for the second or third. Nor did the motivation that first aroused the rescuer to action necessarily remain the same during the course of the behavior, even in relation to the same person or people being helped. A normocentric initial motivation sometimes became more empathic as bonds formed between the rescuer and rescued. The same was true for principled rescuers. As one rescuer motivated by the principle of justice explained it, "I began to like the people I was helping and became very distressed at what was happening to them."

What is of final importance is that receptivity to such diverse catalysts did not suddenly emerge in the context of the traumas of the Holocaust. Rather, preparation began long before in the emotions and cognitions through which rescuers normally and routinely related to others and made their decisions. Thus, their responses were less explicit conscious choices than characteristic ways of attending to routine events. Already attuned to conferring meaning on events through their particular moral sensibilities, they depended on familiar patterns to discern the significance of the unprecedented events at hand. To a large extent, then, helping Jews was less a decision made at a critical juncture than a choice prefigured by an established character and way of life. As Iris Murdoch observes, the moral life is not something that is switched on at a particular crisis but is rather something that goes on continually in the small piecemeal habits of living. Hence, "at crucial moments of choice most of the business of choosing is already over." Many rescuers themselves reflected this view, saying that they "had no choice" and that their behavior deserved no special attention, for it was simply an "ordinary" thing to do.

Alice M. Isen
Paula F. Levin

# Effect of Feeling Good on Helping: Cookies and Kindness

The research by Isen and Levin is a fairly basic, but now classic, study in which they were interested in determining the effect of mood on helping. The authors led some people to feel good, either by giving them a cookie or arranging for them to find a dime in a pay phone, and then set up situations in which they might offer assistance or not. Consistent with their predictions, those people enjoying a temporarily positive mood state helped more in both of the studies they performed. After reading this article, you might consider why mood should affect helping and ask how this factor compares to other determinants of helping.

Recent investigations of determinants of helping have begun to focus on the role of mood state in producing differences in helpfulness. The first studies that indicated the relevance of a potential helper's internal affective state used reports of success and failure at a task as their independent variable. A study by Berkowitz and Connor (1966) indicated a relationship between success and helping, when the beneficiary was dependent on the subject. A later study (Isen, 1970) also indicated a link between success and helping, where there was no relationship between the people involved and where helping was a low-cost, naturalistic, behavioral measure. It was postulated that in just such a situation (i.e., nonsolicited, low-cost helping), an important determinant of helpfulness may be the potential helper's positive affective state or "warm glow of success" (Isen, 1970). In addition, even though their success/failure manipulation was not aimed specifically at affecting internal mood state, Berkowitz and Connor (1966) also made reference to a "glow of goodwill" in their discussion. In both of these studies which suggested that "feeling good" may be a determinant of helping, positive affective state was induced via a report of success. However, report of success may not be an entirely satisfactory way of manipulating mood, since induced affective state may be confounded with estimates of competence.

Several recent studies have indicated that manipulation of affective state in ways other than via success/failure also results in differential helping, thus lending credibility to the hypothesis that a relationship between feeling good and helpfulness does exist. Two naturalistic experiments seem to indicate that good feeling aroused through positive verbal contact results in increased aid, both solicited (Berkowitz & Macaulay, as cited in Aderman, 1971) and nonsolicited (Isen, Becker, & Fairchild).

Studies by Aderman (1971) and Aderman and Berkowitz (1970), while conducted in an experimental setting, manipulated mood state in several novel ways. In the Aderman and Berkowitz study, the subject's mood state was varied by having him observe one of several interactions between two male college students, one who needed aid and one who was a potential helper. The experimental condition varied according to the person with whom the subject was instructed to empathize, the helping response of the second person (helped or did not help), and the reaction of the helped person (thanked the helper or did not). The subject then filled out a mood questionnaire and finally was given an opportunity to comply with the experimenter's request for help. The results of the experiment, though complex, tended to support the idea that feeling good can be related to increased helping under some circumstances (empathy with the thanked helper), while feeling bad can be associated with increased helping under other circumstances (empathy with the nonhelped person in need).

In the study by Aderman (1971), elation or depression was induced in subjects by having them read sets of mood statements. Aderman found that following the reading of the cards, subjects in the elation condition wrote more numbers for the experimenter, when this task was presented as a favor rather than a requirement of the experiment. In addition, elation subjects volunteered more often for a future experiment. Such findings do lend credence to the "glow" hypotheses, yet one complexity of the findings is that the "help" was solicited.

A further question remaining is whether success, or good mood, leads specifically to helping or, more generally, to increased activity and/or productivity. In other words, does the good feeling lead to an increased desire to do something nice for someone else, or would subjects who have been made to feel good, as opposed to those who have not, engage in more or any subsequent activity?

Using a 2 × 2 design, we performed an experiment that attempted to answer the two questions posed above: First, whether feeling good leads to increased helping; second, whether, following the induction of good feeling, the response to an opportunity to help differs from the response to an opportunity to engage in some other activity. We predicted an interaction between the two independent variables such that those subjects who were feeling good would subsequently be more willing to help but less willing to hinder (distract) than those not made to feel good.

## STUDY I

*Method*

### Subjects

The study, which spanned five sessions, was conducted in the libraries of a university and two colleges in the Philadelphia area. Fifty-two male college students who were studying in individual carrels served as subjects.

### Procedure

At the beginning of the session, a coordinator randomly assigned rows of carrels to the feeling good or to the neutral condition. The assignment to condition was based on rows, rather than on individuals, in order to insure that subjects would be unaware that two conditions existed.

To induce good mood, confederates distributed cookies along the rows that had been assigned to the feeling good condition, while they merely walked by the rows in the neutral condition. This task was performed by a male and female pair of confederates in two of the sessions and by a female confederate in the remaining three sessions.

The coordinator also randomly divided subjects in each condition into "help" or "hinder" groups. The experimenter was told this assignment of "help" and "distract" subjects, but was kept unaware of whether a particular row was "cookie" or "no cookie." Similarly, the coordinator was careful to withhold from the confederates information as to help or distract condition of the subjects.

A few minutes after the confederates returned following the distribution or nondistribution of cookies, the experimenter approached each subject individually and asked if, and for how many 20-minute sessions, the subject would serve as a confederate in a psychology experiment. In the help condition, the purpose of the experiment was given as an investigation of creativity in students at examination times, as opposed to other times during the year. The confederate was needed in this experiment to act as helper to subjects who would be attempting to conceive of novel uses for ordinary items. The confederate's aid, which involved holding and manipulating the items, was described as "something which the subjects usually found very helpful to them." In the distract condition, the job of the confederate was described as a distracter of a randomly chosen, unwitting student who happened to be studying in the library. As distracter, he would stand near the subject and drop books, make noises, rattle papers, all while the experimenter unobtrusively recorded the subject's reactions. The purpose of such an experiment was given as an investigation of distractibility of students at examination time as opposed to other times during the year. In addition, the experimenter cautioned each subject in the distract condition by saying, "I think it only fair to tell you before you decide to act as distracter, that the subjects find the distraction to be an unpleasant annoyance." Thus, in the help condition the role that the subject was invited to play was clearly that of a helper, one appreciated greatly by the creativity subjects; in contrast, the role that a confederate would play in the distract condition was clearly described as that of an annoying distracter of unsuspecting students studying in the library.

A debriefing and discussion period followed each subject's reply. Subjects' reports indicated that the independent and dependent manipulations were plausible, and that they had not been associated in the subjects' minds prior to the debriefing.

## Results

Since the five sessions yielded comparable results, the data were combined. Table 1 shows the proportion of subjects volunteering in each condition and means of number of minutes volunteered. A *t* test for proportions revealed subjects receiving cookies volunteered to help more, but to distract less, than those not receiving cookies.

For the data on number of minutes volunteered in each condition, the transformed scores indicated with cookie subjects volunteering more time to help, but less to distract, than no-cookie subjects.

## Discussion

The results of this experiment indicate that in terms of both number of subjects volunteering and amount of time volunteered, subjects who have unexpectedly received cookies help more, but distract less, than do those who have not received cookies. Thus, feeling good, induced naturalistically and in a way other than via report of success, seems to lead to increased helping, and to helping specifically, rather than to general activity.

Although this finding provides evidence for the "warm glow" hypothesis—people who feel good themselves are more likely to help others—an alternative interpretation is possible. Following from a modeling or a normative explanation, cookie subjects might have been more helpful simply because they had just been exposed to a helpful model (the person passing out the cookies) who may have reminded them of norms of kindness to others.

**TABLE 1** Study I: Means of Amount of Time (in Minutes) Volunteered and Proportion of Subjects Volunteering in Each Condition

| Condition | Help | Distract |
|-----------|------|----------|
| Cookie | | |
| M | 69.00 | 20.00 |
| P | .69 (9/13) | .31 (4/13) |
| | | |
| No cookie | | |
| M | 16.70 | 78.60 |
| P | .50 (6/12) | .64 (9 1/4) |

Furthermore, a few aspects of the dependent measure complicate the warm glow interpretation. Although the independent manipulation was more naturalistic than that found in many experiments, the dependent measure was one of *solicited* helpfulness. In addition, help was only volunteered, rather than actually performed.

Thus, a second study was conducted to determine whether nonsolicited, low-cost helpfulness increases following the induction of good feeling, without the good mood being directly brought about by another person. The question was, Does feeling good lead to increased helping, even if there is no helpful model? In the "dime" study, which is directed at this question and which is presented below, good feeling was induced in a subject by the discovery of an unexpected dime in the coin return slot of a pay telephone. The dependent measure was that of helping a young woman pick up papers which she had just dropped.

## STUDY II

*Method*

### Subjects

Subjects were 24 female and 17 male adults who made calls from designated public telephones located in enclosed shopping malls in suburban San Francisco and Philadelphia. Excluded from the subject pool were those shoppers who were not alone and those who were carrying packages.

### Procedure

Telephone booths were "set up" in the following manner. The experimenter made an incomplete call, ostensibly took her dime from the return slot, and left the booth. In actuality, the dime was left in the coin return slot for a randomly selected half of these trials. Thus, subjects using such telephones received an unexpected 10¢ when they checked the coin return before, during, or upon completion of their calls; these subjects constituted the experimental group. The control group was made up of individuals who used a telephone that had not been "stocked" with a dime and who therefore did not receive unexpected money.

The experimenter set up the experimental and control telephones without informing the confederate as to condition. This was done in order to eliminate any possible systematic bias in the confederate's performance of the paper dropping. The experimenter also checked to make sure that all subjects did look in the coin return slot. Only a few subjects failed to meet this requirement, and these were not included in the data analysis. This was done in order to avoid ultimately obtaining a sample of subjects which was inadvertently selected for attention. For this reason, no subject who was at an "experimental" condition telephone and simply failed to see his dime was included in the control group.

During the call, the confederate was able to observe the outline of the subject unobtrusively by pretending to "window shop," while actually watching the subject's reflection in one of the store windows. The aim of this surveillance was simply to know when the subject was leaving the telephone. When the subject did leave, the confederate started in the same direction as the subject and, while walking slightly ahead and to the side of him or her, dropped a manila folder full of papers in the subject's path. The dependent measure was whether the subject helped the female confederate to pick up the papers.

*Results*

Table 2 shows the number of males and females helping in each condition. A Fisher exact test on the data of the females indicated a significant relationship between getting a dime and helping. A similar finding was obtained for the males.

*Discussion*

These results indicate that differential unsolicited helping occurs even when good mood is induced in an impersonal manner. The finding appears to be less pronounced for males than for females, but the smaller number of male subjects may be responsible in part for this apparent difference. Because our society has specific norms applying to this particular helping situation for males, one might have expected the behavior of the males, more than that of females, to reflect not only the independent manipulation but also these norms for courtesy. The data show that while no females in the control condition helped, one male in the same condition did help. However, it must also be noted that two males in the experimental condition failed to help, while no female experimental subjects failed to help. Thus, while it is true that the behavior of the males may be more complex than that of the females, the simple courtesy expectation is not supported.

The results of the two studies taken together provide support for the notion that feeling good leads to helping. Because feeling good has been generated in a variety of ways and settings, and since the type of helping measure and the source of the subject populations have also varied, this relationship seems to have some empirical generality. We recognize, however, that the question of why feeling good leads to helping, or more properly, what

**TABLE 2**  Study II: Number of People Helping in Each Condition

| Condition | Females | | Males | |
|---|---|---|---|---|
| | Helped | Did not help | Helped | Did not help |
| Dime | 8 | 0 | 6 | 2 |
| No dime | 0 | 16 | 1 | 8 |

mediates the relationship between the two, remains to be answered. More-over, such an answer may provide some insights into the more general and important issue of how the observed determinants of helping, such as success, feeling good, feeling bad in some circumstances, guilt, verbal contact, and the presence or absence of other people, relate to one another. That is, while these states or events may seem unrelated as determinants of helping, they may have some common aspects in that capacity. If so, then the determination of helping may be more parsimoniously understood in terms of broader con-cepts, such as maintenance of positive affective state, perception of costs and rewards, or both, and this possibility is now under investigation.

## References

Aderman, D. (1971)Effect of prior mood on helping behavior. Unpublished doctoral dissertation, University of Wisconsin.

Aderman, D., & Berkowitz, L. (1970) Observational set, empathy, and helping. *Journal of Personality and Social Psychology*, 14, 141–148.

Berkowitz, L., & Connor, W. H. (1966) Success, failure, and social responsibility. *Journal of Personality and Social Psychology*, 4, 664–669.

Berkowitz, L., & Macaulay, J. (1971) Ideals, ideas and feelings in help-giving. Unpublished manuscript, University of Wisconsin. Cited by D. Aderman. Effect of prior mood on helping behavior. Unpublished doctoral dissertation, University of Wisconsin.

Isen, A. M. (1970) Success, failure, attention, and reaction to others: The warm glow of success. *Journal of Personality and Social Psychology*, 15, 24–301.

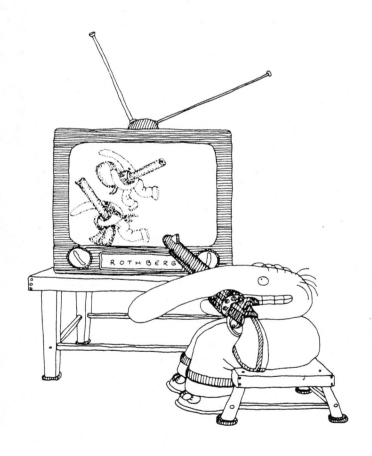

# 8

# Aggression: The Nature and Sources of Harm

Violence seems to be a part of our lives. It is impossible to read the newspaper or watch television without running head on into it. Alongside the debate over whether a violent instinct exists among humans, psychologists and others have asked how we can control, reduce, or even eliminate aggressive behavior.

Edward Donnerstein is a Professor in the Department of Communication at the University of California at Santa Barbara. He is widely recognized as a leading expert in mass media violence, especially sexual violence. He has testified at numerous governmental hearings and has recently published *The Question of Pornography* (with Daniel Linz and Steven Penrod) and *Big World, Small Screen* (with several colleagues).

Our conversation covered a number of topics from America's violent nature to issues of the media. Prof. Donnerstein points out ways that social psychologists can become involved in reducing violence and offers an optimistic view that we can have a significant impact.

## A CONVERSATION WITH
## EDWARD DONNERSTEIN
*University of California
at Santa Barbara*

**Krupat:** *Human beings seem to be pretty aggressive creatures. Do we have aggressive instincts, do we learn it, or just how does aggression come about?*

**Donnerstein:** This is an issue where there are a lot of differing opinions. I serve on the American Psychological Association's Commission on Violence and Youth, and our report will be issued sometime in the near future. We take the position that there might be some hardwired, biological possibilities, but even if that is the case there are very strong cultural and societal factors influencing aggression. For instance, you could take the position that males are more aggressive than females, yet we can certainly find cultures where it's just the opposite. My feeling is that societal norms and pressures interact with many of these other biologically based factors. By taking the position that the environment plays a very strong role, I think that's a more optimistic outlook. Obviously, if aggression is learned, it can be unlearned.

**Krupat:** *When I first asked the question, I was asking about people in general. How about the United States in particular. Why is this such a violent society?*

**Donnerstein:** People have argued that, if you look at the history of this country and how we were founded, there is a sense that violence is acceptable. It's interesting, in my own area of research on the mass media, that in the U.S. violence is highly acceptable yet sexual material is not—whereas it is just the opposite in most other places on the globe. When I go to international film conferences, people from other societies ask what is it about America that makes us produce these sorts of things. I am against censorship, but when our movies go to other countries they do cut a lot of the violence out. They are really appalled by it, and they have this fear of coming here, which might be justified unfortunately. Of course I can point to places in Europe and the Middle East that are just as violent in some ways. But on a day-to-day basis, we have a culture that is very accepting.

**Krupat:** *Are there other factors?*

**Donnerstein:** Certainly the availability of firearms plays a strong role. Where the United States is more violent than other places is in terms of homicides and aggravated assaults, and I think the availability of guns increases this substantially. There are also issues of poverty, discrimination, and racism which very much reinforce societal norms that violence is acceptable in this particular culture. But we are not unique. You don't have to look vary far to see some of the same things played out all over the world.

**Krupat:** *Let's go back then and start with young children. To the extent we believe that violence is learned, how exactly is it communicated? How does a one-year-old get enrolled in Violence 101?*

**Donnerstein:** Obviously, it can be communicated by parents. There is a whole body of literature suggesting that children who are abused have a very good chance to become abusers themselves. A recent report from the National Academy of Sciences argues that the best predictor of adult aggressive behavior is being a victim as a child. Another factor is witnessing violence in the family, which seems to be a very good predictor, as well as witnessing violence within the community. There is a lot of research going on in the inner city in terms of how the daily viewing and experience of violence can have an effect on a general callousness toward violence.

**Krupat:** *If violence is to be learned, does it have to happen early?*

**Donnerstein:** The general feeling now is that socialization, working with hardwired tendencies, is really going to take its effect in childhood. Beyond that, the chances of becoming a violent individual are fairly remote because the processes that have been developing from early on are now fairly stable. Again, the best predictor of adult aggressive behavior seems to be childhood aggressive behavior.

**Krupat:** *To move into the area of media as an influence, many students say to me, "I watched Saturday morning cartoons, I've seen violent movies, and I'm not violent."*

**Donnerstein:** For whatever reasons, certain kids are predisposed to some form of aggression. Those children search out this kind of material or find the material reinforcing their value system. These are kids who tend to be having trouble in school or are already having run-ins. So it's a perpetual cycle. For most of us it just isn't having that effect. We can watch a lot of violence and have no problem. Psychologists are still trying to answer questions such as which children are most susceptible and what the underlying processes are.

**Krupat:** *Well, what are some of the mechanisms that account for the apparent link between violent media and violence in real life?*

**Donnerstein:** There are a number of potential processes. One argument is that violence in the media teaches children certain scripts about how one deals with conflict in interpersonal relations. So that process is initially taking place. You could also talk about desensitization, which makes you less aroused to violence so it becomes a little easier to perpetuate violence. Another process would be simple learning or imitation where certain individuals who are predisposed come to model or imitate aggressive acts. So if we look at all of research together, there's a general feeling that there's a sort of a desensitization that creates a callousness, there is a reinforcing of values and behaviors which children are learning, and there's some sort of direct imitation. Although direct imitation is really for those individuals who are very much predisposed to aggressive behavior to start with.

**Krupat:** *You mentioned desensitization briefly. That seems like a very important mechanism. Could you elaborate on that some more?*

**Donnerstein:** What we tend to find is initially when people view violent or sexually violent material, not pornographic but just R rated material, desensitization occurs. You become less bothered by what you see, less aroused, less concerned, less upset—a classic type of habituation. There's also a change in your perceptions of violence. You tend to see less violence in the material with the passage of time. An important finding is that exposure to this type of material can actually change your perceptions of real victims of violence. For instance, in some of our research we have people act as jurors in a mock rape trial, and a couple of days later they see an actual victim of rape. We actually find in some of these studies less empathy or sympathy towards the rape victim. They see less pain and suffering on the part of the victim. It is not that these people are going to go out and commit violent acts, but they just aren't bothered by what they're seeing. We are really concerned about children who are growing up with a steady diet of witnessing violence in the media, or in the home, or in the neighborhood. It makes it that much easier to be violent because you're not as aroused or as sympathetic, and you cannot easily empathize with your victim. I think all of these can really make for a very lethal type of combination.

**Krupat:** *I can hear a Hollywood producer responding by saying, "But you are blaming everything wrong with society on my movies."*

**Donnerstein:** No, not all. Our position would be: Look, violence is a part of society. It is not that violence shouldn't be presented at all; it's how and the context in which it is presented. There is a big difference between the movies *Platoon* and *Rambo* in terms of how war and the Vietnam War is presented. Nobody sees *Platoon* and says, "Let's go back there." *Rambo* is just the opposite. You can present violence without glamorizing it, without glorifying it, without making it gratuitous and excessive. Nobody is suggesting regulation or censorship. Not at all. I just wish they would stop and think, "What are the messages you are sending about violence?" And some of these can be very, very subtle messages.

**Krupat:** *And I assume these messages can especially have an effect on young children.*

**Donnerstein:** And on those who are predisposed. Think for the moment about violent films such as *Batman.* It was R rated, but it was obviously directed at an incredibly young audience. MacDonald's was giving away cups, and every promo was made for young kids. In terms of how the violence was portrayed, it was exactly the kind that creates problems. It was excessive and gratuitous, it was performed by heroes as part of a fantasy, there were no consequences, and it was used to solve conflict. It had everything that is wrong about violence mixed up in it.

**Krupat:** *Is there something good to be said for media violence? For instance, what's become of the idea of catharsis, the notion that viewing violence can drain off your own aggressions?*

**Donnerstein:** That hopefully has died, although it is still brought up by the movie industry. There are many myths about violence, and one of those is that catharsis is an effective process. That's fine, except there is no empirical evidence for it at all. There are other myths, for example, that violence has always been in literature and entertainment throughout history. People will cite Shakespeare and things of that nature, but they forget that the violence was always offstage, whereas today it is obviously right in front of you and quite graphic and high tech, which produces a much different effect.

**Krupat:** *It sounds to me like what we have here is a vicious cycle. How do you turn it around? How can we go about reducing violence?*

**Donnerstein:** My feeling is that we need very early intervention. There should be media literacy, violence courses, conflict resolution courses, intervention programs at a very early age. Very young children have to learn that there are alternatives to deal with conflict other than violence. That's only one step, dealing with the individual. Other issues have to be dealt with—political issues, economic issues, educational issues all have to be part of the solution if people really want to accomplish something. There's the drug problem and large disparities in terms of equal opportunity among individuals, and all sorts of social problems. Teaching conflict resolution is great, but it's not going to do much when those kids go back to their neighborhood where there are drive-by shootings. I think we've got to deal with the issues on many levels.

**Krupat:** *As a social psychologist, how do you feel about entering a world that likely goes well beyond your early training?*

**Donnerstein:** I see myself much more as an applied social psychologist than ever before. I have an interest not only in laboratory findings, but in the policy implications of our findings and the use and misuse of social science data. I have a much stronger feel now for the need for social psychologists to have input into the policy arena, the legal arena, and into the industry to make their findings known for society as a whole. We should be asking ourselves how can we take what we know to turn it around, to mitigate the effects of violent media? This means that we have an obligation to work effectively on a real multidisciplinary level, not only with our colleagues in many fields, but also with the industry that produces the material we are interested in.

**Krupat:** *Would you consider yourself at all optimistic about the future in this area?*

**Donnerstein:** On yes, I always am. When I give talks on violence prevention and media literacy, people sometimes say "You're a bit naive to think educational interventions will work." That is fine, but I believe there is a lot of excitement out there for social psychologists. And I am optimistic that we can do something about it if we realize that we're going to have to act on a very applied level with many types of groups—environmental groups, industry groups, and academicians in an interdisciplinary, multifaceted way. That is new and that is exciting, and it does make me optimistic in terms of being able to deal with the question of violence.

Alan S. Reifman
Richard P. Larrick
Steven Fein

# Temper and Temperature on the Diamond: The Heat-Aggression Relationship in Major League Baseball

Social psychologists have long been interested in the relationship between temperature and aggression, and conflicting data exist as to whether aggression continues to climb as the thermometer does. Although much of the research has focused on crime and urban riots, the authors here take an unusual look at this issue by considering the relationship between heat and the number of times pitchers hit batters in major league baseball. Using records from the 1986–88 baseball seasons, the authors are able to rule out several alternative interpretations of their data and conclude that there is a direct and positive relationship between temper and temperature on the baseball diamond.

Mark Twain, among others, observed that everybody talks about the weather. One aspect of weather that people have talked about for centuries is its effects on human behavior. Probably the most discussed idea regarding the effects of weather on people's behavior is the idea that very hot weather is associated with aggression and violence. This idea has been expressed many times, from the classic works of the theater, such as Shakespeare's *Romeo and Juliet*, to contemporary film, such as Spike Lee's *Do the Right Thing*. Indeed, the metaphors of anger and aggression, such as "hot under the collar," "steamed," and "blood boiling," are replete with imagery of heat.

This long-standing idea that heat and aggression are related has recently inspired a growing body of research that aims to test this hypothesis scientifically and to determine how and why they are related. During the last 2 decades numerous studies—both correlational and experimental—have found that aggressive behavior increases as a function of increasing ambient temperatures (for a review, see Anderson, 1989). Although the basic heat-aggression relationship appears well established, research on this problem continues today on several fronts. One important issue concerns the range of domains to which the relationship can be extended. Anderson (1987) has stated that only through the cumulation of results using different operationalizations and different social contexts can the authenticity of a heat-aggression relationship be confirmed. Thus far, however, most of the field/archival studies on this topic have examined crime statistics as the measure of aggression (e.g., Anderson, 1987), although other domains have begun to be explored, such as horn honking among drivers (Baron, 1976; Kenrick & MacFarlane, 1984). One domain in which the heat-aggression relationship has not been investigated is that of sports. This is an important domain because much of our leisure time is spent participating in or watching others engage in sports and, depending on the nature of the sport, there is often the opportunity for aggression and even violence to manifest itself during the course of a game. An examination of the heat-aggression relationship in sports would be valuable both because of the ubiquity of sports in our culture and because the measures of aggression therein would not be associated with extraneous factors (e.g., socioeconomic variables, number of people outdoors) that plague much of the archival research, nor would they be as trivial as some of the measures of aggression used in field and laboratory research. The present authors were especially interested in examining the heat-aggression relationship in the sport of baseball. Baseball offers the advantages of typically being played outdoors and in the summertime. Furthermore, it is a game in which much of what occurs on the field is easily quantified. Indeed, major league baseball fans are notorious for their love of baseball statistics.

A second issue with which research on heat and aggression is concerned is how heat and aggression are related. Specifically, what is the shape of the relation? Several shapes have been suggested, including a straight linear function, a J-shaped function, an inverted-U-shaped function, and an M-shaped function (Anderson, 1989). Because major league baseball is played form midspring to midfall, games are played in a great variety of temperatures. Although games are rarely played in uncomfortably cold temperatures, they are played in temperatures that are as hot as the weather ever gets in most places in the United States and Canada. Therefore, data from major league baseball games offer a good naturalistic test of some of the theories concerning the shape of the heat-aggression relationship.

Although we are aware of no previous research that has investigated the issue of heat and aggression in sports, some research has been conducted on other variables affecting aggression in sports. For example, Frank and Gilovich (1988) found that professional football and ice hockey teams with black uniforms received more penalties over a period of several years than teams with nonblack uniforms. It may be interesting to note that Dick Butkus, one of professional football's most aggressive linebackers of all time, responded to this finding by saying, "All I know was that we wore dark in the hot weather, dark colors attract heat, and it was uncomfortable" (Boxer, 1989, p. 56).

In the present study aggression was operationalized as the number of times major league baseball pitchers hit batters with pitched balls. In recent years, batters being hit by pitches has been a serious and highly publicized problem in baseball. Baseball players and analysts have suggested numerous causes, such as pitchers' frustration and need to intimidate hitters (Hersch, 1987; Lopresti, 1987). A goal of the present research was to determine whether heat, independent of these other factors, may be a significant factor that has been largely overlooked by the baseball community. Specifically, using the individual baseball game as the unit of analysis, we examined whether the number of hit batters was related to ambient temperature in a large sample of major league games.

Because factors other than ambient temperature might contribute to the rate of batters being hit by pitches, the most plausible of these were incorporated into the analyses as control variables. Partly on the basis of the speculations of baseball players and experts about the causes of batters being hit by pitches (e.g., Hersch, 1987; Lopresti, 1987), the following potential predictors of the number of batters hit by pitches during a game were recorded for each game: the total number of walks, the total number of wild pitches, the total number of passed balls, the total number of errors, the total number of home runs, and the attendance. The number of walks and wild pitches in a game may serve as an index of pitcher inaccuracy or wildness and thus may correlate with the number of batters hit by pitches. Errors are a measure of inaccuracy or wildness displayed by all the players on the team in fielding and throwing. Passed balls may serve as an index either of pitcher wildness or of inaccuracy displayed by the catcher. Home runs are likely to covary with the number of batters hit by a pitch in a game for two reasons that have frequently been cited by baseball analysts. One is that allowing home runs is a source of frustration for pitchers and they may vent their frustrations by hitting batters. A second reason is strategic. After allowing a home run, pitchers need to reclaim their authority on the mound by intimidating the hitters and preventing them from taking their best swings. Finally, attendance was used as an index of the importance or intensity of a game. It was thought that the more important a game, the more aggressively it would be played, perhaps leading to an increased number of hit batters. Because temperature and perceived importance of a game are likely to covary (games played in August have both higher temperatures and higher perceived importance than games played in April), this control variable is particularly important.

Concerning the shape of the heat-aggression relationship, the existing literature would suggest a priori hypotheses of both linearity and curvilinearity. The latter would arise if aggression increased with temperature up to a point but then declined owing to debilitation or to the opportunity to escape the hot environment rather than aggressing. Other curvilinear functions besides this inverted-U might also be possible (for a discussion of these issues, see Anderson, 1989).

## METHOD

Microfilm issues of major daily newspapers were consulted to obtain data on weather and major league baseball games. Random samples of games were taken from three major league baseball seasons: 1986, 1987, and 1988. The 1986 sample included every 10th game played during the season ($n = 215$ games). Every 7th game during the season was included for the 1987 ($n = 304$) and 1988 ($n = 307$) samples. For each game sampled, the number of players hit by a pitch (HBP) was recorded. Within the same newspaper issue, the high temperature (°F) in the home city the day of the game was also recorded. The numbers of walks, wild pitches, passed balls, errors, home runs, and fans in attendance in each game were recorded as control variables.

## RESULTS

To test the primary prediction that the number of HBPs in a game increases with temperature, a Pearson product-moment correlation between temperature and HBPs was calculated for all the games in our sample from the 1986, 1987, and 1988 seasons. As predicted, this correlation was positive and significant. To determine whether this relationship would be maintained with the potentially confounding variables described above controlled for, we regressed HBP on temperature, walks, wild pitches, passed balls, errors, home runs, and attendance. Supporting our prediction, temperature was positively and significantly related to HBP when the alternative variables were partialed out.

The results of the multiple regression indicate that the temperature-HBP relationship is not mediated by pitcher wildness (as measured by walks, wild pitches, and passed balls). An additional way of understanding this point is to examine the correlations between the measures of pitcher wildness and HBP and between pitcher wildness and temperature. If temperature produces wildness (e.g., resulting from fatigue or a pitcher's slippery hand), and if wildness mediates the temperatures-HBP relationship, then one would expect that (a) temperature would be positively correlated with pitcher wildness and (b) pitcher wildness would be positively correlated with HBP. However, temperature is *negatively* correlated with the measures of wildness. Thus, heat does not lead to greater pitcher wildness, and the alternative explanation that wildness mediates the temperature-HBP relationship is rendered less plausible.

### The Temperature-HBP Relationship in Each of the Home Parks

Although the analyses reported above discredit several potentially trivializing mediators of the temperature-HBP relationship, a final alternative explanation that must be rule out is that this relationship was produced spuriously by incidental differences in the tendency to throw HBPs among the various teams. This alternative explanation arises in part because the 26 home parks of the teams are located in regions that vary greatly in climate. It is possible that the relationship reported between temperature and HBPs could be due simply to the fact that the teams that throw the most HBPs just happen to play in warmer climates and the teams that throw the fewest happen to play in colder climates, for reasons that have nothing to do with temperature.

To examine this issue, we calculated Pearson product-moment correlations between total number of HBPs and temperature for all the games played at each of the 23 home parks that are not domed. These results indicate that batters were not significantly more likely to be hit in one home park than in another.

### Replication of the Relationship in the 1962 Season

The analyses reported thus far concern data from games played during the 1986, 1987, and 1988 seasons. We also collected temperature and HBP data for the 1962 season, using the same sampling procedure as was used for the 1987 and 1988 seasons. We collected these additional data for two reasons. First, this would allow us to examine the generalizability of the temperature-HBP relationship across different periods of time. Second, by looking at a season in which the personnel and the personalities of the teams, and even several of the teams themselves, were very different than among the 26 teams in the 1986–1988 seasons, this would provide an additional test of the alternative explanation that the relationship we found was produced by incidental differences among the pitchers who pitched for the 26 teams between 1986 and 1988.

The Pearson product-moment correlation between temperature and HBP for the 1962 games was positive and marginally significant. As can be seen in Table 1, the correlation for the 1962 season was similar in magnitude to the correlations found for the 1986, 1987, and 1988 seasons. The consistency of these correlations supports the generalizability of the relationship between temperature and HBP. In addition, it further reduces the plausibility of the idea that incidental differences among the pitchers on the 26 teams during 1986–1988 could have produced the temperature-HBP relationship found for those seasons.

**TABLE 1**  Correlations Between Temperature and Number of Players Hit by a Pitch (HBP) for Individual Seasons

|  | 1986 | 1987 | 1988 | 1962 |
|---|---|---|---|---|
| Correlations between temperature and HBP ($n$) | .11 (215) | .09 (304) | .11 (307) | .10 (228) |

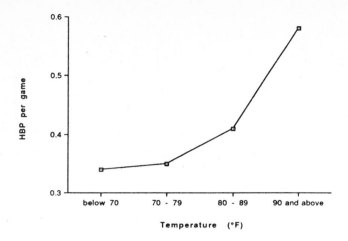

**Figure 1** Mean number of players hit by a pitch (HBPs) in games played below 70 °F ($n$ = 176), between 70 °F and 79 °F ($n$ = 315), between 80 °F and 89 °F ($n$ = 224), and at 90 °F and above ($n$ = 111).

*The Shape of the Temperature-HBP Relationship*

One of the issues that has been important in the heat-aggression literature is the shape of the function that relates heat to aggression. In order for the reader to examine the shape of the relationship between temperature and HBP, we have displayed in Figure 1 the mean numbers of HBPs in games from our 1986–1988 sample that were played at four levels of temperature.

The shape of the relationship between temperature and HBP was analyzed by applying a set of orthogonal polynomial contrasts to the average number of HBPs in games played at the four levels of temperature. These results are most consistent with a linear, rather than a curvilinear, relationship between temperature and HBP.

## DISCUSSION

The results of the present study revealed that mean hit-by-pitch levels rose linearly with temperature. Regression analyses revealed that this relationship remained positive and significant when several variables that have nothing to do with aggression but could plausibly mediate a temperature-HBP relationship were partialed out. Indeed, because the measures of pitcher wildness and inaccuracy were negatively correlated with temperature, the measures of pitcher wildness apparently suppressed, rather than confounded, the temperature-HBP relationship.

Moreover, the results of a series of correlations between temperature and HBPs calculated for each of the nondomed home stadiums and of an analysis looking for significant differences among the mean numbers of HBPs thrown at the various home parks suggest that the observed temperature-HBP relationship was not produced spuriously by incidental differences among the teams. Further discrediting this alternative explanation was the finding of a similar temperature-HBP relationship in the 1962 season, a season featuring none of the players—and not all of the teams—who were included in the 1986–1988 samples. Though not reported in the Results section, one final piece of evidence arguing against the alternative explanation is that only 50% of the pitchers who pitched in the major leagues for all three seasons, 1986–1988, played for the same team throughout (MacLean, 1989). Indeed, this figure underestimates the turnover rate because it does not take into account the rookies who entered and the players who retired from the leagues at various points during the three seasons.

This study provides further evidence for the existence of a relationship between heat and aggression, and it extends our knowledge of this relationship to the domain of sports. In addition, the results of this study lend some support to the idea that the shape of the heat-aggression relationship is linear. Of course, no major league baseball games are played in extremely cold temperatures, and few are played in temperatures that exceed 100 °F. Therefore, the data from our study cannot allow us to rule out the possibility that heat and aggression are related in a nonlinear fashion at temperatures more extreme than in our range. It should be noted, however, that our sample does accurately represent the range of temperatures present in the summer months in most of the United States and southern Canada.

Heat-aggression effects have usually been explained in terms of the major theories of aggression, such as excitation-transfer/misattribution and cognitive neoassociation (for this type of discussion, see Anderson, 1989). A recently proposed theory of emotion also offers an interesting insight into the possible mechanisms underlying the heat-aggression relationship. In their vascular theory of emotional efference, Zajonc, Murphy, and Inglehart (1989) suggest that brain temperature—which is partially regulated by a venous structure in the nose—and temperature-related neurochemistry may underlie heat-aggression effects. Proposed mechanisms such as these are clearly far away from our level of data collection. They do, however, represent useful hypotheses about the nature of the relationship of temperature to negative affect and aggression, as well as suggest possible interventions to reduce aggression in naturalistic settings such as sports.

In addition to their theoretical implications, the results have practical significance. Although the magnitude of the correlation is rather small, the slope of the temperature-HBP function is fairly steep in the higher temperatures. In fact, there is approximately a two-thirds greater chance of a batter's being hit in a game played when the temperature is in the nineties or above than in a game played when the temperature is in the seventies or below. Considering that during the course of one full baseball season 2,106 major league baseball games are played, numerous batters will suffer the consequences of the relationship between heat and aggression. Given the potential for serious injury whenever a batter gets hit with a pitch traveling approximately 90 miles per hour, any statistical relationship found between heat and batters being hit must be regarded as noteworthy.

These results suggest that the current trends in major league baseball of a greater number of night games and a greater number of domed stadiums, trends that have aroused the ire of many a baseball purist, may prove to decrease the number of batters being hit by pitches, and such a decrease could save some careers or even lives. Although the authors do not call for the abolishment of summer day games in nondomed stadiums, we do suggest that baseball players should take care to keep cool during games played in hot weather. Indeed, the many nonprofessional athletes who flock to the recreational fields and courts as the weather gets warm every spring and summer should also be careful of rising temperatures and tempers. It may be that talking about the weather, and specifically about what effects it can have on human behavior, can save many from pain and remorse.

## References

Anderson, C. A. (1987). Temperature and aggression: Effects on quarterly, yearly, and city rates of violent and nonviolent crime. *Journal of Personality and Social Psychology, 52,* 1161–1173.

Anderson, C. A. (1989). Temperature and aggression: Ubiquitous effects of heat on occurrence of human violence. *Psychological Bulletin, 106,* 74–96.

Baron, R. A. (1976). The reduction of human aggression: A field study of the influence of incompatible reactions. *Journal of Applied Social Psychology, 6,* 260–274.

Boxer, S. (1989, April 17). Dark forces. *Sports Illustrated,* pp. 52–56.

Frank, M. G., & Gilovich, T. (1988). The dark side of self- and social perception: Black uniforms and aggression in professional sports. *Journal of Personality and Social Psychology, 54,* 74–85.

Hersch, H. (1987, July 20). It's war out there! *Sports Illustrated,* pp. 14–17.

Kenrick, D. T., & MacFarlane, S. W. (1984). Ambient temperature and horn-honking: A field study of the heat/aggression relationship. *Environment and Behavior, 18,* 179–191.

Lopresti, M. (1987, July 30). Homer-stung pitchers fight back. *USA Today,* pp. C1–C2.

MacLean, N. (Ed.). (1989). *Who's who in baseball.* New York: Who's Who in Baseball Magazine Co.

Zajonc, R. B., Murphy, S. T., & Inglehart, M. (1989). Feeling and facial efference: Implications of the vascular theory of emotion. *Psychological Review, 96,* 395–416.

Edward I. Donnerstein
Daniel G. Linz

# The Question of Pornography

In this article, Donnerstein (along with his colleague Linz) follows up on some of the ideas he suggested in the conversation. The authors take exception with some of the conclusions of the 1986 Commission on Pornography, suggesting that the commission misinterpreted some of the research available to them. They note that violence against women does not have to occur in a sexually explicit context to have a negative effect on attitudes about rape and violent behavior. More generally, the authors assert that it is violence, whether or not accompanied by sexual content, that has the most damaging effect on those who are exposed to it.

In July 1986, the United States Attorney General's Commission on Pornography issued its final report on a subject that is as complex as the human condition. While many people have commented upon the report, few have actually read it and fewer still understand its implications.

As social scientists and two of the researchers whose work was cited throughout the two-volume work, we feel it necessary to point out that the report fell short of our expectations in several important respects. First, there are factual problems with the report, representing serious errors of commission. Several of the contentions made in its pages cannot be supported by empirical evidence. Some commission members apparently did not understand or chose not to heed some of the fundamental assumptions in the social science research on pornography. Second, and perhaps more importantly, the commission members have committed a serious error of omission. The single most important problem in the media today, as clearly indicated by social science research, is not pornography but violence.

The report begins with some history about previous attempts to examine the question of pornography. One of the most important of these was the President's Commission on Obscenity and Pornography, which issued its final report in 1970. "More than in 1957, when the law of obscenity became inextricably a part of constitutional law, more than in 1970, when the

President's Commission on Obscenity and Pornography issued its report . . . we live in a society unquestionably pervaded by sexual explicitness," the current report states. It goes on to point out, quite rightly, that the most dangerous form of pornography is that which includes specifically violent themes. But then the report adds: "Increasingly, the most prevalent forms of pornography . . . fit this description. . . . It is with respect to material of this variety that the scientific findings and ultimate conclusions of the 1970 Commission are least reliable for today, precisely because material of this variety was largely absent from that Commission's inquiries."

It is popularly assumed—and the members of the commission appear to share this assumption—that images of violence have become more prevalent in pornography in recent years. Interestingly, there has never been a systematic content analysis of X-rated books, films and magazines that would be needed to support such a conclusion. But there are a handful of studies, concentrating on specific media, that at least call this notion into question.

One of the most recent of these was undertaken by sociologist Joseph E. Scott of Ohio State University. He examined the content of cartoons in *Playboy* magazine from 1954 to 1983 and found that there was indeed a period— around 1977—when the violent content peaked. But just as there had been an increase in violence in the years before 1977, there has been a like decrease since. Further, he notes that sexually violent material seems to occur on an average of about 1 page in every 3,000 and in fewer than 4 pictures out of 1,000—a level that would have to be considered barely noticeable.

In addition, there is evidence indicating a different sort of trend in sexually oriented videocassettes. Psychologist Ted Palys of Simon Fraser University analyzed the content of 150 randomly selected home videos, most of which were produced between 1979 and 1983. He divided these films into "Triple X," in which sexual activity is explicit and graphic, and "Adult," in which no explicit sex is shown but nudity and "implied" sexual behavior is allowed.

Palys found that the Adult films actually portrayed a higher percentage of aggressive scenes and more severe and graphic forms of aggression than did the Triple X videos. More important, there was no increase in aggressive images between 1979 and 1983 for either type of video. In fact, as Palys notes, the difference between these two types of videos may be widening over time, primarily because of decreases in sexual violence in the Triple X category.

At least for now we cannot legitimately conclude that pornography has become more violent since the time of the 1970 Pornography Commission. The results of the few studies that have been done are inconclusive and inconsistent, but at least a few of them point in the opposite direction. Perhaps it is because all forms of pornography are more prevalent now than they once were that we are more aware of the sexually violent forms of pornography.

What is so particularly evil about violent pornography? Here, the commission does not mince words: "In both clinical and experimental settings, exposure to sexually violent materials has indicated an increase in the likelihood of aggression." The commission goes on to state that "finding a link between aggressive behavior toward women and sexual violence . . . requires assumptions not found exclusively in the experimental evidence. We see no reason, however, not to make these assumptions." The assumptions include the idea (in the commission's words) that "increased aggressive behavior towards women is causally related, for an aggregate population, to increased sexual violence."

One persuasive reason to be careful about an intuitive leap like this, however, is a closer examination of the empirical evidence—what it says and what it does not say. We have no argument with the commission on its first point. Experiments by psychologist Neil Malamuth at the University of California, Los Angeles, suggest that, especially when the experimenter appears to condone aggression against women, men act more aggressively toward women in a laboratory after having been exposed to sexually violent stories. But a question that the prudent reader might rise is: "How long do these effects last?" In the vast majority of studies, aggressive behavior is measured almost immediately after exposure to the violent pornographic films. But is the effect cumulative or does it disappear over time?

In one study by Malamuth and psychologist Joseph Ceniti, college-aged men were exposed to violent and nonviolent sexual material over a four-week period. They watched two feature-length films each week and read similar materials. About seven days later, they were (according to the researchers' plan) angered by a woman working with the researchers and then given an opportunity to act aggressively against her. Contrary to expectations, the men who had been exposed to pornography were no more aggressive against her than were those not exposed to pornography. For the moment, then, we do not know if repeated exposure has a cumulative effect or if such effects are only temporary. But the evidence, such as it is, points toward the latter conclusion. This fact seems not to have been given sufficient consideration by the commission.

In addition, there is evidence that particular themes in pornography might be especially harmful. Recent research indicates that it is specifically the message that women find force or aggression pleasurable that seems to be important in influencing men's perceptions and attitudes about rape. For example, in a study Donnerstein conducted with psychologist Leonard Berkowitz, men were shown one of two films, both aggressively violent and sexually explicit. In both, a young woman arrives at the home of two young men to study. She is shoved around, tied up, stripped, slapped and ultimately raped by both men. In one version of the film ("positive ending"), the woman is shown smiling at the end and in no way resisting. A narrative added to the film indicates that she eventually becomes a willing participant. In the version with a "negative ending," the reaction of the woman is not clear, but the voiceover indicates that she found the experience humiliating and disgusting.

Men who saw the positive-ending film interpreted the film itself as less aggressive and said that the woman suffered less, enjoyed herself more and was more responsible for what happened than did the men who saw the negative ending. This seems fairly clear evidence that the different messages in the two films affected the men's attitudes in different ways.

But this literature can be tricky to interpret. In one study by Malamuth, researcher Scott Haber and psychologist Seymour Feshbach, for example, men read several stories, some of which were about a woman being raped. When the men were asked how likely they would be to behave as the rapist did if they knew they would not be caught, more than half indicated some likelihood of behaving that way. Many assume that this surprisingly high percentage was due to the effects of men being exposed to violent pornography. As the commission report concludes, "substantial exposure to sexually violent materials . . . bears a causal relationship to anti-social acts of sexual violence and, for some subgroups, possibly to unlawful acts of sexual violence."

Yet nothing could be further from the truth. In none of the studies by Malamuth has a measure of motivation such as "likelihood to rape" ever changed as a result of exposure to pornography. If the men reported feeling this way, it might be because they were generally callous about rape to begin with. As Malamuth has noted, men who indicate some likelihood that they might commit rape (if not caught) are more sexually aroused by and more attracted to violent materials, but there is no reason to think that exposure to violent pornography is the cause of these predispositions.

Malamuth and psychologist James Check again asked men to read two stories. Some first read a story with a "positive ending," in which the woman becomes sexually aroused; others read a story with a negative ending; then all of the men read a realistic depiction of a rape. But first, the researchers classified the men as "more likely to rape" or "less likely to rape" based upon their answer to the question, "Would you rape if you knew you would not be caught?"

While both groups were more likely to view the woman in the second story as enjoying rape if they had read the positive-ending story first, the "more likely to rape" men seemed much more affected by exposure to this sort of pornography. They agreed much more frequently with statements suggesting that women enjoy rape and enjoy being forced into having sex than did those who were "less likely to rape" to being with. This indicates to us that exposure to violent pornography is not necessarily causing callous attitudes about rape but rather may reinforce and strengthen already existing beliefs and values. If aggressive pornography is not the cause of the negative attitudes, then it ought not be blamed for them.

What we have is a picture of violent pornography that is somewhat different from that drawn by the commission. We do not, as yet, know if the detrimental effects of watching pornography are long-lived or only fleeting. We do know that it is specifically the pornographic materials that depict women "enjoying" rape that are especially damaging, but it remains unclear whether all men are affected equally even by these bizarre scripts. Finally, it remains to be seen whether changes in attitudes about women and rape revealed in relatively small-scale tests have any applicability to rape and aggression in the real world.

There is some evidence from the work of Malamuth that these attitudes do have some relationship to real-world aggression, but again, these are attitudes that people already have. The commission members were obviously aware of these issues. In fact, these conclusions, well-grounded in scientific research, are briefly summarized deep within their report, which makes it even more perplexing that they ignore the data in making their 92 recommendations.

Our major criticism of the report and its authors, however, has to do with a subject that has been glossed over in the commission's 1,960-page report. The commission has ignored the inescapable conclusion that it is violence,whether or not accompanied by sex, that has the most damaging effect upon those who view it, hear it or read about it. This is an extremely important distinction, with direct relevance to the work of the commission, because it has implications far beyond violent pornography and pornography in general.

Sexual violence and depictions of women "desiring" rape are not limited to X-rated films, books and magazines. In the popular film *The Getaway*, for example, one of the robbers kidnaps a woman (portrayed by Sally Struthers) and her husband. He rapes the woman, but she is portrayed as a willing participant. Struthers's character becomes the kidnapper's girlfriend and the two of them taunt her husband until he finally commits suicide. The woman then willingly continues with the assailant. Far from being consigned to dingy X-rated theaters, this film, originally produced in 1972 and shown in cinemas all over the country, is still shown occasionally on commercial television.

Malamuth and Check tried to determine whether the mildly explicit sexual violence in *The Getaway* and in *Swept Away*, another film with similar content, influenced viewers' attitudes toward women and rape. When the researchers questioned college students who saw both films and students who saw nonviolent films or no films at all, they found that the men who saw violent movies more readily accepted interpersonal violence and more frequently believed that women enjoy rape.

In another study we did with Berkowitz, men saw different versions of a film. The first version contained a scene of sexual aggression in which a woman is tied up, threatened with a gun and raped. The second version contained only the violent parts of the scene, with the sexually explicit rape omitted. The third version contained only the sexually explicit rape scene with the violence deleted.

The most callous attitudes about rape and the largest percentage of subjects indicating some likelihood of raping or using force were found among those men who had seen only the violent coercion. Subjects who saw the X-rated version without violence scored the lowest on both measures, and those who saw both the explicit sex and the violence scored somewhere in between.

Taken together, these studies strongly suggest that violence against women need not occur in a pornographic or sexually explicit context to have a negative effect upon viewer attitudes and behavior. But even more importantly, it must be concluded that violent images, rather than sexual ones, are most responsible for people's attitudes about women and rape.

As should be obvious to anyone with a television set, the mass media contain an abundance of such nonsexually explicit images and messages. These ideas about rape are so pervasive in our culture that it is myopic to call them the exclusive domain of violent pornography. In fact, one would not have to search much farther than the local 7-Eleven to find numerous bloody murder mysteries in detective magazines that reinforce this point.

And this is where we have our strongest disagreement with the Commission on Pornography. Granted that the charter of the group was to examine the pernicious effects of pornography on society. Granted also that the time, money and other resources of the commission were limited. But it seems appropriate to note that if the commissioners were looking for the most nefarious media threat to public welfare, they missed the boat. The most clear and present danger, well documented by the social science literature, is all violent material in our society, whether sexually explicit or not, that promotes violence against women. Let us hope that the next commission will provide a better example by disentangling sexuality from violence, therefore yielding more useful conclusions.

Richard Gelles

# Basic Training for Violence

In this selection, Gelles proposes that, of all the factors that determine violent behavior, the home is the most important. It is, as it has been said, the "cradle of violence." He notes that those who commit acts of violence toward their spouses have often been witness to or victim of violence in the home as children. He suggests that parents serve as role models for children who witness them acting violently, that they justify violence, and that they even show that it is an approved way of handling problems. In effect, this communicates norms and values accepting of violent behavior and even teaches children how and when to use violence to get their way.

The family, more than any other social institution, is the primary mechanism for teaching norms, values, and techniques of violence. If we want to understand and explain violence (be it in the street or in the home), our attention ought to be directed towards the family more than, for example, to the effects of television violence on children (Larsen, 1968) or the impact of corporal punishment in the school. The empirical data (discussed in the following pages) on homicide, assault, child abuse, violent crimes, and violence between family members definitely tend to indicate that violent individuals grew up in violent families and were frequent victims of familial violence as children. The theoretical work on violence also points to the family as a major factor that contributes to violence by providing basic training for violence.

In our own research we found that many of the respondents who had committed acts of violence towards their spouses had been exposed to conjugal violence as children and had been frequent victims of parental violence. This exposure and experience often provided role models for the use of violence, and situations where accounting schemes were learned that justified and approved of violence. This chapter posits that the family serves as basic training for violence by exposing children to violence, by making them victims of violence, and by providing them with learning contexts for the commission of violent acts. Finally, the family inculcates children with normative and value systems that approve of the use of violence on family members in various situations.


## SOCIALIZATION AND VIOLENCE

A common factor throughout the research on violent individuals is that they had a high level of physical brutality inflicted on them throughout childhood and adolescence. Guttmacher's (1960) conclusion of a discussion about a group of murderers is that their common experience was the high level, of violence inflicted on them by parents when they were growing up. Guttmacher (1960) states that this victimization produced a hostile identification by the victims (the eventual murderers) with their brutal aggressors and the murderers learned by conscious example that violence was a solution to frustration. Tanay's study of homicidal offenders finds that 67% had histories of violent child rearing (1969: 1252–1253). Palmer (1962) suspected that mothers of murderers were more aggressive towards them than their brothers. His data reveal that a slightly greater number of murderers than control brothers were beaten by their mothers (p. 76). In addition, fathers beat the murderers severely as opposed to control brothers (Palmer, 1962: 76). Palmer's later work on violence (1972) concludes that the early life histories of those who later commit homicides are characterized by extreme physical frustration (p. 53). Leon's study of violent bandits in Colombia (1969) adds cross-cultural support to the relationship between violence received as a child and violence committed as an adult. Studying the childhood history of violent bandits, Leon observes that fathers of these bandits used brutal punishment in order to assert dominance over the family.

The literature on child abuse presents strong evidence that abusive parents were raised in the same style that they have re-created in the pattern of rearing their own children (Steele and Pollock, 1968: 111). Abused children are likely to become abusive adults (Bakan, 1971: 114; Kempe, 1962: 18; Gil, 1971: 641; Gelles, 1973).

Given the experience of violent individuals with violence when they were growing up, what is the mechanism that leads to them becoming violent adults? Theories and students of violence posit that the family serves as an agent of socialization in teaching violent behavior. Not only does the family expose individuals to violence and techniques of violence, the family teaches approval for the use of violence. Bakan asserts that every time a child is punished by violence he is being taught that violence is a proper mode of behavior (Bakan, 1971: 115). Goode (1971) concurs with this position by arguing that children are taught that violence is bad but shown by parents that violence can be used to serve one's own ends. Gold (1958) explains that modes of aggression vary among social classes as a result of different socialization experiences. These different socialization experiences are the different types of punishment meted out by parents of misbehaving children (p. 654).

Where physical punishment is used (in the lower classes) it serves to identify this type of behavior as approved behavior when one is hurt or angry. The punishing parent serves as a model for aggressive behavior (Gold, 1958: 654).

Other theoretical and empirical work further emphasizes the position that the family plays a major role in teaching violent behavior and proviolent norms. Bandura, Ross, and Ross (1961) would assert that children viewing their parents' acts of violence towards each other might imitate this behavior as children and in later life. And Guttmacher cites the fact that a number of murderers observed violence in a parent (1960: 61). A study of exposure to violence and violence approval (Owens and Straus, 1973) reveals a high correlation between observation of and experience with violence as a child and violence approval. Another discussion of violence asserts along the same line that violence is learned through childhood experience with violence and viewing the parent as a role model of violence (Singer, 1971; Gelles, 1973). This approach proposes that interpersonal violence reflects the shared meanings and role expectations of the person and others with whom he interacts. Self-attitude theory (Kaplan, 1972), structural theory (Coser, 1967; Etzioni, 1971), and culture of violence theory (Wolfgang and Ferracuti, 1967) all state, to a greater or lesser degree, that patterns endorsing violent responses are transmitted to children in the course of parent-child interaction and day-to-day family life.

## EXPERIENCE WITH VIOLENCE

Based on the theoretical and empirical work on violence we expected to find that: first, respondents who had observed violence between their parents would engage in more conjugal violence as adults than respondents who had not observed violence between their parents; and second, respondents who had been victims of violence in childhood would be more likely to engage in conjugal violence as adults than individuals who had not been victims of childhood violence or who had been victimized less.

The respondents who had observed their parents engaging in physical violence were in fact much more likely to physically fight with their own spouses than the people we interviewed who never saw their parents physically fight (Figure 1).

The data for victimization as a child and later violence with a spouse are not as clear-cut. Those respondents who had been frequent victims of violence as children were more likely to be violent toward their spouses than people who were never hit as children. However, the individuals who were hit infrequently as children were *less* likely to hit their spouses than either the no-experience or frequent-experience with violence groups. Why this is the case is extremely difficult to explain.

The two hypotheses that introduced this section are generally supported by the data. Observation of and experience with violence as a child are more likely to lead to later conjugal violence than are no observation and no experience with violence. The question still remains—why? What are the

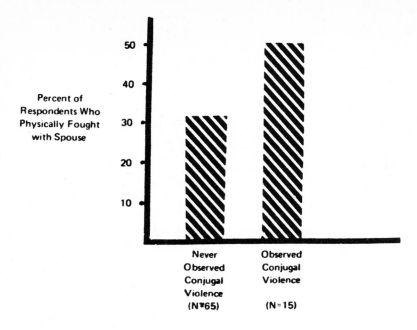

**Figure 1** Percent of Respondents who Physically Fought with Spouse by Respondent's observation of Conjugal Violence in Family of Orientation.

mechanisms by which these observations and experiences are translated into violent actions as an adult? Singer (1971: 31) provides the initial rationale for positing that these observations and experiences have a deep and lasting effect on eventual violent behavior towards family members:

> In new situations where a child is at loss for what to do he is likely to remember what he saw his parents do and behave accordingly, even to his own detriment. Indeed, adults when they become parents and are faced with the novelty of the role revert to the type behavior they saw their parents engage in when they were children sometimes against their current adult judgement.

Children growing up are witness to the trials and frustrations of married life by viewing the actions of their parents. They see how to react to frustration and crisis. They learn how to raise and to punish children, and they learn how a husband treats his wife and how a wife treats her husband. In our society, there are no other institutions that teach these lessons (with the minor exception of the "preparation for marriage" courses taught in some universities and the role models presented by television family shows).

Our conversations with the members of 80 families indicated that basic training for violence consists of a learning situation that takes place where observation and experience with violence can lead to later conjugal violence. Techniques of violence, approval of violence, and accounting schemes for violence all are learned in the family by seeing one's own parents fight and by being struck as a child.

## LEARNING THE SCRIPT: TECHNIQUES, APPROVAL, ACCOUNTING SCHEMES OF VIOLENCE

The interviews yielded some important insights into the process by which experience with violence leads to intrafamily violence. In many cases, these insights are drawn from the discussions of how the respondent acts towards his or her spouse and children and the discussions of life in the respondent's family of orientation. It was evident that many of the techniques of intrafamily violence are passed on from generation to generation. Where one mother uses a belt on her children, we found that she had been hit by a belt by her parents. If a wife slaps her husband, she may have observed her mother do the same thing to her father. Also, a very strong theme in the interviews was how approval and justification for violence is taught. Many discussions of "normal violence" between husband and wife and parents and children were followed later in the interview by the respondent recalling a time when he was hit, or when his father hit his mother, and how these incidents happened because the victim "deserved to be hit." Finally, there is the subtle teaching of the entire script of intrafamily violence in the accounting schemes that are learned. The homily of "sparing the rod and spoiling the child," the justifications for violence, and the whole approval of violence in the family comprised a detailed accounting scheme which, for the respondents, explained much of the violence that they either committed as adults or were victims of in their childhood.

### Techniques of Violence

Although there were some discussions of techniques of conjugal violence learned from observing or experiencing violence in the family, the most lucid discussions came when the topic was how one behaved towards his own child and how he was treated by his own parents. Individuals learn much about how to be physically violent by being hit or watching someone else being hit. First, the particular methods and instruments of violence are learned. Whether an individual uses his hand, a belt, a curtain rod, or a yardstick is greatly determined by how he was hit as a child and what techniques were deployed by his parents on each other and on the other children. When respondents stated how they hit their children and then, later in the conversation, discussed how they were treated by their parents, the instruments were sometimes identical. It must be pointed out that these discussions were not connected and occurred at completely different times in the conversation. In addition, the interviewers never referred to what the respondent said previously about how he punished his child when the discussion concerned how he was punished as a child. For example, Mrs. (2) first discussed how she punishes her children. Later, she talked about the types of punishment she received.

> **Mrs. (2):** I rant and rave and sometimes I get my yardstick. Sometimes if they are close I haul off with my hand. But they are getting so big that it's too painful.
> **Interviewer:** What kind of punishment or discipline would your parents let out to you?
> **Mrs. (2):** We usually got the yardstick.

Some respondents made the connection that they used the same method to raise their children that their parents used on them.

> **Mrs. (20):** I guess she punished us the same way I do my kids—with probably a belt or do without things.

In addition to teaching the use of particular instruments, the family also teaches *why* an instrument or technique is deployed. In Mrs. (47)'s family the instrument was not as important as its impact—it had to sting to be effective.

> **Mrs. (47):** I used to spank them. I used to have, you know, those yardsticks. Of course, they're not really heavy or anything, but they sting, you know.

When she talked about how she was punished she said:

> **Mrs. (47):** I think that's the only time he used a razor strap on me. The other times we had to go out and pick our own peach tree switch, you know, because they're very strong and they sting like mad!

The learning of techniques of violence also applies to learning *when* to employ these techniques. We talked about a calculus that parents develop to determine when and where to use force and violence. These calculi are often learned from one's own parents and by using one's own childhood as a guideline. Mr. (42) gets upset by his children's talking back. When they do this they get a slap in the mouth:

> **Mr. (42):** They talk back—that gets me upset. . . . One of them talked back to me once, about three years ago and I hit him in the mouth.

To understand why Mr. (42) gets upset when his children talk back and why they get slapped in the mouth for this, we can examine Mr. (42)'s experience as a child.

**Mr. (42):** I never got a spanking. I can remember talking back to my mother once—my father never hit us. I can remember my mother giving me a belt in the mouth. That was the only time I ever talked back to my mother.

The accounts of the respondents add further evidence to the assertion made in the research of Bandura and his colleagues on imitative and modeling behavior, which show that children and young adults imitate the behavior of aggressive models (Bandura, Ross, and Ross, 1961). For those who are less than convinced that role models do lead to imitation, there is the story told by Mrs. (10):

**Mrs. (10):** My daughter would sit down with a little blanket she had and she would put it between her legs and she would say that daddy hit mother like this and she would bang on the blanket, you know.

Individuals not only imitate in later life the behavior they witnessed as children, they also learn how to hit, what to hit with, what the impact should be, and what the appropriate circumstances are for violence.

*Approval of Violence*

A recent analysis of data from a national survey conducted in 1968 for the President's Commission on the Causes and Prevention of Violence revealed that approval of interpersonal violence is highly related to experiencing violence as a child (Owens and Straus, 1972: 13). Our interview data confirm this finding and demonstrate that observing violence and being a victim of violence as a child can lead to approval of the use of interpersonal violence among family members. Mrs. (75), who has been hit by her husband, learned as a child that sometimes a wife deserves to be hit.

**Mrs. (75):** My father spanked my mother when I was about 5 years old. I don't know what it was for, but I know my mother told me father spanked her. That's the only time he ever laid a hand on her—she must have done something to deserve a spanking.

Being a victim of violence also contributes to an "I deserved it" outlook, which leads to approval of the use of interpersonal violence in the family.

**Mrs. (1):** The only time my father ever hit is when I swore at my mother. And I deserved it, you know. He slapped me across the mouth when he was really mad. You know, I deserved to be hit, I realized that.

Thus, our respondents provide a vivid demonstration of how observation and experience with violence as a child can be translated into violence approval as an adult.

### Violence and Accounting Schemes

A major problem in positing that experience with violence leads to approval of violence is that this does not necessarily mean that it causes violent actions. As most students of attitudes and behavior know, there is no one-to-one relationship between attitudes toward a particular behavior and engaging in that behavior. Thus, if an individual approves of violence, he may not necessarily engage in a violent act towards a family member. We would argue, however, that a plausible sequence is that approval of violence contributes to the development of an accounting scheme that family members can use to explain or justify incidents of intrafamily violence. Moreover, the existence of this accounting scheme may facilitate violent behavior by providing, in advance, acceptable accounts that serve to justify the behavior despite cultural prescriptions and proscriptions about intrafamily violence. An example of an accounting scheme for parental violence that has been passed down for three generations and is now being taught to a fourth, is given by Mrs. (19):

**Mrs. (19):** The rules were set and they were to be followed. If I did something wrong I was given a beating on the spot. My mother was a church-going woman. She went to church. She'd say I don't have time, but when I come back I'm going to hunt you down and spank you. We got it right then and there—right on the nose because that was the promise she made. I also believe that when I'm raising my children—I should be a little more lenient—but with my leniency I also believe that when I tell my girls to be home at a certain time, I expect that. But see then too, I also raised my children on faith and trust which I guarantee this from every mother and father. I really do. I never had much education and I don't believe in reading out of books or this sort of thing because I wasn't raised up on no book. I just believe in knowledge. I love my children. I raised them and even my little grandchild— when I see her doing something wrong I'm going to spank her. I mean it's as simple as that, you know.

## VIOLENCE AS LEARNED BEHAVIOR

The conclusion of this discussion is that violence is learned behavior. We have been asserting that violence, and violence towards family members in particular, is learned by experiencing violence while growing up in a family. Where an individual experiences violence as a child he is more likely to engage in violence as an adult.

**Mrs. (48):** He's (her husband) very rough. Always pushing me around.

You know, not hitting, you know, but just putting his hand against me and just shoving or stuff like grabbing. I was always black and blue from where he grabbed me. He was this way. He never knew anything gentle. He was very, very rough and this was the way he handled everything. And it wasn't something, you know, he didn't always do it out of temper most of the time. He did it because this was what he learned. He never knew any different.

When individuals do not experience violence in their families as they are growing up, they are less likely to be violent adults.

## References

Bakan, D. (1971) *Slaughter of the Innocents: A Study of the Battered Child Phenomenon.* Boston: Beacon Press.

Bandura, A., D. Ross, and S. Ross (1961) Transmission of aggression through imitation of aggressive models. *Journal of Abnormal and Social Psychology* 63 (3): 575–582.

Coser, L. A. (1967) *Continuities in the Study of Social Conflict.* New York: Free Press.

Etzioni, A. (1971) Violence, pp. 709–741 in Robert K. Merten and Robert Nisbet [eds.] *Contemporary Social Problems.* 3rd ed. New York: Harcourt Brace Jovanovich.

Gelles, R. J. (1973) Child abuse as psychopathology: a sociological critique and reformulation. *American Journal of Orthopsychiatry,* 45 (July): 611–621.

Gil, D. G. (1971) Violence against children. *Journal of Marriage and the Family* 33 (November): 637–648.

Gold, M. (1958) Suicide, homicide and the socialization of aggression. *American Journal of Sociology* 63 (May): 651–661.

Goode, W. J. (1971) Force and violence in the family. *Journal of Marriage and the Family* 33 (November): 624–636.

Guttmacher, M. (1960) *The Mind of the Murderer.* New York: Farrar, Straus, and Cudahy.

Kaplan, H. B. (1972) Toward a general theory of psychosocial deviance: the case of aggressive behavior. *Social Science and Medicine* 6 (5): 593–617.

Kemper, C. H. et al. (1962) The battered child syndrome. *Journal of the American Medical Association* 181 (July 7): 17–24.

Larsen, O. N. [ed.] (1968) *Violence and the Mass Media.* New York: Harper & Row.

Leon, C. A. (1969) Unusual patterns of crime during 'la Violencia' in Colombia. *American Journal of Psychiatry* 125 (11): 1564–1575.

Owens, D. J. and M. A. Straus (1973) Childhood violence and adult approval of violence. Paper presented to the 1973 meetings of the American Orthopsychiatric Association.

Palmer, S. (1962) *The Psychology of Murder.* New York: Thomas Y. Crowell Co.

Palmer, S. (1972) *The Violent Society.* New Haven: College and University Press.

Singer, J. (1971) *The Control of Aggression and Violence.* New York: Academic Press.

Steele, B. F. and C. B. Pollock (1968) A psychiatric study of parents who abuse infants and small children. Pp. 103–147 in Ray E. Helfer and C. Henry Kempe [eds.] *The Battered Child.* Chicago: University of Chicago Press.

Tanay, E. (1969) Psychiatric study of homicide. *American Journal of Psychiatry* 125 (9): 1252–1258.

Wolfgang, M. E. (1957) and F. Ferracuti (1967) *The Subculture of Violence.* London: Tavistock Publications.

# 9

# Stereotypes and Prejudice: Devaluing Others

Stereotypes abound—of racial and ethnic groups, of students and professors, of lawyers and politicians. Social psychologists have long tried to understand what accounts for them and how they fit into the study of group prejudice. Earlier approaches to these issues greatly emphasized the role of emotions and irrational thinking in prejudice. However, the modern approach focuses more on a cognitive analysis, on the manner in which we organize, process, and remember information about groups.

Patricia Devine of the University of Wisconsin at Madison has quickly become one of the leading researchers in this field. Her analysis of the ways in which people who are high and low in prejudice differ has provided researchers with new insights and suggested interesting directions for interventions to reduce prejudice and discrimination.

In our conversation, we covered a range of issues about the manner in which stereotypes tend to resist change and the ways in which social psychologists might help to bring that change about.

## A CONVERSATION WITH
## PATRICIA DEVINE
*University of Wisconsin*
*at Madison*

**Krupat:** *If we are going to talk about stereotypes, let me start out by asking you exactly what they are.*

**Devine:** Well, I think you'll find some disagreement about what one is. A lot of people define stereotypes as a set of beliefs that individuals have about members of a minority group or an otherwise stigmatized group. I tend to think about stereotypes a little bit differently because I like to draw a distinction between one's *knowledge* of a stereotype and *believing* the stereotype. That actually turns out to be a central distinction in my work because you can have a high degree of knowledge about what the stereotype is and think it completely inappropriate to apply that knowledge to a member of a particular group. In fact, I think prejudice very often is a characteristic that differentiates who is willing and ready to use stereotypes in making judgements about others—people high in prejudice—and who is not—those low in prejudice.

**Krupat:** *What accounts for the content of stereotypes? Why does one group get labeled sly and another lazy?*

**Devine:** When you take a given group and watch how their stereotype has developed over time, I think one unfortunate answer is that they support political motives. If you were to follow, for example, the development of the black stereotype over time, you would see that the changes in it very closely follow changes in political tides and changing roles that blacks have played in our society. When blacks were enslaved by the white majority, the characteristics commonly ascribed to them were that they were happy-go-lucky, lazy, and really enjoyed their lot in life. That could the justify the institution of slavery. "You know, they're not very smart, and so you have to give them guidance," and all that kind of stuff. After they were freed, in order to deal with this group who have rights, yet still rationalize the institution of slavery, you find very strategic changes in the characteristics ascribed to black people. To see them as animalistic and criminal-like justifies being scared of them and also provides a justification for slavery because "You have to have them enslaved to keep them under control" and so on. So the dramatic changes in the stereotype, I think, were very often to justify white supremacy. And I think you can see some of the same kinds of changes with stereotypes of women if you were to follow those over time with the changing nature of their roles in society. You cannot understand the nature of contemporary race relations or gender relations without understanding the historical context out of which they grew. It's just not possible.

**Krupat:** *But, as we both know, the current stereotypes of these groups don't reflect reality any more than the old ones did. How do people come to believe stereotypes even though they are not accurate?*

**Devine:** Unfortunately, these things begin to take on a life of their own, and because they're so well entrenched in our culture, they become part of our consensually shared knowledge. They get transmitted just like any other belief systems and set of values from one generation to the other. I think that they're very often learned in extraordinarily subtle ways. Careful analysis of the media and the portrayal of various minority groups reveals how the media often contribute to the support of culturally defined stereotypes. Now we see some efforts to try to challenge those kinds of things, but the history of the mass media has more often contributed to the persistence of stereotypes. So one of the things that turns out to be difficult is that kids, for example, often learn these stereotypes at a very young age.

**Krupat:** *How young?*

**Devine:** It has been suggested as young as three and four. Children may not have the fully articulated notion, but what they know is there's a difference between groups and that one group is valued whereas another is devalued. So they learn to associate good and bad, positive and negative, with the stereotypes, sometimes through classical conditioning techniques, through observing the reactions of their parents, and putting two and two together. You know, "I get in trouble when I play with this kid. My mom hasn't said it directly, but hey, I'm smart enough that I can see that something negative will happen to me if I play with this group, so they must be negative." And so the decisions about the validity of the stereotype and a personal decision to accept or not accept these ideas comes much later.

**Krupat:** *But do the stereotypes persist even when the child or adult comes into contact with contradictory evidence?*

**Devine:** This has turned out to be one of the great puzzles in the study of stereotypes and prejudice. Indeed, many hoped that one route to reducing prejudice would be to modify stereotypes by challenging them with contradictory evidence. However, a great deal of research suggests that stereotypes are tenacious and highly resistant to change. The question is why. Some researchers believe that people are highly motivated to believe the stereotype, while others suggest that cognitive processing biases may also contribute to the stereotype's resistance to change. For example, if you've got a stereotype of a black person and your stereotype is that they're not all that intelligent or motivated, what happens when you come in contact with a black physicist? This person clearly challenges any stereotypic conception that you might have of the characteristics of black people, but the problem is that the person's too different. The person's so different from the stereotype that you can subtype that person, store that person separately in memory, and then there's no serious challenge to the stereotype. You don't even treat that person as being relevant to the stereotype. You understand this person as an exception, but the rule stays intact, or you think about this person as a physicist instead of as a black person. So you lump that person in with your physicist stereotype, whatever that might be, and then your racial stereotype remains intact.

**Krupat:** *So does that mean that people who don't even agree with the stereotypes may still buy into them without ever realizing it?*

**Devine:** Yes, I think very often people decide that stereotypes are an inappropriate way to make judgements about other people. The problem is they've been so well learned and they are so highly accessible as cognitive structures that they get in the way. We can say, "I think it's wrong and I'm going to try not to do it." The problem is that it's a kind of habit; it's rather automatic, spontaneous, or involuntary. We just see the member of the group or think about contact with them, and those ideas come to mind, whether it be the stereotypic ideas or the fearful, uncomfortable kind of reaction that you learned while you were growing up.

**Krupat:** *Does this differ for people who we would classify as more versus less prejudiced?*

**Devine:** No, not entirely. That is, both low- and high-prejudiced people are prone to experience such negative reactions. What differentiates the low- from the high-prejudiced people is how they feel as a consequence of these negative reactions. For example, low-prejudiced people have internalized nonprejudiced values and have established personal standards that require nonprejudiced responses toward members of stigmatized groups. They are committed to responding consistently with these standards. It's part of their self-concept; they feel it is self-defining. When they transgress these internalized standards, they feel guilty, they feel angry and annoyed with themselves. In my work, I have referred to this as prejudice with compunction.

**Krupat:** *And how about the more highly prejudiced people?*

**Devine:** Well, first it's important to recognize that their personal standards permit higher levels of prejudice in their reactions to members of stigmatized groups. But they too often respond with more prejudice than their standards permit. In comparison to their low-prejudiced counterparts, however, high-prejudiced people are not as committed to responding consistently with their standards, and their standards are not as self-defining. So, when they violate these standards, they feel uncomfortable, but they do not internalize the negative emotion. They don't feel guilty or direct negative emotion toward themselves.

**Krupat:** *Can I assume that this is "prejudice without compunction?"*

**Devine:** That's right. We've just recently found—and this is kind of scary and unfortunate—that, whereas low-prejudice people feel angry, annoyed, and irritated with themselves, the higher-prejudiced people feel angry, annoyed, and irritated with others. And when we ask them who those others are, most often it's the target group (such as blacks or homosexuals).

**Krupat:** *Give the perspective you have offered, how can we go about reducing prejudice?*

**Devine:** Just as we learned stereotypes, we can learn to control them. If they become a habitual response, we can break this habit, just like people break the nail-biting habit. It's not going to be easy, and it's going to take time and practice, but I will argue that prejudice is a habit that can be broken. This ties into some of my earlier comments about people feeling guilty and feeling compunction when they respond in stereotypic or negative ways when they say they should not. If you believe that it's inappropriate and you've got nonprejudiced values and beliefs and they're important to you, then what you're going to have to do is to learn how to short-circuit those stereotypic types of responses. You have to learn to push them out of the way in a sense, somehow inhibit them, and then replace those habitual responses with responses that are more consistent with your personal beliefs, values, and standards. It's not easy, but it can be done.

**Krupat:** *How?*

**Devine:** The first step is establishing the nonprejudiced standards, understanding that it's important to do that for yourself. The second step is internalizing those standards, integrating them into your core value system. Once you do that, then violations are going to be meaningful. And that's where I think the self-directed guilt, the compunction, comes from. When you find yourself responding in a way that challenges your values, challenges your personal standards, then people get this kind of self-inflicted punishment. Step three, which is the real difficult one, is to learn how to respond consistently with your nonprejudiced standards. And the reason that that one's difficult is it's very involved. This is the breaking-the-habit part of it. You have to learn to recognize when the stereotype or these negative reactions are going to exert their influence, you have to learn how to cut them off, and then you have to learn, especially in the early stages of prejudice reduction, how to intentionally and deliberately replace those negative reactions with responses that are more consistent with your nonprejudiced standards. It's very difficult. It takes a lot of effort, attention, intention, and time.

**Krupat:** *If I am hearing you correctly, it suggests that reducing prejudice is something that we do one person at a time. Wouldn't many people say that this is a very slow way to get a society to change its ways?*

**Devine:** It's not necessarily going to be quick, and I don't think we can expect it to be. Back in the sixties, we tried to desegregate schools through forced busing and so on. We said here's a solution—put blacks and whites into contact, then we're dealing with the problem. It'll be quick ad it'll be clean. Well, it was naive. I understand that it was a positive attempt and it was necessary to do something at that time, but we didn't think about the psychological reality of the people who had to deal with the situation. And I think that's exactly where we are in the nineties. If you look at the history of efforts to try to change people's prejudiced attitudes using large-scale efforts, so far they have failed.

**Krupat:** *Have you been applying the results of your research in an attempt to reduce prejudice among people in the real world?*

**Devine:** I think one of the things that I find exciting about working in this area and the work that I've been doing over the past few years is that there does seem to be the potential for application. I was trained in the tradition of doing good, basic experimental work, and I highly value that. My belief is that you can only develop good interventions and good applications by having a solid, well-tested set of theoretical ideas, so I'm not wanting to jump into application right away. But I see that down the line, and I find that very appealing.

**Krupat:** *Of all the things you have learned from your research, what are some of the most important messages?*

**Devine:** I want people to understand that prejudice is a hard habit to break, but they should try, that it's worth the effort. Your earlier question asked whether change must proceed at the individual level, on a person-by-person basis. Although this may not be the most efficient route to societal change, we've seen through history that very often this can be an effective strategy. It's something that at least we can take advantage of, and then perhaps we can set good examples that may set the stage for future change. I think the worst conclusion would be to just shrug our shoulders and say, "Oh well, it can't be done, let's just get on with the rest of life." I think that these issues are too important for us to take that kind of helpless approach.

# The Nature of Prejudice: What Is the Problem?

Originally published in 1954, Gordon Allport's classic book, *The Nature of Prejudice*, was one of the first sources of clear, scientific thinking about this topic. This selection, which was taken from that book, points out that prejudice involves prejudgement and generalization, two processes that are common and not *necessarily* bad. However, when the generalization is faulty and inflexible and when a person is judged just because of his or her membership in a group, then we are dealing with prejudice. While prejudice involves beliefs, Allport notes that discrimination involves unfair treatment and represents the acting out of prejudice.

The word *prejudice,* derived from the Latin noun *praejudicium,* has, like most words, undergone a change of meaning since classical times. There are three stages in the transformation.

(1) To the ancients, *praejudicium* meant a *precedent*—a judgment based on previous decisions and experiences.
(2) Later, the term, in English, acquired the meaning of a judgment formed before due examination and consideration of the facts—a premature or hasty judgment.
(3) Finally the term acquired also its present emotional flavor of favorableness or unfavorableness that accompanies such a prior and unsupported judgment.

Perhaps the briefest of all definitions of prejudice is: *thinking ill of others without sufficient warrant.* This crisp phasing contains the two essential ingredients of all definitions—reference to unfounded judgment and to a feeling-tone. It is, however, too brief for complete clarity.

In the first place, it refers only to *negative* prejudice. People may be prejudiced in favor of others; they may think *well* of them without sufficient warrant. The wording offered by the New English Dictionary recognizes positive as well as negative prejudice:

*A feeling, favorable or unfavorable, toward a person or thing, prior to, or not based on, actual experience.*

While it is important to bear in mind that biases may be *pro* as well as *con*, it is none the less true that *ethnic* prejudice is mostly negative. A group of students was asked to describe their attitudes toward ethnic groups. No suggestion was made that might lead them toward negative reports. Even so, they reported eight times as many antagonistic attitudes as favorable attitudes. In this volume, accordingly, we shall be concerned chiefly with prejudice *against,* not with prejudice *in favor of,* ethnic groups.

The phrase "thinking ill of others" is obviously an elliptical expression that must be understood to include feelings of scorn or dislike, of fear and aversion, as well as various forms of antipathetic conduct: such as talking against people, discriminating against them, or attacking them with violence.

Similarly, we need to expand the phrase "without sufficient warrant." A judgment is unwarranted whenever it lacks basis in fact. A wit defined prejudice as "being down on something you're not up on."

It is not easy to say how much fact is required in order to justify a judgment. A prejudiced person will almost certainly claim that he has sufficient warrant for his views. He will tell of bitter experiences he has had with refugees, Catholics, or Orientals. But, in most cases, it is evident that his facts are scanty and strained. He resorts to a selective sorting of his own few memories, mixes them up with hearsay, and overgeneralizes. No one can possibly know *all* refugees, Catholics, or Orientals. Hence any negative judgment of these groups *as a whole* is, strictly speaking, an instance of thinking ill without sufficient warrant.

Sometimes, the ill-thinker has no first-hand experience on which to base his judgement. A few years ago most Americans thought exceedingly ill of Turks—but very few had ever seen a Turk nor did they know any person who had seen one. Their warrant lay exclusively in what they had heard of the Armenian massacres and of the legendary crusades. On such evidence they presumed to condemn all members of a nation.

Ordinarily, prejudice manifests itself in dealing with individual members of rejected groups. But in avoiding a Negro neighbor, or in answering "Mr. Greenberg's" application for a room, we frame our action to accord with our categorical generalization of the group as a whole. We pay little or no attention to individual differences, and overlook the important fact that Negro X, our neighbor, is not Negro Y, whom we dislike for good and sufficient reason; that Mr. Greenberg, who may be a fine gentleman, is not Mr. Bloom, whom we have good reason to dislike.

So common is this process that we might define prejudice as:

an avertive or hostile attitude toward a person who belongs to a group, simply because he belongs to that group, and is therefore presumed to have the objectionable qualities ascribed to the group.

This definition stresses the fact that while ethnic prejudice in daily life is ordinarily a matter of dealing with individual people it also entails an unwarranted idea concerning a group as a whole.

Returning to the question of "sufficient warrant," we must grant that few if any human judgments are based on absolute certainty. We can be reasonably, but not absolutely, sure that the sun will rise tomorrow, and that death and taxes will finally overtake us. The sufficient warrant for any judgment is always a matter of probabilities. Ordinarily our judgments of natural happenings are based on firmer and higher probabilities than our judgments of people. Only rarely do our categorical judgments of nations or ethnic groups have a foundation in high probability.

Take the hostile view of Nazi leaders held by most Americans during World War II. Was it prejudiced? The answer is No, because there was abundant available evidence regarding the evil policies and practices accepted as the official code of the party. True, there may have been good individuals in the party who at heart rejected the abominable program; but the probability was so high that the Nazi group constituted an actual menace to world peace and to humane values that a realistic and justified conflict resulted. The high probability of danger removes an antagonism from the domain of prejudice into that of realistic social conflict.

In the case of gangsters, our antagonism is not a matter of prejudice, for the evidence of their antisocial conduct is conclusive. But soon the line becomes hard to draw. How about an ex-convict? It is notoriously difficult for an ex-convict to obtain a steady job where he can be self-supporting and self-respecting. Employers naturally are suspicious if they know the man's past record. But often they are more suspicious than the facts warrant. If they looked further they might find evidence that the man who stands before them is genuinely reformed, or even that he was unjustly accused in the first place. To shut the door merely because a man has a criminal record has *some* probability in its favor, for many prisoners are never reformed; but there is also an element of unwarranted prejudgment involved. We have here a true borderline instance.

We can never hope to draw a hard and fast line between "sufficient" and "insufficient" warrant. For this reason we cannot always be sure whether we are dealing with a case of prejudice or nonprejudice. Yet no one will deny that often we form judgments on the basis of scant, even nonexistent, probabilities.

*Overcategorization* is perhaps the commonest trick of the human mind. Given a thimbleful of facts we rush to make generalizations as large as a tub. One young boy developed the idea that all Norwegians were giants because he was impressed by the gigantic stature of Ymir in the saga, and for years was fearful lest he meet a living Norwegian. A certain man happened to know three Englishmen personally and proceed to declare that the whole English race had the common attributes that he observed in these three.

There is a natural basis for this tendency. Life is so short, and the demands upon us for practical adjustments so great, that we cannot let our ignorance detain us in our daily transactions. We have to decide whether objects are good or bad by classes. We cannot weigh each object in the world by itself. Rough and ready rubrics, however coarse and broad, have to suffice.

Not every overblown generalization is a prejudice. Some are simply *misconceptions*, wherein we organize wrong information. One child had the idea that all people living in Minneapolis were "monopolists." And from his father he had learned that monopolists were evil folk. When in later years he discovered the confusion, his dislike of dwellers in Minneapolis vanished.

Here we have the test to help us distinguish between ordinary errors of prejudgment and prejudice. If a person is capable of rectifying his erroneous judgments in the light of new evidence he is not prejudiced. *Prejudgments become prejudices only if they are not reversible when exposed to new knowledge.* A prejudice, unlike a simple misconception, is actively resistant to all evidence that would unseat it. We tend to grow emotional when a prejudice is threatened with contradiction. Thus the difference between ordinary prejudgments and prejudice is that one can discuss and rectify a prejudgment without emotional resistance.

Taking these various considerations into account, we may now attempt a final definition of negative ethnic prejudice—one that will serve us throughout this book. Each phrase in the definition represents a considerable condensation of the points we have been discussing:

> Ethnic prejudice is an antipathy based upon a faulty and inflexible generalization. It may be felt or expressed. It may be directed toward a group as a whole, or toward an individual because he is a member of that group.

The net effect of prejudice, thus defined, is to place the object of prejudice at some disadvantage not merited by his own misconduct.


## ACTING OUT PREJUDICE

What people actually do in relation to groups they dislike is not always directly related to what they think or feel about them. Two employers, for example, may dislike Jews to an equal degree. One may keep his feelings to himself and may hire Jews on the same basis as any workers—perhaps because he wants to gain goodwill for his factory or store in the Jewish community. The other may translate his dislike into his employment policy, and refuse to hire Jews. Both men are prejudiced, but only one of them practices *discrimination*. As a rule discrimination has more immediate and serious social consequences than has prejudice.

It is true that any negative attitude tends somehow, somewhere, to express itself in action. Few people keep their antipathies entirely to themselves. The more intense the attitude, the more likely it is to result in vigorously hostile action.

We may venture to distinguish certain degrees of negative action from the least energetic to the most.

1. *Antilocution.* Most people who have prejudices talk about them. With like-minded friends, occasionally with strangers, they may express their antagonism freely. But many people never go beyond this mild degree of antipathetic action.
2. *Avoidance.* If the prejudice is more intense, it leads the individual to avoid members of the disliked group, even perhaps at the cost of considerable inconvenience. In this case, the bearer of prejudice does not directly inflict harm upon the group he dislikes. He takes the burden of accommodation and withdrawal entirely upon himself.
3. *Discrimination.* Here the prejudiced person makes detrimental distinctions of the active sort. He undertakes to exclude all members of the group in question from certain types of employment, from residential housing, political rights, educational or recreational opportunities, churches, hospitals, or from some other social privileges. Segregation is an institutionalized form of discrimination, enforced legally or by common custom.
4. *Physical attack.* Under conditions of heightened emotion prejudice may lead to acts of violence or semiviolence. An unwanted Negro family may be forcibly ejected from a neighborhood, or so severely threatened that it leaves in fear. Gravestones in Jewish cemeteries may be desecrated. The Northside's Italian gang may lie in wait for the Southside's Irish gang.
5. *Extermination.* Lynchings, pogroms, massacres, and the Hitlerian program of genocide mark the ultimate degree of violent expression of prejudice.

This five-point scale is not mathematically constructed, but it serves to call attention to the enormous range of activities that may issue from prejudiced attitudes and beliefs. While many people would never move from antilocution to avoidance; or from avoidance to active discrimination, or higher on the scale, still it is true that activity on one level makes transition to a more intense level easier. It was Hitler's antilocution that led Germans to avoid their Jewish neighbors and erstwhile friends. This preparation made it easier to enact the Nürnberg laws of discrimination which, in turn, made the subsequent burning of synagogues and street attacks upon Jews seem natural. The final step in the macabre progression was the ovens at Auschwitz.

From the point of view of social consequences much "polite prejudice" is harmless enough—being confined to idle chatter. But unfortunately, the fateful progression is, in this century, growing in frequency. The resulting disruption in the human family is menacing. And as the peoples of the earth grow ever more interdependent, they can tolerate less well the mounting friction.

Susan Basow

# Gender Stereotypes and Roles

In this selection, Basow discusses gender stereotypes—the overgeneralizations that we make about men and women, boys and girls. Basow notes that stereotypes of males and females are surprisingly consistent across cultures, revolving around competence and assertiveness for men and warmth and expressiveness for women. She notes that one effect of believing in these stereotypes is that they may give rise to actual differences in behavior or at least in the perception of these differences. After reading this, consider the extent to which your behavior and that of your friends is or is not consistent with these stereotypes and to what degree you consciously accept or resist them.

If you were giving a toy to a girl, would you give her a doll? A catcher's mitt? A coloring book? A chemistry set? Which of these toys would you give to a boy? Such choices tap our basic assumptions about boys and girls, males and females. Although for a particular child your choice may not reflect the typical assumptions we make about female and male interests, how about your response for an unknown boy or girl? If that distinction makes a difference, you have come face to face with the meaning of the term *stereotype*. Stereotypes are strongly held overgeneralizations about people in some designated social category. Such beliefs tend to be universally shared within a given society and are learned as part of the process of growing up in that society. Not only may stereotypes not be true for the group as a whole because they are oversimplifications (most boys may not want a chemistry set), but they also are unlikely to be true for any specific member of the group (Johnny Doe, in particular, may not want a chemistry set). Even when a generalization is valid (that is, it does describe group averages), we still cannot predict an individual's behavior or characteristics. For example, if we know that men are taller than women, we still don't necessarily know that John Doe is taller than Jane Doe. Stereotypes, because they are more oversimplified and more rigidly held than such generalizations, have even less predictive value.

When we speak of *gender* or *sex role stereotypes,* we are speaking of those "structured sets of beliefs about the personal attributes of women and men" (Ashmore & Del Boca, 1979, p. 222). These beliefs are *normative* in the sense that they imply that gender-linked characteristics not only exist but also are desirable. Gender stereotypes exist both on the cultural level (for example, as reflected in the media) and on a personal level (for example, our implicit personality theory regarding the attributes linked with being female or male) (Ashmore, Del Boca, & Wohlers, 1986). We acquire gender stereotypes as we acquire information about the world and our roles in it.

## GENDER STEREOTYPES

A number of aspects of gender stereotypes need examining—their content, their implications, their bases, and their effects. We will begin with the content of gender stereotypes.

### What Are the Gender Stereotypes?

List as many descriptors as you can for the terms *masculine* and *feminine.* If you're like most people, a number of descriptors come readily to mind. See if they match the ones listed in Table 1.

For most people, masculinity is associated with competency, instrumentality, and activity; femininity is associated with warmth, expressiveness, and nurturance. Studies conducted during the late 1960s and early 1970s with nearly 1000 males and females (I. Broverman, Vogel, Broverman, Clarkson, & Rosenkrantz, 1972; Rosenkrantz, Vogel, Bee, Broverman, & Broverman, 1968) demonstrated a broad consensus regarding the existence of different personality traits in men as compared with women. This consensus was found regardless of the age, sex, religion, educational level, or marital status of the respondents. More than 75% of those asked agreed that 41 traits clearly differentiated females and males. Table 1 lists these traits in the two categories suggested by statistical analysis: 29 male-valued items (competency cluster) and 12 female-valued items (warmth-expressiveness cluster). Similar clusters have been found by more recent researchers as well (for example, P. A. Smith & Midlarsky, 1985; Spence & Spence & Sawin, 1985). In general, using Bakan's (1966) terminology, women most often are characterized as communal (that is, selfless and other-oriented); men most often are characterized as agentic (that is, assertive and achievement-oriented).

Children as young as 7 years make these distinctions (Davis, Williams, & Best, 1982; Hensley & Borges, 1981), and even cross-cultural research finds considerable generality in those characteristics seen as differentially associated with women and men (Ward, 1985; Zammuner, 1987). For example, in all 25 of the countries sampled by J. E. Williams and Best (1990), men were associated with such descriptors as "adventurous" and "forceful," whereas women were associated with such descriptors as "sentimental" and "submissive."

**TABLE 1** Stereotypic sex role descriptors (responses from 74 college men and 80 college women, 1972)

*Competency Cluster: Masculine Pole Is More Desirable*

| Feminine | Masculine |
|---|---|
| Not at all aggressive | Very aggressive |
| Not at all independent | Very independent |
| Very emotional | Not at all emotional |
| Does not hide emotions at all | Almost always hides emotions |
| Very subjective | Very objective |
| Very easily influenced | Not at all easily influenced |
| Very submissive | Very dominant |
| Dislikes math and science very much | Likes math and science very much |
| Very excitable in a minor crisis | Not at all excitable in a minor crisis |
| Very passive | Very active |
| Not at all competitive | Very competitive |
| Very illogical | Very logical |
| Very home-oriented | Very worldly |
| Not at all skilled in business | Very skilled in business |
| Very sneaky | Very direct |
| Does not know the way of the world | Knows the way of the world |
| Feelings easily hurt | Feelings not easily hurt |
| Not at all adventurous | Very adventurous |
| Has difficulty making decisions | Can make decisions easily |
| Cries very easily | Never cries |
| Almost never acts as a leader | Almost always acts as a leader |
| Not at all self-confident | Very self-confident |
| Very uncomfortable about being aggressive | Not at all uncomfortable about being aggressive |
| Not at all ambitious | Very ambitious |
| Unable to separate feelings from ideas | Easily able to separate feelings from ideas |
| Very dependent | Not at all dependent |
| Very conceited about appearance | Never conceited about appearance |
| Thinks women are always superior to men | Thinks men are always superior to women |
| Does not talk freely about sex with men | Talks freely about sex with men |

*Warmth-Expressiveness Cluster: Feminine Pole Is More Desirable*

| Feminine | Masculine |
|---|---|
| Doesn't use harsh language at all | Uses very harsh language |
| Very talkative | Not at all talkative |
| Very tactful | Very blunt |
| Very gentle | Very rough |
| Very aware of feelings of others | Not at all aware of feelings of others |
| Very religious | Not at all religious |
| Very interested in own appearance | Not at all interested in own appearance |
| Very neat in habits | Very sloppy in habits |
| Very quiet | Very loud |
| Very strong need for security | Very little need for security |
| Enjoys art and literature | Does not enjoy art and literature at all |
| Easily expresses tender feelings | Does not express tender feelings at all easily |

From "Sex Role Stereotypes: A Current Appraisal," by I. Broverman, S. R. Vogel, D. M. Broverman, F. E. Clarkson, and P. S. Rosenkrantz, *Journal of Social Issues*, 1972, 28(2), 59–78. Copyright 1972 by the Society for the Psychological Study of Social Issues. Reprinted by permission of the author and publisher.

*Variations in Gender Stereotypes*

Despite general agreement on a number of sex-stereotypic traits, variations in gender stereotypes do occur (Lii & Wong, 1982; J. E. Williams & Best, 1990). The specific traits listed in Table 1 appear to be based on people's image of a prototypic male and female. In the United States, the prototype basically is White, middle-class, heterosexual, and Christian. For groups that differ from the prototype, different stereotypic traits exist. For example the stereotypes of African-American males and females are more similar to each other in terms of expressiveness and competence than are the stereotypes of Anglo-American males and females (Millham & Smith, 1981; P. A. Smith & Midlarsky, 1985). Compared with White women, Black women are viewed as less passive, dependent, status conscious, emotional, and concerned about their appearance (Landrine, 1985; Romer & Cherry, 1980). Compared with White men, Black men are viewed as more emotionally expressive and less competitive, independent, and status conscious.

Less research has been done on gender stereotypes of other racial or ethnic groups, but cultural images of women suggest other variations do exist. Hispanic women tend to be viewed as more "feminine" than White women in terms of submissiveness and dependence (Vazquez-Nuttall, Romero-Garcia, & De Leon, 1987). A similar stereotype holds for Asian women, but with the addition of exotic sexuality (Chow, 1985). Native-American women typically are stereotyped as faceless "squaws"—drudges without any personality (Witt, 1981). And Jewish women are stereotyped as either pushy, vain "princesses" or overprotective, manipulative "Jewish mothers" (S. W. Schneider, 1986).

Besides racial differences in gender stereotypes, there are social class differences, sexual orientation differences, and age differences (Cazenave, 1984; Del Boca & Ashmore, 1980; Kite & Deaux, 1987; Landrine, 1985). For example, working-class women are stereotyped as more hostile, confused, inconsiderate, and irresponsible than middle-class women; male homosexuals are stereotyped as possessing feminine traits while lesbians are stereotyped as possessing masculine traits.

What these variations in gender stereotypes suggest is that gender is not the only variable by which people are stereotyped. Each one of us is situated in sociological space at the intersection of numerous categories—for example, gender, race or ethnicity, class, sexual orientation, and able-bodiedness. These social categories interact with each other in complex ways A woman who is White, working class, lesbian, and differently abled will be viewed very differently from a Black, middle-class, heterosexual, able-bodied woman.

Stereotypes are not fixed but respond, albeit slowly, to cultural changes. Since the 1970s, distinct subtypes of both female and male stereotypes have appeared (Ashmore, Del Boca, & Wohlers, 1986; Deaux & Kite, 1987; Deaux, Winton, Crowley, & Lewis, 1985; Six & Eckes, 1991). For women, there are at least three distinct stereotypes: the housewife (the traditional woman), the professional woman (independent, ambitious, self-confident), and the Playboy bunny (sex object). Although the subtypes are perceived as differing on many traits, behaviors, and occupations, they still share commonalities. For example, all three subtypes are expected to be concerned with having and caring for children.

Subtypes of the male stereotype are less clear, partly because less research has been done on this topic, partly because the image of "man" seems less differentiated than the image of "woman," and partly because women and men may hold slightly different subtypes (see also Hort, Fagot, & Leinbach, 1990). The traditional man stereotype has been found to be comprised of three main factors: status (the need to achieve success and others' respect), toughness (strength and self-reliance), and antifemininity (avoidance of stereotypically feminine activities) (E. H. Thompson & Pleck, 1987). In addition, the traditional man is seen by men as sexually proficient. Women, however, distinguish a sexual man subtype—the stud or Don Juan. For many people, a liberated man stereotype also exists that incorporates such stereotypically feminine traits as gentleness and sensitivity (Ehrenreich, 1984; Keen & Zur, 1989; Kimmel, 1987a; Pleck, 1981b). Some writers in the emerging field of men's studies argue for use of the term *masculinities* rather than *masculinity* to acknowledge the pluralism in definitions based on race, class, sexual orientation, and so on (for example, Brod, 1987). Still, when most people think of a typical man or woman, they apparently have the traditional (White) middle-class stereotype in mind.

Although most research on gender stereotypes has focused on personality traits, Deaux and Lewis (1984) and others (J. Archer, 1989; P. A. Smith & Midlarsky, 1985; Spence & Sawin, 1985) have shown that gender stereotypes exist in at least three other areas as well. Not only can one talk about masculine and feminine traits (such as independence and gentleness, respectively), but one can also talk about masculine and feminine roles (such as head of household and caretaker of children, respectively), masculine and feminine occupations (such as truck driver and telephone operator, respectively), and masculine and feminine physical characteristics (such as broad shoulders and grace, respectively). The four components, although related, can operate relatively independently. A graceful individual can be male or female, independent or gentle, a head of household or a caretaker of children, and a truck driver or a telephone operator. Of all the domains (personality, role behaviors, occupations, and physical appearance), the most important in terms of eliciting an individual's gender belief system is the physical (Deaux & Lewis, 1984; Freeman, 1987). For example, if the only information people are given about a man is that he has a slight build, people are likely to predict that he has stereotypically feminine traits, is employed in a feminine occupation, and possibly is homosexual. Such far-reaching predictions would be much less likely if all we knew about the man was that he was gentle. Given the fact that the first thing we notice or know about a person is her or his physical appearance, it's clear that gender stereotypes can get activated very quickly.

## Implications of Gender Stereotypes

A number of issues regarding gender stereotypes merit further consideration: their social desirability, the opposition they imply between the two sexes, and their all-or-none categorizing.

**Social desirability** The general social desirability of masculine and feminine traits is related to gender stereotypes. Traditionally, stereotypically masculine traits have been viewed more positively and as more socially desirable than stereotypically feminine traits (I. Broverman et al., 1972; Rosenkrantz et al., 1968). Masculine traits are viewed as showing more strength and activity than feminine traits (Ashmore et al., 1986; J. E. Williams & Best, 1990), and the qualities of strength and activity have been highly valued by Western cultures. Traditionally, the only exceptions to this pattern have been the few feminine traits that relate to sensitivity to the needs of others. These few traits have been rated more highly than any masculine ones (S. L. Bem, 1974).

More recently (since 1980), increased value has been attached to certain stereotypically feminine traits, especially by women (Eagly & Mladinic, 1989; P. A. Smith & Midlarsky, 1985; P. D. Werner & LaRussa, 1985). This increased valuation probably has stemmed from a deliberate attempt by many feminists and nonfeminists alike to counteract the "masculinization of values" that occurred as a product of the women's movement during the 1970s. The women's movement during the 1970s seemed to emphasize women moving into traditionally male roles (for example, the executive suite) and adopting traditionally male traits (for example, assertiveness and dominance). The other side of social change—men moving into traditionally female roles and adopting traditionally female traits—was relatively neglected. Consequently, during the 1980s we saw the rise of attempts to valorize the feminine traits involved with being relational (communal)—in moral reasoning (Gilligan, 1982), in cognitive processes (Belenky, Clinchy, Goldberger, & Tarule, 1986), and in personality in general (Chodorow, 1978; J. B. Miller, 1976, 1984). The irony of this attempt is that arguing for the value of stereotypically feminine traits strengthens the stereotypes themselves. The identification of these traits with women rather than as valuable but "human" ones perpetuates the myth that these traits are indeed sex-linked (see M. Crawford, 1988, and Hare-Mustin & Marecek, 1988, for an interesting discussion of the debate between maximizing and minimizing claims of gender differences).

Today, although a number of stereotypically feminine traits are viewed more positively than stereotypically masculine traits, especially by women, a number of stereotypically feminine traits are still viewed extremely negatively, such as being submissive, emotional, easily influenced, sneaky, and unambitious. Of course, a number of stereotypically masculine traits (such as restricted emotionality, aggressiveness) are viewed negatively as well, at least by women. Thus, the value attached to stereotypic gender traits appears to be changing, at least for women. Still, masculine traits are culturally supported more than feminine traits and are associated with power and control. In contrast, feminine traits are associated with powerlessness and being controlled.

**The "opposite" sex.** The traits listed in Table 1 reveal another common finding related to gender stereotypes: the characteristic traits for men and women are commonly viewed as being opposite each other. Thus, whereas males are thought of as dominant and objective, females are thought of as submissive and subjective. This all-or-none distinction may have been a function of the questionnaire used by the Broverman group (Brannon, 1978). The items were presented as two endpoints on a line, and each respondent was asked to check where on the line the typical male or female could be placed. Thus, a female could only be rated as either submissive or dominant, not as more or less submissive, or more or less dominant. Even when responses are free form, however, nearly identical lists and distinctions emerge; for example, males are strong, females weak; females are emotional, males are unemotional. Furthermore, as many researchers (Deaux & Lewis, 1984; Foushee, Helmreich, & Spence, 1979) have found most people think that masculinity and femininity are negatively related—that is, that being low on masculine traits implies being high on feminine traits.

If sex-typed traits were opposites, we would expect a strong inverse relationship between how a person scores on stereotypically masculine traits and how she or he scores on stereotypically feminine traits. However, research that has correlated individual scores on the masculinity and femininity scales has found little relationship between the two (S. L. Bem, 1974; Marsh, Antill, & Cunningham, 1989; Spence & Helmreich, 1978). How high someone scores on masculinity is unrelated to how high he or she scores on femininity. Thus, the bipolar model of masculinity and femininity, which postulates that instrumentality and expressivity fall at opposite ends of a single dimension, is not completely correct. However, a few aspects of the gender stereotypes may be bipolar. In particular, ratings of the terms *masculine* and *feminine* do seem to be negatively correlated; that is, people who rate themselves high on one tend to rate themselves low on the other (Marsh et al., 1989).

**All-or-none categorizing** The all-or-none categorizing of gender traits is misleading. People just are not so simple that they either possess all of a trait or none of it. This is even more true when trait dispositions for groups of people are examined. Part a of Figure 1 illustrates what such an all-or-none distribution of the trait "strength" would look like: all males would be strong, all females weak. The fact is, most psychological and physical traits are distributed according to the pattern shown in Part b of Figure 1, with most people possessing an average amount of that trait and fewer people having either very much or very little of that trait. Almost all the traits listed in Table 1 conform to this pattern.

To the extent that females and males may differ in the average amount of the trait they possess (which needs to be determined empirically), the distribution can be characterized by *overlapping normal curves,* as shown in Part c of Figure 1. Thus, although most men are stronger than most women, the shaded area indicates that some men are weaker than some women and vice versa. The amount of overlap of the curves generally is considerable. Another attribute related to overlapping normal curves is that differences within one group are usually greater than the differences between the two groups. For example, although males on the average may be more aggressive than females on the average, greater differences may be found among males than between males and females.

This concept of overlapping normal curves is critically important in understanding gender stereotypes because it undermines the basis of most discriminatory regulations and laws. Although most men are stronger than most women, denying women access to jobs requiring strength simply on the basis of sex is unjustified, because some women are stronger than some men (see shaded area in Part c of Figure 1.). Thus, if most of the stereotypic traits are actually distributed in normal curves along a continuum (that is, people may be more or less dominant, more or less submissive) rather than distributed in an all-or-none fashion—dominant or submissive—then setting up two opposite and distinct lists of traits for females and males is entirely inappropriate and misleading.

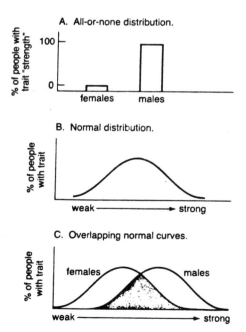

**Figure 1** Three types of distributions for the trait "strength."

With reference to gender stereotypes, then, it can be concluded that (1) people cannot be viewed simply as collections of consistent traits, because situations also are important; (2) males and females specifically cannot be viewed as having unique traits that are opposite each other; and (3) whatever attributes are thought of as distinctly masculine or feminine are also possessed by at least some members of the other sex.

## Bases of Gender Stereotypes

If women and men are not accurately described solely as collections of feminine or masculine traits, respectively, and, in fact, if the application of trait terms to personality is generally not appropriate, on what are the stereotypes based? Two basic theories exist regarding the origin of gender stereotypes: the "kernel of truth" theory and social-role theory. The *"kernel of truth" theory* rests on the assumption that gender stereotypes have some empirical validity—that is, there are real differences in behavior between the sexes that the stereotypes just exaggerate. This approach suggests that the differences exist first and that the stereotypes simply reflect them. In this case, what have been called stereotypes would be simple generalizations. Carol Martin (1987) examined this question and found that most of the gender stereotypic traits were indeed oversimplifications and exaggerations of minor group differences. Polling 139 college students regarding which of 32 gender-typed traits they viewed as typical of male college students and which as typical of female college students, Martin found significant differences on all of them, in the expected direction. For example, a very large sex difference was expected for the trait "loves children." (This trait was viewed as much more characteristic of women than of men.) However, when these same students were asked to rate these 32 traits as either descriptive or not descriptive of themselves, male and female students differed on only 5: male students were more likely than female students to see themselves as egotistical and cynical; female students were more likely than male students to see themselves as aware of others' feelings, whiney, and fussy. Although these 5 differences were as predicted, the major finding was of gender similarity on the 27 other sex-typed traits, including "loves children." Thus, although a few gender differences might exist with respect to personality traits, people expect many more. Unger and Siiter (1975) found similar exaggerations made by college students with respect to values. Gender stereotypes, thus, may not be based on statistically significant differences between the sexes, but, at best, are exaggerations of a grain of truth.

The *social-role theory* of gender stereotypes (Eagly, 1987b; Eagly & Steffen, 1984) maintains that the stereotypes arise from the different social roles typically held by women and men. Males are likely to play with guns, know how to change a flat tire, mow the lawn well, and be employed when they are adults. Females are likely to bake well, change diapers, play with baby dolls, and be homemakers as well as employed when they are adults. Eagly and Steffen (1984, 1986b) argue that it is *because* men and women typically do different things that people make assumptions about men's and women's innate traits and abilities. These researchers found that people's beliefs that females possess more communal (concerned with others) and fewer agentic (masterful) qualities than men are a result of perceiving women as homemakers and men as full-time employees. When women are specifically described as full-time employees, they are perceived as more similar to men in terms of communal and agentic qualities (low communal, high agentic). When men are described as full-time homemakers, they are perceived as more similar to (traditional) women (high communal, low agentic). Other research confirms that when men and women are in identical roles, they are perceived as similar (L. A. Jackson & Sullivan, 1990). Therefore, it is the division of labor and tasks between women and men that accounts for the content of gender stereotypes.

*Effects of Gender Stereotyping*

What are the consequences of the gender stereotypes themselves? As we have just seen, rather than reflecting real behavioral differences, it is more likely that belief in the stereotypes may give rise to some behavioral differences. If the stereotypes function as part of sex role expectations, then people will learn them and be influenced by them. Even though sex-typed distinctions between the sexes may not fit individuals, stereotypes themselves have power as standards to which to conform, against which to rebel, or with which to evaluate others.

One way stereotypes operate is by serving as *perceptual filters* though which we see individuals. We're actually more likely to notice and remember stereotype-consistent behaviors than other behaviors (Bodenhausen, 1988; Stangor, 1988). If we see a White man acting assertively, we're more likely to remember that incident than if we see the same behavior in an Asian woman. When it comes to promotion time, who might be seen as the better candidate for a leadership position? This perceptual filter function of stereotypes also explains why stereotypes are so resistant to change. If we observe someone conforming to the stereotype (for example, a woman being helpless about changing a tire), we notice and remember it ("Isn't that just like a woman!"). Consequently, the stereotype (in this case, of helplessness) is strengthened. If, however, we observe someone not conforming to the stereotype (for example, we see a woman competently changing a tire), we either don't notice or remember it, or we view it as an exception to the "rule." ("Oh, *she's* just different. Most women can't take care of their cars.") The strength of the stereotype itself is undiminished. The self-perpetuating nature of stereotypes is further enhanced by the finding that even if we only *imagine* that an individual conforms to stereotypes, we remember the imagining as an actual confirmation (Slusher & Anderson, 1987).

Another way stereotypes operate is by setting up a *self-fulfilling prophecy.* If females are viewed as having more negative characteristics than males, some females may view themselves this way and may, in fact, develop those very characteristics. For example, if females are expected to be less rational than males, some may view themselves that way and not participate in problem-solving activities or take advanced math courses, since such behaviors are not gender-appropriate. As a result, some females may indeed develop fewer problem-solving abilities than some males who have had those experiences, thereby fulfilling the stereotype. Such beliefs can powerfully influence behavior in either a negative way, if the expectations are negative, or a positive way, if the expectations are positive (M. Snyder, Tanke, & Berscheid, 1977).

An example of the critical role of other people's expectancies in determining our own behavior was demonstrated by Skrypnek and Snyder (1982). In a laboratory study, males were led to believe that they were paired with either another male or a female in a task requiring a division of labor. Males selected more gender-stereotypic activities for themselves and for their partner when the partner was thought to be female than when the partner was thought to be male. More important, the female partner later chose more stereotypically feminine tasks when her partner believed that she was female, even though she wasn't informed directly of his expectations. Thus, other people's expectations become fulfilled.

As this study suggests, another way gender stereotypes affect us is through *impression management*. All of us, at some level, want to be socially acceptable, at least to some people. To the extent that we desire such approval, we may engage in impression-management strategies in order to obtain it. That is, we will try to present ourselves (our image) in a way that we think is acceptable to another person. Zanna and Pack (1975) found that female Princeton undergraduates when meeting a man they viewed as a desirable partner would present themselves as extremely conventional women when the ideology of the man was conventional and as more liberated women when his ideology was nontraditional. When the man was viewed as undesirable, his views did not have much impact on the images presented by the women.

## References

Archer, J. (1989). The relationship between gender-role measures: A review. *British Journal of Social Psychology, 28*, 173–184.

Ashmore, R. D., & Del Boca, F. K. (1979). Sex stereotypes and implicit personality theory: Toward a cognitive-social psychological conceptualization. *Sex Roles, 5*, 219–248.

Ashmore, R. D., Del Boca, F. K., & Wohlers, A. J. (1986). Gender stereotypes. In R. D. Ashmore and F. K. Del Boca (Eds.), *The social psychology of female-male relations: A critical analysis of central concepts* (pp. 69–119). New York: Academic Press.

Bakan, D. (1966). *The duality of human existence.* Chicago: Rand McNally.

Belenky, M. F., Clinchy, B. M., Goldberger, N. R., & Tarule, J. M. (1986). *Women's ways of knowing: The development of self, voice, and mind.* New York: Basic Books.

Bem, S. L. (1974). The measurement of psychological androgyny. *Journal of Consulting and Clinical Psychology, 42*, 155–162.

Bodenhausen, G. V. (1988). Stereotypic biases in social decision making and memory: Testing process models of stereotype use. *Journal of Personality and Social Psychology, 55,* 726–737.

Brannon, R. (1978). Measuring attitudes toward women (and otherwise): A methodological critique. In J. Sherman & F. Denmark (Eds.), *The future of women: Issues in psychology* (pp. 647–709). New York: Psychological Dimensions.

Brod, H. (Ed.) (1987). *The making of masculinities: The new men's studies.* Boston: Allen & Unwin.

Broverman, I., Vogel, S. R., Broverman, D. M., Clarkson, F. E., & Rosenkrantz, P. S. (1972). Sex role stereotypes: A current appraisal. *Journal of Social Issues, 28*(2), 59–78.

Cazenave, N. A. (1984). Race, socioeconomic status, and age: The social context of American masculinity. *Sex Roles, 11,* 639–656.

Chodorow, N. (1978). *The reproduction of mothering: Psychoanalysis and the sociology of gender.* Berkeley: University of California Press.

Crawford, M. (1988). Agreeing to differ: Feminist epistemologies and women's ways of knowing. In M. Crawford & M. Gentry (Eds.), *Gender and thought: Psychological perspectives* (pp. 128–145). New York: Springer-Verlag.

Davis, S. W., Williams, J. E., & Best, D. L. (1982). Sex trait stereotypes in the self- and peer descriptions of third grade children. *Sex Roles, 8,* 315–331.

Deaux, K., & Kite, M. E. (1987). Thinking about gender. In B. B. Hess & M. M. Ferree (Eds.), *Analyzing gender: A handbook of social science research* (pp. 92–117). Newbury Park, CA: Sage.

Deaux, K., & Lewis, L. (1984). Structure of gender stereotypes: Interrelationships among components and gender label. *Journal of Personality and Social Psychology, 46,* 991–1004.

Deaux, K., Winton, W., Crowley, M., & Lewis, L. L. (1985). Level of categorization and content of gender stereotypes. *Social Cognition, 3,* 145–167.

Del Boca, F. K., & Ashmore, R. D. (1980). Sex stereotypes through the life cycle. In L. Wheeler (Ed.), *Review of Personal and Social Psychology,* Vol. 1. (pp. 163–192). Beverly Hills, CA: Sage.

Eagly, A. H. (1987). *Sex differences in social behavior: A social-role interpretation.* Hillsdale, NJ: Erlbaum.

Eagly, A. H., & Mladinic, A. (1989). Gender stereotypes and attitudes toward women and men. *Personality and Social Psychology Bulletin, 15,* 543–558.

Eagly, A. H., & Steffen, V. J. (1984). Gender stereotypes stem from the distribution of women and men into social roles. *Journal of Personality and Social Psychology, 46,* 735–754.

———(1986). Gender stereotypes, occupational roles, and beliefs about part-time employees. *Psychology of Women Quarterly, 10,* 252–262.

Ehrenreich, B. (1984, May 20). A feminist's view of the new man. *New York Times Magazine,* pp. 36–41, 44, 46, 48.

Foushee, H. C., Helmreich, R. L., & Spence, J. T. (1979). Implicit theories of masculinity and femininity: Dualistic or bipolar? *Psychology of Women Quarterly, 3,* 259–269.

Freeman H. R. (1987). Structure and content of gender stereotypes: Effects of somatic appearance and trait information. *Psychology of Women Quarterly, 11,* 59–67.

Gilligan, C. (1982). *In a different voice: Psychological theory and women's development.* Cambridge, MA: Harvard University Press.

Hare-Mustin, R. T., & Marecek, J. (1988). The meaning of difference: Gender theory, postmodernism, and psychology. *American Psychologist, 43* 455–464.

Hensley, K. K., & Borges, M. A. (1981). Sex role stereotyping and sex role norms: A comparison of elementary and college age students. *Psychology of Women Quarterly, 5,* 543–554.

Hort, B. E., Fagot, B. I., & Leinbach, M. D. (1990). Are people's notions of maleness more stereotypically framed than their notions of femaleness? *Sex Roles, 23,* 197–212.

Jackson, L. A., & Sullivan, L. A. (1990). Perceptions of multiple role participants. *Social Psychology Quarterly, 53,* 274–282.

Keen, S., & Zur, O. (1989, November). Who is the new ideal man? *Psychology Today,* pp. 54–60.

Kimmel, M. S. (Ed.). (1987). *Changing men: New directions in research on men and masculinity.* Newbury Park, CA: Sage.

Kite, M. E., & Deaux, K. (1987). Gender belief systems: Homosexuality and the implicit inversion theory. *Psychology of Women Quarterly, 11,* 83–96.

Landrine, H. (1985). Race × class stereotypes of women. Sex Roles, 13, 65–75.

Lii, S., & Wong, S. (1982). A cross-cultural study on sex-role stereotypes and social desirability. *Sex Roles, 8,* 481–491.

Marsh, H. W., Antill, J. K., & Cunningham, J. D. (1989). Masculinity and femininity: A bipolar construct and independent constructs. *Journal of Personality, 57,* 625–663.

Martin, C. L. (1987). A ratio measure of sex stereotyping. *Journal of Personality and Social Psychology, 52,* 489–499.

Miller, J. B. (1976). *Toward a new psychology of women.* Boston: Beacon Press.

———(1984). *The development of women's sense of self* (Work in Progress, No. 12). Wellesley, MA: Wellesley College, The Stone Center.

Millham, J., & Smith, L. E. (1981). Sex-role differentiation among Black and White Americans: A comparative study. *Journal of Black Psychology, 7* 77–90.

Pleck, J. H. (1981). *The myth of masculinity.* Cambridge, MA: MIT Press.

Romer, N., & Cherry, D. (1980). Ethnic and social class differences in children's sex-role concepts. *Sex Roles, 6,* 245–263.

Rosenkrantz, P., Vogel, S. R., Bee, H., Broverman, I. K., & Broverman, D. M. (1968). Sex role stereotypes and self-concepts in college students. *Journal of Consulting and Clinical Psychology, 32,* 287–295.

Schneider, S. W. (1986). Jewish women in the nuclear family and beyond. In J. Cole (Ed.), *All-American women: Lines that divide, ties that bind* (pp. 198–215). New York: Free Press.

Six, B., & Eckes, T. (1991). A closer look at the complex structure of gender stereotypes. *Sex Roles, 24,* 57–71.

Skrypnek, B. J., & Snyder, M. (1982). On the self-perpetuating nature of stereotypes about women and men. *Journal of Experimental Social Psychology, 18,* 277–291.

Slusher, M. P., & Anderson, C. A. (1987). When reality monitoring fails: The role of imagination in stereotype maintenance. *Journal of Personality and Social Psychology, 52,* 653–662.

Smith, P. A., & Midlarsky, E. (1985). Empirically derived conceptions of femaleness and maleness: A current view. *Sex roles, 12,* 313–328.

Snyder, M., Tanke, E. D., & Berscheid, E. (1977). Social perception and interpersonal behavior: On the self-fulfilling nature of social stereotypes. *Journal of Personality and Social Psychology, 35,* 656–666.

Spence, J. T., Helmreich, R. L., & Holahan, C. K. (1979). Negative and positive components of psychological masculinity and femininity and their relationship to self-reports of neurotic and acting out behaviors. *Journal of Personality and Social Psychology, 37,* 1673–1682.

Spence, J. T., and Sawin, L. L. (1985). Images of masculinity and femininity: a reconceptualization. In V. O'Leary, R. Unger, & B. Wallston (Eds.), *Women, gender and social psychology* (pp. 35–66). Hillsdale, NJ: Erlbaum.

Stangor, C. (1988). Stereotype accessibility and information processing. *Personality and Social Psychology Bulletin, 14,* 694–708.

Thompson, E. H., Jr., & Pleck, J. H. (1987). The structure of male role norms. In M. S. Kimmel (Ed.), *Changing men: New directions in research on men and masculinity* (pp. 25–36). Newbury Park, CA. Sage.

Unger, R. K., & Siiter, R. (1975). Sex role stereotypes: The weight of a "grain of truth." In R. Unger (Ed.), *Sex-role stereotypes revisited: Psychological approaches to women's studies* (pp. 10-13). New York: Harper & Row.

Vazquez-Nuttall, E., Romero-Garcia, I., & DeLeon, B. (1987). Sex roles and perceptions of femininity and masculinity of Hispanic women: A review of the literature. *Psychology of Women Quarterly, 11,* 409–425.

Ward, C. (1985). Sex trait stereotypes in Malaysian children. *Sex Roles, 12* 35–45.

Werner, P. D., & LaRussa, G. W. (1985). Persistence and change in sex-role stereotypes. *Sex Roles, 12,* 1089–1100.

Williams, J. E., & Best, D. L. (1990). *Measuring sex stereotypes: A multination study* (rev. ed.). Newbury Park, CA: Sage.

Witt, S. H. (1981). The two worlds of native women. In S. Cox (Ed.), *Female psychology* (2nd ed.) (pp. 149–155). New York: St. Martin's.

Zamunner, V. L. (1987). Children's sex-role stereotypes: A cross-cultural analysis. In P. Shaver & C. Hendrick (Eds.), *Sex and gender* (pp. 272–293). Newbury Park, CA: Sage.

Zanna, J. J., & Pack, S. J. (1975). On the self-fulfilling nature of apparent sex differences in behavior. *Journal of Experimental Social Psychology, 11,* 583–591.

Charles F. Bond, Jr.
Clarisse G. DiCandia
John R. MacKinnon

# Responses to Violence in a Psychiatric Setting: The Role of Patient's Race

This article investigates the response of the staff at a state psychiatric hospital to violent acts committed by white and non-white adolescent patients. Although the authors found no differences in the overall number or kinds of offenses committed by white and black patients, black patients were forcibly restrained four times as often. The authors suggest that the reactions of the staff represent a form of not-so-subtle discrimination. They believe that the predominantly white staff may have interpreted the acts of white patients more innocently, while attributing more negative and aggressive intent to the same acts when performed by black patients.

Scholars have been following American race relations for generations. In recent decades, they have noted some ameliorative trends, including an institutional movement toward legal equality (Pettigrew, 1985) and a reduction in overt expressions of prejudice (Taylor, Sheatsley, & Greeley, 1978). Still, racial tensions remain.

There are racial differences in crime. Larger-scale surveys reveal that Blacks commit a disproportionate number of violent offenses (Chilton & Galvin, 1985) and receive harsher punishments than Whites (Petersilia, 1985). Interracial crimes are prevalent (Wilbanks, 1985); sanctions are most severe when the offender is Black and the victim White (Savitz, 1973).

Social psychologists have used experimental methods to study interracial aggression. In one program of research (Donnerstein & Donnerstein, 1976), White college students administered electric shock to a male target person who was represented as either Black or White. Results reveal that the Black received more shock, unless he was in a position to retaliate by shocking the subject. Ancillary findings showed that these college students shared a stereotype: They expected Blacks to be aggressive.

Stereotypes color interpretations of behavior. In a study by Sagar and Schofield (1980), sixth graders heard stories about Whites or Blacks whose actions were ambiguous but slightly aggressive. Later, when asked to judge the story characters, these subjects rated Blacks as meaner and less friendly than Whites. Research by Duncan (1976) makes a similar point. White college students saw a videotape of one person shoving another, then were asked to describe what they saw. Students who had seen a Black shove someone described the behavior as violent; students who had seen a White act identically described the behavior as "playing around." Outside the laboratory, the two races rarely act identically. Racial differences in gaze, touching, and inter-personal distance (Patterson, 1983) increase the potential for cross-racial misunderstanding.

Jones (1983) criticized the experimental literature on race relations, noting that it is impossible to manipulate a person's race. Blacks are rarely studied in the experimental literature. More often, experimenters observe White subjects who encounter Black or White stimulus persons. In experiments, the subject and stimulus person seldom interact. At best, the subject spends a few minutes with a preprogrammed confederate (Rogers, 1983). More often, the target is depicted on a videotape (Donnerstein & Donnerstein, 1976), in a photograph, or as a stick figure (Sagar & Schofield, 1980). No Black-White relationship can develop. No two-way influence ensues. Because of these limitations, Pettigrew (1985) calls for race relations research in institutional settings.

There are problems with experimentation on aggression. Experimenters rarely study violent people. Their college-student subjects come from nonviolent backgrounds. The students know that they are in an experiment and know that aggression is socially proscribed. In the standard paradigm, subjects administer shock to a confederate. Some may administer high levels of shock because they have inferred experimental demands; others may withhold shock because they fear the experimenter's disapproval (Schuck & Pisor, 1974). Interracial aggression is especially reactive: When a camera is trained on White subjects, aggression against a Black declines (Donnerstein & Donnerstein, 1976). In light of these threats to experimental validity, Bertilson (1983) advises that aggression be studied with multiple methods, including archival techniques.

In this article, we report a study of naturally occurring interracial violence. The violence punctuates ongoing relationships and entails mutual influence. We conducted the study at an institution in which violence is prevalent, using an archival method that should have minimized reactivity. From the accumulated literature, we expected high rates of interracial violence.

Scholars have discussed the effects of interracial contact. Many surmised that contact would improve race relations, but it was Allport (1954) who advanced a specific hypothesis. Allport believed that interracial contact would reduce prejudice, but only if the contact was between individuals of equal status who were working toward a common goal. Research has supported this *contact hypothesis* (Amir, 1976; Clore, Bray, Itkin, & Murphy, 1978; Miller & Brewer, 1984).

Our research permitted a study of interracial contact under less favorable circumstances. We observed contact between nonequals—high-status Whites and low-status Blacks who were often in violent conflict. Like Allport (1954), we assumed that unpleasant Black-White interactions would promote no positive interracial attitudes. Even so, we wondered how contact would influence individuals' conceptions of one another. Previous research suggested an interesting possibility—that with extended contact (even unpleasant contact), individuals of different races would come to accept one another (Amir, 1976). They would retain their negative stereotypes while making exceptions for individuals they knew (Taylor, 1981). In our study of interracial violence, we assessed this possibility by tracking the relationships of Black and White individuals over time.

## METHOD

### The Setting

The study was conducted at Altobello Youth Center, a state-run psychiatric facility located in Meridan, Connecticut. Altobello services lower- to lower-middle-class adolescent residents of the eastern two-thirds of Connecticut, aged 14 to 18. At Altobello, patients live on two locked wards, served by separate staffs, which can accommodate 16 and 26 patients, respectively. Males and females reside on each ward. Ward assignment is based on the availability of space at the time of a patient's admission.

We had reason to suspect that violence would be prevalent at Altobello Youth Center. Lewis, Shanok, Cohen, Kligfeld, and Frisone (1980) studied another Connecticut state psychiatric facility and concluded that its adolescent inpatients were as violent as the adolescents incarcerated at a nearby correctional school.

### The Archives

The administration of Altobello Youth Center records demographic and psychiatric information about each adolescent admitted to the facility. These patient records are supplemented by nurses' daily reports. Nurses are required by law to end each 8-hour shift at Altobello by summarizing significant incidents that occurred during the shift, including all incidents of violence. The latter were of interest in our research.

At Altobello Youth Center, methods for dealing with violence have been institutionalized. For their violent offenses, patients can receive two negative sanctions: temporary seclusion and physical restraint. Patients can be secluded in a small, barren "time-out room." Seclusion is usually voluntary and rarely lasts more than an hour. Patients can also be physically restrained. They can be placed in a camisole (that is, a "strait-jacket") or tied to a bed with sheets. Physical restraint is a more severe sanction than seclusion. By state law, physical restraints can be imposed only under a physician's order, only upon a patient whom the physician has deemed "dangerous," and only when all other sanctions have failed. Physical restraints often exacerbate the angry patient and occasion screaming, cursing, and head banging. After being restrained, most patients are forcibly injected with a major tranquilizer that renders the patient unconscious.

*Procedure*

The second author secured permission from the director of Altobello Youth Center for a study on the use of physical restraints. In January 1984, she retrospectively examined all activities on the two locked wards of the facility for 85 days just prior to data collection: that is, for the period extending from October 15, 1983 to January 7, 1984. From patients' records and nurses' daily reports during these 85 days, the second author noted each incident that precipitated the use of a negative sanction. For each incident, she recorded the following data: (a) the patient's race (White, Black, Puerto Rican, or Hispanic), (b) the patient's sex (male or female), (c) the patient's ward, (d) the patient's commitment status (voluntary or involuntary commitment), (e) the patient's diagnosis (as determined upon admission to the hospital by a White psychiatrist), (f) the patient's medication (exclusive of medications administered at the time of physical restraint), (g) the patient's length of hospitalization (prior to the incident), and (h) the type of sanction (seclusion or restraint).

In reporting incidents of violence, nurses did not identify the staff members who had ordered the use of sanctions. However, employee records indicate that at this time the Altobello Youth Center staff consisted of White, middle- to lower-middle-class nurses and aides of both sexes who resided in Connecticut. Although physicians were telephoned prior to each imposition of physical restraints, they were rarely in the wards on these occasions.

Some of the patients who resided in the Altobello Youth Center were sanctioned for no offense between October 15, 1983 and January 7, 1984. We included these "model patients" in our sample, alongside patients who had been reported secluded or restrained.

## RESULTS

From October 15, 1983 to January 7, 1984, 70 adolescents resided in the locked wards at Altobello. Of these patients, 56 were White; 9 were Black; 3 were Puerto Rican, and 2 were Hispanic. In all, 40 of the patients were male; 30 were female. Only 15 of the patients were on medication, and medication was unrelated to all other variables. On the average, these patients were 15.7 years old.

From October 15, 1983 to January 7, 1984, nurses recorded 453 incidents in which sanctions were used on patients. On 370 occasions, a patient was secluded in the time-out room; on 83 occasions, a patient was physically restrained.

We planned to relate a patient's characteristics to the use of sanctions on that patient. A number of patients entered and left the institution over the 85 days studied. Hence individuals were under study for varying lengths of time. For statistical analyses, we noted the number of days each patient was in Altobello between October 15, 1983 and January 7, 1984, and expressed this observation interval in months. We then defined a patient's *seclusion rate* as the number of times the patient was confined to the time-out room, divided by the duration of the patient's stay at Altobello over our 85-day study, and a patient's *restraint rate* as the number of times the patient was physically restrained, divided by the duration of the patient's hospitalization over these 85 days. Overall *sanction rate* is the sum of seclusion and restraint rates. It indicates the number of times per month that a patient was sanctioned for an offense.

A preliminary analysis indicated that patient's sex was unrelated to sanction usage and did not interact with patient's race. A second analysis revealed a heavier use of sanctions on one of the wards than the other. Hence ward is included in the analyses below and sex is not. Previous research had focused on race relations between Whites and Blacks, not Whites and other minority groups. Thus the analyses below include data from 56 White patients and 9 Black patients; excluded are 3 Puerto Ricans and 3 Hispanics. The number of Puerto Rican and Hispanic patients is, in any case, too low to warrant extensive analysis.

*Patient's Race*

We wondered if a patient's violence would be related to the patient's race. It was not. The mean number of offenses per month was 4.28 for Whites and 4.36 for Blacks.

Although Blacks committed no greater number of violent offenses, they received harsher sanctions than Whites. The staff tended to restrain Black patients more often than White patients (Ms = 2.32 vs. .65 restraints per month for Blacks and Whites, respectively); they secluded Black and White patients equally often (Ms =2.04 and 3.63 seclusions per month for Blacks and Whites).

We conducted a supplementary analysis to test for the differential use of sanctions. Forty-five of the patients in our study (40 Whites and 5 Blacks) were sanctioned for at least one offense between October 15, 1983 and January 7, 1984. We compared Whites and Blacks in this subsample, using as a dependent measure the percentage of offenses that ended with the patient in restraints. This revealed a strong effect of Race, with Blacks restrained for

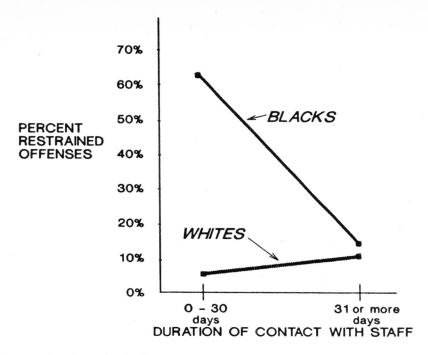

**Figure 1.** Restrained offenses, by patient's race and contact with staff.

35.49% of their offenses and Whites restrained for only 9.58% of theirs. As these means show, Blacks were restrained nearly four times as often as Whites.

Perhaps the Blacks in our sample had violent, belligerent personalities. If so, we might expect them to have resisted admission to a psychiatric hospital, to have received an involuntary commitment, and to have been diagnosed as violent. The data do not support these expectations. In the current sample, Blacks were no less likely to have volunteered for admission to the hospital than were Whites, nor were Blacks more likely to have been diagnosed as violent or aggressive. If anything, diagnoses suggested that Blacks were slightly less violent than White patients (upon admission to the hospital, 22.1% of the Blacks and 33.9% of the Whites received a diagnosis that mentioned belligerence or aggression).

*Interracial Contact*

According to Allport's hypothesis (1954), interracial contact should reduce prejudice, but only if the contact is between individuals of equal status who are working toward a common goal. At Altobello, these conditions are not met.

Black patients have lower status than White staff members; moreover, patients are often in conflict with the staff.

To study the impact of interracial contact under these untoward circumstances, we distinguished patients who had arrived at Altobello recently (and were unknown to the staff) from those who had resided at the institution for some time (interacting with the staff daily). For purposes of analysis, we defined *new arrivals* as patients who were in their first month at Altobello and *old-timers* as ones who had been at the hospital for more than 30 days.

Upon their arrival, Blacks were restrained more often but secluded no more often than Whites. The mean number of restraints in the first month was 2.89 for Blacks and .33 for Whites. The mean number of seclusions in this first month was .62 for Blacks and 3.14 for Whites. These results are more dramatic if expressed as percentages. During their first month at Altobello, Blacks were restrained for 61.11% of their offenses, Whites for only 6.33% of their offenses. We wondered if this differential use of restraints would change with the passage of time.

After interacting with the staff for a month, Blacks were restrained no more often than Whites and there was no racial difference in rates of seclusion. Among old-timers, the mean number of restraints per month was 1.03 for Blacks and .74 for Whites; the mean number of seclusions per month was 4.11 for Blacks and 3.53 for Whites. These results are similar if expressed as percentages. Among old-timers, 13.11% of Black offenses and 11.05% of White offenses ended with the patient in physical restraints. Apparently, contact improved relations between individual Blacks and Whites. Relevant results appear in Figure 1.

## DISCUSSION

In our study, we examined archives at a Connecticut state psychiatric hospital for adolescents. The archives revealed a high incidence of violence—over five violent acts a day in wards that housed barely 40 patients. Earlier research (Lewis et al., 1980) had prepared us for the high incidence of violence, but not for its intensity or for the institutionalized staff response.

We were interested in the role of patients' race in violence. The hospital archives indicated no difference in the number of offenses by White and Black patients. There was a racial difference at this psychiatric institution, but it was a difference in the sanctions applied to violence. Often, patients were forcibly restrained and tranquilized. Blacks received this treatment four times as often as Whites. Restraints were most often imposed on Blacks who were new to the institution. Blacks fared better after interacting with the staff for a month.

We will consider two interpretations for these results: racial differences in the severity of offenses and racial discrimination in the staff's response. The Black patients in our sample may have behaved more violently than their

White counterparts. Although the Blacks committed no greater number of offenses, perhaps their offenses were more severe. If the Blacks perpetrated assaults as the Whites engaged in horseplay, the sanctions would be understandable.

According to psychiatric diagnoses, the Black patients in our sample were not dispositionally violent. Their aggression emerged at a White-run hospital. Perhaps Blacks had difficulty adapting to the predominantly White institution, felt threatened, and reacted with hostility. When a White staff member intervened to abort friction, the Black's violence escalated—rendering seclusion insufficient to control the incident, thereby prompting the imposition of restraints. According to this interpretation, there was a racial difference in patients' terminal level of violence—after the patient had interacted with a White staff member who expected aggression from Blacks. Blacks were confirming the White's expectation (Snyder, 1984). The racial difference in patient behavior dissipated as Black individuals became assimilated into the ward and learned what the staff would tolerate. Whites had been better prepared to be patients, knowing the limits from the outset.

This interpretation is consistent with earlier research. Kuhlman, Telintelo, and Winget (1982) studied violence in a sample of emergency psychiatric patients. Some of these patients were violent before entering the emergency room, but there was no racial difference in preexisting violence. The difference came in violence that evolved from patient interviews with a White therapist: During the interview, Blacks tended to become violent.

There may be racial differences in the severity of patients' offenses, but we note a second interpretation for the current results—that sanction usage reflects racial discrimination by the White staff. Black patients were not particularly violent; yet they engendered an unusually harsh response.

Discrimination has cognitive and affective roots. Like Whites, Blacks enter psychiatric hospitals because of their abnormal behavior. Yet when Whites act in ambiguous ways, their behavior is given an innocent interpretation; when Blacks act identically, they are attributed with aggressive intent (Duncan, 1976; Sagar & Schofield, 1980). Having attributed aggression to Black psychiatric patients, a White staff member would feel justified in imposing physical restraints. The White could then vent covert hostilities from a position of superior power (Crosby, Bromley, & Saxe, 1980), regressing angrily to an old-fashioned racism (Rogers, 1983) without threatening an egalitarian self-concept (Gaertner & Dovidio, 1986). Racial ambivalence would underlie this exaggerated response (Katz, 1981).

Interracial contact may reduce discrimination against individual minority group members. As the White staff at Altobello became familiar with individuals' expressive styles, perhaps they were less likely to infer aggressive intent. And after a month-long exposure, the staff may have come to like particular minority group members. Either the cognitive or the affective trend could explain the salutary effect of contact on staff-patient race relations. It is noteworthy that the effect did not generalize beyond the individuals involved.

Despite their experiences with Black individuals, the staff continued to restrain new arrivals. As previous research shows, interracial contact causes no general reduction in prejudice, unless the contact is between equals working cooperatively toward a superordinate goal (Amir, 1976). Here perceivers retained their stereotypes by regarding individuals as exceptions (Taylor, 1981). This is a common construal. Indeed, Bond and Brockett (1987) maintain that all acquaintances are conceived as deviations from a social stereotype.

We observed unstaged interracial aggression that dissipates with the passage of time. Although our observations were limited to a single setting in which Blacks were in a minority, they complement experimental results and illustrate long-term race relations.

## References

Allport, G. W. (1954). *The nature of prejudice*. Reading, MA: Addison-Wesley.

Amir, Y. (1976). The role of intergroup contact in change of prejudice and ethnic relations. In P. A. Katz (Ed.), *Towards the elimination of racism*. New York: Pergamon Press.

Bertilson, H. S. (1983). Methodology in the study of aggression. In R. G. Geen & E. I. Donnerstein (Eds.), *Aggression: Theoretical and empirical reviews* (Vol. 1, pp. 213–246). New York: Academic Press.

Bond, C. F., Jr., & Brockett, D. R. (1987). a social context-personality index theory of memory for acquaintances. *Journal of Personality and Social Psychology, 52*, 1110–1112.

Chilton, R., & Galvin, J. (1985). Race, crime, and criminal justice. *Crime & Delinquency, 31*, 3–14.

Clore, G. L., Bray, R. M., Itkin, S. M., & Murphy, P. (1978). Interracial attitudes and behavior at a summer camp. *Journal of Personality and Social Psychology, 36*, 107–116.

Crosby, F., Bromley, S., & Saxe, L. (1980). Recent unobtrusive studies of black and white discrimination and prejudice: A literature review. *Psychological Bulletin, 87*, 546–563.

Donnerstein, E., & Donnerstein, M. (1976). Research in the control of interracial aggression. In R. G. Geen & E. C. O'Neal (Eds.), *Perspectives on aggression* (pp. 133–168). New York: Academic Press.

Duncan, B. L. (1976). Differential social perception and attribution of intergroup violence: Testing the lower limits of stereotyping of blacks. *Journal of Personality and Social Psychology, 34*, 590–598.

Gaertner, S. L., & Dovidio, J. F. (1986). The aversive form of racism. In S. L. Gaertner & J. F. Dovidio (Eds.), *Prejudice, discrimination, and racism* (pp. 61–89). New York: Academic Press.

Jones, J. M. (1983). the concept of race in social psychology: From color to culture. In L. Wheeler & P. Shaver (Eds.), *Review of Personality and Social Psychology: 4* (pp. 117–150). Beverly Hills, CA: Sage.

Katz, I. (1981). *Stigma: A social psychological analysis*. Hillsdale, NJ: Lawrence Erlbaum.

Kuhlman, T., Telintelo, S., & Winget, C. (1982). Restraint use with emergency psychiatric patients: A new perspective on racial bias. *Psychological Reports, 51*, 343–347.

Lewis, D. O., Shanok, S. S., Cohen, R. J., Kligfeld, M., & Frisone, G. (1980). Race bias in the diagnosis and disposition of violent adolescents. *American Journal of Psychiatry, 137*, 1211–1216.

Miller, N., & Brewer, M. B. (1984). *Groups in contact: The psychology of desegregation*. Orlando, FL: Academic Press.

Patterson, M. L. (1983). *Nonverbal behavior: A functional perspective.* New York: Springer-Verlag.

Petersilia, J. (1985). Racial disparities in the criminal justice system: A summary. *Crime & Delinquency, 31,* 15–34.

Pettigrew, T. F. (1985). New black-white patterns: How best to conceptualize them? *Annual Review of Sociology, 11,* 329–346.

Rogers, R. W. (1983). Race variables in aggression. In R. G. Geen & E. I. Donnerstein (Eds.) *Aggression: Theoretical and empirical reviews* (Vol. 2, pp. 27–50). New York: Academic Press.

Sagar, H. A., & Schofield, J. W. (1980). Racial and behavioral cues in black and white children's perceptions of ambiguously aggressive acts. *Journal of Personality and Social Psychology, 39,* 590–598.

Savitz, L. D. (1973). Black crime. In K. S. Miller & R. M. Dreger (Eds.), *Comparative studies of blacks and whites in the United States.* New York: Seminar Press.

Schuck, J., & Pisor, K. (1974). Evaluating an aggression experiment by the use of simulating subjects. *Journal of Personality and Social Psychology, 29,* 181–186.

Snyder, M. (1984). When belief creates reality. In L. Berkowitz (Ed.), *Advances in experimental social psychology* (Vol. 18, pp. 247–305). New York: Academic Press.

Taylor, D. G., Sheatsley, P. B., & Greeley, A. M. (1978). Attitudes toward racial integration. *Scientific American, 238,* 42–49.

Taylor, S. E. (1981). A categorization approach to stereotyping. In D. L. Hamilton (Ed.), *Cognitive processes in stereotyping and intergroup behavior* (pp. 83–114). Hillsdale, NJ: Lawrence Erlbaum.

Wilbanks, W. (1985). Is violent crime intraracial? *Crime and Delinquency, 31,* 117–128.

Jean's parents were hoping for a son and were a bit disappointed when she was born. She was soft and cute and she loved it when her mother dressed her. up and called her Sugar. As she grew up she got lots of dolls to play with and spent most of her time indoors playing house.

At school Jean was a good reader and speller, and her teacher always praised her for being so neat and polite. In her science books she saw many pictures of famous men who had done important things, so she decided quite early that she could not be like them and wanted to be a teacher when she grew up. By the fourth grade she was as bright as anyone else in the class, but she was upset that when she did well, especially in math or science, other kids teased her and called her a bookworm.

By the time she was in junior high and high school, she noticed that her interest and her grades in many academic subjects were dropping, and she doubted her ability to make it in college. After four years of college as an education major with a C+ average, Jean met a brilliant young man and they settled down to have a family.

All in all, Jean was pleased with her life. Her husband provided her with the tangible means to live in a style she enjoyed, and she knew that the people around her respected her as a good mother and wife.

Gene's parents were hoping for a son and were quite pleased when he was born. He was strong and sturdy, and he loved it when his father tossed him up and called him Tiger. As he grew up he got lots of blocks to play with and spent most of him time outdoors playing ball.

At school Gene was a good reader and speller, and his teacher always praised him for being so accurate and smart. In his science books he saw many pictures of famous men who had done important things, and he decided quite early that he could be like them and wanted to be an engineer when he grew up. By the fourth grade he was as bring as anyone else in the class, and he was pleased that when he did well, especially in math or science, other kids respected him and called him a genius.

By the time he was in junior high and high school, he noticed that his interest and his grades in many academic subjects were rising, and he was optimistic about his ability to make it in college. After four years of college as a chemistry major with a B+ average, Gene met a beautiful young woman and they settled down to have a family.

All in all, Gene was pleased with his life. His wife provided him with the love and support to work at the pace he enjoyed, and he knew that the people around him respected him as a hardworking professional.

# 10

# Applied Social Psychology: Health and the Law

In recent years, social psychologists have branched out in a wide range of directions. Businesses are guided by the principles of group dynamics as developed in social psychological laboratories, juries are selected based on social psychological research, dormitories are designed in consultation with social psychologists, and physicians are trained to relate to patients using basic principles of social interaction.

Andrew Baum is Professor of Medical Psychology at the Uniformed Services University of the Health Sciences in Bethesda, Maryland. He is the editor of the *Journal of Applied Social Psychology* and associate editor of *Health Psychology*. After gaining a reputation as a leading researcher in environment psychology, he made the transition into health psychology through his research on stress-provoking events, such as the Three Mile Island nuclear reactor incident. In our conversation Prof. Baum considers the unique contributions that social psychologists can make and lays out a whole series of issues for social psychology to address.

## A CONVERSATION WITH
## ANDREW BAUM
*Uniformed Services University
of the Health Sciences*

**Krupat:** *The topic of applied social psychology seems to come up a great deal. What is applied social psychology, and what does it deal with?*

**Baum:** Social psychology has many different focuses. Applied social psychology is the use of basic social psychological theories and findings to investigate and solve social issues and problems of society. The best current example that I can think of is in the struggle against the AIDS virus. Given that this disease has no cure as far as we know, and there is no vaccine that effectively prevents one from becoming infected, the most important tools that we have in combating the disease are techniques that really involve social influence and persuasion. If we can convince people not to do certain things that encourage the spread of the virus and give them social skills and techniques to avoid infection, we may be able to halt its progress and minimize lives lost.

**Krupat:** *Why are social psychologists involved in applied research? What kinds of unique contributions can we make?*

**Baum:** Social psychology has two important aspects that are particularly useful in this effort. One is that the body of knowledge and the areas of investigation that social psychologists are interested in are basic and central to our interactions in our daily lives. Social psychologists have staked out a domain of behavior that is central to almost everything that goes on in human life. The second and perhaps more important thing is that social psychologists use unique methodologies in understanding the problems that they study. Because of the nature of the phenomena that they are studying, social psychologists are forced to use laboratory studies and field studies, as well as a host of imaginative techniques. I think that the combination of this unique focus on content and this unusual methodological approach makes social psychology particularly important in applications to social problems.

**Krupat:** *How does this research translate into action?*

**Baum:** Intervention is one of the goals of a lot of research that goes on within social psychology. Let's consider the AIDS virus in relation to college students. One goal is to come up with an intervention, something that we can deliver to college students that will make it easier for them to avoid becoming infected with the virus. So a social psychologist might do research on the best persuasion techniques that seem to create long-term behavior change or at least create intentions to change behavior. Then they might focus on providing social skills that will make people more successful in avoiding infection. The work would build toward creating an intervention, which in this case might be a training program or an educational program, and an evaluation of the intervention.

**Krupat:** *Are we doing much more applied psychology now than we ever were, or are there cycles in the history of the field?*

**Baum:** Right now I think that we are doing a lot of applied work, but to some extent this does come in cycles, which are a product of the demands of the world that we live in. An early period of very active application of social psychology occurred during World War II, and this was a function of the demands created by the war. Another surge in applied work occurred in the late sixties through the mid-seventies, when the society we were living in was in turmoil, when environmental issues were suddenly of great concern, and a number of changes in the society demanded new knowledge and new application. Currently, there is a combination of forces, one of which is again a demand on science to try to answer some of the questions that people have been unable to answer in other ways. In general, I think the distinctions between basic and applied psychology have become less clear, and I see the whole field moving a bit toward the applied dimension.

**Krupat:** *Which I assume you think is a good direction?*

**Baum:** I think it's a good direction as long as it doesn't go too far toward the other extreme.

**Krupat:** *I agree. What do you think of the feelings expressed by some critics that social psychology runs in fads, that areas such as health psychology are popular now, but soon we will move on. How would you respond to that?*

**Baum:** I really don't see social psychology in the guise of an ambulance chaser. Health is going to be an important issue for a long time, whether or not social psychologists are contributing to the effort to prevent and heal disease. Back in the middle and late eighties, there was concern in organized psychology that most researchers were not particularly interested in the AIDS problem, when in fact we were getting messages from the Surgeon General and others that understanding behavior change and social influence was absolutely vital to the solution of the AIDS problem. And yet as a group, psychologists seemed somewhat reluctant to become involved. A series of meetings took place, and I wrote a paper with one of my students for the *American Psychologist,* attempting to show psychologists some of the things that we needed to do and all that could be done. Today there is greater interest in HIV disease and AIDS. I'm certainly not suggesting that the article or even the meetings had much to do with this increased interest, but people didn't suddenly wake up one day and say, "Gee, that's a hot area. Let's get involved in it." It took some coaxing and some cautious examination of the potential of social psychological research in this area. I think that, if you look carefully at the history of application in social psychology, you'll see that it is really not a matter of going after hot topics, but rather of the right people finding the right matches between what they do and the kinds of problems that need solutions.

**Krupat:** *When social psychologists get involved in these issues, they often end up working with physicians and lawyers or architects. How has that collaboration gone?*

**Baum:** It has been very exciting. My experience has been that psychologists are uniquely trained to be able to interact across these different disciplinary lines. I have found instances where I have been in a group of biomedical scientists who have less in common with each other than I have in common with each of them. Part of that has to do with the nature of what psychologists study. There is a certain inescapability of mental and behavioral processes in almost all of these issues, so that a virologist might be studying only a small piece of a problem, whereas the psychologist may be involved in almost all of it. And that has led in my experience to psychologists becoming very central in these clusters of interdisciplinary scientists.

**Krupat:** *Are there cases where you have found that others have been skeptical of your contributions?*

**Baum:** Sure. There's a certain skepticism that is built in whenever other people are dealing with a discipline that describes something that's very common to everyone. Part of what social psychologists have to deal with is the perception that a lot of what we do has a certain common sense quality to it, and that people find it difficult to take social psychology seriously at times. There is also a skepticism that's not just unique to psychology, but is more globally applied to scientists in general. A lot of lawyers, for example, approach these collaborations with a sense that we are "ivory tower" scientists. They are not as familiar with scientists who are out there in the real world getting their hands dirty with the kinds of problems that we work on.

**Krupat:** *But don't lawyers sometimes wonder how a psychologist can be telling them how to present evidence? Or don't physicians question what psychologists can tell them about clinical reasoning?*

**Baum:** There is some of that, although my experience has been that, if they have figured out that they need the expertise, they are likely to be open to the advice. Lawyers and physicians who ask for help usually have a positive attitude toward the kind of contribution that can be made before they go ahead and ask.

**Krupat:** *Do we have to wait until people ask?*

**Baum:** We shouldn't. But frequently that's the way that things get started. Certainly we shouldn't have needed to be asked to become involved with HIV disease and heart disease, but in many cases we did.

**Krupat:** *You are based in a medical school. Most social psychologists are still in standard psychology departments, but others are now in law schools and business schools. Some are completely outside of academia. What advantages or disadvantages for the field or the individual lie in having these different kinds of affiliations?*

**Baum:** Where you are located affects who you interact with on a daily basis and what kinds of cross-fertilizations are likely to occur. In a medical school environment, there are few other social scientists, and almost everyone else is a natural or life scientist. What you get in your daily interactions is very different from what you would get if you were in a liberal arts college where there are lots of other psychologists as well as sociologists, political scientists, and economists. I'm not sure that this is good or bad, just different. The point is, the interactions and collaborations differ, and these affect the directions that research and theory may take. I find that the interactions I have in the medical school setting are essential to my continued growth and have influenced my research. I miss a lot of the other kinds of interaction, but I try to make up for that by maintaining a network of colleagues that I talk with. I think that the overall proliferation of psychology into these different areas is good for the science of psychology in that in provides us with new opportunities by virtue of contacting different kinds of people and researchers. And it also broadens the base of the field so that now we are not just an academic discipline with its roots exclusively in psychology departments.

**Krupat:** *I agree with you. But how about extending even further and talking about social psychologists in ad agencies, government positions, and all sorts of nonacademic settings?*

**Baum:** I haven't had a lot of experience with ad agencies, but I do know it is good for government agencies to have a lot of different types of people in them. When there are enough people with different kinds of perspectives to keep each other "honest," it discourages narrow thinking or even a groupthink type of phenomenon. My guess is that in most of the nonacademic settings it is not only good for the field, but it is good for the product as well. It provides a different perspective on what things should be done and how things might be done.

**Krupat:** *Within health psychology, which is the field that you have been involved in, what kinds of specific issues and problems have social psychologists become involved in?*

**Baum:** We can start with stress research, which is ubiquitous because stress is involved in almost all health processes and it has a large social component. Consider things such as social support, which is one of the very basic buffers of stress. There is also the study of coping and how we deal with stressful events. Perceived control, which is derived directly from basic research in social psychology, has proven important not just in response to environmental stressors, but also in things like preparation for surgery. There are also areas such as compliance with medical regimens—how do you get patients to do what their health care professionals prescribe for them? If you've got a high-risk individual who needs to go for hypertensive screening every year or if you have someone who needs to go on a diet to lose weight, how do you go about convincing them, making sure that they understand and remember what they are supposed to do, and seeing to it that they actually do this? The compliance problem is enormous; about 50 percent of all people on antihypertensive medication drop out by about a year after they begin their treatment. And that is going to affect their health and the outcome of therapy that is being prescribed. So that's another area where I think social psychologists have very specific and essential expertise. There are also disease-specific areas. There is research on heart disease, much of which has social and personality psychological components, and cancer research is becoming more and more influenced by psychological and social psychological constructs. The AIDS epidemic, of course, also requires this kind of work. There is also smoking, health promotion, diet, eating behaviors, exercise, and managing chronic illness. I could go on and on.

**Krupat:** *I ask half seriously how these fields ever existed without us.*

**Baum:** It's a really good question. And the answer to it is that they did, and they are better now because the information we are providing them is being incorporated. I can tell you from personal experience that major institutions investigating health and disease, such as comprehensive cancer centers all across the country, have added biobehavioral or psychosocial units to help not only in patient care but also in the basic and applied research they are doing.

**Krupat:** *I hear you saying that, while social psychology, especially as it relates to health care, has arrived only recently, it has assumed a highly important place. So what is the future like?*

**Baum:** The future is difficult to predict now because of all the changes that are going on around us in health care reform. Sometimes it feels as if the ground we are standing on is moving as we speak. I see the psychological and social psychological study of health as continuing to grow, particularly as we see major diseases and major health problems in our society being problems of lifestyle or diseases that are influenced by behavioral variables. As long as cancer, heart disease, HIV disease, and others like them are primary problems that we have to deal with and as long as people are people and we have difficulties with compliance and other health behaviors, I can't imagine that we won't have behavioral research directed toward these problems.

Andrew Baum
Sarah E. A. Nesselhof

# Psychological Research and the Prevention, Etiology, and Treatment of AIDS

In this article, Baum (along with Nesselhof) expands on one issue raised in our conversation, the need for psychology to contribute to the understanding of HIV disease and to direct interventions relating to prevention, control, and care. Although this article speaks to all of psychology, a quick look through the issues and approaches raised clearly places the focus on social psychology. Efforts at changing behavior, for instance, must be informed by an understanding of attitude change, education, and peer influences, all basic social psychological concerns. Concepts such as stress, social support, control, and patient blame, all discussed by Baum and Nesselhof, again lie at the very heart of social psychology.

Acquired immune deficiency syndrome (AIDS) is one of the most important diseases of the last quarter century. Although it kills fewer people than do heart disease, cancer, and other illnesses common in our society, it is newer and, unlike these other killers, is communicable. It is not a disease of life-style, like heart disease, but is associated with certain life-styles by virtue of its routes of transmission. Like cancer, it involves the immune system, but rather than evolving when the immunosurveillance function breaks down or in spite of natural defenses against it, AIDS attacks the heart of immunity. AIDS is not caused by diet, lack of exercise, or environmental toxins—factors that can be difficult to identify and control. Instead, the disease is caused by a virus (human immunodeficiency virus [HIV]) that is spread by sexual contact and exposure to infected blood or blood products. For behavioral scientists, AIDS may prove a watershed for the application of preventive programs targeted at stopping the spread of HIV. It also provides an opportunity to study further many basic and applied issues related to the etiology, progression, and treatment of AIDS, as well as a number of other health problems. In this article, we consider some of the research opportunities afforded by the AIDS epidemic, as well as the pressing needs for study and application that are needed to fight it.

The fact that there are no vaccines against AIDS, no cures for it, and few effective treatments makes the medical and behavioral aspects of AIDS equally important. Knowledge about the etiology and progression of the disease, activity of the virus, and behavioral factors that contribute to the spread of the disease are all crucial to developing preventive and curative regimens. Most work in the behavioral sciences has been concerned with the latter issue: How can we social scientists use what we know about behavior influence to alter people's behavior that places them at risk for AIDS or otherwise contributes to the spread of the disease? However, there are a number of other issues that derive from the AIDS epidemic that have behavioral aspects, and there is much to be learned about basic cognitive, behavioral, and psychophysiological processes as a "by-product" of research to halt the spread of AIDS. Using prevention, etiology, and treatment issues as organizing themes, we provide an overview of some of these problems and consider a few of the many issues needing study.

## PREVENTION

The contribution of behavioral scientists is central in the prevention of AIDS and HIV infection. Because there is no effective vaccine, psychosocial models may provide the only tools to stem the spread of AIDS. People come in contact with HIV by exchange of bodily fluids—primarily through sex, shared drug paraphernalia, and transfusions. It is generally believed that the behaviors that lead to contact and infection are modifiable if the proper tactics are used. The possibility of changing behaviors that increase risk of infection, thereby helping to control the spread of AIDS, is a clear imperative for behavioral research. However, the success of interventions to increase health-promoting behaviors has been limited and, in some cases, disappointing.

On the surface, the task looks easy. We know what causes AIDS, and we know how it is spread. So, if we can prevent people from having unprotected sex, or if we can prevent healthy people from having sex with HIV-positive people, the epidemic might be controlled. Or if we can get intravenous (IV) drug users to use clean needles and prevent their exposure to infected blood or blood products, we can reduce new cases of HIV infection to near zero and focus on the subsequently stable population of HIV-positive people. Hearst and Hulley (1988) have suggested that "the single most important message for patients is to have sex only with partners who they know are at low risk of carrying HIV infection" (p. 2431). The problem, of course, is that people do not know this in many cases: There are no clear markers of risk-group membership, nor any assurance that potential partners will tell the truth about themselves.

We need to know more about the processes by which risky behaviors are generated and decisions are made and about the ways in which fear, knowledge, stress, and other factors affect their ability to intervene. There is some evidence that recognition of the risks associated with unprotected sex or promiscuity has led to behavior change that reduces the risk of infection (e.g., McKusick, Horstman, & Coates, 1985). The effects of intervention to reduce fear, increase knowledge about AIDs, and provide clear behavioral recommendations suggest, however, that a substantial number of people are knowingly or inadvertently exposing themselves to risk for HIV infection (e.g., Temoshok, Sweet, & Zich, 1987).

## EDUCATION

Efforts designed to increase people's knowledge about AIDS have several goals. One is to decrease fear by providing a clear understanding of the nature of the disease and how infection can be prevented. By reducing fear, one may be better able to intervene in other ways. However, it is unclear whether (a) information reduces fear, (b) fear affects receptivity to information, or (c) a decrease in fear has much impact on behavior (e.g., Sherr, 1987; Temoshok et al., 1987). Other objectives of informational campaigns include increasing knowledge about specific preventive behaviors (e.g., condom use) in the hope that this will increase these behaviors and reduce infection risk. The extent to which such campaigns affect actual behavior, however, is not solely deter-mined by the appropriateness of their goals. The effectiveness of the campaign itself is determined by a host of cognitive and social psychological variables. Regardless of how relevant fear reduction and information gains are for AIDS prevention, ineffective campaigns will produce negative results simply by not reaching or influencing people in an effective way.

Cognitive effects of various aspects of educational campaigns might have important implications for design of these interventions. Many of these informational issues are basic to psychological research on cognition, persua-sion, and health behavior. Is information structured or stored differently when different educational campaigns are used? Are these changes in knowledge more or less likely to be associated with behavior change? What is the role of strong affective responses in the cognitive changes that result from educa-tional efforts? The mechanisms governing how one goes about getting people's attention may be as important as how the information is received, and the source of information as well as the audience to which it is directed may help to determine this.

The issue of audience is particularly important because a number of "subculture" groups, differentiated by a number of variables, may be of interest. Historically, male homosexuals and IV drug users have been the highest risk groups in this country. Because they are different from one another, the same educational style, focus, content, or source may not prove equally effective with both groups. In addition, other groups of people may be at risk but not fully realize it. Adolescents, for example, may be considered at risk because they are becoming sexually active and because research suggests that they do not, as a group, take adequate risk behavior precautions against pregnancy and sexually transmitted diseases (e.g., Wiesse, Nesselhof, Fleck-Kandath, & Baum, in press). The fact that, by age 21, many young adults will have experimented with sex with several partners, often not well known to them, suggests that HIV infection may be a grim reality for some of them. Like drug users, adolescents have proven resistant to educational campaigns, though there is some indication that school-based sex education can reduce risk of teenage pregnancies (e.g., Weisse et al., in press). The reasons are different, though, and research must determine the context for interventions, including the needs, life-styles, and prevailing attitudes in each group.

Clearly, interventions directed toward reducing risk of infection and spread of the HIV will continue, as will the related controversy. However, basic to any such efforts will be information about general high-risk behavior, sexual behavior, drug abuse, developmental stage, and so on. Among the questions that must be addressed are the common naive theories of the illness as they relate to preventive behavior, the impact of self-regulation on risk taking, impulse control and overall effectiveness in behavior change, and different strategies that may be needed for varying stages of the disease. More complete understanding of behavioral factors that may alter the effectiveness of interventions on the long- and short-term adoption of preventive recommendations is necessary and must be considered both independently and in the context of the AIDS epidemic.

*Risk Assessment*

Perceptions of risk and the decision to engage in risky behaviors are governed by complex processes that produce results that are often at odds with what one would expect. Expert and layperson assessments of risk are often discrepant, and risk-taking appears not to be based on rational decision-making systems (e.g., Slovic, Fischhoff, & Lichtenstein, 1981). The role of heuristics such as availability in determining judgments of probability figure prominently in risk assessments that do not match "reality." What factors affect this process and the accuracy of risk assessment? Are there reliable ways of surveying people about how they assess their own risk? How is assessment of risk related to the spread of AIDS? Do different stages of development affect these perceptions? At some level, the processes that yield inaccurate judgments of risk are important in any behavior that carries a health risk, such as cigarette smoking, unprotected sex, or drug use. These processes, as well as factors specific to sexual behavior, are also of great importance in understanding why people may expose themselves to risk of HIV infection.

### Sexual Behavior

By better understanding the determinants of sexual behavior and by identifying patterns that vary across cultural, ethnic, age, gender, or other background dimensions, social scientists may be better able to curtail risky sexual activity. As a primary mode of communication of HIV, sexual activity is a central issue in the prevention of AIDS. Yet relatively little is known about human sexual behavior. Sexuality is difficult to study for many reasons and is typically not studied by direct observation. Though the past decade has seen important advances in the study of sexual behavior, there is still much to learn. The AIDS epidemic provides a new reason to continue this study. Information drawn from studies of contraception and birth control as well as prevention of sexually transmitted diseases has already proven useful.

Among the issues needing study are the basic determinants of sexual behavior and their associations with risk taking. In adults and adolescents, a better understanding of these factors may enhance efforts to alter sexual behavior to reduce risk of HIV infection. What are the relations between sexual attitudes and behaviors? Study of attitudes toward birth control, maladaptive sexual behaviors, and the effects of changes in sexual activity on relationships between sexual partners may provide important information for preventive interventions.

Continued development of methods of determining individual sexual behavior and investigation of the positive and negative effects of the AIDS epidemic on sexual relationships are also important in this regard. Further study of basic aspects of sexuality, factors that influence the adoption of monogamous relationships, developmental influences on sexual activity, methods for changing high-risk sexual behavior, and methods of assessing sexual predispositions will be important adjuncts to the investigation of how sexual behavior has been affected by the AIDS epidemic.

### Development

Do developmental variables affect adjustment to HIV infection or receptivity to information about AIDS? People of any age and stage of development may become infected by the AIDS virus; infants have been born with HIV infection, and sexually active adolescents and adults of any age are potentially at risk. Developmental issues are important in crafting interventions as well as for understanding and shaping response to them. Study of perceptions of invulnerability among children and adolescents is crucial to gaining the attention of young people, and the attitudes and behaviors of older people are important in determining their attention to and acceptance of interventions and in shaping the context in which interventions are designed and supported. What factors contribute to perceptions of invulnerability at different ages, and how can these perceptions be modified?

We need to know much more about developmental aspects of sexual behavior, about maturation and risk-taking behavior, and about the ways in which parent-child relationships affect a range of behaviors. We still must discover the specific ages or stages of development at which sexual attitudes are most influenced, and we need to learn more about the effects of explicit sex education on psychosocial development. The effects of sex education on attitudes toward sexual activity and other aspects of development are also important, as is a more complete understanding of powerful peer influences that affect health behavior in other realms. The existing methods of caring for infants born with AIDS and the similar strategies used for seropositive infants or seronegative infants born to infected mothers need to be evaluated. The concerns of siblings and their influence on infected children are also important. Studies of children, adolescents, and adults, evaluations of school, familial, and peer influences on development, and assessment of cognitive, social, and behavioral changes over the life span will provide much new information about development of the human organism as well as about prevention of AIDS.

The role of schools as sources of preventive information is crucial. Educators must learn what types of curriculums are most appropriate for educational campaigns against AIDS and who should provide this information. Methodologies for evaluating the effectiveness of school-based campaigns, the important elements of AIDS education evaluation for both students and teachers, methods of intervention and evaluation for learning disabled or emotionally disturbed youngsters, and methods of educating teachers, administrators, parents, and others must be developed and studied.

Worksite health promotion may be as important for adults as are school-based programs for children. Still to be discovered are effective methods of education about AIDS at the worksite, different methods useful for occupational settings varying in professional level, size, type of work, and management system, and appropriate responses to employee concerns about AIDS, including working with others who are HIV-positive or who have AIDS-related complex (ARC) or AIDS. The development of attitudes about AIDS in the workplace, perceptions of financial responsibility for financing health care, discrimination against employees with AIDS, and the insurance implications of the epidemic are among the issues needing study in these settings. On a larger scale, how will economic changes in the health care system affect mental health as well as behavior by employers and workers?

## ETIOLOGY

AIDS has at least two clear biological consequences: impaired immune system function and neuropsychological deficits. The tendency of the virus to attack the immune system has a variety of negative effects on immunosurveillance, allowing opportunistic infections to develop. In these infections, the virus apparently is carried into the brain and, once there, appears to cause a number of cognitive and attentional problems. To the extent that psychosocial variables affect these processes, they will contribute to the development of AIDS and to the manner in which it progresses.

*Immunity and Stress*

One of the more commonly held assumptions about psychosocial influences on physiological functioning is that stress and the immune system are linked. Research supports this hypothesis, documenting relations between stress and immune system changes or subsequent illness (e.g., Jemmott & Locke, 1984; Kiecolt-Glaser & Glaser, 1987; Rahe, 1975). However, clear evidence of simultaneous stress-induced immunosuppression and illness has not been reported. A number of studies have suggested that stress can have immunosuppressive effects, but clear demonstrations that stress-related immunosuppression leads to illness have not been reported. There are studies that have demonstrated immunosuppressive and tumorogenic effects of stress (e.g., Riley, 1981), but because of the many ways in which stress may increase tumor growth, the consequences of stress-related immunosuppression are still not clear. Coupled with methodological limitations and other qualifying factors, this makes the conclusion that stress suppresses both immune function and health tentative at best and suggests that further study is needed.

The study of immunity and stress in the HIV-positive, ARC, or AIDS patient can provide important information about the nature of the stress-immunity relation as well as about the disease itself. The HIV appears to remain in a latent stage after it enters the body and may not become "active" or induce ARC or AIDS for some time. The length of time between infection and onset of one of these two syndromes is variable and could be a function of several factors. One factor might be stress: Research has suggested that stress plays a role in the activation of latent herpes viruses, presumably by weakening immunoregulation of the virus (Kiecolt-Glaser & Glaser, 1987). The same could be true of the HIV (the virus may not be "held in check" by an immune system weakened by stress), and the role of stress in the immunological consequences of HIV infection is an important topic for study. Normal variations in stress, compounded by events and upsets associated with the HIV (e.g., learning that one is HIV-positive, seeing someone else become ill and die) may interact with the physical course of HIV and in that way affect the progression of the disease.

The possibility that stress affects the course of HIV infection suggests a number of corollary questions: Do variables that affect stress or the systems through which it works also affect HIV disease? Do psychosocial assets such as social support, rich coping repertoires, or positive coping styles affect the progression of the virus by modifying stress load? Are stress-related neuroendocrine changes mechanisms by which general immune system changes occur and by which HIV may be influenced? Though it may be premature to begin to consider stress-management or exercise interventions for HIV-positive individuals and AIDS or ARC patients, it is probably desirable to do so. First, study of the effects of stress management or fitness training may provide more information about stress and immune function, as have studies of stress reduction and immunity in other populations (e.g., Kiecolt-Glaser, Stephens, Lipetz, Speicher, & Glaser, 1985). Second, though we do not know that stress reduction will affect immune status and disease state among HIV-positive individuals, the possibilty that it may do so is sufficient to justify exploratory studies.

Stress can affect health either by direct physiological changes or by changes in behaviors that affect health or immunity independently (e.g., cigarette smoking, alcohol use). We know little about how AIDS may affect motivational systems: How might eating, drinking, sleep, sexual activity, and other behaviors be affected by the virus or by the knowledge that one is HIV-positive, and how might these changes affect progression of the disease? The role of sexually transmitted diseases in the etiology and progression of AIDS, recently identified as an important cofactor (Weber et al., 1986), needs to be studied, as do differential rates of progression across subgroups of patients.

*Neuropsychological Changes*

Stress provides one possible key to identification of those mechanisms by which bodily and psychological changes associated with stress mediate the rate and nature of spread of the HIV in the brain. The effects of stress on damage by the HIV once it begins to act also remain to be identified. However, resolution of basic problems of neuropsychological assessment must precede much of this work. Is it possible, for example, that traditionally crafted batteries of tests may not be the most effective means of assessing HIV-related impairment or central nervous system (CNS) damage? Functional assessments based on hypotheses regarding the locus of CNS effects may prove more useful, but consistency of measurement needs to be achieved as well. Increased use of new technology for assessing brain function should also help in refining measurement. At present, it is difficult to get a good sense of the findings from research on neuropsychological aspects of AIDS. The role of the CNS in HIV disease and the consequences of CNS effects of the virus and their role in further progression of the illness are important unresolved issues in the fight against AIDS. The virus reaches the brain at some phase of infection, but the time course of this process has not been reliably determined, and consistency of reported effects has not always been what one would hope. We need to improve assessment techniques and monitoring of the course and nature of HIV-related neuropsychological changes and identify the mechanisms by which CNS function is impaired and by which these effects influence the course of the illness.

Advances in assessment of the CNS effects of the HIV should generate a number of questions about the relation between HIV activity in the periphery and its effects on the CNS. If CNS effects are more or less independent of peripheral manifestations and consequences for immunity, can evidence of disease be detected before the onset of classic symptoms and the drastic compromising of immunity? Can changes in emotionality be tied to changes in disease status, and can they be used to diagnose progression from one disease stage to another?

Identification of the pattern or patterns of neuropsychological deficits associated with HIV infection and study of behavioral correlates may ultimately provide important information about how CNS problems affect preventive and treatment behavior and whether observable behavior changes provide indications of CNS deficits, as well as about the nature of neuroregulation of behavior. If AIDS produces specific brain abnormalities, can observable changes in behavior provide indications of brain-behavior relation? Clear criteria for AIDS dementia must be developed to aid in clinical care of patients, better screening devices should be created, and long-term studies of neuropsychological changes during AIDS are needed.

## PATIENT CARE

Once someone has tested positive for HIV antibodies, indicating exposure to the virus, or once a seropositive individual begins to experience the symptoms of ARC or AIDS, what can be done for this individual? The development of medical treatments for AIDS patients has had some positive effects, but there is little published on patient care, prevention of the progression from HIV-positive status to ARC and AIDS, and psychological treatment of these people. This belies the potential importance of behavioral aspects of treatment approaches.

Can psychological knowledge be applied to treatment so that stress can be managed, well-being enhanced, and psychosocial exacerbation of the physical course of illness minimized? A recent article (Morokoff, Holmes, & Weisse, 1987) describes a model program for education and care of newly diagnosed HIV-positive individuals, but, for the most part, care has been unsystematic or programs largely unreported. Application of behavioral principles to the care of HIV-positive, ARC, and AIDS patients, reduction of distress, countering or treating of neuropsychological deficits, and other aspects of patient care are important focuses for psychosocial research and practice. At the same time, these efforts may provide valuable information about management of chronic illness, psychological decline, and improvement of well-being among victimized populations.

### Social Support

In studying the effect of social support on adjustment to HIV infection, well-being during illness, and the manner in which AIDS progresses, social variables such as support, perceived control, and attributional tendencies need to be examined. Social support is recognized as an important mediator of stress and morbidity (e.g., Cohen & Wills, 1985) but may not be as available to ARC or AIDS patients as to people with other diseases. The effects of loss of social support or noncontingent social regard are important variables, and, although they have been considered, they require more thorough investigation. The effects of loneliness on immune function, the potential stress-enhancing effects of low levels of support, and the disturbing effects of noncontingent regard all point to the importance of this dimension (Coates & Wortman, 1980; Cohen & Wills, 1985; Kiecolt-Glaser et al., 1986).

## Perceived Control

The role of perceived control is also important, both as a presumed mediator of social support and as a stress-related variable. Do cognitive variables related to the ways in which information is processed or interpreted affect the nature or course of HIV disease, and what happens to perceived control when someone is infected with HIV or when the disease progresses? The extent to which neuropsychological deficits affect perceived control or to which localized brain damage affects these perceptions, the effects of control and uncertainty on disease progression, and the similarities and differences between coping with AIDS and with other diseases or forms of victimization are also of significance.

## Assignment of Blame

Assignment of blame or responsibility may prove to be an important variable as well. There is a large literature suggesting that under some conditions, self-assignment of some responsibility or avoiding the tendency to blame others for victimization may have positive effects on adjustment (e.g., Baum, Fleming, & Singer, 1983; Bulman & Wortman, 1977; Janoff-Bulman & Frieze, 1983). However, self-attribution of blame by victims of AIDS may not be positive and may carry with it additional stigma, reluctance to seek help, and barriers to treatment. Further, others' opinions regarding the cause of one's infection may carry negative connotations and may lead to negative outcomes. The admission that one is HIV-positive or that one has AIDS may carry with it disclosure of life-styles that have been previously kept secret, and the reaction of others to this news may deter people from being tested for the virus or taking action once they know they have AIDS. The ways in which society treats AIDS patients and seropositive individuals should be studied to learn what factors contribute to the development of fair treatment of victims, ways in which victims are tested, and methods of dealing with the illness and risky behavior.

## Social Response

Clearly, social variables relate to other areas of research and practice in the face of this epidemic. The decision to be tested for HIV may be a difficult one, and a number of factors may contribute to this action. The social dynamics of communities may change because of AIDS, and a thorough knowledge of how they change may be useful in treating and preventing the disease.

The epidemiology of AIDS and sexually transmitted diseases could affect community willingness to be involved in locally based activities, and appropriate community program evaluations suited to the AIDS epidemic may need to be developed. The emergence of credible neighborhood leaders and community-based attempts to curb the spread of AIDS are very important variables, as are the characteristics of networks and resource allocation within the community. Social influence variables and personality may also affect the decision to engage in risky behavior and may determine the appropriateness and effectiveness of educational campaigns and other preventive efforts. A more complete understanding of these processes will result from and contribute to the treatment and prevention of AIDS.

### Patient Intervention

Among the key aspects of patient care in the AIDS epidemic are those associated with clinical care and application of behavioral technology to the prevention and treatment of the disease. Stress management, as noted earlier, is potentially important as a means to "slow down" progression from HIV-positive status to ARC or AIDS, as well as being a valuable goal among patients in its own right. The identification of management technologies that are useful across victimized groups, as well as those more or less useful with specific victim groups, will not only facilitate stress reduction among patients but may also yield information about the general design of stress management programs.

How are the mental health needs of patients with ARC or AIDS different from those of HIV-positive individuals, and do they differ from those of the general population or patients with other illnesses? Are these needs individually based, or are certain needs associated with specific groups of AIDS patients or high-risk groups? Are there special considerations in providing mental health care to AIDS patients? The process of coping with being seropositive or having ARC or AIDS may be different from that associated with other life-threatening conditions. The psychological consequences of seropositivity and AIDS and how they vary with individual characteristics such as personality and mode of infection need to be identified, as do other techniques and variables that fail to help victims of AIDS and those that are more effective in reducing distress, altering risky behavior, and so on.

Comparison of AIDS with other diseases may yield useful information. Identification of factors that contribute to different coping styles and abilities including health status, preexisting physical and psychological status, and concurrent life stressors may help us learn more about treatment of HIV-positive individuals and ARC and AIDS patients. The issue of attribution is again important, as patterns of assignment of responsibility may be different and may have different consequences for AIDS than for other diseases. Attention to these issues may affect the progression of the illness or the well-being of patients.

Much can be learned about family dynamics and multitarget treatments by addressing the unique problems of those who have a friend or family member ill with AIDS. The development of "new" therapies to deal with these and other AIDS-related problems should advance the practice of psychotherapy and help to identify the characteristics of seropositive people, the needs of these and other patients, and the psychological sequelae of powerful victimization. Finally, it is important to develop therapeutic regimens for health care workers who are experiencing difficulties treating AIDS patients.


## CONCLUSIONS

We have considered some of the issues that should be studied as part of the effort to fight AIDS. The blurring of distinctions between basic and applied research that has characterized the emergence of health psychology, community psychology, and other "newer" areas of behavioral science has occurred in AIDS-related research. This work typically has aspects of both basic and applied research in that studies reveal information about basic psychosocial or psychophysiologic functioning and provide a basis for intervention, care, and prevention.

Several issues have not been discussed in detail. For example, issues involving drug use—effects on severity of illness and receptivity to prevention efforts, patterns of sexual behavior among drug users, and the general issue of the effects of withdrawal from drugs on the physical and psychological sequelae of HIV disease—are important as well. Likewise deserving of attention are the barriers to research in this area, such as the reluctance of many investigators to become involved because of fear of contagion, ethical issues, and the strains of working with the seriously ill.

Some have suggested that behavioral scientists have been slow to react to the AIDS epidemic and that, despite the steady growth of psychological research on AIDS, they have yet to make substantial contributions to efforts to prevent or treat the disease. Many might dispute this notion. Regardless, we should focus on ways in which this research can continue to expand, including tracing links between basic research and applied investigations in the study of AIDS. Recognition of the many potential areas of application of psychological knowledge to the fight against AIDS and the ways in which research on HIV-positive individuals and ARC and AIDS victims can contribute to basic research may provide an impetus for expansion of relevant research.

There are a number of reasons to study AIDS or AIDS-related processes. We have highlighted areas where research on AIDS may provide important insight into basic processes and have explored some ways in which basic research on a number of non-AIDS related populations may provide useful data for the effort to curb the spread of the epidemic. The most compelling rationale for biopsychosocial studies of AIDS-related issues is that they are crucial to the fight against AIDS. Without such research, the role of psychological variables in the etiology, progression, treatment, and prevention of the disease will not be identified, and the overall effort to combat the disease will be hampered.

# References

Baum, A., Fleming, R., & Singer, J. E. (1983). Coping with victimization by technological disaster. *Journal of Social Issues, 39*(2), 117–138.

Bulman, R. J., & Wortman, C. B. (1977). Attribution of blame and coping in the "real world": Severe accident victims react to their lot. *Journal of Personality and Social Psychology, 35*, 351–363.

Coates, D., & Wortman, C. (1980). Depression maintenance and inter-personal control. In A. Baum & J. E. Singer (Eds.) *Advances in environmental psychology* (Vol. 2, pp. 149–182). Hillsdale, NJ: Erlbaum.

Cohen, S., & Wills, T. A. (1985). Stress, social support, and the buffering hypothesis: A critical review. *Psychological Bulletin, 98*, 310–357.

Hearst, N., & Hulley, S. B. (1988). Preventing the heterosexual spread of AIDS. *Journal of the American Medical Association, 259*, 16, 2428–2432.

Janoff-Bulman, R., & Frieze, I. H. (1983). A theoretical perspective for understanding reactions to victimization. *Journal of Social Issues, 39*(2), 1–18.

Jemmott, J., & Locke, S. (1984). Psychosocial factors, immunologic mediation, and human susceptibility to infectious diseases: How much do we know? *Psychological Bulletin, 95*, 78–108.

Kiecolt-Glaser, J. K., & Glaser, R. (1987). Psychosocial moderators of immune function. *Annals of Behavioral Medicine, 9*(2), 16–20.

Kiecolt-Glaser, J. K., Glaser, R., Strain, E. C., Stout, J. C., Tarr, K. K., Holliday, J. E., & Speicher, C. E. (1986). Modulation of cellular immunity in medical students. *Journal of Behavioral Medicine, 9*, 5–21.

Kiecolt-Glaser, J. K., Stephens, R. E., Lipetz, P. D., Speicher, C. E., & Glaser, R. (1985). Distress and DNA repair in human lymphocytes. *Journal of Behavioral Medicine, 8*(4), 311–320.

McKusick, L., Horstman, W., & Coates, T. (1985). AIDS and sexual behavior reported by gay men in San Francisco. *American Journal of Public Health, 75*, 493–496.

Morokoff, P. J., Holmes, E., & Weisse, C. S. (1987). A psychosocial program for HIV-seropositive persons. *Patient Education and Counseling, 10*, 287–300.

Rahe, R. H. (1975). Life changes and near-future illness reports. In L. Levi (Ed.), *Emotions: Their parameters and measurements* (pp. 511–530). New York: Raven.

Riley, V. (1981). Psychoneuroendocrine influences on immunocompetence and neoplasia. *Science, 212*, 1100–1109.

Sherr, L. (1987). An evaluation of the UK Government Health Education Campaign. *Psychology & Health, 1*, 61–72.

Slovic, P., Fischhoff, B., & Lichtenstein, S. (1981). Perception and acceptability of risk from energy systems. In A. Baum & J. E. Singer (Eds.), *Advances in environmental psychology* (Vol. 3, pp. 155–170). Hillsdale, NJ: Erlbaum.

Temoshok, L., Sweet, D. M., & Zich, J. (1987). A three city comparison of the public's knowledge and attitudes about AIDS. *Psychology and Health, 1*, 43–60.

Weber, J. N., Wadsworth, J., Rogers, L. A., Moshtal, O., Scott, K., McManus, T.,

Berrie, E., Jeffries, D. J., Harris, J. R. W., & Pinching, A. J. (1986). Three year prospective study of HTLV-III/LAV infection in homosexual men. *The Lancet, 24,* 1179–1182.

Weisse, C. S., Nesselhof, S. E., Fleck-Kandath, C., & Baum, A. (in press). Psychosocial aspects of AIDS prevention among heterosexuals. In J. Edwards et al. (Eds.), *Applied social psychology annual.* Beverly Hills, CA: Sage.

Larry Bernard
Edward Krupat

# The Patient-Practitioner Relationship

In this article, Bernard and I take a basic understanding of social relationships and apply this to the medical realm in discussing the patient-practitioner relationship. For instance, just as in any relationship, there must be open communication and good information sharing. We review the different kinds of relationships that doctors and patients form, asking if one kind or another is the best. In general, research has indicated that patients are most satisfied when they are treated with warmth and respect and as whole people, not just medical conditions. Ask yourself how satisfied you are with your primary physician. What are some of the things he or she does that make you most or least pleased?

Modern medicine has progressed to a point beyond the imagination of early health practitioners. Technological advances and medical breakthroughs have given the physician the ability to diagnose and treat that would have been considered science fiction only years ago. Yet, in spite of these great discoveries—or in part because of them—all is not well with modern medicine. For all the growth we have witnessed on the technical side of medicine, the interpersonal side, involving the human element of care, has not kept pace. In fact, several observers, including doctors, have asked whether this aspect of medical care has suffered with the advent of modern technological and bureaucratic medicine.

## THE ART AND SCIENCE OF MEDICINE

The idea of treating the body by attending to the spirit has always caused tension in medicine. Although the philosopher Descartes expounded on the duality of body and mind, early physicians relied heavily on their interpersonal skills. In fact, sometimes they could offer little more than compassion, hope, and an effective bedside manner. The early Greek Hippocrates, known as the father of medicine, once wrote that it is possible that a patient "may recover his health through his contentment with the goodness of his physician."

In modern health care, the general practitioner and the small town doctor who ministered to all of a family's problems, physical as well as personal, are quickly disappearing. Increasingly, patients are being seen in large medical complexes by teams of highly specialized practitioners who diagnose via computer and treat using the latest technology. As a result, the technical quality of care has improved, but patients often report that "something is missing" in their relationship with their physician. As stated by one concerned physician, "Increasingly, people feel that their doctors do not or cannot listen, and are too caught up in struggles for money, status, knowledge, and power. . . . The patient and doctor no longer know and appreciate each other as people, working toward a common goal." (Roter & Hall, 1992)

This discussion underlines the distinction between the *art* and the *science* of medicine (Bloom, 1963; DiMattero, 1979), between the tasks of *caring* versus *curing*. Yet, health psychologists feel strongly that the interpersonal and technical sides of medicine cannot be separated, that a health professional must combine both in order to provide effective treatment. In referring to the perspective of health psychologists, Friedman and DiMatteo (1979) have stated:

> They are not merely saying that the physician should smile, as did the old family physician, while prescribing a particular treatment regimen. Nor are they saying that modern physicians should remember that the patient is a person with feelings, and should be treated as such as a matter of civility. Rather they are proposing that interpersonal relations are a part of the basic process of healing. . . . Ignoring these factors is not an error of ethics or courtesy; it is a scientific error (p. 4).

## THE NATURE OF THE PATIENT-PRACTITIONER RELATIONSHIP

It is curious that the term "relationship" has been used to describe what goes on between a physician and a patient. Some people have preferred to use the more neutral term "encounter" (Anderson & Helm, 1979) or the term "health transaction" (Stone, 1979) to capture its more business-oriented or problem-centered side. The concept of relationship does fit, however, because it captures the essential elements of what goes on in all relationships: Two people come together and enter into an agreement to engage in some form of exchange with the purpose of accomplishing one or more goals. When a patient and practitioner enter into a relationship, their goals may be well defined or vague; mutually agreed upon or not; and the interaction may differ in terms of its length, commitment, or intensity. Still, a bond is formed between the two participants about a key issue for them both, the patient's health (Krupat, 1983).

## The Szasz-Hollender Models

In a classic paper, Szasz and Hollender (1956) have described three different types or models of patient-practitioner relationship. In the first, the model of activity-passivity, a great asymmetry of power exists, almost like the relationship between a parent and a very young child. The doctor is in complete control, and the patient is passive, little more than a work object to whom things are done. The treatment of the patient is almost totally determined by the physician and takes place independent of any preferences or contributions of the patient. Clinically, this might be appropriate in cases of acute trauma where the patient is bleeding, or when the patient is anesthetized or in a coma.

The second model, guidance-cooperation, underlies much of modern medical practice, especially in the treatment of acute illness. In this model, the patient's thoughts, feelings, and desires are made known, yet they still only serve as background for the choice of the physician. The patient has a problem and seeks answers from a knowledgeable health professional, readily willing to cooperate with the solution generated. An asymmetry of power still exists, but in contrast to the activity-passivity model, it is closer to that between a parent and adolescent.

The third model is mutual participation. This relationship is characterized by mutual respect, information sharing, and a decision-making process in which both participants have equal input. This is the sort of adult-to-adult partnership more likely found in the treatment of chronic disease, and it is often advocated by those who have taken a more activist stance.

## The Consumer Model

Although it is difficult to estimate how common each of these models has become, there has been a clear trend away from patient passivity. The old authority relationship in which absolute trust was placed in the physician is slowly but surely eroding, and in its place we see one in which the physician's automatic right to govern is being challenged, and the patient's rights to participate and decide are being demanded (Haug & Lavin, 1983). Conceptualizing these models somewhat differently, Roter and Hall (1992), have included a consumerist model, which was not even considered by Szasz and Hollender when they were writing in the 1950s (see Table 1).

The consumerist model goes one step beyond the mutual participation model in reversing the balance of power between patient and practitioner. It envisions a health care relationship in which the practitioner is more of a skilled consultant who responds to the directives and needs of an informed and increasingly skeptical health care consumer. The consumerist model has been embraced by many but criticized by others for going too far. Its critics argue that those who take this orientation may underutilize the health

**TABLE 1**  Types of Doctor-Patient Relationships

| Patient Control | Physician Control | |
| --- | --- | --- |
| | Low | High |
| Low | Default | Paternalism |
| High | Consumerist | Mutuality |

Source: Roter, S. L., & Hall, J. A., 1992, Doctors talking with patients—Patients talking with doctors, Westport, CT: Auburn House.

professional's skills and expertise, placing themselves in a position of conflict and lack of trust (Steward & Roter, 1989).

*Patient versus Disease Centeredness*

Parallel to the Szasz-Hollender models, which focus on the issues of power and control, other researchers have looked at this relationship from a different angle, contrasting a patient-centered style with a disease-centered orientation (Henbest & Stewart, 1990; Byrne & Long, 1976; Mishler, 1984). The *disease-centered* perspective is dominated by "the voice of medicine" (Mishler, 1984). It reflects a scientific and detached attitude, in which the physician's main goals are to understand the patient's problem in relation to organic pathology and to make an accurate diagnosis. The focus is on *the body* rather than *the person*, wherein the physician determines what information is relevant and what is not. If the patient is to gain an understanding of the problem it is by entering into and accepting the practitioner's perspective on the problem.

A patient-centered orientation implies a more participatory or partnership-oriented relationship (Balint et al., 1970; Levenstein et al, 1989). In adopting this style, "the physician tries to enter the patient's world, to see the illness through the patient's eyes by behavior that invites and facilitates openness." (Levenstein et al., 1989, p. 111) Four key elements in this approach are: (a) understanding patients' ideas about what is wrong with them; (b) eliciting their feelings about their illness, especially their fears; (c) determining the impact of their problems on their everyday functioning; and (d) exploring their expectations about what should be done (Weston, Brown, & Steward, 1989).

## PATIENT SATISFACTION

At the heart of the discussion of patient-practitioner relations are two basic questions: To what extent are people satisfied with the medical care that they receive? And what aspects or elements are they most satisfied and dissatisfied with? These questions have been difficult to answer for several reasons. First, different studies of satisfaction have defined and measured satisfaction in unique ways, making cross-study comparisons difficult. Second, the degree of satisfaction found differs somewhat depending on how specifically the

**TABLE 2** Overall Ranking of Satisfaction with 10 Specific Aspects of Medical Care Based on 107 Studies

| Aspects | Rank |
| --- | --- |
| Humaneness | 1 |
| Competence | 2 |
| Outcome | 3 |
| Facilities | 4 |
| Continuity of care | 5 |
| Access | 6 |
| Informativeness | 7 |
| Cost | 8 |
| Bureaucracy | 9 |
| Attention to psychosocial problems | 10 |

Source: Hall, J. A., & Dornan, M. C., (1988b).

question is asked. The more specific the question ("How satisfied are you with your last visit with your doctor?" versus "Are you satisfied with the health care system?"), the more satisfied people report that they are (Hall & Dornan, 1988a). Third, the level of satisfaction reported depends on whom is asked, and when (Ross, Wheaton, & Duff, 1981).

Recently, Judith Hall, Debra Roter, and their colleagues (Hall & Dornan, 1990; 1988a; 1988b; Hall, Roter & Katz, 1988) have applied the method of meta-analysis, a statistical technique that allows the results of many different studies to be combined and compared, to summarize the results of more than 200 satisfaction studies. Overall, they found very high levels of satisfaction, averaging 81% and ranging from a high of 99% to a low of 43% (Hall & Dornan, 1988a).

Satisfaction has been divided into many different categories (Ware & hays, 1988; Ware, Davies-Avery, & Stewart, 1978; Pascoe, 1983). In Table 2, we present the 10 specific aspects of care evaluated by Hall and Dornan ranked according to patient satisfaction. In spite of concerns about the interpersonal skills of physicians, humaneness is the factor with which patients are most satisfied, followed closely by the competence of physicians and the outcomes of care. In the bottom half, we find two types of issues. The first involves the patient's relationship to the system, as represented by concerns over cost, access to care, and bureaucracy. The second deals with the amount of information patients receive, and whether they are treated by their doctors as something more than a narrowly defined medical problem.

## DOCTOR-PATIENT COMMUNICATION

Patients seem to be least satisfied with the degree to which doctors address their psychosocial concerns, treating them as whole people within the broader context of their lives. For instance, a study of 75 women who were receiving radiotherapy following a mastectomy showed that one third developed sexual problems and one quarter showed signs of clinical depression within a year of their operations. However, none of the sexual problems were identified by their physicians, and only half of the depressed women were identified and treated for this problem (McGuire et al., 1978). It is easy to see how these psychological and sexual problems might be missed if we assume that the physicians were taking a disease-centered approach. When physicians define the problem narrowly according to the biomedical model, they may look no further than the malignancy and miss other important aspects or consequences of the illness experience that are not technically a part of the physical ailment.

*Information Sharing*

Information giving, which is the single variable that best predicts satisfaction, ranked 8 out of the 10 dimensions measured (Hall, Roter, & Katz, 1988). During a typical visit, doctors and patients do not spend a great deal of time together, an average of 16.5 minutes according to research by Howard Waitzkin (1984). Of that time, 1 minute and 18 seconds, less than 10%, involves information given by doctor to patient. Still, when asked how much time they had spent giving information, on the average the doctors responded almost 9 minutes, overestimating by a factor of almost 7. And when asked how much information their patients wanted, the physicians underestimated the amount desired in 65% of the cases.

Although it might be easy to blame doctors for this lack of information giving, patients typically ask no more than 3 or 4 questions per visit (Roter, 1984), and question-asking time ranges form 0 to 97 seconds, averaging an unbelievably low 8 seconds (Waitzkin, 1984). Still, patients report that they would like more information about their diagnosis, the prognosis for recovery, and the origins of their condition (Kindelan & Kent, 1987), as well as more complete disclosure about the risks of procedures and medications (Faden et al., 1981; Keown, Slovic, & Lichtenstein, 1984).

**Information and power** To explain the lack of time allotted to information giving and question asking, a broad range of possibilities exists. Several noted researchers (Waitzkin, 1985; Waitzkin & Stoeckle, 1976; Freidson, 1970) believe that doctors avoid giving information and leave patients in a state of uncertainty to preserve power, that the doctor-patient relationship is a "micropolitical situation" in which the doctor withholds information to maintain dominance and patients seek it to challenge that dominance. Yet, to the extent that the doctor and patient are in a "struggle" over information, much of the evidence suggests that patients do not put up much of a fight. Many patients hesitate to ask for information, clarification, or additional information for fear of appearing ignorant, while others fear that they are taking time from more pressing requirements of the doctor or other more needy patients (Tuckett et al, 1985).

Although some doctors may withhold information to maintain power, the patient's desire for information is not necessarily accompanied by a desire to challenge the physician's right to make decisions (Beisecker & Beisecker, 1990). When technical knowledge is needed for decision making, people are generally willing to let the person with more expertise do so. However, when a choice must be made between equally effective treatments, in this case patients want some control over the decision (Kaplan, 1991; Pitts et al. 1991).

**Patient characteristics**   Another explanation for the lack of information exchange between patient and provider focuses on the characteristics of the patient (Clark, Potter, & McKinlay, 1991). In general, patients who are white, older, or female, as well as those with greater education and from the middle and upper classes, are given more time, ask more questions, and get more explanations. The more serious the diagnosis and the longer the doctor and patient have known each other, the greater the exchange of information as well (Hall, Roter, & Katz, 1988; Waitzkin, 1985). These findings suggest that physicians probably spend more time with people with whom they are most comfortable, and they dispense more or less information according to how much they believe patients want or can benefit from it. However, these assessments may often be inaccurate when they are based on stereotypes about race, sex, and class.

### Quality of Doctor-Patient Communication

More than the mere *quantity* of information conveyed,what can we say about the *quality* of doctor-patient communication? In a classic study, Barbara Korsch and her colleagues (Korsch, Gozzi, & Francis, 1968) tape recorded 800 pediatric visits in a hospital outpatient clinic and then conducted follow-up interviews with the mothers. The communication tone of the visits was generally very technical and narrowly focused—that is to say, disease centered. The mothers reported that their emotional concerns were rarely addressed, and approximately one quarter did not have the opportunity to express the single most important problem on their minds. Twenty percent felt they were not given a clear explanation of what was wrong with their child, and almost half were unsure of what had caused their child's illness. Although these interactions involved white American, middle-class physicians with patients who were predominantly poor and black, similar findings have been reported in a wide variety of settings and with different patient populations in different countries (Ben-Sira, 1985; Clark, Potter, & McKinlay, 1991; Pendleton & Bochner, 1980).

Even when information is conveyed from doctor to patient, it is not always understood. In another classic study, Bonnie Svarstad (1976) observed patients at a neighborhood health center reputed to be one of the best of its kind. She found that more than three out of four times the physicians failed to give explicit instructions about how prescribed drugs should be taken, and when they did, the instructions were often ambiguous. In fact, more than half of the patients interviewed misunderstood the very purpose for which they were taking their medications. Some of the patients who had received prescriptions to control their blood pressure reported that the drug was meant to treat symptoms as diverse as asthma, palpitations, and lower back pain. Even more notably, Svarstad reported that many times she herself could not understand the directions offered to the patients. Even for something as basic as naming a condition, Hadlow and Pitts (1991) report that patients often misunderstand a range of terms such as "eating disorder," "migraine," and "stroke."

**Medical jargon**  Some of the failure of communication between patient and practitioner can be traced to the use of medical jargon. Defined as the specialized or technical language of a trade, jargon allows doctors to speak to one another in a strange dialect that is all their own. Pediatrician Perri Klass (1987), telling of her experience in learning this new language, offers one such example:

> "Mrs. Tolstoy is your basic L.O.L. in N.A.D. admitted for a soft rule-out M.I.," the intern announces. I scribble that on my patient list. In other words Mrs. Tolstoy is a Little Old lady in No Apparent Distress who is in the hospital to make sure she hasn't had a heart attack (rule out myocardial infarction). And we think it's unlikely that she has had a heart attack (a soft rule-out). (p. 73)

Physicians even use terms that laypeople cannot understand even when there are simpler ways of saying things. They might say, "He had a pneumonectomy" instead of, "He had a lung removed." At other times they may communicate almost completely in numbers, noting that "his $PO_2$ is 45; $pCO_2$, 40; and pH 7.4" (Johnson, 1980). After a while, "doctor talk" becomes so natural that physicians forget when they are speaking it.

Jargon serves several purposes for health professionals. It allows them to communicate with one another in a fast, efficient manner and creates a sense of professional spirit and identification among people who are working under daily stress. Jargon helps to distance health professionals from the strong emotions that come with their work, yet it can distance them from their patients as well. When patients hear their doctors talking to one another about them in technical language, or when they are offered explanations in terms that they cannot understand, it makes them feel left out and leaves them frustrated.

Waitzkin (1984) has recommended that the communication ability of physicians be assessed according to how often physicians use *multilevel explanations* and *nondiscrepant responses*. Multilevel explanations offer a technical explanation accompanied by an explanation in everyday terms. In this way the physician educates the patient in the jargon, while at the same time offering understandable information. Nondiscrepant responses are answers given by physicians at the same level of technicality as the question asked by the patient. By giving complex answers to complex questions (and vice versa), physicians indicate that they have listened carefully, and they offer useful information by speaking in a language that matches the patient's level of sophistication.

**Nonverbal communication** In addition to the content of verbal communication, we have become increasingly aware of the importance of nonverbal communication. The messages that gestures, tone of voice, posture, and facial expressions convey can be every bit as important as those communicated by words. Physician behaviors that express a warm social climate such as sitting close, maintaining eye contact, leaning forward, and nodding in response to patient comments are associated with patient satisfaction (Hall, Roter, & Katz, 1988). In addition, physicians who have greater nonverbal sensitivity both in their ability to decode patients' emotions and to express their own feelings have more satisfied patients (DiMatteo, Hays, & Prince, 1986; DiMatteo et al., 1980; Friedman, 1982).

In sum, what do patients want from their doctors? A simple answer is difficult because patients differ according to their orientations, values, and needs. Some desire an active, involved relationship while others are satisfied to remain passive (Haug & Lavin, 1983; Krantz, Baum, & Weideman, 1980; Woodward & Wallston, 1987). However, we can make some generalizations that hold for a large part of the populace. People want to be treated with warmth and respect, to be given good technical care but related to as "whole people," not just as medical conditions. When they begin to interact with a physician in what is known as the history section of a medical encounter, they want the opportunity to express their concerns in their own words. And at the end, in the conclusion section, they want to be provided with information and have the chance to engage in feedback exchanges that build a partnership between doctor and patient (Stiles et al., 1979a, 1979b).

## IMPROVING DOCTOR-PATIENT RELATIONS

Doctor-patient communication and patient satisfaction are not just topics of academic interest. Dissatisfied patients are more likely to shop around for doctors, to change health plans, to fail to follow medical advice, and even to sue (Kaplan & Ware, 1989). Conversely, greater patient involvement and satisfaction have been directly associated with better patient health outcomes (Greenfield, Kaplan, & Ware, 1985; Greenfield et al., 1988).

Several programs to improve satisfaction and communication have been initiated. One focus has been on the training of physicians. Medical schools such as those at Harvard, the University of New Mexico, and McMaster in

Canada have been leaders in integrating the behavioral sciences into medical study and in highlighting the teaching of communication skills (Nooman, Schmidt, & Ezzat, 1990; Tosteson, 1990). At Long Beach Memorial Medical Center in California, residents are actually required to spend time as hospital patients to truly appreciate the patient's perspective.

Programs working with practicing physicians have also been effective. At the Johns Hopkins Hospital, a series of tutorial sessions were set up for physicians using the Health Belief Model as a guide for interviewing. The doctors were asked to inquire about patients' attitudes, beliefs and perceptions concerning their condition rather than focusing on physical signs and complications. After a single session, the physicians in this program were found to spend more time on patient teaching and to generate greater patient knowledge than physicians who did not receive this training (Inui, Yourtee, & Williamson, 1976). Bertakis (1977) encouraged physicians to end their medical sessions by having patients repeat information in their own words, clarifying anything that was confusing or adding relevant information that was omitted. When questioned later on, patients were not only more satisfied, but recalled 20% more information than a control group.

Other programs have focused on the patient rather than on the physician. Roter (1984) encouraged patients to identify questions they would like answered during their visit. She reported that this intervention increased question asking compared to a control group, although on the average patients did not end up asking as many questions as they initially intended. More recently, Thompson, Nanni, & Schwankovsky (1990) had one group of women write down questions to ask their doctor before a visit. A second group received a brief note from their doctor encouraging question asking, and a third (control) received no special treatment. The researchers found that both intervention groups were more likely to ask what was on their minds, felt more in control, and were also more satisfied with their visits.

Using a more comprehensive approach, Greenfield, Kaplan, & Ware (1985) reviewed patients' medical records with them, went over methods of treatment, and coached them in how to discuss and negotiate with their doctors. Patients who received this 20-minute coaching session were significantly more active and assertive with their doctors, received more information, and indicated that they liked taking a more active role. Most important, they reported fewer physical limitations during the 8 weeks following the study.

Programs such as these, which involve only small investments of time on the part of patients and doctors, have been quite successful and are likely to grow in the future. They acknowledge that every encounter between a doctor and patient represents a therapeutic opportunity, and that technical skill and knowledge must be accompanied by equal amounts of caring and communication. As we incorporate this into everyday practice, the doctor-patient relationship will improve, and so will medical care.

# References

Anderson, W. T. & Helm, D. T. (1979). The physician-patient encounter: A process of reality negotiation. In E. G. Jaco (Ed.) *Patients, physicians, and illness* (3rd ed.). New York: Free Press.

Balint, M., Hung, J., Joyce, D., Marinker, M., and Woodcock, J. (1970). *Treatment or diagnosis: A study of repeat prescription in general practice.* Toronto: J. B. Lippincott.

Beisecker, A. E. and Beisecker, T. D. (1990). Patient information-seeking behaviors when communicating with doctors. *Medical Care, 28,* 19–28.

Ben-Sira, Z. (1985). Primary medical care and coping with stress and disease: The inclination of primary care practitioners to demonstrate affective behavior. *Social Science and Medicine, 21,* 485–498.

Bertakis, K. D. (1977). The communication of information from physician to patient: A method for increasing patient retention and satisfaction. *Journal of Family Practice, 5,* 217–222.

Bloom, J. R. (1982). Social support, accommodation to stress, and adjustment to breast cancer. *Social Science and Medicine, 16,* 1329–1338.

Byrne, P. S. & Long, B. E. L. (1976). *Doctors talking to patients.* London: Royal College of General Practitioners.

Clark, J. A., Potter, D. A. & McKinlay, J. B. (1991). Bringing social structure back into clinical decision-making. *Social Science and Medicine, 32,* 853–866.

DiMatteo, M. R. (1979). A social psychological analysis of physician-patient rapport: Toward a science of the art of medicine. *Journal of Social Issues, 35,* 12–33.

DiMatteo, M. R., Hays, R. D., & Prince, L. M. (1986). Relationship of physicians' nonverbal skill to patient satisfaction, appointment non-compliance, and physician workload. *Health Psychology, 5,* 581–594.

DiMatteo, M. R., Taranta, A., Friedman, H. S., & Prince, L. M. (1980). Predicting patient satisfaction from physicians' nonverbal communication skills. *Medical Care, 18,* 376–387.

Faden, R. R., Becker, C., Lewis, C., Freeman, J., & Faden, A. I. (1981). Disclosure of information to patients in medical care. *Medical Care, 19,* 718–733.

Freidson, E. (1970). *Profession of medicine. A study in the sociology of applied knowledge.* New York: Dodd, Mead.

Friedman, H. S. (1982). Nonverbal communication in medical interaction. In H. S. Friedman & M. R. DiMatteo (Eds.) *Interpersonal issues in health care.* New York: Academic Press.

Friedman, H. S. & DiMatteo, M. R. (1979). Health care as an interpersonal process. *Journal of Social Issues, 35,* 1–11.

Greenfield, S., Kaplan, S. H., & Ware, J. E., Jr. (1985). Expanding patient involvement in care: Effects on patient outcomes. *Annals of Internal Medicine, 102,* 520–528.

Greenfield, S., Kaplan, S. H., Ware, J. E., Jr., Yano, E. M., & Frank, H. J. (1988). Patient participation in medical care: Effects on blood sugar control and quality of life in diabetes. *Journal of General Internal Medicine, 3,* 448–457.

Hadlow, J., & Pitts, M. (1991). The understanding of common health terms by doctors, nurses, and patients. *Social Science and Medicine, 32,* 193–196.

Hall, J. A., & Dornan, M. C. (1988a). Meta-analysis of satisfaction with medical care: Description of research done in and analysis of overall satisfaction levels. *Social Science and Medicine, 26,* 637–644.

Hall, J. A., & Dornan, M. C. (1988b). What patients like about their medical care and how often they are asked: A meta-analysis of the satisfaction literature. *Social Science and Medicine, 27,* 935–939.

Hall, J. A., & Dornan, M. C. (1990). Patient sociodemographic characteristics as predictors of satisfaction with medical care: A meta-analysis. *Social Science and Medicine, 30,* 811–818.

Hall, J. A., Roter, D. L., & Katz, N. R. (1988). Meta-analysis of correlates of provider behavior in medical encounters. *Medical Care, 26,* 657–675.

Haug, M. R., & Lavin, B. (1983). *Consumerism in medicine: Challenging physician authority.* Beverly Hills, CA: Sage.

Henbest, R. J. & Stewart, M. (1990). Patient-centeredness in the consultation. 2: Does it really make a difference? *Family Practice, 7,* 28–33.

Inui, T. S., Yourtee, E. L., & Williamson, J. W. (1976). Improved outcomes in hypertension after physician tutorials: A controlled trial. *Annals of Internal Medicine, 84,* 646–651.

Johnson, D. (1980). Doctor talk. In L. Michaels & C. Ricks (Eds.), *The state of the language.* Berkeley, CA: University of California.

Kaplan, R. M. (1991). Health-related quality of life in patient decision-making. *Journal of Social Issues, 47,* 69–90.

Kaplan, S. H., & Ware, J. E., Jr. (1989). The patient's role in health care and quality assessment. In N. Goldfield & D. B. Nash (Eds.), *Providing quality care.* Philadelphia: American college of Physicians.

Keown, C., Slovic, P., & Lichtenstein, S. (1984). Attitudes of physicians, pharmacists, and laypersons toward seriousness and need for disclosure of prescription drug side effects. *Health Psychology, 3,* 1–2.

Kindelan, K., & Kent, G. (1987). Concordance between patients' information preferences and general practitioners' perceptions. *Psychology and Health, 1,* 399–409.

Klass, P. A. (1987). *Not an entirely benign procedure.* New York: Signet.

Korsch, B. M., Gozzi, E. K., & Francis, V. (1968). Gaps in doctor-patient communication. 1. Doctor-patient interaction and patient satisfaction. *Pediatrics, 42,* 855–871.

Krantz, D. S., Baum, A., & Weideman, M. V. (1980). Assessment of preferences for self-treatment and information in health care. *Journal of Personality and Social Psychology, 39,* 977–990.

Krupat, E. (1983). The doctor-patient relationship: A social psychological analysis. In R. F. Kidd & M. J. Saks (Eds.), *Advances in Applied Social Psychology* (Vol. 2). Hillsdale, NJ: Erlbaum.

Levenstein, J. H., Brown, J. B., Weston, W. W., Stewart, M., McCracken, E. C., & McWhinney, I. (1989). Patient-centered clinical interviewing. In M. Steward & D. Roter (Eds.), *Communicating with medical patients.* Beverly Hills, CA: Sage.

Maguire, G. P., Lee, E. G., Barington, D. J., Kuchemann, C. S., Crabtree, R. J., & Cornell, C. E. (1978). Psychiatric morbidity in the first year after mastectomy. *British Medical Journal, 1,* 963–965.

Mishler, E. G. (1984). *The discourse of medicine: Dialectics of medical interviews.* Norwood, NJ: Ablex.

Nooman, Z. M., Schmidt, H. G., & Ezzat, E. S. (1990). *Innovation in medical education: An evaluation of its present status.* New York: Springer-Verlag.

Pascoe, G. C. (1983). Patient satisfaction in primary health care: A literature review and analysis. *Evaluation and Program Planning, 6,* 185–210.

Pendleton, D., & Bochner, S. (1980). The communication of medical information as a function of patients' social class. *Social Science and Medicine, 14A,* 669–673.

Pitts, J. S., Schwankovsky, L., Thompson, S. C., Cruzen, D. E. Everett, J., & Freedman, D. (1991, August). *Do people want to make medical decisions?* Paper presented at the annual meeting of the American Psychological Association, San Francisco.

Ross, L.E., Wheaton, B., & Duff, R.S. (1981). Client satisfaction and the organization of medical practice: Why time counts. *Journal of Health and Social Behavior, 22,* 243–255.

Roter, D. L. (1984). Patient question asking in physician-patient interaction. *Health Psychology, 3,* 395–410.

Roter, D. L., & Hall, J. A. (1992). *Doctors talking with patients—patients talking with doctors.* Westport, CT: Auburn House.

Stewart, M., & Roter, D. (1989). Introduction. In M. Stewart & D. Roter (Eds.), *Communicating with medical patients.* Beverly Hills, CA: Sage.

Stiles, W. B., Putnam, S. M., James, S. A., & Wolf, M. H. (1979a). Dimensions of patient and physician roles in medical screening interviews. *Social Science and Medicine, 13A,* 335–341.

Stiles, W. B., Putnam, S. M., Wolf, M. H., & James, S. A. (1979b). Interaction exchange structure and patient satisfaction with medical interviews. *Medical Care, 17,* 667–681.

Stone, G. C. (1979). Health and the health system: A historical overview and conceptual framework. In G. C. Stone, F. Cohen, & N. E. Adler (Eds.), *Health psychology—A handbook* (pp. 1–17). San Francisco: Jossey-Bass.

Svarstad, B. (1976). Physician-patient communication and patient conformity with medical advice. In D. Mechanic (Ed.), *The growth of bureaucratic medicine.* New York: Wiley.

Szasz, T. S., & Hollender, M. H. (1956). The basic models of the doctor-patient relationship. *Archives of Internal Medicine, 35,* 156–184.

Thompson, S. C., Nanni, C., & Schwankovsky, L. (1990). Patient-oriented interventions to improve communication in a medical visit. *Health Psychology, 9,* 390–404.

Tosteson, D. C. (1990). New pathways in general medical education. *New England Journal of Medicine, 322,* 234–238.

Tuckett, H. D., Boulton, M., Olson, C., & Williams, A. (1985). *Meetings between experts: An approach to sharing ideas in medical consultations.* London: Tavistock.

Waitzkin, H. (1984). Doctor-patient communication. *Journal of American Medical Association,* *252,* 2441–2446.

Waitzkin, H. (1985). Information giving in medical care. *Journal of Health and Social Behavior,* *26,* 81–101.

Waitzkin, H., & Stoeckle, J. D. (1976). Information control and the micropolitics of health care: Summary of an ongoing research project. *Social Science and Medicine, 10,* 263–276.

Ware, J. E., Jr., Davies-Avery, A., & Stewart, A. L. (1978). The measurement and meaning of patient satisfaction. *Health and Medical Care Services Review, 1,* 2–15.

Ware, J. E., Jr., & Hays, R. D. (1988). Methods for measuring patient satisfaction with specific medical encounters. *Medical Care, 26,* 393–402.

Weston, W. W., Brown, J. B., & Stewart, M. (1989). Patient-centered interviewing. Part I: Understanding patients' experiences. *Canadian Family Physicians, 35,* 147–151.

Elizabeth F. Loftus
John C. Palmer

# Reconstruction of Automobile Destruction: An Example of the Interaction Between Language and Memory

The article by Loftus and Palmer represents a simple demonstration of the way in which the reconstruction of an event in memory can be biased. Its findings are so clear and implications so strong that it is one of the most cited pieces of research in the area of eyewitness testimony. Loftus and Palmer showed students films of auto accidents and then asked them how fast the cars were going at the time. By using verbs such as "collided" or "smashed" versus "bumped" or "hit," they were able to affect the speed that people reported, and, even though there was *no* broken glass in the film, a week later those who were asked about the cars that "smashed" were more likely to recall having seen glass at the scene.

How accurately do we remember the details of a complex event, like a traffic accident, that has happened in our presence? More specifically, how well do we do when asked to estimate some numerical quantity such as how long the accident took, how fast the cars were traveling, or how much time elapsed between the sounding of a horn and the moment of collision?

It is well documented that most people are markedly inaccurate in reporting such numerical details as time, speed, and distance (Bird, 1927; Whipple, 1909). For example, most people have difficulty estimating the duration of an event, with some research indicating that the tendency is to overestimate the duration of events which are complex (Block, 1974; Marshall, 1969; Ornstein, 1969). The judgment of speed is especially difficult, and practically every automobile accident results in huge variations from one witness to another as to how fast a vehicle was actually traveling (Gardner, 1933). In one test administered to Air Force personnel who knew in advance that they would be questioned about the speed of a moving automobile, estimates ranged from 10 to 50 mph. The car they watched was actually going only 12 mph (Marshall, 1969, p. 23).

Given the inaccuracies in estimates of speed, it seems likely that there are variables which are potentially powerful in terms of influencing these estimates. The present research was conducted to investigate one such variable, namely, the phrasing of the question used to elicit the speed judgment. Some questions are clearly more suggestive than others. This fact of life has resulted in the legal concept of a leading question and in legal rules indicating when leading questions are allowed (*Supreme Court Reporter*, 1973). A leading question is simply one that, either by its form or content, suggests to the witness what answer is desired or leads him to the desired answer.

In the present study, subjects were shown films of traffic accidents and then they answered questions about the accident. The subjects were interrogated about the speed of the vehicles in one of several ways. For example, some subjects were asked, "About how fast were the cars going when they hit each other?" while others were asked, "About how fast were the cars going when they smashed into each other?" As Fillmore (1971) and Bransford and McCarrell (in press) have noted, *hit* and *smashed* may involve specification of differential rates of movement. Furthermore, the two verbs may also involve differential specification of the likely consequences of the events to which they are referring. The impact of the accident is apparently gentler for *hit* than for *smashed*.

## EXPERIMENT I

*Method*

Forty-five students participated in groups of various sizes. Seven films were shown, each depicting a traffic accident. These films were segments from longer driver's education films borrowed from the Evergreen Safety Council and the Seattle Police Department. The length of the film segments ranged form 5 to 30 sec. Following each film, the subjects received a questionnaire asking them first to, "give an account of the accident you have just seen," and then to answer a series of specific questions about the accident. The critical question was the one that interrogated the subject about the speed of the vehicles involved in the collision. Nine subjects were asked, "About how fast were the cars going when they hit each other?" Equal numbers of the remaining subjects were interrogated with the verbs *smashed, collided, bumped*, and *contacted* in place of *hit*. The entire experiment lasted about an hour and a half. A different ordering of the films was presented to each group of subjects.

*Results*

Table 1 presents the mean speed estimates for the various verbs. Some information about the accuracy of subjects' estimates can be obtained from our

**TABLE 1**  Speed Estimates for the Verbs Used in Experiment 1

| Verb | Mean speed estimate |
| --- | --- |
| Smashed | 40.8 |
| Collided | 39.3 |
| Bumped | 38.1 |
| Hit | 34.0 |
| Contacted | 31.8 |

data. Four of the seven films were staged crashes; the original purpose of these films was to illustrate what can happen to human beings when cars collide at various speeds. One collision took place at 20 mph, one at 30, and two at 40. The mean estimates of speed for these four films were: 37.7, 36.2, 39.7, and 36.1 mph, respectively. In agreement with previous work, people are not very good at judging how fast a vehicle was actually traveling.

*Discussion*

The results of this experiment indicate that the form of a question (in this case, changes in a single word) can markedly and systematically affect a witness's answer to that question. The actual speed of the vehicles controlled little variance in subject reporting, while the phrasing of the question controlled considerable variance.

Two interpretations of this finding are possible. First, it is possible that the differential speed estimates result merely from response-bias factors. A subject is uncertain whether to say 30 mph or 40 mph, for example, and the verb *smashed* biases his response towards the higher estimate. A second interpretation is that the question form causes a change in the subject's memory representation of the accident. The very *smashed* may change a subject's memory such that he "sees" the accident as being more severe than it actually was. If this is the case, we might expect subjects to "remember" other details that did not actually occur, but are commensurate with an accident occurring at higher speeds. The second experiment was designed to provide additional insights into the origin in the differential speed estimates.

## EXPERIMENT II

*Method*

One hundred and fifty students participated in this experiment, in groups of various sizes. A film depicting a multiple car accident was shown, followed by a questionnaire. The film lasted less than 1 min; the accident in the film lasted 4 sec. At the end of the film, the subjects received a questionnaire asking them first to describe the accident in their own words, and then to answer a series of questions about the accident. The critical question was the one that interrogated the subject about the speed of the vehicles. Fifty subjects were asked, "About how fast were the cars going when they smashed into each other?" Fifty subjects were asked, "About how fast were the cars going when they hit each other?" Fifty subjects were not interrogated about vehicular speed.

One week later, the subjects returned and without viewing the film again they answered a series of questions about the accident. The critical question here was, "Did you see any broken glass?" which the subjects answered by checking "yes" and "no." This question was embedded in a list totalling 10 questions, and it appeared in a random position in the list. There was no broken glass in the accident, but, since broken glass is commensurate with accidents occurring at high speed, we expected that the subjects who had been asked the *smashed* question might more often say "yes" to this critical question.

*Results*

The mean estimate of speed for subjects interrogated with *smashed* was 10.46 mph; with *hit* the estimate was 8.00 mph. Table 2 presents the distribution of "yes" and "no" responses for the *smashed, hit,* and control subjects. The probability of saying "yes" to the question about broken glass is .32 when the verb *smashed* is used, and .14 with *hit.* Thus *smashed* leads both to more "yes" responses and to higher speed estimates. It appears to be the case that the effect of the verb is mediated at least in part by the speed estimate. The question now arises: Is *smashed* doing anything else besides increasing the estimate of speed? To answer this, the function relating P(Y) to speed estimate was calculated separately for *smashed* and *hit.* If the speed estimate is the only way in which effect of verb is mediated, then for a given speed estimate, P(Y) should be independent of the verbs. Table 3 shows that this is not the case. P(Y) is lower for *hit* than for *smashed*; the difference between the two verbs ranges from .3 for estimates of 1–5 mph to .18 for estimates of 6–10 mph. The average difference between the two curves is about .12.

**DISCUSSION**

To reiterate, we have first of all provided an additional demonstration of something that has been known for some time, namely, that the way a question

**TABLE 2**  Distribution of "Yes" and "No" Responses to the Question, "Did You See Any Broken Glass?"

| | Verb condition | | |
|---|---|---|---|
| Response | Smashed | Hit | Control |
| Yes | 16 | 7 | 6 |
| No | 34 | 43 | 44 |

**TABLE 3** Probability of Saying "Yes" to, "Did You See Any Broken Glass?" Conditionalized on Speed Estimates

| Verb condition | Speed estimate (mph) | | | |
|---|---|---|---|---|
| | 1–5 | 6–10 | 11–15 | 16–20 |
| Smashed | .09 | .27 | .41 | .62 |
| Hit | .06 | .09 | .25 | .50 |

is asked can enormously influence the answer that is given. In this instance, the question, "About how fast were the cars going when they smashed into each other?" led to higher estimates of speed than the same question asked with the verb *smashed* replaced by *hit*. Furthermore, this seemingly small change had consequences for how questions are answered a week after the original event occurred.

As a framework for discussing these results, we would like to propose that two kinds of information go into one's memory for some complex occurrence. The first is information gleaned during the perception of the original event; the second is external information supplied after the fact. Over time, information from these two sources may be integrated in such a way that we are unable to tell from which source some specific detail is recalled. All we have is one "memory."

Discussing the present experiments in these terms, we propose that the subject first forms some representation of the accident he has witnessed. The experimenter then, while asking, "About how fast were the cars going when they smashed into each other?" supplies a piece of external information, namely, that the cars did indeed smash into each other. When these two pieces of information are integrated, the subject has a memory of an accident that was more severe than in fact it was. Since broken glass is commensurate with a severe accident, the subject is more likely to think that broken glass was present.

There is some connection between the present work and earlier work on the influence of verbal labels on memory for visually presented form stimuli. A classic study in psychology showed that when subjects are asked to reproduce a visually presented form, their drawings tend to err in the direction of a more familiar object suggested by a verbal label initially associated with the to-be-remembered form (Carmichael, Hogan, & Walter, 1932). More recently, Daniel (1972) showed that recognition memory, as well as reproductive memory, was similarly affected by verbal labels, and he concluded that the verbal label causes a shift in the memory strength of forms which are better representatives of the label.

When the experimenter asks the subject, "About how fast were the cars going when they smashed into each other?", he is effectively labeling the accident a smash. Extrapolating the conclusions of Daniel to this situation, it is natural to conclude that the label, smash, causes a shift in the memory representation of the accident in the direction of being more similar to a representation suggested by the verbal label.

# References

Bird, C. The influence of the press upon the accuracy of report. *Journal of Abnormal and Social Psychology*, 1927, 22, 123–129.

Block, R. A. Memory and the experience of duration in retrospect. *Memory & Cognition*, 1974, 2, 153–160.

Bransford, J. D., & McCarrell, N.S. A sketch of a cognitive approach to comprehension: Some thoughts about understanding what it means to comprehend. In D. Palermo & W. Weimer (Eds.), *Cognition and the symbolic processes*. Washington, D.C.: V. H. Winston & Co., in press.

Carmichael, L., Hogan, H. P., & Walter, A. A. An experimental study of the effect of language on the reproduction of visually perceived form. *Journal of Experimental Psychology*, 1932, 15, 73–86.

Clark, H. H. The language-as-fixed-effect fallacy: A critique of language statistics in psychological research. *Journal of Verbal Learning and Verbal Behavior*, 1973, 12, 335–359.

Daniel, T. C. Nature of the effect of verbal labels on recognition memory for form. *Journal of Experimental Psychology*, 1972, 96, 152–157.

Fillmore, C. J. Types of lexical information. In D. D. Steinberg and L. A. Jakobovits (Eds.), *Semantics: An interdisciplinary reader in philosophy, linguistics, and psychology*. Cambridge: Cambridge University Press, 1971.

Gardner, D. S. The perception and memory of witnesses. *Cornell Law Quarterly*, 1933, 8, 391–409.

Marshall, J. *Law and psychology in conflict*. New York: Anchor Books, 1969.

Whipple, G. M. The observer as reporter: A survey of the psychology of testimony. *Psychological Bulletin*, 1909, 6, 153–170.

*Supreme Court Reported*, 1973, 3: Rules of Evidence for United State Courts and Magistrates.

Saul M. Kassin
Lawrence S. Wrightsman

# The American Jury on Trial: Inside the Jury Room

This selection by Kassin and Wrightsman is about jury deliberations, but it is just as much about the social psychology of
social influence and group behavior. Noting that opinions
can differ widely in a jury, the authors utilize basic theory and
research to explain some of the reasons behind the acceptance
of influence and allow us to understand better who accepts
influence from whom. The "sounds of deliberation" that they
discuss follow directly from the principles of conflict resolution and illustrate how these same concepts can describe the
stages that any groups, whether families or warring nations,
might follow in trying to come to a reasonable resolution.

It is often said that the distinctive power of the system is that the jury functions
as a *group*. Is it? How do jurors carrying different opinions manage to converge
on a single verdict? Indeed, what does transpire behind the closed doors of
the jury room? We will see that although the jury meets in total privacy, the
courts have articulated a clear vision of what the dynamics of deliberation
should look like. Basically, there are three components to this ideal.

The first component is one of independence and equality. No juror's vote
counts for more than any other juror's vote. A 12-person jury should thus
consist of 12 *independent* and *equal* individuals, each contributing his or her
own personal opinion to the final outcome. The courts attempt to foster this
ideal in a number of ways. For example, judges instruct jurors to refrain from
discussing the trial with each other until they retire for their deliberations. In
this way, each juror develops his or her own unique perspective on the case,
uncontaminated by others' views. This ensures not only the independence of
individual members but also the diversity of the group as a whole.

Unlike other task-oriented groups, the jury's role is ideally structured to
advance the cause of equal participation. The cardinal rule of jury decision
making is that verdicts be based only on the evidence introduced in open
court. By limiting the task as such, jurors are discouraged from basing their

arguments on private or outside sources of knowledge. Because they experience the same trial, and because they are provided with identical information, jurors are placed on an equal footing. To further promote equality, the courts often exclude from service people who are expected to exert a disproportionate amount of influence over other jurors. Lawyers or others who are particularly knowledgeable about trial-relevant subjects are thus excluded despite their otherwise welcome expertise. Several years ago, Edmund G. Brown, then Governor of California, was among those picked at random from a pool of 219 prospective jurors in Sacramento. At least publicly, nobody questioned his impartiality. But wouldn't his presence on the panel overwhelm other jurors? Despite the voir dire, the defense lawyer asked a prospective juror, "Would you hesitate to disagree with him in deliberation?" she replied, "No, I've disagreed with him before." In the end, Brown was seated on the jury and elected foreperson.

The second component of the deliberation ideal is an openness to informational influence. Once inside the jury room, jurors have a duty to interact and discuss the case. They should share information, exchange views, and debate the evidence. Thus, when an Indianapolis juror locked herself in the ladies' room after 20 hours of deliberation and refused to talk after having been called a "big mouth," the judge was forced to declare a mistrial. Two essential characteristics of an ideal jury follow from the requirement of deliberation. One is that jurors maintain an open mind, that each juror withhold judgment until "an impartial consideration of the evidence *with his fellow jurors.*" Openmindedness is such an important aspect of an ideal deliberation that if a juror dies before a verdict is announced, then the jury cannot return a verdict even if all the remaining jurors indicate that the deceased had agreed with their decision. The reasoning behind this rule is that "the jurors individually and collectively have the right to change their minds prior to the reception of the verdict."

The second is that consensus should be achieved through an exchange of information. Jurors should scrutinize their own views, be receptive to others', and allow themselves to be persuaded by rational argument. One juror advances a proposition; the others either accept it, challenge it, or modify it on publicly defensible grounds. As the Supreme Court put it almost a century ago, "The very object of the jury system is to secure unanimity by a comparison of views, and by arguments among the jurors themselves. . . . It cannot be that each juror should go to the jury-room with a blind determination that the verdict shall represent his opinion of the case at that moment; or that he should close his ears to the arguments of men who are equally honest and intelligent as himself."

The third component of the deliberation ideal follows from the second. Although juries should strive for a consensus of opinion, it should *not* be achieved through heavy-handed normative pressure. Obviously, jurors who dissent form the majority position should not be beaten, bullied, or harangued into submission. Indeed "no juror should surrender his honest conviction as to the weight or effect of the evidence solely because of the opinion of his fellow jurors, or for the mere purpose of returning a verdict." The reason for discouraging juries from securing unanimity through social pressure is simple. Jurors are expected and, in fact, instructed to vote with their conscience. If they change their minds because they are genuinely persuaded by new information, fine. But if they comply with the majority just to avoid being rejected or to escape an unpleasant experience, then their final vote will not reflect their true beliefs. In the Supreme Court's words, "the verdict must be the verdict of each individual juror, and not a mere acquiescence in the conclusion of his fellows."

## A Social-Psychological Analysis

It is rare for all jurors to agree on a verdict at the outset of their deliberations. For that reason, the process of deliberation is, by and large, a study in persuasion and social influence. With that in mind, the legal system is clear in its prescriptions for how its juries should manage the inevitable tension between minority and majority viewpoints; between individual expression and independence on the one hand, and the collective need for consensus, on the other. How should jurors influence and be influenced? What kinds of pressure comport with the ideals of deliberation? Before evaluating the extent to which juries meet the courts' standards, let us look at the psychology of group influence.

In a now classic series of experiments, social psychologist Solomon Asch confronted people with the following awkward situation. Subjects were scheduled in small groups to participate in a study of visual discrimination. Upon their arrival, they were seated around a table and instructed that they would be making a series of simple judgments. Presented with a single vertical line on one board and three lines of varying length on another, subjects were asked to decide which of the three comparison lines was the same as the standard. Because the task was straightforward, the experimenter remarked, he would save time by having subjects announce their judgments out loud in order of their seating position. Actually, there was only one real subject in the group—the others were "confederates" posing as subjects but working for the experimenter. The first two judgments passed uneventfully. The discriminations were simple and all subjects agreed on the correct answer. Then on 12 of the next 16 trials, the first confederate gave what clearly seemed to be the wrong answer. The next four did the same. With all eyes on the subject, how does he respond? Much to Asch's surprise, subjects conformed with the incorrect majority 37 percent of the time. Only when they had an ally, or even another member who dissented from both their own and others' judgments, were subjects able to resist the pressure to conform.

Asch's study raised important questions, the first being, why did people conform as often as they did? By interviewing his subjects, Asch discovered that they followed the majority for different reasons. Some claimed they actually agreed with what the majority had reported; others became uncertain of their own perceptions; still others maintained their original beliefs but went along anyway. Shortly after Asch's initial demonstration, social psychologists Morton Deutsch and Harold Gerard repeated the experiment with one significant modification. In one condition, subjects were separated by partitions and prevented from communicating with one another. And instead of publicly announcing their answers, they indicated their judgments by pressing a button. Do people still conform, even when protected by their anonymity within the group? The answer is, yes and no. Deutsch and Gerard found that subjects who participated in this anonymous condition were less likely to follow the incorrect majority than those who were in the face-to-face situation created by Asch. But they were sill more likely to make incorrect judgments than a group of subjects who completed the line-judgment task alone.

Deutsch and Gerard concluded from this study that people are influenced by others for two distinct reasons—informational and normative. Through *informational* social influence, people conform because they want to be correct in their judgments and expect that when others agree with each other, they must be right. Thus in Asch's visual discrimination task, it is natural for subjects to assume that ten eyes are better than two. Through *normative* social influence, however, people conform because they fear the negative consequences of appearing deviant. Wanting to be accepted and well liked, they avoid behaving in ways that make them stick out like a sore thumb. And for good reason. Decision-making groups often reject, ridicule, and punish individuals who frustrate a common goal by adhering to a deviant position.

The distinction between normative and informational social influence is critical not just for an understanding of why people conform, but because it produces two very different types of conformity: public compliance and private acceptance. The term *public compliance* refers to a superficial change in behavior. Often, people will publicly vote with the majority, even though privately they continue to disagree. "To get along, go along," as they say. In contrast, as the term *private acceptance* indicates, there are times when people are genuinely persuaded by others' opinions. In these instances, they change not only their overt behavior, but their minds as well. Obviously, public compliance is a weaker and less stable outcome of social influence than private acceptance. The individual who complies without truly sharing the group's views is likely to revert to his or her own real attitude as soon as the promise of reward or threat of punishment are no longer in effect (for example, when he or she is not being observed).

The social psychology of group influence provides a framework and, as we will see, an empirical literature with which we can evaluate the ideals of jury deliberation. As the courts have long recognized, an ideal jury enters the jury room with diverse opinions and open minds. Through a vigorous exchange of viewpoints, a majority faction develops. It then strives toward unanimity through a process of informational influence until the final hold-outs come to accept that position. In the ideal, then, a jury's final verdict reflects each individual's vote of conscience. In contrast to this information-acceptance model, there is what might be called the normative-compliance model of deliberation. It is characterized by the use of heavy-handed social pressure that leads dissenters to publicly support the jury's verdict while privately harboring reservations. As the poet Ferlinghetti put it, "Just because you have silenced a man does not mean you have changed his mind." In this less-than-ideal model, the jury completes its task unanimous in vote but not in conscience.

There are important reasons to protect individual jurors from the kinds of normative pressure that would force merely their compliance. To begin with, justice itself is undermined when a jury renders a verdict not supported even by its own membership. Criminal defendants should not be convicted by juries that are plagued by a reasonable doubt within its membership. There is also danger that people's perceptions of justice are undermined as well by deliberations that follow a normative-compliance model. How much faith in the legal system can a juror have after voting against his or her conscience? The following case illustrates the point.

In 1981 a Miami jury deliberated for more than six hours on whether four defendants had paid undercover agents $220,000 for 15 pounds of cocaine. At one point the jurors reported they were deadlocked, so the judge asked that they try further to reach agreement. Three hours later they returned with verdicts: three convictions and an acquittal. When the judge began polling them in open court as to whether they agreed in conscience with their decisions, the very first juror said, "no." The judge sent them back to the jury room. A few minutes later, they returned with the same verdicts. Polled again, the first juror agreed, but juror #5 said, "No, it's not my verdict." Again, the judge sent them back. This time, they returned and confirmed the verdicts. But one of the defense lawyers said, "We noticed juror #11 kick the back of juror #5's chair when it was her turn." Polled separately, jurors 1 and 5 both repudiated their verdicts. Sent back a fourth time, the jurors deliberated half an hour more, returned with the same verdicts, and stood by them. Then when the trial had ended, jurors 1 and 5 approached two of the defendants and apologized for their convictions. According to their report, two jurors insisted on concluding that night because they had vacation plans. One of them swung at another juror, and four who initially had voted for acquittal were "brow-beaten into submission."

Now that we have a clear image of the informational-acceptance and normative-compliance models of deliberation, we should add that they rarely appear in their pure form. Most decision-making groups achieve a consensus of opinion through a combination of forces. Juries are no exception. As Kalven and Zeisel noted, the deliberation process "is an interesting combination of rational persuasion, sheer social pressure, and the psychological mechanism by which individual perceptions undergo change when exposed to group discussion." With that reality in mind, it is clear that the ideals of deliberation should be stated in relative terms: *A jury verdict meets the courts' standards if, following a vigorous exchange of information and a minimum of normative pressure, it accurately reflects each of the individual jurors' private beliefs.*

## BEHIND CLOSED DOORS: WHO SAYS WHAT TO WHOM?

If only the walls of the jury room could talk, what would they say? By carefully observing mock jury deliberations, by interviewing actual jurors, and by analyzing trial verdict records, it is possible to piece together what transpires during deliberations. How is the foreperson elected? Who does the talking? What is said, and to whom is it said? How and when are votes taken? How do factions develop? These are among the many questions jury researchers have tried to answer.

### Leaders, Participants, and Followers

Juries should consist of 12 independent and equal individuals, each contributing to the final outcome. Let us consider whether that is a realistic ideal. Many trial lawyers do not think so. Robert Duncan, an experienced Kansas City attorney, asserts that "most juries consist of one or two strong personalities with the rest more or less being followers. Thus, often the jury trial actually consists of a one of two person jury." Looking at the empirical literature, it is clear there is an element of truth to that observation. In virtually all kinds of small-group discussions, the rate of participation among individual members is very uneven—a few people do almost all the talking. Exactly the same pattern seems to characterized how juries function. In one study more than 800 people watched a reenactment of a murder trial and then participated in one of 69 mock juries. By video-taping the deliberations and then counting the number of statements contributed by each juror within each group, the experimenters were able to measure how equally the individuals had participated in their respective groups. The results of this analysis were clear. In each group a few jurors controlled the discussion, while the others spoke at a much lower rate. In fact, most groups included as many as three members who remained virtually silent through deliberations, speaking only to cast their votes. Add to that pattern the fact that the more a juror speaks, the more he or she is spoken to and the more persuasive he or she appears to the others, and it is apparent that dominance hierarchies develop in juries just as they do in other groups.

With juries stratifying into leaders, participants, and followers, it is natural to ask—what constitutes leadership on a jury, or any other kind of group for that matter? What kinds of people emerge as leaders, and under what circumstances? Social scientists have two ways of answering that general question. One is to focus on stable personal qualities that distinguish those in power from everyone else. The idea is that leaders are born, not made; that the history of nations and social movements is a history of great individuals; that to identify leaders, one must study their abilities, their character, their appeal, and their personality. The second approach is to focus on transient situational forces that propel certain individuals into positions of power and leadership. From this perspective, leadership is determined by current events, the needs and resources of a particular group, and the nature of the task that needs to be performed. A person who is prepared to lead in one situation may be ill equipped in another group at another time.

When it comes to small decision-making groups, everyday observation and empirical research have shown that leadership consists of two discrete components or—to put it differently—there are two types of leaders. In order to achieve a specific objective, groups need a *task-oriented leader*, one who takes charge, defines a substantive and procedural agenda, establishes a network of communication, and drives the group toward its destination. For the maintenance of interpersonal harmony, however, groups need a *socioemotional* leader, one who reduces tensions created by decision-making conflicts, provides emotional support to individual members, and helps to increase the cohesiveness and morale of the group as a whole. Both task and socioemotional roles are important. Within a group's life cycle, the relative needs for the two types of leadership change according to circumstances.

Turning to the jury, it is common for people to assume that the foreperson is the jury's leader. That is true only in a limited sense. The foreperson holds a position of responsibility that cannot be denied. Selected for the role by the judge, by random assignment, or by the jury itself, the foreperson announces the verdict in open court and acts as a liaison between the judge and jury. Although a leader in this formal sense, however, the foreperson is not necessarily the most influential juror in either a task-oriented or socioemotional sense.

Who are these forepersons and how are they selected? Research shows that juries spend little time at it. Forepersons are often chosen by acclamation and without dissent. People do not seem to seek the position actively. In fact, chances are the first juror who says "what should we do about a foreman?" is immediately chosen. It is interesting that although the selection process is rather casual, its outcomes follow a predictable pattern. To begin with, the foreperson is, quite literally, a *foreman*. All sexist language aside, men are more likely to be selected than women. This finding was not particularly shocking when it appeared in the 1950s, at a time when traditional sex roles were intact. But the bias toward male forepersons continues even in today's era of greater equality for women. Apparently, people assume (erroneously, we might add) that men make better leaders than women. To illustrate how dramatic the difference is, a recent study of 179 trials held in San Diego revealed that although 50 percent of the jurors were female, 90 percent of the forepersons were male.

Other systematic patterns are evident too. For example, forepersons tend to be better educated and hold higher status jobs than the average juror. Those who have previous jury experience are also selected at a higher-than-expected rate. Then there is an interesting, less obvious selection bias. In 1961, jury researchers Fred Strodtbeck and L. H. Hook published a paper entitled "The social dimensions of a 12-man jury table." Looking at the most common geometrical layout, the rectangular table, they discovered that foreperson selections were predictable from where jurors were seated. Those who sat at the heads of the table were by far the most likely to be chosen, whereas those located in the middle were the least likely. Since it also turns out that jurors of higher status naturally tend to take more prominent seats, it appears that this dimension adds even further to the development of a dominance hierarchy within the jury.

Research has thus shown that although juries are casual about their choice of a foreperson, the selections follow systematic patterns. But research has also shown that it does not really matter who fills that role. To be sure, the foreperson is usually the most active member of the jury. Several of the Chicago Jury Project studies reported in the 1950s and 1960s found that, on the average, the foreperson accounts for approximately 25 percent of the statements made during deliberations. It turns out, however, that although forepersons carry a disproportionate amount of influence over the process of deliberation, they do not have the same kind of impact over its outcome. In one study, for example, forepersons contributed a great deal at first on primarily procedural matters (calling for votes or rereading judges' instructions), but then behaved like the more average participants as the deliberations progressed. Another study revealed that while forepersons raised organizational matters at five times the rate of other jurors, they were less likely to express an opinion concerning the verdict. This latter result suggests that it may be more accurate to think of the foreperson not as the jury's leader, but as a referee or moderator.

If the foreperson does not lead the jury to its verdict, who does? The answer to this question is simple. By and large, the same characteristics that are associated with foreperson selections are also related to opinion leadership: sex, employment status, jury experience, and seating position. Male and female jurors, for example, play very different roles in the jury room. Consistent with traditional sex roles, men assume a primarily task-oriented role, offering information and expressing opinions; women assume the more socioemotional role, agreeing with others' statements, offering support, and helping to reduce interpersonal tensions. Needless to say, male jurors are rated by their fellow panelists as more persuasive than their female counterparts.

Experienced and novice jurors are not equivalent in their levels of participation, either. When Dale Broeder interviewed jurors after their trials, he came across several experienced jurors who had taken on an air of expertise and tried to control the rest of the group. As an example, he described a woman who, immediately upon entering the jury room, cut paper ballots, explained that it was standard procedure to open with a secret vote, and "did everything but suggest that she be elected foreman." More controlled research with mock juries lends support to Broeder's observations. In one study, subjects who had previously served on a real jury talked more during deliberations than those who had not. These kinds of effects appear even when the subject's experience consists of having earlier participated in a mock jury. In this situation, the first author, in collaboration with Ralph Juhnke, found that new subjects reportedly participated less and made less persuasive comments than their more experienced peers. We also found that new subjects conformed to their groups more when they deliberated with others of experience than when they participated in fully inexperienced groups. Finally, consistent with the more situational theories of leadership, we suspect that individual jurors will lead or follow depending upon their suitability and expertise for a particular trial. In principle, all jurors are supposed to be created equal. In practice, however, this egalitarian ethic is seldom if ever realized. The fact of the matter is that dominance hierarchies develop that mirror the differences of status in the real world. Thus, despite the forces designed to place all jurors on an equal footing and neutralize individual differences, juries still consist in predictable ways of leaders, participants, and followers.

## The Sounds of Deliberation

Imagine that you just sat through a full trial, having listened to several witnesses, lawyers, and the judge. You still have not communicated your thoughts and impressions to anyone else, nor do you know what the others on the panel are thinking. You may have formed some opinions, and you are probably filled with questions. Finally, the door of the jury room closes, and you find yourself with 11 strangers. Where do you begin? How do juries structure their discussions and what do they talk about? In short, what are the sounds of deliberation? Kalven and Zeisel offer the following colorful description:

> There is at first, in William James' phrase about the baby, the sense of buzzing, booming, confusion. After a while, we become accustomed to the quick, fluid movement of jury discussion and realize that the talk moves with remarkable flexibility. It touches an issue, leaves it, and returns again. Even a casual inspection makes it evident that this is interesting and arresting human behavior. It is not a formal debate; nor, although it is mercurial and difficult to pick up, is it just excited talk.

Social psychologists interested in how groups solve problems describe the process through series of stages. According to this view, a group begins in an open ended, not very well defined *orientation* phrase. During these opening moments, the group defines its task and perhaps even a strategy for discussion. Questions are raised, issues are explored, and tentative views are expressed in general terms. Formally or informally, a vote is eventually taken. Differences of opinion are thus revealed, factions develop, and the group enters an *open conflict* phase. At this point, the discussion takes on a more focused, serious tone. With individuals taking sides in a debate, only points of disagreement are addressed. During this critical and often lengthy period, discussion is best characterized in social influence terms, with both informational and normative pressures operating. In most groups, a sizeable majority eventually emerges, and a mutually acceptable decision appears imminent. When that happens, the group enters a period of *conflict resolution and reconciliation*. If one or two individuals continue to hold out in the face of attempts to convert them through rational argument, then they become the targets of increasing pressures to conform. If and when unanimity is achieved, the group then goes through a period of reconciliation designed to heal the wounds of battle, express support and reassurance, and affirm its satisfaction with the final outcome.

Judges and lawyers are forever wondering about what jurors talk about in their deliberations. Do they stick like glue to the evidence, or do they allow themselves to wander onto topics prohibited by the judge? How much time do they spend talking about their own personal experiences? To answer these kinds of questions, sociologist Rita James Simon transcribed 10 mock-jury deliberations and then classified all statements made according to their content. She found that jurors spent most of their time talking about trial evidence and their reactions to that evidence. After that they were most likely to talk about procedures for deliberating, experiences from their daily lives, and the judge's instructions. For all categories, Simon found that jurors' statements were, for the most part, relevant, accurate, and helpful for reaching a verdict.

The problem with Simon's analysis is that it represents the deliberation process in static rather than dynamic terms. Do juries' discussions really sound the same in the opening and closing moments? Obviously not, according to the stage-like analysis described earlier. And what do juries do with their statements about evidence, instructions, procedure, and so on? Surely, the decision-making process does not consist of an unrelated string of sentences. More recent studies of jury deliberation are providing answers to these questions. In one study, psychologists Reid Hastie, Steven Penrod, and Nancy Pennington had more than 800 people participate in mock juries and deliberate until a verdict was reached. On the average, deliberations lasted for almost two hours. In order to monitor how discussions change from beginning to end, each deliberation was divided into five units of time. This analysis revealed a very consistent pattern about how juries operate.

As a first step, they spend a good deal of time exchanging views about the case facts and the credibility of the various witnesses. Then they struggle to make sense of the evidence by transforming it into a story of what probably happened. Storytelling, they found, is an important part of deliberation. Confronted with fragments of evidence, juries try to reconstruct the events in question. As with other stories, what they usually come up with is a linked series of episodes that has a beginning, a middle, and an end. To construct these narratives, juries lean heavily on the evidence they find most compelling. Wanting to establish a coherent story, they might then fill in missing details, make inferences about the actors' goals, motives, and intentions, and reject evidence that is incompatible with their views.

As the deliberations progress, jurors become increasingly focused on the judge's instructions concerning the law, the requirements of proof, and the kinds of verdicts they could reach. They might argue about the differences between first and second degree murder, or about how to interpret the concept of an implied contract, or about how much doubt should be considered reasonable. In short, juries appear to shift, generally, from a concern for fact-finding (the "what happened?" stage) to an application of the law (the "what do we do now?" stage).

### The Drive Toward Unanimity

So far, the deliberation process sounds quite rational and orderly. Juries find facts, construct stories, and apply legal principles. But the jury does not speak with one voice. Indeed it is not a "collective mind" but a collection of individuals. Often, individual jurors express a legitimate disagreement with prevailing opinion. Others are ineloquent in their dissent, but just plain stubborn. How do juries ever achieve a consensus and, in the end, a unanimous verdict?

Before trying to answer that question, it is important that we first take the mystique out of popular, romanticized images of jury dynamics. To begin with, the majority almost always wins. Thus, to predict the outcome of deliberations with a fair degree of certainty, one need only know where the 12 individuals stand before they enter the jury room. Kalven and Zeisel found convincing support for this phenomenon in their research. Through posttrial interviews with jurors in 225 criminal juries, they were able to reconstruct how juries split on their very first vote. In all but 10 cases, there was at least a slight majority favoring a particular verdict. Out of these, only six juries reached a final decision that was not predictable from this initial breakdown. From that rather striking result, Kalven and Zeisel concluded that "the deliberation process might well be likened to what the developer does for an exposed film: It brings out the picture, but the outcome is predetermined. . . . The deliberation process, though rich in human interest and color appears not to be at the heart of jury decision making."

Though not a frequent occurrence, minorities sometimes manage to prevail. There are two rather distinct strategies that enable nonconformists to turn others around. One strategy, identified by Serge Moscovici and his colleagues, is to adopt right from the start a staunch, consistent, and unwavering position. Confronted with this self-confident opponent, those in the majority will sit up, take notice, and rethink their own positions. There is a second, very different strategy that can be taken. Based on the fact that dissent often breeds hostility, Edwin Hollander maintains that people who challenge the majority immediately, without having first earned the others' respect, run the risk of becoming alienated and powerless. Based on his own research, Hollander concludes that individual dissenters become influential by first conforming to the majority and establishing their credentials as accepted members of the group. Having accumulated enough "idiosyncrasy credits" (or brownie points), the individual is in a better position to exert influence.

### Alternate Routes: Informational and Social Pressure

When jurors speak, what they say often conveys two messages. They provide information that could persuade others but, at the same time, they also reveal where they stand on the verdict. Suppose a juror says "I don't understand how the witness could have seen the defendant at 5:30, if his wife claims he returned home, which is almost half an hour away, at 5:45." A second juror then adds, "And how could the defendant have been on the street so early, anyway, when he was at work that day?" These statements contribute information *and* they indicate a preference, without a formal vote, for a not guilty verdict. If a third juror subsequently changes his vote from guilty to not-guilty, is that because he came to accept the position implied by the arguments, or is it because he came to realize that, like in Asch's situation, he held an unpopular opinion?

We turn to Kaplan's program of research for an answer. To test the relative effects of informational and normative influence processes, Kaplan developed an artificial but interesting method of "deliberation." Subjects read either a strong- or weak-evidence version of a manslaughter case and indicated whether they thought the defendant was guilty or not. In order to control the subsequent discussion, Kaplan had jurors, each seated in their own cubicles, communicate with each other by passing notes. Actually, all the original notes were intercepted and replaced with others written by the experimenter. Now imagine that you are a subject in this experiment and you believe the defendant is guilty. You write down your opinion, you write down the facts you used to form that opinion, and then you receive notes from other jurors who supposedly did the same. After reading all the notes, you find out that your colleagues either agree or disagree with your verdict. You also learn about facts that either support or refute that verdict. Finally, you are asked again for your judgment. What influences whether you adhere to or change your original position? How do you react if the facts you read about support your guilty verdict, but the other jurors favor an acquittal? Conversely, what if you were supported by others' opinions but not by the facts? Consistently, subjects were more responsive to new, substantive information than they were to the strictly normative pressures.

Research on other decision-making groups yields the same comforting conclusion: people change their minds and their votes according to information and rational argument. That does not mean, of course, that interpersonal forces are inoperative, especially in situations that involve truly important decisions. Kaplan and others are unwilling to close the door on the normative-compliance component of jury decision making. We would have to agree.

Informational and normative influences are not endpoints of a single continuum; they are two independent dimensions. The drive toward unanimity is not characterized by one or the other, but by both. With that in mind, we reiterate our working definition of the ideal deliberation as one in which the information influences are strong and the normative influences are weak. Some degree of social pressure is inevitable and perhaps even desirable. It is a fact of life not just on juries, but in the board room, the classroom, the social club, and the laboratory. The question is, how much pressure is too much? Opinions differ. We certainly part company with an Ohio judge who said, "When you get twelve people in one room, and they all have to reach one decision, things happen. I've known fist fights to break out in the jury room. Abuse that one juror gives to the other is not a reason to turn over a just verdict." A just verdict? How can a verdict be just when one or more jurors was coerced into the final vote? Consistent with a social-psychological perspective, a simple rule applies: Normative influence exceeds an acceptable level whenever it leads people to vote against their true beliefs.

Research has shown that juries fulfill at least half of the deliberation ideal: they are responsive to informational influence. But then there is the other half. One cannot help but wonder about the pressures toward uniformity, and about jurors who appear to abandon their true convictions in order to avoid the role of being deviant. Stories can be found to illustrate both the more and less desirable versions of the deliberation process. Thus, following one trial in which the jury acquitted the defendant of rape and murder, several jurors expressed their pride and satisfaction with the way they had reached a verdict. As one participant put it, "It was not an easy decision to come to. I honestly think the verdict could have gone either way. And even if there was a little shouting, we all tried to listen to what other people are saying. There were shifts of opinion, but we tried not to pressure anyone."

In contrast, jurors sometimes succumb under the weight of inordinate pressure. Take as an example a 1986 trial of two New York City police officers charged with torturing a prisoner with an electric stun gun. Concluding two days of deliberation, a jury of seven women and five men announced a verdict of guilty. Afterwards, one of the jurors reported in an affidavit that she had agreed to the verdict only because she had been intimidated and abused for holding out. "When I argued that the defendants had to have engaged in 'knowing and intentional' conduct before they could be found guilty of any of the crimes charged, the foreman screamed at me words to the effect: 'How would you like a policeman to do this to you?' and, thereupon, he squeezed my left thigh. This physical touching put me in fear of further physical abuse, so I voted guilty on the first count that the jury took up for consideration."

As we have argued, isolated anecdotes and case studies do not provide an adequate basis for evaluating the jury system. Every story has its counterpart. What, then, is the incidence of undue normative pressure? How frequently do jurors exhibit public compliance without private acceptance? In one study, interviews with former jurors revealed that as many as 10 percent of those sampled admitted that they felt pressured into their verdict, and had lingering doubts even as the vote was announced. Since people are generally reluctant to admit their own weaknesses, this figure might even underestimate the problem.

# Source Acknowlegments

*Cognition in Social Psychology* Susan Fiske & Shelly Taylor. From Susan Fiske and Shelly Taylor, *Social Cognition*, 2E (1991). Copyright © 1991. Reproduced with permission of McGraw-Hill, Inc.

*Judgmental Heuristics and Knowledge Structures* Richard Nisbett & Lee Ross. From Richard Nisbett/Lee Ross, *Human Inference: Strategies and Shortcomings of Social Judgment*, © 1980, pp. 17–28. Reprinted by permission of Prentice Hall, Englewood Cliffs, New Jersey.

*They Saw a Game—A Case Study* Albert H. Castorf & Hadley Cantril. From "They Saw a Game: A Case Study" by Albert H. Hastorf and Hadley Cantril in *Journal of Abnormal and Social Psychology*, Vol. 49 (1954), pp. 129–134. Copyright 1954 by the American Psychological Association. Reprinted by permission.

*Embracing the Bitter "Truth": Negative Self-Concepts and Marital Commitment* William B. Swann, Jr., J. Gregory Hixon & Chris De La Ronde. From *Psychological Science*. Copyright © 1992. Reprinted by permission of Cambridge University Press.

*Race and the Schooling of Black Americans* Claude M. Steele. Copyright © 1992 by *The Atlantic Monthly*. Reprinted by permission of the author and *The Atlantic Monthly*.

*William James, the Self, and the Selective Industry of the Mind* Jerry Suls & Christine A. Marco. From *Personality and Social Psychology Bulletin*. Copyright © 1990 by the Society for Personality and Social Psychology, Inc. Reprinted by permission of Sage Publications, Inc.

*To BIRG or to CORF, that is the question* David Gelman. From NEWSWEEK, February 1, 1993. © 1993 Newsweek, Inc. All rights reserved. Reprinted by permission.

*Social Proof: Monkey Me, Monkey Do* Robert Cialdini. From *Influence (3rd edition)*. Copyright © 1993 by Robert Cialdini. Reprinted by permission of HarperCollins College Publishers.

*If Hitler Asked You to Electrocute a Stranger, Would You?* Philip Meyer. From *Esquire*, February 1970. Copyright © 1970 by Esquire Publishing Inc. Used by permission of *Esquire*.

*The Role of Source Legitimacy in Sequential Request Strategies of Compliance* Michael E. Patch. From *Personality and Social Psychology Bulletin*. Copyright © 1986 by the Society for Personality and Social Psychology, Inc. Reprinted by permission of Sage Publications, Inc.

*Attitudes and Opinions* Stuart Oskamp. Stuart Oskamp, *Attitudes and Opinions*, 2e, © 1991, pp. 1-11. Reprinted by permission of Prentice Hall, Englewood Cliffs, New Jersey.

*Central and Peripheral Routes to Advertising Effectiveness: The Moderating Role of Involvement* Richard E. Petty, John T. Cacioppo & David Schumann. From *Journal of Consumer Research*, 1983, 10. Copyright © 1983. Reprinted with permission of University of Chicago Press.

*The Fear Appeal* Anthony Pratkanis & Elliot Aronson. From: *Age of Propaganda: The Everyday Use and Abuse of Persuasion* by Anthony Pratkanis and Elliot Aronson. Copyright © 1992 by W. H. Freeman and Company. Reprinted with Permission.

*Cognitive Dissonance Theory Alive and Well* Tori DeAngelis. Copyright © 1990 by the American Psychological Association. Reprinted by permission.

*The Question of Quality Circles* Mitchell Lee Marks. Reprinted with permission from *Psychology Today Magazine* Copyright © 1986 (Sussex Publishers, Inc.).

*The Role of Evaluation in Eliminating Social Loafing* Stephen G. Harkins & Jeffrey M. Jackson. From *Personality and Social Psychology Bulletin*, Copyright © 1985 by the Society for Personality and Social Psychology, Inc. Reprinted by permission of Sage Publications, Inc.

*Group Decision Fiascoes Continue: Space Shuttle Challenger and a Revised Groupthink Framework* Gregory Moorhead, Richard Ference & Chris Neck. From *Human Relations*, pp. 539–550, 1991. Copyright © 1991. Reprinted with permission of Plenum Publishing Corp.

*Near and Dear: Friendship and Love Compared* Keith Davis. Reprinted with permission from *Psychology Today Magazine* Copyright © 1985 (Sussex Publishers, Inc.)

*Impact of Couple Patterns of Problem Solving on Distress and Nondistress in Dating Relationships* Caryl Rusbult, Dennis Johnson & Gregory Morrow. Copyright © 1986 by the American Psychological Association. Reprinted by permission.

*Similarity and Satisfaction in Rommate Relationships* Linda Carli, Roseanne Ganley & Amy Pierce-Otay. From *Personality and Social Psychology Bulletin*, Copyright © 1991 by the Society for Personality and Social Psychology, Inc. Reprinted by permission of Sage Publications, Inc.

*When Bystanders Just Stand By* R. Lance Shotland. Reprinted with permission from *Psychology Today Magazine* Copyright © 1985 (Sussex Publishers, Inc.)

*The Altruistic Personality: Concern into Action* Samuel P. Oliner & Pearl M. Oliner. From *The Altruistic Personality* by Samuel P. Oliner and Pearl M. Oliner. Copyright ©1988 by Samuel P.

# Index

## A

Aderman, D., 261
Advertising effectiveness, 134–49
  central and peripheral routes to,
    138–43
  involvement and, 135–38
Affleck, G., 71
Aggression, 270–74
  affect of temperature on, 275–82
AIDS (acquired immunodeficiency
    syndrome), 338–40, 343
  education efforts, 345–48
  etiology of, 348–51
  patient care, 351–54
  prevention of, 344–45
Ajzen, I., 129, 131, 147
Allport, Gordon, 126, 128, 305–10,
    326–27, 330
Altobello Youth Center, 327–33
Altruism, 241–45
  personality for, 252–59
Anderson, C.A., 276
Applied social psychology, 338–42
Apsler, Robert, 136
Aronson, Elliot, 152–61
Asch, Solomon, 100, 378–79
Attitudes, 120–24
  change in
      and fear tactics, 152–57

and involvement, 134–43
definitions of, 127–29
reasons for studying, 125–27
separate entities viewpoint, 131–
    32
tri-componential viewpoint, 129–
    30
Attraction, 198–202
Attribution theories, 17–18
Authority, 83
Automobile accident reconstruc-
    tion, 370–75

## B

Bain, Read, 126
Bakan, D., 290
Ballachey, E., 130
Bandura, A., 291, 295
Basow, Susan, 311–21
Batson, Daniel, 240–45
Baum, Andrew, 338–55
Bay of Pigs, 193
Bergloff, Paula, 208
Berkowitz, L., 260–61, 285, 287
Bernard, Larry, 357–66
Bernstein, R.J., 73
Berscheid, Ellen, 198–202, 227
Bettelheim, Bruno, 64

# P

Pack, S.J., 321
Palmer, John C., 370–75
Palmer, S., 290
Palys, Ted, 284
Participant observation, 82
Patch, Michael E., 112–16
Patient-practitioner relationship, 357–66
  communication in, 361–65
  consumer model, 359–60
  disease-centered model, 360
  improving, 365–66
  nature of, 358–60
  patient satisfaction with, 360–61
  Szasz-Hollender models, 359
Penner, Louis, 248
Pennington, Nancy, 385
Penrod, Steven, 385
People's Temple, 95–98
Perceptual filters, 320
Perry, Ralph Barton, 72
Pettigrew, T.F., 326
Petty, Richard, 120–24, 134–49
Pfeiffer, C., 71
Phillips, David, 90–94
Physical restraints, 328
Pierce-Otay, Amy, 226–34
Pitts, M., 364
Plato, 130
*Playboy*, 284
Pornography, 283–88
Powers, Francis Gary, 110
Pratkanis, Anthony, 152–57
Prejudice, 302–4
  acting out, 308–10
  definition of, 305–8
President's Commission on Obscenity and Pornography, 283–84
President's Commission on the Causes and Prevention of Violence, 295
Princeton University, 32–39

Principled motivation, 256–58
*Principles of Psychology* (James), 67
Problem solving in dating relationships, 210–23
  distressed relationships model, 212–14
  exit-voice-loyalty-neglect typology, 211–12
  methodology, 214–17
  results, 217–19
Prosocial behavior, 240–45

# Q

Quality circles, 170–76

# R

Rands, Marilyn, 208
Read, S.J., 71
Reaves, Andrew, 61
Reciprocation, 82
Reifman, Alan S., 275–82
Relationships, 201–2
Report of the Presidential Commission on the Space Shuttle Accident, 187–92
Rescue behavior, 252–59
Reykowski, Janusz, 253
Roberts, Mary K., 208
Roomate relationships, 226–34
Roosevelt, Franklin D., 155
Ross, D., 291, 295
Ross, Lee, 22–30
Ross, S., 291, 295
Roter, Debra, 361, 366
Rowe, J., 71
Rubin, Zick, 206, 216
Rusbult, Caryl E., 210–23
Ryan, Leo R., 95

# S